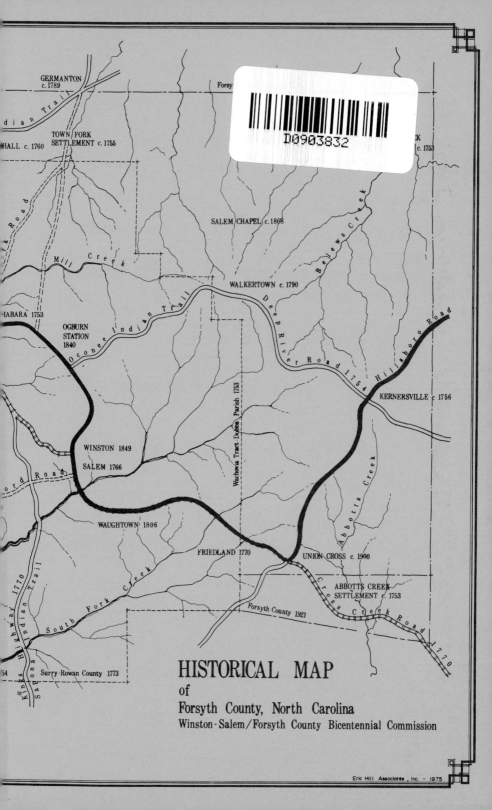

GERMANTON
c. 1789

Forsy

TOWN FORK
SETTLEMENT c. 1755

HALL c. 1760

K
c. 1753

Indian Trail

Mill Creek

SALEM CHAPEL c.1868

Belews Creek

WALKERTOWN c. 1790

HABARA 1753

Oconee Indian Trail

OGBURN
STATION
1840

Deep River Road 1754

Hillsboro Road

KERNERSVILLE c 1756

WINSTON 1849

Wachovia Tract Dobbs Parish 1753

SALEM 1766

Abbotts Creek

ord Road

WAUGHTOWN 1806

FRIEDLAND 1770

UNION CROSS c. 1900

ABBOTTS CREEK
SETTLEMENT c. 1753

South Fork Creek

Cross Creek Road 1770

Forsyth County 1921

54

Kings Highway 1770

Saxona Indian Trail

Surry-Rowan County 1773

HISTORICAL MAP
of
Forsyth County, North Carolina
Winston-Salem/Forsyth County Bicentennial Commission

Eric Hill Associates, Inc. – 1975

Forsyth

The History of a County on the March

Forsyth

The History of a County on the March

ADELAIDE FRIES
Contributor and Editor of the First Edition

STUART THURMAN WRIGHT
Contributor and Compiler of the Revised Edition

J. EDWIN HENDRICKS
Contributor and Editor of the Revised Edition

The University of North Carolina Press
Chapel Hill
1976

Copyright © 1949, 1976 by
The University of North Carolina Press
Manufactured in the United States of America
All rights reserved
ISBN 8078-1273-0
Library of Congress Catalog Card Number 76-22212

Library of Congress Cataloging in Publication Data
Main entry under title:

Forsyth: the history of a county on the march.

  Bibliography: p.
  Includes index.
  1. *Forsyth Co., N.C.—History. I. Wright, Stuart T*
II. *Hendricks, James Edwin, 1935–*
F262.F7F67   1976   975.6'67   76-22212
ISBN 0-8078-1273-0

Table of Contents

Illustrations

Illustrations

Foreword

JAMES A. GRAY, JR., chairman of the Forsyth County Centennial Committee, said in his foreword to the 1949 edition of *Forsyth, A County on the March,* "Dr. Adelaide Fries and her able associates in the writing of this book not only have given us an accurate history of our County but also have captured magnificently the energy of its founders, the surge of its new blood, and the cooperative spirit of its people."

Twenty-five years later, as the nation prepared to celebrate its bicentennial, it seemed appropriate to revise and expand the county history, long out of print. Under the leadership of the Winston-Salem/Forsyth County Bicentennial Commission's co-chairmen, M. C. Benton, Jr., and Mrs. John Eller, Jr., a publications committee was formed with Dr. J. Edwin Hendricks of Wake Forest University as chairman, and set about its task. James A. Gray, Jr., Charles N. Siewers, and Mrs. Z. T. Bynum, Jr., who contributed to the 1949 volume, agreed to assist in the updating and have been most helpful. Dr. Francis Atkins and Mrs. Louise S. Hamilton were asked to represent the black community. John Woodard brought his knowledge of archives and the history of religious groups to the committee and Robert Prongay contributed a valuable knowledge of the local business community and of the photographic art. Dr. Edwin L. Stockton, Jr., ably represented the Wachovia Historical Society. Mrs. Ruth Mills Kipp, bicentennial coordinator for the city/county commission, provided invaluable assistance. Dr. Larry Tise, then area coordinator for the state bicentennial program and now director of the North Carolina Division of Archives and History, provided able assistance and encouragement.

The publications committee was indeed fortunate when The University of North Carolina Press agreed to publish the revised history. Then came assurances of financial support as the Wachovia Historical Society and the Forsyth County Board of Commissioners agreed to advance the funds necessary for publication. Stuart T. Wright was employed as primary author and compiler for the new material.

Much of the material from the 1949 volume has been integrated into the revised version. Dr. Adelaide Fries was a master of the historian's craft and it was decided that much of what she had written and edited could not be surpassed. Stuart Wright was able in many areas to provide coverage for additional topics, new factual or interpretative information not available to Dr. Fries and her other committee and, on occasion, to insert material from one of her other publications or those of other authors.

The cooperative nature of local history meant that many people were called on to provide information or to write sections of the manuscript. All those who were approached responded graciously but special notes of appreciation are due Russell Brantley for the material on Wake Forest University and Roger Rollman for the material on the North Carolina Baptist Hospital and Wake Forest's Bowman Gray School of Medicine. Dr. Francis Atkins and Mrs. Louise S. Hamilton deserve particular appreciation for their labors in identifying leaders and providing information about the black community in Forsyth County. Mrs. Hamilton contributed most of the material for the section on the black community in Chapter 9. Miss Charlotte Pepper of Salem College and John Woodard of Wake Forest University graciously provided materials relating to the history of churches in the county. Mrs. Ruth Mills Kipp, bicentennial coordinator, not only provided information relating to some of the smaller settlements in the county but has also provided unfailing support and assistance. Portions of the section on Joseph Winston appeared earlier in an article by J. Edwin Hendricks in the Summer 1968 *North Carolina Historical Review*.

Monumental tasks were performed willingly and expertly by

Stephen J. Bennett, director of the Forsyth County Information Office, and Nancy Wolfe, director of the Office of Public Relations for Winston-Salem, who compiled the sections in Chapter 14 which deal with their respective governmental agencies and the wide range of their operations. The introductory and concluding passages of the section on county government were written by Nicholas Meiszer, Forsyth County manager. Mr. Meiszer deserves a special note of gratitude also for his support of the county history project from its inception.

Frank Jones, late photographer for the *Winston-Salem Journal and Sentinel*, had agreed to serve as photographic editor of the book and to make available his collection of historical and recent photographs. After his death his executor Oscar Hege and the directors of the Wachovia Historical Society, repository for the collection, generously agreed to facilitate the use of the photographs. Robert Prongay of Piedmont Engraving and Studio One assisted in selecting representative photographs and provided the necessary prints for publication. Wake Forest University provided generous assistance to both Stuart Wright and me as a part of its contribution to the local bicentennial effort.

J. EDWIN HENDRICKS
Wake Forest University

Forsyth
The History of a County on the March

CHAPTER 1

Forsyth, the Beginning

MORE THAN EIGHT THOUSAND YEARS before the first white man set foot in what is today Forsyth County, roving bands of Indian hunters established themselves amid the gently rolling, wooded hills and abundant streams. Archaeologists to date have located more than two hundred shelters and base camps used by these Indians, their descendants, and other migratory bands. Usually these sites were situated on clay or sandy-loam knolls overlooking a small but reliable water source that served to lure the hunter's prey. Larger bodies of water, such as the Yadkin River, posed an obstacle to their constant movements.

A rock shelter located just below the great bend of the Yadkin River, some thirteen miles northwest of Winston-Salem, is the earliest known evidence of human habitation in Forsyth County. This site was probably a temporary camp for the wandering huntsmen who first appeared in the area. Radiocarbon analysis of several charcoal specimens suggests that its occupation dates as far back as 6600 B.C. Over the next five thousand years, at least, this rock shelter was seasonally occupied by hunters or farmers from the many villages located along the bottom lands in the Donnaha area. Projectile points discovered at the site "constitute the oldest stratigraphically dated material in the Piedmont," according to Prudence Rice in her paper, "The Bottoms Rock Shelter," and she continues "it is likely that they represent the earliest men in the Piedmont area."

The environment found in Forsyth more than adequately met the needs of the aboriginal inhabitants who came and settled here. The hilly terrain and numerous streams provided many possible campsites. Outcroppings of chert and quartz or quartzite, used for stone tools and projectile points, were located throughout the county. Important also to the early Indians, who practiced a hunting-and-gathering type of subsistence, were the naturally growing wild food plants, particularly the many wild berries and acorns that cover this area even today. Hunting was made quite easy by the vast resources of game—black bear, white-tailed deer, bison, fresh-water mussels (found in the Yadkin River as recently as the mid-nineteenth century), turkey, quail, pheasant, squirrels, rabbits, foxes, and badgers. In fact it is suggested that agriculture was adopted by Forsyth's Indians quite late and perhaps even then reluctantly because of the unusually large amount and variety of game to be had. A mild climate producing a frost-free growing season of over two hundred days was also of importance to the later, more permanent occupants of Forsyth.

About the time of the birth of Christ the Indians of Piedmont North Carolina reached something of an equilibrium with their environment. They practiced a crude form of maize horticulture and fashioned simple containers from soapstone to hold the corn they grew and the wild fruits they collected. Over the next thousand years the Indian population enlarged and concentrated in smaller areas. The bow and arrow replaced the spear as their chief weapon and hunting implement. Dogs guarded the fields and campsites; carefully buried canine skeletons have been located in some of the Forsyth County Indian sites, dating from 1100 or 1200 A.D.

Then, about 1540, the Indians of the Carolina Piedmont were suddenly thrust from prehistory into history by the coming of European explorers and traders, first Hernando de Soto, then hundreds more over the next two centuries.

The Siouan-speaking Tutelo and Saponi dominated the area which is now Forsyth County at the time of the coming of the first white men. The Tutelo moved from the headwaters of the Dan River in Virginia to the upper Yadkin around Pilot Mountain (present-day Forsyth and Stokes counties). Donnaha Village on the Yadkin River likely was occupied by the Tutelo as they passed through this area. The other group, the Saponi, temporarily resided in what is now Forsyth as they moved southward to the Trading Ford just above the present location of Salisbury.

Archaeological evidence suggests that physically these Indians were quite robust with large bones and well-developed muscles. Except for the obvious there was little difference in the males and females of the tribe. The men averaged about five feet three inches in height and the women were something under one inch shorter. In 1728 William Byrd encountered members of the Saponi nation who had left the Yadkin River for Virginia about 1700. Among this group were four young "Ladies" who "had more the Air of cleanliness than any copper-colour'd Beauties" he had ever seen. The men, according to Byrd's description, "had something great and Venerable in their countenances, beyond the common Mien of Savages." He reported that by "uncommon Circumstance" the Indians traveled on horseback: "the Men rode more awkwardly than any Dutch Sailor" and the women "bestrode their Palfreys a la mode de France, but were so bashful about it, that there was no persuading them to Mount till they were quite out of our Sight."

Actually, according to Dr. Douglas L. Rights in *The American Indian in North Carolina*, the Indians encountered by Byrd were much less than the noble creatures he described. The "pitiful remnants of the Saponi," through contact with their neighbors, had been greatly degraded. Long before the white man arrived in the area now known as Forsyth County, his diseases had preceded him, carried by Indians infected and driven from the eastern part of the colony. Measles and smallpox in particular decimated much of the Indian population of the Carolina Piedmont. Professor Ned Woodall of Wake Forest University notes that the singular lack of beads, trinkets, and other items of barter suggests that the early white traders and settlers did not fear the Indians here.

In *The Siouxan Tribes of the East*, James Mooney in 1894 wrote that "war, pestilence, whiskey, and systematic slave hunts had nearly exterminated the aboriginal occupants before anybody had thought them of sufficient importance to ask who they were, how they lived, or what were their beliefs and opinions." Indeed much of what is known and written about the Indian inhabitants of

Forsyth, both prehistoric and historic, is of necessity based on archaeological evidence. Many early accounts of contact with the Indians are unreliable; time and amateur diggings have taken their respective tolls with artifactual evidence. The average man is now just beginning to ask seriously the questions posed by Mooney over seventy years ago. Around 1825 one young student at the Salem Boys School wrote the following passage in his exercise book:

Not many generations ago, this country was inhabited by the wild and fearless indians. Along the banks of these rivers, their paths were made to their huts. They traversed these hills and plains, with their bow and arrow, in pursuit of the deer and buffalo for their support. The sound of their war whoop echoed, and reechoed from hill to hill, and their resounding voices broke the silence of the night. But where are they now? Where are those warriors of other days, who were once the undisputed owners of this country? They are gone forever. . . . Their vast hunting ground is now in possession of the white man, and is under cultivation and is bringing forth productions, which rear men who are ready to pursue the feeble remnants of that once mighty people, and to blot forever, their race from the Earth. Their voices are no longer heard among these hills. They are beyond the penetrating power of the Sun that once emitted its rays to them in these lonely groves. They have been overcome by the subsequent inhabitants and driven to the wild forests of the west, but before the Earth revolves many more times around the burning luminary of heaven they will be driven to the utmost bounds of the Continent and submerged by the mighty deep of the west. They are gone forever.

Early Explorations and First Settlers

North Carolina was a part of the original Virginia grant of 1606, but no serious attempts were made to settle this "very fruitful and pleasant country" until much later. In 1629 Charles I of England conveyed by patent all the land south of Virginia between 31° and 36° north latitude to Sir Robert Heath, his attorney general. Heath failed to take any initiative in exploring these vast lands, though settlers from Virginia were already beginning to enter the area by 1660. Charles II, the "merrie monarch," gave Heath's land to eight of England's leading men—the soon-to-be lords proprietors of

Carolina—and the original patent was declared void for nonuse. An additional charter in 1665 extended "Carolina" one-half degree to the north and two degrees to the south. Immigration was encouraged by liberal legislative measures and by the "Fundamental Constitutions" for the colony drawn up by John Locke in 1669.

The failure of proprietary rule over the colony resulted in the resale of some of the land to the crown in 1728; John, Lord Carteret, Earl Granville, retained his share. When a survey of Granville's lands had been completed, it was determined that almost one-half of present North Carolina fell within its boundaries; a full two-thirds of the colony's inhabitants were also included.

Though Granville never came to America, his agents collected for him an annual quitrent of four shillings "proclamation" money or three shillings sterling for each one hundred acres of claimed land. It was upon these lands of Lord Granville that many of the immigrants from Pennsylvania, New Jersey, Maryland, and Virginia settled—most with land grants, but some without. The land that later became Forsyth County was a part of the Granville District.

The North Carolina wilderness claimed by agents of the Moravian church, the area's first major settlers, was vast, uncharted, and unsettled. There were, or had been, a few settlers prior to the arrival of the Moravians. William Byrd found scattered settlements in the interior; moreover, the first Moravians occupied an abandoned settler's cabin. Even in late 1752 Bishop August Gottlieb Spangenberg, as he prepared to enter the Carolina Piedmont in search of a home for the Moravians, wrote that there was "no map of North Carolina that is now at all accurate." It is true that gold-seeking Spaniards had explored the state's western section in the sixteenth century, but, as always, Eldorado lay elsewhere. In the seventeenth century adventurous explorers and traders sought new routes to the west and better sources of goods from the Indians. The names of early explorers and chroniclers—John Lederer, John Lawson, Arthur Needham, William Dougherty, and Henry Hatcher—are thus intimately associated with this area; each of these traveled near if not through

Forsyth. But, by 1707, although more than a century of English settlement in America had passed, the Anglicans, Quakers, and Puritans all clung resolutely to the coastal plain and şeldom ventured from the friendly bays and broad rivers which provided contact with the mother country. Lands lying to the west were virtually unexplored, inhabited only by scattered Indian settlements.

Bishop Spangenberg wrote in his diary that, since 1728, when the dividing line between North Carolina and Virginia was drawn, and since Lord Granville's District had been surveyed, "men have traveled more, and have learned more about it [the Granville District]." Yet the settlers had not come in great numbers; the forests of the western Piedmont of North Carolina remained "as tractless as an ocean" and uninhabited. Hostile Indians whose lands had been taken from them were joined by other tribes who were also "resentfull and take every opportunity to show it." In 1752 Bishop Spangenberg recorded that "one must needs fear them." He further noted that isolation created immense difficulties: "Life is hard for those living *alone* and *for themselves.*"

No earlier than 1740 were there a few families located along the Hyco, Eno, and Haw rivers in the central Piedmont; not until six years later were settlers found west of the Yadkin. These brave men and women who ventured to the western Piedmont were largely of Scotch-Irish or German stock. They came from Maryland's Eastern Shore and from Pennsylvania. The reason for their migration was basically twofold: in Maryland, the soil had reached a point of virtual depletion, and in Pennsylvania the price of land had risen beyond the means of many of its inhabitants. In the Carolina "frontier," as the Piedmont was then called, land was still available at a good price and there were greater amounts of fertile soil free from the competitive interests of the east. Also, religious agitation in Pennsylvania and in the region between East Jersey and Maryland's western shore brought other settlers. Religious freedom was a sine qua non.

The route along which the settlers traveled was the Great Wagon Road that ran from Pennsylvania down the Shenandoah Valley, through the Roanoke Gap into Forsyth County, passing near Bethabara.

The lands surrounding the future site of Wachovia were

settled within the decade preceding the arrival of the Moravians. To the east, a few families lived on the headwaters of Alamance and Stinking Quarter creeks by 1745, though fixed settlements probably did not predate 1749. Likewise, the region lying to the south (which would become Davidson County) did not receive its first permanent settlers until roughly the same period. Farther south, settlers were found in the backcountry chiefly along the Yadkin, Eno, and Catawba rivers on 1,200,000 acres warranted to Henry McCulloh and Arthur Dobbs in 1737. As late as 1754, only 854 persons were to be found on these lands. To the west and northwest, settlers were found above the Shallow Ford on the Yadkin in 1747, and along the headwaters of the Catawba and Yadkin rivers slightly later.

It is surprising that in 1753 the Moravians were able to locate and acquire a large tract of land in the middle of an otherwise settled area. Why had one group of settlers using the wagon route from Pennsylvania or another traveling along a branch of the Indian trading path (both of which traversed what is now Forsyth County) not squatted or established themselves here? The answer can only be speculative.

First, it is likely that, when possible, new settlers would seek out lands lying in close proximity to areas that were already partially developed. Second, more convenient routes of transportation must in part account for the earlier settlement of outlying areas. The major artery of northeast-southwest travel was the Indian trading path. Explorers and traders had followed its course (passing south of modern Forsyth) for almost a century before Wachovia was deeded to the Moravians. The branch path that did pass through Forsyth was not so frequently traveled; it did not lead to sources of Indian trade, but it did wind its way to other settlements. The Yadkin River, which forms the current western boundary of Forsyth County and might have provided water transportation, shoals near enough to the Wachovia tract that the shipment of large amounts of goods would be difficult or impossible. The shoals did provide a place to cross the river if one were traveling farther west.

Despite the quality of the land with its abundant streams and game, Forsyth, prior to the coming of the Moravians, was a wilderness largely unsettled.

CHAPTER 2

The Establishment of the Moravian Settlements in Forsyth

IN LATE SUMMER OF 1752, in accordance with instructions received from the leaders of the Moravian church (see Chapter 4 for a discussion of the Moravians) in England, Bishop August Gottlieb Spangenberg and five Brethren set out on horseback from the Moravian community at Bethlehem, Pennsylvania, commissioned to find a suitable tract for settlement. This mission followed a suggestion from Lord Granville that the Moravians buy land in his section of North Carolina and establish a settlement there. They rode along the coast of Maryland and Virginia, crossed into North Carolina, stopped at Edenton to interview Francis Corbin, Lord Granville's agent, and, accompanied by the Granville surveyor, William Churton, set out toward the west. The journey was long and adventuresome.

Spangenberg's Tour of Exploration

Brother Joseph, as Spangenberg was affectionately called by the Brethren, and his party left Edenton the third week in September of 1752. The object of their journey, locating "100,000 acres in one tract," took them westward through what was then Granville and Anson counties. Somewhat discouraged, Spangenberg recorded that the land he had encountered was not particularly good, "and yet we are told that it has all been taken up." Proceeding on, following a southwesterly course, they reached the Catawba River and followed it from the last settlement into the "bush." Tracts were surveyed along the Little River and in what is now Alexander County. Spangenberg's band then returned to the Catawba (instead of crossing the Brushy Mountains) and followed the river to its headwaters, all along claiming other pieces of land that seemed desirable. From the headwaters of the Catawba they planned to continue across to the headwaters of the Yadkin, but their guide lost his way and took them too far to the west beyond the crest of the Blue Ridge, then northward to what proved to be the headwaters of New River. A change in direction brought them back to the southeast; taking the mountains as they came, the men proceeded on to what was doubtless the Lewis Fork of the Yadkin. Following the river to a point near where Wilkesboro now stands, they measured off two additional pieces of land. It was here, "sixty miles from any house," that they heard of the tract of land later known as Wachovia.

Two and a half weeks later, on the "three forks of Muddy Creek," a final survey was made. According to Spangenberg, this "body of land" was the "best left in North Carolina"; indeed, it seemed to "have been reserved by the Lord for the Brethren." His description of the tract follows:

It lies in Anson County, about ten miles from the Atkin [Yadkin], on the upper road to Pennsylvania, some twenty miles from the Virginia line. A road is being built from here to a Landing [Springhill, three miles below the present site of Fayetteville, North Carolina], to which goods can be brought in boats from Cape Fear, and then be hauled further into the country. It is said to be about 150 miles to this Landing, 350 miles to Edenton, and 19 miles to the nearest mill.

This tract lies particularly well. It has countless springs, and numerous fine creeks; as many mills as may be desired can be built. There is much beautiful meadow land, and water can be led to other pieces which are not quite so low. There is good pasturage for cattle, and the canes growing along the creeks will help out for a couple of winters until the meadows are in shape. There is also much lowland which is suitable for raising corn, etc. There is plenty of upland and gently sloping land which can be used for corn, wheat, etc.

On part of the land the hunters have ruined the timber by fire, but this is no disadvantage, for a wise farmer will cultivate this part first, as it is already cleared, and will so spare the fine woodland.

There is also a good deal of barren land, and it would probably be correct to say that the tract is one half good, one quarter poor, and one quarter medium. But all the land in North Carolina is mixed this way, one can hardly find 600 acres that do not include some barren land. There is also stone here, suitable for building purposes, and Br[other] Antes thinks millstones can also be found. . . .

The hills here are not large, and not to be compared with those in the other tracts we have taken up. Most of it is flat, level, land; the air is fresh and healthful; the water good, especially from the springs, which are said never to fail in summer.

The laws of this country reserve to us the rights of pasturage, hunting and fishing on our land, excluding all other persons. In the beginning we will need a good, true, untiring, trustworthy forester and hunter, for the wolves and bears must be exterminated if cattle raising is to succeed. The game which is found here, however, will help supply the table of the first settlers.

The entire tract . . . contains from 72,000 to 73,000 acres [actually 98,985]. We have surveyed it in fourteen pieces, not of exactly the same size, and yet not very different. All these pieces are adjoining, and together are about ten miles long and eleven miles wide, the width varying somewhat with the windings of the Creek. . . . Each piece has water, wood, meadow, and farm land.

Everybody who knows the country says that this is the only place where we could find so much good land together, and decidedly the best land yet vacant. Our impression is the same.

Spangenberg's words provide a superlative picture of the physical layout of the land and also the clearly reasoned justification for choosing this particular tract. Spangenberg knew that life would not be easy at first, but at least the essentials of subsistence were present—good land, abundant streams, excellent drinking water, natural materials for building, much wild game, and favorable laws to protect their property.

Spangenberg suggested the name *Der Wachau* for this tract because he thought that its hills and valleys resembled the terrain in an estate of that name in south Austria, an estate which belonged to the family of Count Nicolaus Ludwig von Zinzendorf, who did so much for the Moravian church in the eighteenth century. This name was used for many years whenever the Moravian settlers wrote in the German language, but they preferred the Latin form of the name, *Wachovia*, when they wrote in English. Traced on a modern map of Forsyth County, the Wachovia tract would extend from Rural Hall a few feet north of Friedberg Moravian Church; the east line would touch Walkertown; on the west would be a series of angles west of Muddy Creek. The survey rules of 1752 permitted only straight north-south, east-west lines and right angles.

The purchase of so large a tract—£500 sterling plus £148 9s. 2 1/2 d. annual quitrent—and the initial expenses of settlement would have laid an impossible burden upon the Moravian church, already staggering under the expense of its rapidly expanding continental work and its scattered mission fields. Therefore it was financed through a specially organized land company. Shareholders, of whom there were twenty-six, would pay "a definite proportion of these initial expenses and the annual quitrent, and [were] to receive two thousand acres in the 'Establishment' in return." A temporary loan to cover immediate needs was acquired from a Swiss gentleman, Rudolph Oehs. Spangenberg and Cornelius van Laer were elected directors of the company; in London formal instructions were drawn up and full powers of attorney were signed for the two directors. By the end of 1757 the purchase price and initial expenses had been paid.

Of the original twenty-six shareholders, only one, Traugott Bagge, actually came to Wachovia. His land lay at the northeast corner of the tract, in what is now Salem Chapel township. The shares of some of the shareholders were sold for them through the years; others presented their shares to the Moravian church, which sold the land as it deemed wise.

Founding A Civilization in the Wilderness

The thoroughness of Moravian planning, which is typified by Spangenberg's journey, is further reflected in the definite plan of settlement that followed. On 8 October 1753, after all the negotiations between Lord Granville and the church authorities had been completed, twelve unmarried Brethren set out from Bethlehem,

Pennsylvania in a large wagon bound for the Wachovia tract. Professor R. D. W. Connor wrote of them that "no better evidence is needed of the shrewd, common sense of those German settlers than the simple fact that this small band, whose mission was to lay the foundation of civilization in the wilderness, consisted of a minister of the Gospel, a warden, a physician, a tailor, a baker, a shoemaker and tanner, a gardener, three farmers, and two carpenters." Their journey to North Carolina was long and not without great difficulties; bad roads, swollen rivers, defective bridges, impassable terrain, and sickness persisted throughout. Finally, a little after noon on 17 November, the band reached Wachovia. They found a deserted cabin formerly occupied by a frontiersman named Hans Wagner. Crowded into this welcome shelter, they celebrated their arrival with a love feast and sang a hymn composed for the occasion:

> We hold arrival love feast here
> In Carolina land,
> A company of Brethren true,
> A little Pilgrim Band,
> Called by the Lord to be of those
> Who through the whole world go,
> To bear Him witness everywhere,
> And naught but Jesus know.

The hymn was sung to the accompaniment of wolves howling in the wilderness.

Within three weeks of their arrival in Wachovia, these stout Germans had cleared and planted six acres of winter wheat; during the first year, not less than fifty acres were prepared for agricultural purposes. The harvest of the first summer yielded wheat, corn, flax, millet, barley, oats, buckwheat, turnips, cotton, and tobacco, in addition to the usual garden vegetables. Fruit trees and various kinds of medicinal herbs also were planted. In short, the activities relative to subsistence in the frontier preceded those of building, as noted in their diary: "Dec. 19th [1753] We are not to undertake any building just yet, but push the clearing of land, that as soon as possible we may be able to eat our own bread."

Once preparations had been made for the season's planting and the Wagner cabin was adequately repaired, more attention was given to building and industry. Their little clearing, Bethabara ("house of passage"), was slowly becoming a center of attraction to all the surrounding country, with the services of the physician and the tailor being greatly needed by the scattered and badly equipped population. Thus the closing months of 1754 saw not only new roads that had been cut, but also the establishment of such diversified industries as a carpenter shop, a flour mill, a pottery, a cooperage works, a tannery, a blacksmith shop, and a shoe shop. Construction had commenced on a guest house and a two-story Single Brothers House; by May 1754 both were well under way.

Professor Cornelius Cathey, in *Agricultural Developments in North Carolina, 1783–1860*, points to the fact that the Moravians, "more than any other group, recognized the dangers of isolation," and as one contemporary observer remarked: "They have no idea of sitting down in a wilderness, and growing wild in it." The settlers had, in less than one year, laid the foundation of a European-style civilization where none had existed. And though the "house of passage" may not have been intended as a permanent venture, as its name indicates, Bethabara did continue to prosper throughout the latter part of the eighteenth century.

The Growth of Bethabara

Perhaps the greatest undertaking of these first settlers was the building of a mill. The magnitude of this project is evident when one considers that all the needed articles had to be made. After the site was selected, a dam had to be built and the race constructed. Next, the wheel had to be fashioned; forging the necessary wheel bearings was no small task. Millstones were then located, quarried, shaped, and dressed. The stone was discovered on Muddy Creek near the future location of Friedberg. It was a full two years before the mill was completed, but soon thereafter roads led to it from all directions.

The population of the Moravians living in Wachovia was increased in November of 1755 by the arrival of seven married couples and ten single men. Lodging for the single men was provided in either the original hut or some later dwelling, and the married couples lived on the first floor of the unfinished Brothers House. Rooms were partitioned with tent cloth which was later replaced by boards. A year later, at the close of 1756, the population of Bethabara numbered sixty-five—eighteen married people, forty-four single Brethren, one boy, and two infants.

Growth and prosperity attracted travelers. It was also known that this outpost ín the wilderness offered hospitality. Located on the ancient trail to Virginia, Bethabara was visited by other settlers and Indians. In 1754, by March the Brethren had 103 guests, and in 1755, not less than 426. Cherokee, Creek, and Catawba Indians halted there, and more than five hundred persons passed through the settlement in 1757 and 1758. The Indians described Bethabara as a place "where there are good people and much bread."

At the time of the Moravian settlement of the Wachovia tract, the Church of England was the established church. Each county was constituted a parish, with a vestry that had charge of the spiritual affairs of the parish. While individual freedom of worship was not usually interfered with, this supervision was unpleasant to the Moravians, who had a very complete system of their own for the government of their congregations and towns. The Wachovia tract was as yet under the care of the church authorities in Bethlehem, Pennsylvania, and in mid-1754, they took advantage of the coming of Arthur Dobbs, the new governor of North Carolina, to petition for special favor in the matter. Pointing to the Brethrens' Wachovia settlement, petitioners Nitschmann and Heyl, each a bishop, stated:

We . . . value nothing so much as Liberty of Conscience and the granting an unlimited Liberty of Conscience to our people will prove a proper encouragement to transplant themselves from these and other parts to North Carolina. . . . Therefore we . . . pray the land called Wachovia may be erected into a separate Parish, and that leave be given to regulate the matters in said Parish according to the Rules, Rites, and Forms of our ancient episcopal protestant church. . . .

The petition was taken to Governor Dobbs, who was urged that without the privilege of ecclesiastical government in Wachovia, "it would be almost impossible to induce more of the Brethren to move there." Dobbs was most open to the request and in October 1755 the General Assembly passed an act making Wachovia a distinct governing unit, Dobbs Parish. The success of this measure meant much to the new settlement, and ultimately it had great weight in establishing the boundaries of the county.

By the spring of 1756, Bethabara was a formidable complex. Indian unrest the previous year had necessitated the construction of a palisade around the settlement, now with at least twelve structures. Entrance was gained through either of two gates, a main gate and a secondary gate located on the southwest side of the palisade on a path leading to God's Acre, the graveyard. As one entered the main gate, the *Gemein Haus*, or congregation house, was located to his right, and the Single Brothers House was directly across from it. There were six other buildings which served as dwellings, with the remainder containing the businesses of various craftsmen. During the Indian unrest of 1755–56 refugees had erected a row of eight log cabins near the stockade, and the back walls of the cabins formed one side of the palisade.

The summer months of 1756 saw no letup in stories of Indian massacre and torture. In July a conference was held in which the pastor, Rauch, informed the Brethren of a collusion between the Cherokees and the French. Bethlehem, Pennsylvania, had already been surrounded by a stockade. After much discussion it was finally decided to erect the stockaded fortification which became the well-known Fort. All other work was suspended in order to construct the triangular-shaped fort which was to contain all the main buildings. Within ten days the structure was complete.

This stockade was recognized throughout the area as a place of refuge, and many unfortunate people were afforded protection here during the Indian wars. No amount of discouragement could prevent outsiders from moving to Bethabara. As John Henry Clewell noted in his *History of Wachovia*, "every house and every place of temporary abode was filled with the terrified refugees."

But despite the impending struggle which seemed to push steadily forward from week to week, the Brethren declined to sign a petition asking the governor for military protection—if they were unwilling to participate in military affairs, and the Brethren in Wachovia were exempt from militia duty, they could not realistically expect military aid. But, as Clewell has pointed out, much of the general fear was unjustified; the numerous bands of Indians that passed through Bethabara in the years 1756–58 were always well behaved, for there they were well treated. Because the Indian population in this area had largely been decimated by disease, one would not expect their activities to be concentrated on a stockaded settlement; rather some lonely, unguarded farmhouse in the wilderness would have been a more likely target. As it was, "by the blessing of the Lord upon their precautionary measures and upon their watchfulness and bravery, all escaped, though murder and bloodshed were all about them during the years that followed."

The Founding of Bethania

Among the refugees who assembled in Bethabara during the Indian wars, there were some who desired to unite with the Moravian settlers. There were also certain Moravians who wished to establish themselves independently instead of sharing in the closely bound cooperative social system of the settlement at Bethabara. Therefore, to accommodate both these groups, plans were made for a new settlement three miles west in a valley location known as Black Walnut Bottom, where a number of "outside friends" were already residing. The exact location of Bethania, as the settlement was to be called, was selected by Bishop Spangenberg, who had just returned to Wachovia for the first time since he had the Wachovia tract surveyed.

On 30 June 1759 the streets and lots of Bethania were laid out. Surveyor Gottlieb Reuter measured thirty town lots, two tracts of meadowland, several acres of upland for gardens and orchards, and about two thousand acres of land set apart for use of the inhabitants.

Moravian settlers who were assigned lots in the lower part of the village were Gottfried Grabs, Balthasar Hege, Charles Opiz, Christopher Schmidt, John Beroth, Adam Kremer, Michael Ranke, and Henry Bieffel. On 18 July the Grabs and their little son

William occupied the first completed cabin. The comforting Scripture for that day was, "I will fear no evil, for Thou art with me." Indeed, there was need of such comfort, for the dangers of Indian warfare still threatened the infant colony. Spangenberg and his party of town-builders rode their horses at a thundering gallop on the road from Bethabara to the new town, and it was well that they did, for Indian warriors were lurking in the forest along the trail, waiting for the opportunity to attack.

Neighbors who were permitted to settle the upper part of the "New Town" (Bethabara became known as "Old Town") were Martin Hauser and his two unmarried sons, George and Michael; Henry Spoenhauer; John Strup; Philip Shaus; Fredrick Shore, a widower; and his son, Henry.

Count Zinzendorf disapproved of the Bethania settlement on a purely doctrinal basis. It was his belief that the "mixture of Brethren and friends" found there did not conform to the idea that the Unity of Brethren was ordained of God to be a "company of workers" (as witnessed at Bethabara), rather than a denomination per se. It was a peculiar asset of those Moravians settling in Pennsylvania and North Carolina that they retained a certain broadness of thinking, so that, when confronted by the many newcomers who sought refuge in their midst, there was no proselyting. Rather, as Zinzendorf advocated, they remained a "company of workers" demonstrating great restraint in the days when, with their good organization, their competent ministry, and their pure gospel, they might have swept whole sections of America into their church.

The settlements at Bethabara and Bethania contained a comparable number of Brethren by the end of 1762, with seventy-five living in Bethabara and seventy-two in Bethania. The non-Moravian population of Wachovia and the immediate vicinity must have been slightly greater at this time, for as early as 1760 more than four hundred persons were present at the Easter Day service at Bethabara. The "time of sorrow" in which the little colony had been stricken by a deadly fever had passed. New settlers had arrived and replenished the population of Wachovia. And lastly, though war raged around them, the peace-loving Moravians and their friends remained untouched. The Church

Book for 1760 recorded: "Among our neighbors more than fifteen were slain. The Indians said later that they had tried to make prisoners here, but had failed; that several times they had been stopped by the sound of the watchman's horn and the ringing of the bell for morning and evening services." Those staunch, God-fearing Brethren had unknowingly discouraged Indian movements simply in the performance of their daily ritual. For as Bishop Spangenberg said to frightened Anna Catharina, who had moved to Wachovia from Bethlehem: "The Lord has brought you here, my child, and He has work still for you to do; wait patiently for the revelation of His will." To those early Moravians, faith did triumph over feeling.

Salem is Founded

Salem, as the central town in Wachovia, was planned from the first purchase of the tract; the name of the town was suggested by Count Zinzendorf six or more years before it was possible to carry out the plan. He probably chose the name, Salem, because it means "peace," and he wanted peace, in the truest and broadest sense, to be a characteristic of the place.

Active planning for the building of Salem began with the arrival of Frederic William Marshall in 1764. The church authorities had appointed him *Oeconomus* (financial director and business administrator). Several months of searching the area finally produced a most suitable site for the new town. Almost at the center of the Wachovia tract, about six miles from Bethabara, a place was chosen halfway up the hill leading from *der Wach* (Salem Creek) to the *Annaberg* (future hilltop site of Winston). The ground sloped in both directions, east and west, but there were several good springs to furnish water and a clear little branch on the west (Tar Branch) to supply their immediate needs until wells could be dug. The town would be high enough up the ridge to be safe in times of flood, when the Wach might, as it occasionally did, rise to a dangerous height. On the other hand, on still higher ground, there were good springs which would make possible a water system when the settlers found time to arrange it.

The original plan for the future town of Salem was drawn in

Europe. It called for certain main structures grouped around a central square, from which streets would radiate like the spokes of a wheel. This rather formal plan was quickly given up for one that was simple and more suitable to the terrain. There would be a main street running north on the crest of the hill, with parallel streets to the east and west, and cross streets at suitable intervals. One of the blocks so formed would serve as the open square around which the chief houses were to stand.

On 6 January 1766, the original diary records: "Monday, a dozen Brethren partly from Bethania, partly from Bethabara, took a wagon and went to the new town site where in the afternoon they cut down the trees on the place where the first house was to stand, singing several stanzas as they worked. . . . Our Text for the day was beautifully appropriate for this little beginning in building: 'I will defend this city.'"

Within a matter of months the first house was built on the main street. It was of frame construction. The available material was not well suited to the building of a log house, and so another method was used. Heavy timbers were erected for the framing; then rude laths, wrapped in a mixture of clay and straw, were inserted horizontally from one grooved upright to another. When pressed down, they made a thick wall, as warm as brick. If the clay began to wash out after years of service, the wall could be weatherboarded and made as good as new. When the first room was finished, Gottfried Praezel moved in and set up his loom, a forecast of Forsyth's textile industry of the future.

The second house on the main street was known for years as "the two-story house." The first house and others of that period were generally of one story, with a high-pitched roof and a cellar. On the first floor of the two-story house was the first meeting hall of Salem. Until it was built, worship services had been held in one of the rooms in the small first house. The immediate preparation of a place of worship indicates the primary purpose for which the Moravians had come to North Carolina—freedom to worship God in their devout, practical way. They had an inherited belief that religion was a personal matter between a man and his God, but they believed also in a religion to be lived every day, seven days a week.

The efforts of the Moravians in North Carolina sought in part to rectify certain misjudgments made in earlier attempts at settlement. In Georgia, the climate had been against them, and some of their number had died; their neighbors had also refused to understand their position in several practical matters. In Pennsylvania, the Brethrens' concern for the conversion of the Indians had been misunderstood, and the Moravian community life of the early years was severely criticized by outsiders, reflecting the animosity shown the Unity in Europe. In North Carolina, surrounded by their own broad acres, the Moravian settlers made immediate arrangements for places of worship, to which they welcomed all visitors who might wish to unite with them in services. And again they made no attempt to proselyte. Rather they sought to hold the leaderless groups steady until pastors of their own various denominations could be sent to them, a fraternal generosity which has seldom been understood.

Before the year 1766 ended, two more of the small houses had been built just north of the first house, and during the next year a potter's shop and a blacksmith's shop were built. Both crafts were of immense value to the town and to the neighborhood. Whenever news spread through the countryside that the Salem potter had burned a kiln of ware, so many persons crowded in that sometimes there were not enough pieces to go around. Good clay was found in a meadow by the creek, now the Salem College athletic field—yellow clay for the making of kitchenware, and gray clay for pipeheads, so long a staple of trade in Salem.

Brick and tile were also made in that meadow, but not by the potter; brickmakers were employed for this service. Salem did not import brick and furniture from Europe, as was done in many cities on the Atlantic seaboard. Salem imported settlers who could make furniture and brick and other things which the residents of a village needed. This made the town largely self-sufficient in the days when the only means of communication were letters carried by passing travelers or by special messengers, and when the only means of transportation inland were carts or wagons. Some things, of course, were brought by wagon from Pennsylvania, or from Petersburg, Virginia, or from Charleston, South Carolina, or from Cross Creek (Fayetteville), still the nearest point to which things could be brought by boat. At those places deerskins and a few other local commodities could be bartered for coffee, tea, window glass, sugar, and other articles handled by the Salem store. Books usually came from England or Germany, where Salem maintained a standing order for the publications of the Unity.

The first extensive building operation in Salem was the erection of the Single Brothers House, which faced the central square from the west. This building housed the workshops, the journeymen, and the apprentices. The Single Brothers had their own organization, their own finances, their own kitchen, their own farm; indeed, for many years the Brothers House was the industrial center of the community. They took possession of their house in 1769, most of them coming from Bethabara, where there had been a similar institution; Bethabara largely became a farming community after Salem was established. The Brothers House was of frame construction, with a difference. In burning brick for chimneys, there were often some bricks which were not hard enough to stand exposure to the weather; therefore the second type of framing omitted the laths with the clay-straw wrapping, added a few more inside braces, and filled the intervening spaces with these softer brick, laid up without mortar.

The third type of building came in with the erection of the *Gemein Haus*, for many years the largest house in the community. The foundation and the first story were of uncut stone, laid up with clay. The walls were made very thick to compensate for lack of lime in the binding, lime being very scarce and hard to get. The second story was of the second type of frame construction, with a high-pitched roof that permitted several rooms on the third floor. In the course of time the entire building was covered with stucco.

On the second floor of the *Gemein Haus* was the meeting hall, which was consecrated on 13 November 1771, the same day the Salem Congregation was formally organized. On the first and second floors at the north end were housekeeping apartments for ministers of the congregation; on the third floor there were guest rooms. The south half of the first and third floors respectively was used by the Single Sisters of the community for living rooms and workrooms.

The next year, 1772, saw much moving from Bethabara to Salem. The community store was moved into the first floor of the two-story house, and the merchant Traugott Bagge settled his family on the second floor. Gottlieb Reuter built a small house for himself and his wife diagonally across from the southwest corner of the square. Matthew Miksch built a small house on Main Street. Miksch, like Praezel, was a forerunner of a most important industry in the city's future development; he manufactured and sold snuff and smoking tobacco. Heinrich Herbst took charge of a tanyard just west of the village. Jacob Meyer and his wife ran the popular tavern. Other small houses were built, and by the end of the year most of the residents of Bethabara had moved to Salem.

Kernersville, Friedberg, Friedland, and Hope

About the time that Salem was established in the center of the Wachovia tract, several other towns sprang up near the borders of what was to become Forsyth County.

Kernersville, the largest of these, was not originally laid out as a town, but gradually grew to such a size. Some time between 1756 and 1760, an Irishman by the name of Caleb Story bought four hundred acres of land some twelve miles east of Salem near the current Guilford County line. Tradition says that he paid for it with four gallons of rum. Story then sold the tract to a man by the name of William Dobson, and from this the place came to be called Dobson's Cross Roads, a name it retained for many years. Located at this important crossroads were an inn and a storehouse. The more important of the intersecting roads was the intercolonial stageline, which was the route the Moravians of Wachovia followed to Bethlehem, Pennsylvania; Dobson's Tavern was the first stopover.

Friedberg, on the lower edge of the county, had a similar beginning. In August 1754, Adam Spach, a native of Pfaffenheim, Alsace, settled about three miles south of the Wachovia line. He speedily made the acquaintance of the Moravians, taking refuge at Bethabara during the Indian wars. Later he urged the Brethren to come and hold services in his home. In 1758 a minister preached to eight families in Spach's home, thus beginning the Friedberg Congregation. This practice continued at intervals until 1766.

With the arrival of several additional families from Pennsylvania in 1769, the church authorities set apart thirty-four acres near the southern boundary of Wachovia for the use of the new congregation, which then numbered fourteen families. The men were Valentine Frey, Christian Frey, George Frey, Peter Frey, George Hartmann, Adam Hartmann, John Mueller, John Boeckel, Frederick Boeckel, Jacob Crater, Martin Walk, Peter Foltz, Adam Spach, and Christian Stauber. Another member later associated with the society was Marcus Hoehns (Hanes). Spach purchased seventy-seven acres, which he added to the original thirty-four. In 1773 about eighty-one acres were purchased for the purpose of building a schoolhouse.

The first meetinghouse of the Friedberg Congregation was consecrated on 11 March 1769, and in January 1772 the Friedberg Congregation of the Unitas Fratrum was formally established.

The settlement at Friedland, near the eastern line of the Wachovia survey, was begun in a different manner. In 1769 six German families arrived in Wachovia. They were part of a company of emigrants from the Palatinate and Württemberg, who, about 1738, had settled near Broadbay in Maine. There they became acquainted with one of the Moravians. Though it was the desire of a small number of their group to establish a congregation, certain legal difficulties concerning their title deeds prevented them from doing so. They resolved to move to North Carolina. Taking the only transportation south, by ship, they unfortunately wrecked off the coast of Virginia. Finally, after great difficulty, they arrived in Wachovia, poor and wayworn, many of them in ill health. They were given temporary homes in Bethabara and Salem. The next year, 1770, they were joined by eight more families who wished to secure their own tract. Therefore, eighteen hundred acres of the Unity's land were sold to them, with the church authorities reserving thirty acres in the center of the tract for a church and a schoolhouse. In February 1772 the cornerstone of the church was laid, and three years later the building was consecrated. The Friedland Congregation was formally recognized in September 1780. The names of the early members of Friedland were John Peter Green (Kroehn), Michael Rominger, Philip Christoph Vogler, Melchior Schneider, John Lanius, Peter Fiedler, George Frederick Hahn, and Jacob Reid.

The first English congregation in Wachovia was Hope, located in the southwestern corner of the tract. Several settlers in that quarter had enjoyed the protection of the "Dutch Fort" during the Indian wars and had afterward joined the congregation at Friedberg. Because they desired an English-speaking church of their own, they began to hold separate meetings, some as early as 1758. In 1775 several additional English families from Carroll's Manor, Maryland, located in their section of Wachovia; soon afterward a meetinghouse was begun, although it was not completed until 1780. Early residents of the community included families named Peddycord, Padget, Chitty, Boner, Goslen, Hamilton, Boyer, Markland, Slater, and Riddle.

Other Settlements

The accounts of the following settlements have been grouped together, not because they are of less importance in the history of Forsyth county, but rather because of their later dates of settlement or a lack of material about them.

The early history of the Belews Creek settlement can be found only in fragments. In 1753 a survey on Belews Creek recorded two hundred acres of land each for Thomas Linville (Linvall), Sr., and Thomas Linville, Jr. Fourteen years later, the county court in Salisbury (Forsyth was a part of Rowan at that time) granted three public roads from Salem, one of which led to "Beloe's Creek." Salem agreed to provide overseers for the maintenance of the first seven miles to "Blewers Creek." The new road to "Beloe's Creek" was opened in 1773. Earlier, in 1772, itinerant Moravian ministers preached at Belews Creek, and later enjoyed the hospitality of settlers Fehr, Saylor (Seeler), and others. A Mr. Hoffman's son from "Bielus Creek" was employed in 1774 as hostler at the Bethabara tavern. Names of early settlers appearing in the records from time to time are Neal, Preston, Pegram, Hester, Dean, Brooks, Strader, and McNally.

Peter Pfaff arrived in Wachovia in 1771 and settled at Friedberg. His son Isaac married Margaret Fulk (Margaretha Volk) in Bethania; they made their home on a farm west of the town. Peter Pfaff was to join them at a later time. It was around this farm that the future Pfafftown was to grow. The first recorded mention of the name appeared in the Bethania records for 1812.

Three miles from Bethania was "Bruxe's Town," later known as Brookstown. As early as 1793, one landowner's name appeared in connection with a ferry on the Yadkin River—Brooks. A connection between this name and that of the settlement seems obvious.

"Hermanus (Harmon) Miller enters one hundred acres of land in Surry County, lying on a Branch of Beaver Dam Creek, beginning on Jacob Lash's Line . . . Jan. 3d, 1778." This entry introduces Beaver Dam, the name first given to the Nazareth Evangelical Lutheran Church of Rural Hall. Records of this church state that the congregation was organized in 1785 and that A. Kiger gave a piece of land for the school located there. Since there was a scarcity of Lutheran ministers, for a score of years from 1796, Moravian ministers served the congregation by request. In time, the railway lines to North Wilkesboro and Mount Airy converged in the town, and the name Rural Hall was bestowed upon the village. A thriving industrial and trading center developed.

The original settlement in the Clemmons area consisted of one square mile of Lord Granville's land, which was purchased in 1757 by a Welshman, William Johnson. This comprises the central portion of Tanglewood Park today. During the Indian uprisings, Johnson surrounded his home with a log fort for protection. With the possible exception of a few scattered settlers who constructed cabins around Johnson's compound, the area remained largely uninhabited until 1800. It was in this year that Peter Clemmons moved nearby from Guilford County. Principally a farmer, Clemmons also owned and operated a store and a mill. The house which he built served as a private residence, a stagecoach stop, and a church. Soon, because of the settlement's growing economic importance, more people moved in, and a new town, Clemmons, sprang up. Clemmons's location on the principal east-west stage route and its proximity to the river plantations made the little town a hub of activity through the first half of the nineteenth century. Peter Clemmons's grandson, Edwin Thomas Clemmons, successfully operated a stage line from 1840 to 1875; his routes included Salem to Raleigh, Clemmons to High Point, and Asheville to Edenton.

Settlements in the Waughtown area date at least back to colonial times. First called Baggetown after Brother Charles Bagge, the village was later known as Charlestown and finally was called Waughtown after James Waugh, a prominent resident.

Across the Town Fork Road from John Armstrong, Robert Walker secured four hundred acres, formerly called the Douglas Place, his grant being dated 1779. This tract was northeast of Salem and is designated on a map of 1771, "Robt. Walker." The name Walker spread throughout the vicinity and it is probable that Walkertown derives its name from this family. Sam Wagner, one of the selectmen who was denied a pardon by Governor Tryon after the troubles of the Regulation, was also listed on a map of 1771. At any rate, the name Wagner, Wagoner, or Waggoner also has long familiarity in the Walkertown neighborhood.

Lewis Lagenauer, a descendant of the Lagenauer family that came to Friedland about 1773, settled in western Forsyth County and there built a substantial brick house. Tradition has it that the village which grew up about his home was called Lewisville, after the first name of its founder.

Close to Lagenauer's settlement, along the Yadkin River, the Williams family set up their plantation at Panther Creek before the American Revolution. Upstream was the Martin plantation. Another small settlement near Lewisville, West Bend, was created by the families Black, Jones, McBride, Hauser, Dinkins, and Nading.

Conclusion

J. F. D. Smyth, a visitor to the Moravian settlements at Wachovia in 1773, noted that "they certainly are valuable subjects, and by their unremitting industry and labor have brought a large extent of wild, rugged country into a high state of population and improvement." Within twenty years of Spangenberg's initial surveys in this area, a civilization had been founded in the wilderness. Unlike other regions of the Piedmont that were still dependent on subsistence farming and the numerous but widespread industries of the Scotch-Irish, the Moravians had established a prospering self-sufficient community. Again, as Smyth observed, "This society, sect, or fraternity of the Moravians have everything in common and are possessed of a very large and extensive property." The mill, the "many excellent and very valuable farms," and the large number of "useful and lucrative manufactures" were joined with great religious zeal and intellectual prowess to make Forsyth's first civilized inhabitants unique in their time and place. They were "all an industrious people."

CHAPTER 3

Forsyth County during the American Revolution

AT THE TIME OF THE AMERICAN REVOLUTION, the Forsyth County area was still relatively isolated from the rest of North Carolina and the other colonies. The revolutionary movement, however, came early and had a lasting impact on both Moravian and non-Moravian settlements. The Moravians as a body tried to stay clear of the ideological and political struggles, but as individuals they were unable to refrain from taking sides. Their attempts to remain neutral were interpreted by both sides as active support of the enemy. More than once during the period 1767–83 this area was on the verge of civil unrest between the Moravian and non-Moravian elements, and sometimes among the Moravians themselves. Whenever politically, economically, or socially expedient, however, during the course of the war, the Brethren drifted with the tide of the Revolution and played a prominent but militarily inactive role in the ensuing events.

The Regulation

Outside the Moravian communities in Wachovia, life was particularly difficult for the early settlers of the backcountry. Geographically, these people were separated from the eastern plain and the seat of colonial government by a sparsely settled region of pine forest which stretched monotonously from the valley of the Roanoke on the north to the Cape Fear valley on the south. Roads which traversed the colony in an east-west direction were frequently impassable. The necessities of life in the wilderness were plentiful, but the luxuries were few. Some old men who had been Regulators told the Reverend E. W. Carruthers around 1820 that "there was not a plank floor, a feather bed, a riding carriage, or a side saddle within the bounds of their acquaintance." Therefore, from time to time, many of these pioneers turned to the relative comforts of the Moravian communities for their wants: tailored and crafted goods, guns, ground meal, pottery, shoes, and the services of the physician, among others. They had taken refuge in the Bethabara complex during the Indian wars and later had willingly sought the pastoral care of the Moravian ministers. All in all there was good rapport between Moravian and non-Moravian groups, and at least a tolerable dependence on the Moravian community, until about 1764 or 1765, when a change in these relations occurred.

The "notorious and intolerable abuses" that the Piedmont settlers suffered as the result of a corrupt and inbred county court system were causing unrest in the backcountry. As the author of the "Nutbush Address," George Sims, declared, it was "not the form of Government, nor yet the body of our laws, that we are quarreling with, but with the malpractices of our County Courts, and abuse which we suffer by those empowered to manage public affairs." The so-called Regulators began to organize and make various requests of the General Assembly; most often the action taken was considered unsatisfactory by the Regulators. Governor Tryon lent a sympathetic ear, for even he realized the need for reform in county government. Tryon and the assembly read and considered a number of their petitions. Still, no dramatic relief was forthcoming, and riots broke out. The years 1765–70 were indeed trying for the colonial government. At the same time that the lowlanders of the east were espousing so loudly the dictum "no taxation without representation," they were exploiting the highlanders of the frontier with unfair taxation. But how did the Brethren fit into this movement?

The Moravian population of Wachovia actually pursued a clear-cut isolationist policy in its attitudes toward colonial government, and did so by choice. Earlier negotiations with the proper authorities secured for the Moravians exemption from militia duty during the French and Indian War. Further, the Moravians said, "[we] humbly [recommend] ourselves into your Excellency's [Governor Tryon's] favor and protection with all our invaluable religious rights and privileges." The governor's reply read: "I shall always be glad to encourage and promote that good order, harmony, and industry which so happily subsists in the Society of the United Brethren." Because the Moravians were good subjects, they did enjoy his "favor and protection in the enjoyment of their religion." A successful journey to Wachovia in 1767 caused Governor Tryon to urge the inhabitants of Dobbs Parish to elect their own representative assemblymen. Wisely, perhaps even knowingly, Brother Loesch answered that such an action might cause "envy and ill will" against them. Governor Tryon knew all too well that such a thing could happen under any circumstances and resentment was already building up.

Without complaint the Brethren had regularly paid their quitrent to Lord Granville's agents; they were the king's friends and exponents of the status quo. Because they were thriving and prosperous in their little settlements and because of their good relations with the colonial government, they saw no need of change.

The year 1768 marked the formal organization of the Regulators. Colonel Fanning noted that Orange County was the "very nest and bosom of rioting and rebellion—The People are now . . . meeting, conspiring, and confederating by solemn oath and open violence." A general unrest created by their activities even raised the suspicion of "an attack from the whole united force of the regulators." Militia was called out in Halifax, Granville, Rowan, Mecklenburg, Cumberland, and Johnston counties. But, as might be expected, the Moravians of Wachovia deplored these "disturbances caused by a Mob," and so recorded in the *Memorabilia* of 1768.

It seems that Forsyth's Regulators were located in three basic areas: at Abbotts Creek, near Walkertown, and along the Yadkin. A particularly large group of them at Abbots Creek refused to take Governor Tryon's oath of allegiance and many of them were summarily declared outlaws. Some time later, in May 1771, a subtle punishment was administered them when General Hugh Waddell requisitioned "Thirty good Steers and Twenty Barrels of good Flour," this being no small amount of food. Sam Wagner from the vicinity of Walkertown distinguished himself as a leader and organizer in the Regulator movement. He was denied the governor's pardon for his activities.

The Regulators along the Yadkin were well organized by 1768; in that year a number of them signed a petition protesting public taxes. Three years later a force about seven hundred strong gathered on the road by the river and stopped all those persons en route to the Salisbury court. Their tactics on this occasion proved so successful that the court session was not held. In March 1771 a group of twelve Regulators from Yadkin came to Bethabara asserting claims to a part of the Wachovia tract. The Brethren simply suggested that they register their claims in court. Of course, since there were no claims, nothing came of the matter.

Two months later, Regulators passed through Bethabara almost daily as they traveled to Orange County for a large gathering. Some, who were quite open and friendly, admitted to the Moravians that they had been forced into going; others, not so friendly, threatened that when they finished with the governor they would take on the Brethren in Wachovia. Again, the threat was nothing more than vocal.

On 16 May 1771, six years of riot and protest culminated in a confrontation between the eastern militia of Governor Tryon and a strong force of Regulators. A *Relation of the Battle fought at Alamance*, written by an unknown member of the Wachovia Brethren, is recorded below. The language used by its author is rather indicative of Moravian sentiment toward the movement.

His Excellency [Governor Tryon] . . . sent one of his Aids du Camps, and the Sheriff of Orange, with a letter to the Rebels, requiring them to lay down their Arms, surrender their outlawed Ringleaders, and submit themselves to the Laws of their County, Allowing them One Hour to accept of the terms to prevent the effusion of Blood which might ensue, as they were at that time in a State of War and Rebellion against their King their Country and their Laws. . . . They called out that he might fire and be damned. . . . It is computed that the Rebels must have had killed in the Battle about One Hundred Men, and upwards of twenty taken prisoners. . . .

This account, though obvious in its reference to "rebels," is not nearly so demonstrative of the Brethren's feelings as this passage from the Wachovia *Memorabilia* of 1771:

With the Savior's help this year has been marked by the maintenance of our good name with those in authority, and their recognition of our loyalty to the existing Government during the tumult and uprising that has existed in almost all the counties of the Province, and they have acknowledged that we took no part whatever in this *insurrection*. Our position brought us into danger that our houses and towns would be destroyed; even our lives were threatened, especially in May, when threats were not only uttered here and there against us, but came also from the Government, to whom false reports had been taken; but even more evidently was the almighty hand of God held over us, and all their evil designs were brought to naught, neither did those in authority cease to trust us, but on the contrary His Excellency Gov. Tryon, and his whole army of about 3,000 men, spent June 4th to 10th here in Bethabara and the adjacent fields and meadows. . . .

An incidental note speaking well not only of the Brethren's treatment of Governor Tryon but also of his regard for them is recorded in the Bethabara Diary for 1771. After taking "tender leave" of a group of well-wishers, the Governor went to speak to the Sisters. "The cook said his face showed as much emotion as though he were bidding farewell to his own family." The Moravians refused to take any payment for services rendered the governor, which "he accepted . . . as a token of regard for him." And in concluding his comments the diarist again confirms the Brethren's loyalty to the colonial government: "We thanked our faithful and merciful Lord from our hearts, that he had not only helped us through all the difficult circumstances, but had given us such favor with our Government."

The Coming of the Revolution

The good favor of the General Assembly was also extended to the Moravians. In 1773, Dobbs Parish was threatened by division. Frederic William Marshall and Traugott Bagge personally delivered a petition to the assembly requesting the members "to do their utmost that Wachovia remain one Parish, belonging to one county only." Again, "these Brethren found favor with those in authority, and carried out their commission with success and blessing." Wachovia remained one undivided parish as confirmed by an act of the assembly that "placed [it] as a whole in Surry County."

Not long after the troubles of the Regulation had ended, more pressing issues confronted all thirteen of the colonies in their relation to the mother country. The First Continental Congress met in September 1774 and adopted the Declaration of Rights, later considered an act of rebellion by Parliament. For all practical purposes the American Revolution was under way by the last month of that year.

Active trouble began in the early summer of 1775 after the Battle of Lexington stirred resentment throughout the colonies. News of this engagement reached Salem by rumor on 8 May; newspapers received the next week reported that there had been a "skirmish near Boston," and that Parliament had declared the Congress meeting in Philadelphia to be in rebellion against the crown.

In the days that followed there was much confusion in Wachovia—mental confusion caused by the uncertainty as to what should or could be done by the colonists who wanted independence, by a flood of rumors with which the loyalists sought to arouse the adherents of the crown, and by economic troubles which resulted from high prices and fluctuating currency.

The Moravians of Wachovia were divided in sentiment. They had no quarrel with England; indeed, they had many friends in that country. Likewise, they had many friends among the colonists who were seeking some sort of solution to the impending struggle. The Brethren refused to attend the election of delegates to a convention in Hillsborough in August, and because of this certain of the Bethabara leaders were interrogated by local officials. At this session the officials were convinced that the Moravians would at least not bear arms against them or the crown. But suspicion of loyalist sentiment prevailed. The Moravians were indeed loyal, to those they believed to be in control of their adopted country.

There must have been many discussions about the best way to meet the impending struggle. Bishop John Michael Graff handled the matter with rare good judgment and with surprising success. He begged the Brethren to refrain from any discussion, especially with strangers who might misquote them. Yet he "left every man free to act according to his conscience" in the matter of militia duty. Salem stood firm for freedom from military service and the inhabitants were willing to pay a threefold tax in lieu thereof (£25 for each eligible person per year). The Broadbayers of Friedland took exactly the opposite position. Other Moravian groups in Wachovia were more or less divided in sentiment, but Graff's unbounded patience, tact, and ability held them all steadfast in their confessed desire for Christian brotherhood.

Traugott Bagge, the Salem storekeeper, was not only the chief spokesman of the Wachovia Brethren during the American Revolution but also the best historian and barometer of the feeling of the times. In writing of the situation in Wachovia, he stated: "The unsettled people of the land had long been wanting a revolution, to free them of all taxes and take possession of property of more wealthy persons. Many of this type became civil and military officers, others aspired to become such, and these were the men who gave the Brethren the most trouble and were the most dangerous, causing them much harm and much sorrow of heart." No better description of the avaricious feelings of the Brethrens' neighbors may be found. They coveted the Moravian holdings as well as their good relations with the colonial government. When the opportunity arose for those neighbors to acquire something for nothing, they wasted no time in attempting to do so.

· Clewell divides the "enemies" of the Brethren into four classes. Those in the first class were "desperadoes" who always flourish in times of civil unrest. A second group, the "hotheads," laid an undue stress on some fancied personal wrong done by the Moravians, for example, when more than once the Brethren refused a "doubtful piece of money" in the store or tavern. The third group was quite large and was made up of people who as yet misunderstood the Moravians with their peculiar customs and speaking a language other than English. Most significant was a fourth group consisting of those "envious, shiftless people" who believed that if by some political tangle the Moravians were banished, the outsiders (*Fremde*) could enter claims for the mills, the trades, the homes, and the well-cultivated farms. Their enmity was based on the prospect of material gain, a fact known to the Brethren, who actually feared exile.

The Brethren's friends were generally among the better-educated classes: their representatives in the Continental Congress and the General Assembly, certain members of the Committee of Safety who had studied them, and army officers, both Continental and royalist.

The Revolution

Certain events of the years 1771–79 confirmed the Moravians' noninvolvement, yet raised suspicion as to their sympathies. The congress which met at Hillsborough in August 1775 authorized the first issue of paper currency without royal authority. This action was followed by other issues in North Carolina and adjoining states. The fiat money depreciated rapidly, thus throwing a heavy burden on the businesses of Salem and eventually bringing them heavy losses. It is no wonder that Moravian businessmen were reluctant to accept the continental currency. The problem facing them was one of simple economics, rather than one of patriotism.

Again, in 1775 Bagge recorded that the "Brethren, especially in Salem and Bethabara, took no part in what was going on, and as our commerce continued while around us it had greatly lessened, and as we still had some stock of goods, jealousy of us constantly increased."

The year 1776 brought the beginning of demands for supplies for militia and Continental troops; pressure for supplies continued throughout the war. Salem was only a small village, and how it could furnish the large quantities of supplies required of it is one of the mysteries of the Brethren's history in Forsyth. Traugott Bagge, though he held no commission, was virtually a purchasing agent for the patriots during the last years of the war and was officially certified as "a true friend to American liberty."

The Halifax Convention of April 1776 forwarded to the Continental Congress its resolution to cooperate in declaring independence. Congress acted on 4 July; on receipt of the official notice of the Declaration of Independence in Salem it was posted in the Salem Tavern. On the following Sunday, petitions for the king were dropped from the litany read in the Salem church, and prayers for the American government were substituted.

The assembly of April 1777 passed a new militia act under which all men from sixteen to sixty years of age were liable for duty. No exceptions were allowed for conscientious scruples. This, and the Confiscation Act of November of the same year, placed the Moravians in a precarious position. Future developments were uncertain until January 1779, when the assembly drew up a form of affirmation of allegiance which the Moravians were willing to accept. That they had "no implements of war" and "did not wish to use violence against this or any other power" was understood. The assembly, "in order to quiet the Consciences and indulge the religious scruples of the Unitas Fratrum," entitled them "to all those Rights, Privileges and Immunities they heretofore respectively enjoyed." In particular the Brethren were happy about their exemption from militia duty, though at the expense of a triple tax. On 4 February 1779 the men of Salem took the affirmation before Justice Dobson: "I . . . do solemnly and sincerely declare and affirm . . . that I will truly and faithfully demean myself as a peaceable Subject of the independent State of North Carolina . . . and that I will not abet or join the Subjects or forces of the King of Great Britain, or other enemies of this State."

This continued reassurance demanded by the authorities must have greatly perplexed the Brethren. Certainly within their own minds collectively, and on paper as early as March 1777, they had affirmed their allegiance to "those in authority over us." As the Salem *Memorabilia* recorded: "We have made it our rule, in these times and under the new [North Carolina] Constitution, to be subject to those in authority over us, and submit to all laws they have made, so far as they are not against our conscience." And, as further recorded in the declaration of the Brethren, 15 February 1776, "we intend to demean ourselves as hitherto as quiet people, who wish the wellfare of the Country and Province, & that we nor either of us will not at any time intermedle in political affairs." Because it was politically expedient, the Moravians chose noninvolvement, a course they had continually taken since Governor Tryon's request for an assemblyman from Dobbs Parish.

By the late 1770s the Moravians of Wachovia, as a united body, had severed their political ties with Great Britain and had affirmed their support of the new state. They continued to remain militarily inactive; they said no more of the conflict than was necessary. Individually, the Brethren expressed their own preference of government. In one instance the Salem Diary recorded that "several of our brethren were taken to task for incautious remarks about the condition of the country, but if they will not listen they must suffer." And, at another place in the diary, "we reproved two boys for unwise enthusiasm, the one hurrahing so loudly for Washington, the other responding in an equally enthusiastic manner for King George!"

In April 1779 Pulaski's Legion was in Salem for four days. The men behaved well, but one of the soldiers had smallpox and this brought the disease into Salem in an epidemic which lasted until October.

The year 1780 was full of difficulty and danger. Trade and handicrafts suffered more loss than they made profit. Currency fell in value. Taxes were three times what they had been the previous year. Fortunately, there was a good harvest on the farms of Wachovia, for besides the never-ending stream of soldiers many poor families passed through Salem, fleeing first in one direction, and then in another, as the English and Tories swarmed over South Carolina and Virginia. All possible kindness was shown to them, though their increased presence placed a severe burden on the slender resources of the town.

In his memorabilia of the Revolution, Brother Bagge recorded that "the English came as far as Camden and the Cheraws. In our neighborhood more than a thousand Tories gathered, who did many deeds of violence. To put a stop to this the militia was called out, and scoured the land pressing horses, arms and provisions, and living at discretion in many places. Our towns were constantly visited, but no payments were made. In addition all sorts of demands were made for provisions."

Search parties that passed through Wachovia placed great impositions on the inhabitants. In August 1780 several hundred Virginia militia were in pursuit of Tories who supposedly were hiding in this vicinity. The Virginians stayed at Bethabara for three weeks, "eating up all the provisions on hand." Also, on 13 September of that same year, Brother and Sister Fritz were "protected from bodily injury when Sixteen Light-Horse broke into the School-house at Hope." Another Tory hunt in October brought five hundred militia to Bethabara: "As it was raining they forced their way into the houses, lived entirely at discretion, committed excesses, and nearly ruined the entire establishment."

The next year, 1781, found Wachovia "in the very theatre of the war." First came parts of Greene's army: ammunition wagons which stopped to load shells, and a field hospital which stayed only one day, but left behind the more seriously wounded men to be cared for by the Salem physician, Jacob Bonn. Then came lawless militia; the Wilkes men especially seemed to delight in excesses of every kind, including personal attacks. Bagge reported that in early February 1781 a preaching service at Friedland was disturbed by "Georgia soldiers [who were joined by the Wilkes men] belonging to General Pickens' troops that plundered several plantations and treated some of our members badly, giving them blows." Each group "tried by deception to draw an admission that we were Tories." Certain members of the Friedberg congregation were even arrested.

The British army, under Lord Cornwallis, camped in Bethania on 9 February 1781. Headquarters were established at the home of George Hauser, a distinguished patriot of the Revolution. Nearly five thousand soldiers, accompanied by as many camp followers, seized almost all available food in that area—chickens, cattle, and hogs—as well as a number of horses. The discovery of several stills outside the town resulted in much drunkenness among the soldiers.

On 10 February the British troops reached Salem. The regulars made many demands and the camp followers stole a great deal, but the diary states that on the whole less damage was done than might have been expected. One particularly unfortunate incident occurred, though, when eight soldiers held Brother Heinzmann of Friedland at bayonet point, "trying to force him to give them food, of which he had none." He was rescued "just in time" by the visit of several Brethren from Salem.

The days following Cornwallis's departure were fairly quiet, but from 15 to 18 February "days of darkness and terror" descended on the inhabitants of Wachovia. First came Major Dixon's troops from Mecklenburg County; they were soon joined by two parties of General Pickens's men and several wandering groups.

"When two parties of the Wilkes militia arrived there was no escape," Brother Bagge's contemporary account records. Again, "on the pretext that we were traitors to the country . . . and that we were carrying on clandestine intercourse with the English," the most terrible excesses were committed. Many of the Brethren thought that "the ruin of our towns had been agreed upon." Some of the Sisters feared for their lives when "loaded guns were held at their breasts." Fortunately, these days ended without serious injury or loss of life, but there was always the chance that the marauders might return.

The battle fought at Guilford Courthouse on 15 March 1781 attracted little attention at the time because it was, the diarist recorded, "another English victory," and Cornwallis held the field. But in fact, though Greene had retired, this battle marked the beginning of the end. On 30 October 1781, Salem received word that Cornwallis had surrendered at Yorktown almost two weeks before. The greatest part of the hostilities in the South were thus ended, but as the Revolutionary *Memorabilia* recorded, "the misery of this period cannot be described, and to all else smallpox was added in Friedberg. In Bethania and in Friedberg, and also in Friedland, highwaymen attacked Brethren in their houses, or on the public roads, on the pretext that they belonged to one or the other party, and robbed and injured them. The more should we praise the wonderful hand of God, who preserved the lives of our Brethren, and finally put an end to the distress." The misery suffered by the Moravians living in Wachovia was as great as that of any group other than those who remained loyal to their king. They were continually the brunt of attacks from both Tories and patriots; more than once they faced starvation because of depleted stores and confiscation of their livestock. Continually threatened by ostracism and exile, they never wavered in their rightful claim to the land on which they lived, nor did they ever think that the God in whom they believed would let them down. The future could be no worse than the past.

Aftermath of the Fighting, and Peace

In November 1781 and again in January 1782 the North Carolina Assembly met in Salem; each time the members failed to transact any business for lack of a quorum. The presence of so many distinguished guests taxed the resources of the town to the limit, but it was of lasting benefit since the assemblymen learned to know and appreciate the Brethren and their beliefs. On 29 November 1781, when the governor and members of the assembly left for their homes, the Salem diarist recorded that "all were satisfied with the treatment received from the Brethren and grateful for their lodging." He continued by saying that through the "gracious ordering of events, . . . we are restored to peace and the usual order of our church services, and can look forward to partaking of the Lord's Supper next Sabbath."

At the next election Traugott Bagge was elected a representative from Surry County. He and Frederic William Marshall attended the April 1782 session of the assembly at Hillsborough. It was here that Marshall had confirmed his standing as proprietor of Wachovia, thus putting to a definite end all danger of confiscation of the Moravian properties. In 1778 all parishes had been done away with, for, as Bagge wrote, "no denomination was to rank above another." Bagge was appointed auditor for Surry County in connection with claims for services and supplies during the war, and together with two auditors from Guilford County sat in Salem as the Committee of Auditors for the Upper Board of Salisbury District. The Moravian position in the revolutionary war was well on the way to a complete vindication.

Peace was officially restored by the Treaty of Paris in 1783. The preliminary treaty, signed on 20 January, affirmed King George's acknowledgment of the independence of the colonies. When the news reached North Carolina, Governor Alexander Martin officially made the announcement to the General Assembly, which in turn instructed the governor to appoint 4 July as a day of public thanksgiving. This he did on 18 June, "enjoining all the Good Citizens of this State to set apart the said Day from bodily labour, and employ the same in devout and religious exercises."

In this first year of peace, North Carolina was the only state to proclaim a holiday in celebration of the colony's independence. The Moravians of the Wachovia settlement were the only North Carolinians to respond to the governor's request for a planned observance. Each community in Wachovia made observance in its own way. The Bethabara Diary for 4 July 1783 contains the following statement:

The Day of Thanksgiving for Peace was Announced early in the morning by the blowing of wind instruments. At ten o'clock there was a service, in which the Te Deum was sung, and there was a sermon on Psalm XLVI. . . . The service closed with a prayer. Some of our neighbors were present. At two in the afternoon the congregation, including the children and some of the neighbors, had a happy lovefeast, during which time the Ode composed in Salem was sung. In the evening, the bell was rung, and the congregation assembled before the Gemein Haus . . . and the congregation marched in procession between the two Brothers Houses and the other houses to the tavern, along the road by Schaub's and back by Spach's to the Gemein Haus, full of praise and thanksgiving. At the close the choir sang the benediction.

At Bethania, the celebration was more in line with the governor's suggestions. Service was held at ten o'clock. The proclamation was read, and a portion of the litany referring to the government of the land was read as the congregation stood. Then, on their knees, they "thanked the Lord of Lords for His gift of Peace." With wonderful historical perspective, "the 46th Psalm was read, as the 12th verse was the Watch-Word for January 20th when Peace was agreed upon in Paris." The diary mentions that an unexpected number of outsiders were also present.

At Friedberg, the congregation "gladly" took their part in observance of a day of thanksgiving. The governor's proclamation was read, and all joined in the singing of "Now Thank We All Our God." The sermon was based on Psalm 46 and, following a lovefeast, hymns of thanksgiving were sung.

Services at Friedland were much like those at Bethania and Friedberg, but the reading "from the history of the Unity the account of the Peace Festival in Herrnhut on March 21st, 1763" was added.

Salem Congregation's diarist made the following entry for 4 July 1783:

According to the order of the government of this State we celebrated a day of thanksgiving for the restoration of peace. The congregation was awakened by the trombonists. At the beginning of the service the Te

Deum was sung, with trombone accompaniment. [The sermon was then preached by Brother Benzien.] The service closed with the singing of: *Glory to God in the highest*. At two o'clock there was a happy lovefeast, during which a Psalm of Joy was sung with thankful hearts. In the evening at eight o'clock the congregation again assembled in the Saal, and the choir sang: *Praise be to Thee, Who sittest above the cherubim*. Then the congregation formed a circle in front of the Gemein Haus, and from there passed in procession through the main street of the town, with music and the antiphonal song of two choirs. The street was illuminated. Returning to the Gemein Haus the congregation again formed a circle, and with the blessing of the Lord was dismissed to rest. Hearts were filled with the peace of God evident during the entire day and especially during the procession, and all around there was silence, even the wind being still.

Conclusion

In the years following the Regulator activities, particularly after 1772, one notes the beginning of a process of Americanization in the Moravian settlements in Wachovia. Prior to 1778 the Moravians referred to the "Continental Army" or "American Army" or "George Washington's Army" in their writings. But, in a letter from Christian Heckewaelder to John M. Graff, dated 1 October 1778, one finds a reference to "our" army—the first such reference from Salem. The following year, the term "our army" is used regularly in the Salem Diary. This is but one example of the growing identification of the Moravians with the patriot cause.

The Moravians of Wachovia celebrated peace in 1783. For almost a decade they had suffered the hardships of civil unrest and economic depression; now peace was restored. During the Revolution their sincere religious beliefs, coupled with a desire to succeed, had led them to a position that was both proper and logical. They had had no quarrel with the crown; they were now content with a new order. One must conclude with James A. Gray, Jr., that "it is impossible for any group, as it was for their group, to insulate itself completely from the forces around it. The Revolutionary War did much to hasten the amalgamation of the Moravians into the American culture as we know it today."

Bethabara

First House, Salem, January 1766

Adam Spach House, Friedberg

Fourth of July float, Salem

Founders Hall, Clemmons School

Main Street through Salem, looking south; Matthew Miksch House on right

Depot Street Graded School for Negroes

West End Graded School, Fourth and Broad Streets

CHAPTER 4

Joseph Winston
and Benjamin Forsyth

Joseph Winston

Joseph Winston was a man of family and property. In the seventeenth century, five Winston brothers of Winston Hall in Yorkshire, England, settled in Hanover County, Virginia. A proliferation of Winstons followed through the eighteenth century leading to Joseph Winston's father, Samuel, of Louisa County, Virginia. Samuel's sister Sarah was the mother of Patrick Henry and the first cousins Joseph and Patrick spent much of their boyhood together.

Born 17 June 1746, Winston grew to manhood during the French and Indian War and, at seventeen, joined a punitive expedition against some border Indians. The expedition was ambushed; Winston was shot twice and left for dead. One of the musket balls remained in his body and pained him periodically for the rest of his life. Winston was active in land speculation as a young man, and the failure of one of his larger Virginia schemes led him to Surry County in the late 1760s. There, on the Town Fork of the Dan River, Winston settled and began raising a family which ultimately included at least twelve children. As early as 1782 he owned 980 acres of land and fifteen slaves. In 1790 he had 1,362 acres and eighteen slaves; and on his death he left a will in which he indicated ownership of some nine hundred acres in Stokes County and eight thousand acres of western lands.

In the process of acquiring land and a family, Winston became a leader in his community, and his neighbors turned to him for direction as the troublesome events of the coming of the Revolution made themselves felt in backcountry North Carolina. The Edenton Tea Party and even the election of delegates to the First Continental Congress were primarily actions of the eastern, more populated areas. But by 1775 committees of safety were being created throughout the state; and another provincial congress was to be held in August, this time at the inland town of Hillsborough. Royal Governor Josiah Martin had taken refuge aboard a vessel of the British Navy and issued protests at the proceedings of the radicals. Winston was elected a delegate to the Hillsborough Congress and with the other Surry County delegates was given the responsibility of forming a committee of safety. As a member of the Congress, Winston signed the Continental Association whereby the colonies declared an economic boycott of England. As a member of the Surry County Committee of Safety he began to make preparations for the coming conflict. The Hillsborough Congress had devised a most elaborate system of government for the state as well as a complex militia organization. Winston was soon second major, then first major of the Surry County militia. In April 1776 he represented Surry in the Halifax Provincial Congress to vote for independence from Britain. Winston and all the delegates present voted for these Halifax Resolves.

Winston's chief area of activity for the next several years was in the military. In February 1776 Winston led a group of volunteers against the Scottish Tories at the battle of Moores Creek Bridge. Later that year he participated in an expedition against the Cherokee Indians. The expedition was successful and Winston was one of four North Carolina commissioners at the Treaty of Long Island of the Holston in July 1777, in which the Cherokees ceded their claim to the lands east of the Blue Ridge along with a corridor through the Cumberland Gap.

Affairs at home continued to take a part of Winston's time. Some of his children were born during these years. He was made entry-taker (register of deeds) for Surry County in 1778 and among other duties he made copies of all the deeds to the Moravian lands in the Wachovia settlement to the south. The Moravians recorded that Winston was "very friendly" and that he went out of his way to assist them. Perhaps this accounts for his later excellent relationship with this group which was suspect during the Revolution because of its neutral position.

Numerous bands of Tories roaming the countryside under arms for the cause of the king gave northwestern North Carolina a real taste of revolutionary violence. Many incidents involving these Tory bands have been recorded, and for almost every local revolutionary figure, there is a traditional story relating his heroism and bravery in such times of stress. One tale about Winston concerns a band of thirteen Tories, a free Negro, and an Englishman who took from one of Winston's neighbors everything but his life and his shirt. The man made his way to Winston's house, from which messengers were then sent out. Fifteen men soon gathered to form a posse. They caught the Tories near the Virginia line, defeated them, and spared only their leader who had been responsible for saving the life of Winston's neighbor from the wrath of his men.

Winston participated in the crucial battle of Kings Mountain in October 1780 and in the battle of Guilford Courthouse in March 1781. At Kings Mountain Winston and a group of Surry County militia served under Winston's uncle, Colonel Ben Cleveland. The Surry group charged up the wrong hill in the early course of the battle but returned to the fight in time to play an important role in the victory of the mountain men over the British and Tories. At Guilford Courthouse, Winston's Surry militia served again with distinction. As part of General Nathanael Greene's first line, they fired at the approaching British and withdrew as ordered. They then engaged a British contingent about a mile from the center of action and continued the fight until the arrival of Tarleton's cavalry brought an end to the engagement. Later the North Carolina legislature awarded Winston an elegant sword for his services.

Of great importance for Winston during this period was his ability to maintain good relations with the Moravians of Wachovia as he commandeered their goods, quartered himself and his troops among them, and sent them his sick and wounded to care for.

Winston conferred with the leaders of the community, controlled his men better than the other commanders—both patriot and British—who passed through, and generally assisted in keeping the peace where possible. Except for instances when Winston improperly confiscated a horse from Salem and when he wanted more than his proper share of some confiscated brandy, the Moravian Brethren regarded him as very friendly. Winston's earlier friendship and his relative fairness in dealing with the peace-loving Unitas Fratrum undoubtedly made the hardships of war more bearable.

As the Revolution came to an end Winston continued his public activities. In February 1784 he met with his neighbors at the Salem Tavern for a general settling of local problems. In 1777 he represented Surry County in the newly formed House of Commons of the North Carolina legislature. He also served in 1779, 1782, and 1783. During this period he voted regularly to keep the governor virtually powerless, voted to allow the upper house of the legislature to be chosen by the electorate, voted for lower taxes, and voted against higher salaries for legislators. He was several times an unsuccessful nominee of the House for the Council of State and worked on his share of legislative committees.

Winston served in both of North Carolina's conventions to consider the ratification of the new federal Constitution. Following the lead of Willie Jones and the majority of the delegates, Winston voted neither to ratify nor to reject the Constitution at Hillsborough in 1788. With the Bill of Rights on its way to ratification, Winston voted with the majority of the delegates at Fayetteville in 1789 to ratify the Constitution.

During the period 1787–89, Winston was in the North Carolina Senate representing Surry County. After securing signatures throughout the county in support of the measure, Winston introduced a bill in November 1789 to divide Surry into two counties. This was a part of the movement of the times and was needed to give the western portion of the state a fairer voice in the state legislature. The act passed, and at the next session Winston represented the newly formed Stokes County in the state senate. He served again in that position in 1791, 1802, 1807, and 1812. In addition he represented his district (consisting of Surry, Stokes, Iredell, Wilkes, and Ashe counties) in the Third Congress, 1793–95, and in the Eighth and Ninth Congresses, 1803–07.

In the state and national legislatures Winston was not an outstanding legislator, but he was a true exponent of Jeffersonian principles. He had an excellent record for attendance, was almost always present on the first day of the session and stayed until it was over, seldom failed to vote, and generally voted along lines one would expect from a Jeffersonian. From the records in the *Annals of Congress* it appears that he never addressed that assembled body either in formal session or in a committee of the whole.

Back home in North Carolina, however, Winston was intimately involved in the political controversies of his day. It was an era of bitter strife and partisan politics. Political battles were intense, and campaigning was frequently unscrupulous. In addition to the usual electioneering problems, Winston had to face the fact that the Salem Moravians generally voted as a bloc. Their minutes reveal that in 1790 they considered voting for Winston's opponent, James Martin, since it appeared that Martin was going to be elected with or without the Moravian votes. Winston won nevertheless and two years later the same Moravian group reported that "Mr. Winston, who is a suitable man and a friend of the Brethren, has announced himself a candidate for the senate."

From the earliest days of his political experience, Winston sought to keep his constituency informed of his actions and the issues involved. In 1787 he called a county meeting at Richmond Courthouse "in order to learn the wish of the people regarding the new Constitution for North America." In 1789 he circulated a petition through Salem and elsewhere to seek support for the division of Surry County. While a congressman, Winston's favorite device for keeping in touch with his constituency was to send a circular letter to the residents of his district. Using popular administrative victories, such as the Louisiana Purchase, in an attempt to enhance his own political position, Winston informed his constituents of the happenings in Washington. Winston served twice as a presidential elector, voting for Jefferson in 1800 and James Madison in 1812.

In addition to his legislative and political life, Winston contributed greatly to the progress of education in North Carolina. He was made a trustee of Salisbury Academy in 1784. In 1807 he was chosen by the legislature to be a trustee of the University of North Carolina for six years. And in 1809 he was a trustee of Germanton Academy, located only a few miles from his home.

On 21 April 1815, he died, and was buried in the family cemetery near Germanton. Winston's body was moved to Guilford Courthouse National Military Park in 1908. At the park, an impressive statue and a large portrait commemorate Winston's contributions. But the most lasting tribute of all is the "Winston" in the city name Winston-Salem, named on its formation for the revolutionary hero.

Benjamin Forsyth

Benjamin Forsyth's date and place of birth are not known, but it is believed that he was born in the early 1760s, probably in Virginia. Family tradition says that he was the son of James and Elizabeth Forsyth and that he lived in St. Martin's Parish, Hanover County, Virginia, before coming to North Carolina. A fairly extensive genealogical description of Forsyth's ancestry and progeny may be found in the 1949 edition of *Forsyth, A County on the March*. Only two deed books in Hanover County escaped destruction during the Civil War, but there are several land transactions involving Benjamin Forsyth between 1786 and 1788. The Benjamin Forsyth who lived in Stokes County, North Carolina, from 1794 to the day on which he left for service in the War of 1812 must have come with money in his pocket, for he first appears in the taking of a deed for a tract bid in for him at a sheriff's sale. This purchase was followed in the same month of December 1794 by the purchase of another tract, for which he paid £260.

For almost two decades Benjamin Forsyth bought and sold land industriously. The Stokes County deed books show thirty-four purchases. Of these, three were at sheriff's sales, nineteen were grants from the state of North Carolina, and twelve were tracts bought from individuals. There are forty of his sales recorded, making a total of seventy-four transactions listed. This is most unusual, for in those days many men did not trouble to probate and record their deeds, since sales and purchases were legal and valid indefinitely without registration. Possession of the land itself held the title.

The rapidity of this turnover of land during his early years in North Carolina indicates that Forsyth carried on a land brokerage business. Some years he listed only a few acres for taxation; in 1802 he listed eight thousand acres. In 1810 he listed three thousand acres, seven black polls, his own white poll, and a lot in Germanton, which he had owned for some years. In 1811 his taxes were "not given in"; perhaps he sold most or all of his slaves and real estate before leaving for the war.

In 1797 Benjamin Forsyth married Bethemia Ladd, daughter of Constantine Ladd. His marriage bond is dated 4 October with Christian Lash signing as bondsman. Lash was a resident of Bethania, but in 1797 he owned a lot in Germanton, and as he was a justice of the peace, he and Forsyth had undoubtedly met in court. The tax books show a number of men listing lots in Germanton who never lived there, and the indications are that there was a considerable amount of speculation in real estate in the new county seat for the next decade. Forsyth and his wife had six children.

In 1807 and 1808 Benjamin Forsyth served in the General Assembly of North Carolina as a representative from Stokes County.

Like all other able-bodied men from sixteen to fifty, Forsyth was required by law to enroll in a militia company and to attend muster and drill. His first commission as an officer was dated 14 April 1800, when he became a second lieutenant in the Sixth Infantry and served in the army for two months. His brief service is likely due to the threats of war between the United States and England at this time. On 1 July 1808 he was commissioned a captain and assigned to the Rifle Regiment. The Salem Diary for 29 April 1809 records: "Captain Forsyth came from Germanton with a recently enlisted volunteer company of riflemen, and will go to New Bern and from there to New Orleans. The captain wished to give his company the pleasure of seeing our town, and at the same time show us their new uniforms and military drill. They marched into town in military order, with trumpet and fife, and paraded and drilled in front of the boarding school."

Forsyth was still a captain when the War of 1812 broke out.

His service in that war was all on the northern border of the state of New York, where he at once established a reputation for personal bravery and for ability as an officer. In his first exploit, in September 1812, Forsyth led a party of men who went down the St. Lawrence River in boats, landed on the Canadian side, destroyed a British storehouse, and returned with many captured military supplies. He lost only one man, with another slightly wounded; the British suffered ten to twenty times as many losses.

On 20 January 1813 Benjamin Forsyth was promoted to the rank of major. His career continued with "dash, vigor, and enterprise." In February of that year, he gathered a force of regulars and volunteers and went up the St. Lawrence River to Morristown. At three o'clock in the morning they crossed the river to Elizabethtown, surprised the guard, and took fifty-two prisoners, including five officers. They captured 120 muskets and other supplies before returning to the post at Ogdensburg, New York. Forsyth's ranks did not suffer a single casualty. Soon after his return, a vastly superior British force drove Forsyth from Ogdensburg, but it is reported that the British suffered severely in their attack and probably lost as many as three times the number of Americans who fell.

In May 1813 Major Forsyth was present at the capture by American forces of Fort George in Canada, and he added greatly to his reputation as a soldier in the battle fought there.

Forsyth was then commissioned a lieutenant-colonel for his "distinguished services" on 15 April 1814. The services were not to continue long, for two months later he was killed in a skirmish near Odeltown, on the Canadian frontier on 23 June 1814. The American general had sent a small party to attack a much larger force of British, but with orders only to attract the attention of the British and then retire, leading them into an ambush. Colonel Forsyth was in command of one part of the ambuscade, and when the enemy appeared he brought his troops out of hiding and gave battle. The British fired twice and retreated, but at the first fire Colonel Forsyth fell, shot through the chest. He exclaimed, "Boys, rush on!" and died a few minutes later. The next day he was buried with the honors of war at Champlain.

The news of Colonel Forsyth's death reached North Carolina, and at the September 1814 session of the Stokes County Court of

Pleas and Quarter Session his widow was appointed administratrix of his estate. The amount of personal property listed in the Forsyth inventory was not large, but it included $302 in cash, which at that time—on the scale of prices prevailing—was enough to support a family for two years. Also listed were fifteen "disparate" notes, which would have been worth over $600 had they been good.

With the filing of this inventory, the Forsyth name disappeared from Stokes court records. No guardians were appointed for the children. No settlement of the estate was made. Forsyth's running account with the Moravian Church in Salem had always been kept in excellent condition while he was in the state. After his death part of it was charged off and the rest gradually liquidated, with the help of the Salem storekeeper.

Mrs. Forsyth moved to Tennessee, taking her children with her. She later married a man named William Cowin.

Justly deserved acclaim was finally awarded Forsyth in 1817. Representing Stokes County in the North Carolina General Assembly of that year were Joseph Winston (son of Major Joseph Winston of Revolutionary fame and namesake of the future town of Winston) and John Hauser of Bethania. It must be presumed that these men personally knew Colonel Forsyth, for they were very eager that the state should honor him as much as it had Captain Johnston Blakeley, of Wilmington. So, on 18 December 1817, Elijah Callaway of Ashe County introduced the following resolution: "That the public services rendered by the late Colonel Benjamin Forsythe [sic] in the late war with the king of Great Britain are well appreciated by the General Assembly of this state." Additional resolutions provided for the care of his widow and children as well as for the presentation of a sword to Forsyth's infant son. The House adopted all these resolutions without delay, and sent them to the Senate, which concurred in them the next day.

The memory of Colonel Benjamin Forsyth was again honored in 1849 when Stokes County was divided into two counties, one of which retained the old name of Stokes, while the new one was named Forsyth.

The Social Order—Religion, Education, and Culture, 1753–1860

Salem in 1791

William Loughton Smith, a Federalist from Charleston and sometime traveling companion of President Washington, visited Salem in May 1791. Journeying west along the road from Guilford Courthouse, he stopped at Dobson's (Kernersville) where he ate breakfast on the morning of 5 May. According to Smith, Dobson had "a very decent house" and served a good meal. Nor was his hospitality wanting: "his wife, who sat down to breakfast with me, is a huge fat woman of about eighty, whom he calls 'Honey.'"

The road from Dobson's Cross Roads to Salem was good, "with a few interruptions of steep and broken hills." Smith noted that "traveling through woods for many days" preceded his arrival at the village of Salem, which after so long a time in the wilderness appeared "highly curious and interesting." He continued: "The first view of the town is romantic, just as it breaks upon you through the woods; it is pleasantly seated on a rising ground, and is surrounded by beautiful meadows, well-cultivated fields, and shady woods."

A citizen of one of the South's most elegant cities, Smith was attracted to the "antique appearance of the houses [of Salem], built in the German style." He recorded delight over the "singular and pleasing effect" of this "beautiful village," the whole prospect of which to him formed "a pastoral scene."

On his arrival in Salem, Smith made the acquaintance of Traugott Bagge, the storekeeper. Bagge took the traveler throughout the village, showing him the "single men's house" and the various trades. Duly impressed with what he saw, Smith wrote that "everyone [was] hard at work; such a scene of industry, perhaps, exists no where in so small a place." The Moravians of Wachovia, Smith wrote, "live in brotherly love and set a laudable example of industry," an example, he continued, unfortunately "too little observed and followed in this part of the country."

Smith noted with some delight that "the Brewery and distillery are considerable; the beer is very good, and a cordial made out of whiskey excellent." His tour then took him to the waterworks, and from the waterworks to the churchyard. "As witness to the universality of the Salem settlers, a medley of nations lie . . . interred" there, he wrote. But more striking than this universality was the apparent good health of the Brethren, who demonstrated "a surprising proof of the good effects of industry, sobriety, temperance, and a good situation." Only sixty persons lay buried in God's Acre, he noted, and among them was "one negro."

William Smith closed his day in Salem by attending a *Singstunde*. There was "singing accompanied by an organ," which he recorded, was "good." His pleasure with the "very orderly and decent appearance of the audience" was also expressed.

With some reluctance, William Smith left the village for "Saulsbury" the next day. He was "very much pleased with Salem, and [had been] recruited by the best bed since I left home." One might well imagine that Smith's sentiments were shared by many more travelers, far from home, and without adequate lodging.

President Washington's Visit to Wachovia

In the course of three separate tours, in 1789, 1790, and 1791, George Washington visited all the states of the newly formed union "in order to become better acquainted with their principal characters and internal circumstances" as well as to seek "advice on political subjects." The southern tour came last, in the spring and summer months of 1791.

It is suggested that Washington chose to include Salem on his tour because of the better condition of the roads in that area and to show his friendliness towards the Moravians, whose sincere neutrality in the Revolution had distinguished them from the loyalist element. Whatever the case, he and his secretary, Mr. Jackson, and "a number of servants" arrived there on 31 May 1791 at five o'clock in the afternoon. The party was greeted by official representatives of the town—Brothers Marshall, Benzien, and Koehler—and "a complete band of music." Though Washington (then on the return phase of his tour) planned only to remain in Salem one night, he learned that Governor Alexander Martin wished to meet him in Salem, so he decided to stay an extra night. Washington's quarters were in the Salem Tavern in the northeast room on the second floor.

During his first day in Salem, described by Washington as a "small but neat village," he visited the shops of the "artizans," the waterworks, and the Boys School. At the school, as an awestruck fellow read from Noah Webster's *American Speller* the words, "A cat may look on a king," the president smiled and remarked to the teacher: "They are thinking that now!" Later in the day he was entertained by "the wind instruments [which] were heard sweetly beside the Tavern" and by a *Singstunde*. Major Jackson, on inquiring as to "the principles of our congregation," was presented a copy of the *History of the Brethren*, probably Lafroke's English translation of Cranz (London: 1780).

The major event of the day was the presentation of a statement to President Washington of the Brethren's patriotic allegiance to the United States. It closes with the words:

The settlement of the United Brethren, though small, will always make it their study to contribute as much as in them lies to the peace and improvement of the United States, and all the particular parts they live in, joining their ardent prayers to the best wishes of this whole continent that your personal as well as domestic happiness may abound, and a series of successes may crown your labours for the prosperity of our times and an example to future ages, until the glorious reward of a faithful servant shall be your proportion.

Washington personally acknowledged this "patriotic sentiment" of "a society whose governing principles are industry and love of order," and wished the Brethren "social and individual happiness."

President Washington and his party left Salem at four o'clock in the morning of 2 June, but before leaving what was to become Forsyth County, they too stopped at Dobson's Tavern and breakfasted.

The People

Coming primarily from Pennsylvania, the Scotch-Irish who settled in and around Forsyth County were descendants of the Lowland Scotsmen who had been "planted" by King James I of England in order to make "Ireland a civil place." Two large migrations brought these doubly transplanted Scots to America in 1717–18 and 1728–29. Most chose Pennsylvania as their new home because of the political, social, and economic freedom it afforded immigrants. But, as has previously been noted, rising land prices and rent forced them to look to new areas for settlement. North Carolina's Piedmont region was well suited to their needs, not only because its farmland was cheap, but because there was still an abundance of it to be taken. By 1755 the numbers of the Scotch-Irish coming to this colony were "dayley increasing."

For the most part, the Scotch-Irish who settled in this section were farmers, though many are known to have engaged in trades, especially those in the north-central and eastern Piedmont. They have been called everything from shiftless, clannish, contentious, and hard to get along with, to fun-loving and playful. In short, contemporary writers seldom agreed about them.

The other principal group that settled in Forsyth was of German stock—the Moravians. Founded after the Hussite Wars by followers of the great Bohemian reformer, John Hus, the ancient Unitas Fratrum, or Unity of Brethren, had known persecution after persecution. The members often suffered martyrdom, as did Hus himself, burned at the stake in 1415 because he would not obey the orders of the Roman hierarchy nor give up his simple belief that men ought to accept the Bible as God's word, declining to obey men who substituted their own will for the divine precept.

In 1722 descendants of members of the ancient Brethren emigrated from Moravia to Saxony and found refuge on the estate of Count Nicolaus Ludwig von Zinzendorf. There the ancient church was reorganized, and from Saxony it spread into various countries of Europe and into England. Burning at the stake had gone out of fashion, but the opposition the Moravians endured was considerable. As a result, there was a movement toward America, first to Georgia, then to Pennsylvania, and finally to North Carolina. The name "Moravian," to designate the church formally known as the Unitas Fratrum, originated in this eighteenth-century development, and it is appropriate today because it is through the Moravian branch of the renewed Unity of Brethren that the church possesses the episcopate, secured in 1467 and handed down without interruption to the Moravian bishops of today.

Customs and Practices of the Moravians

One of the most distinctive features of the social life of the Brethren who settled Wachovia was the choir (*Chor*) system. Age, sex, and marital status determined to which of nine choirs a member belonged: Single Brothers, Single Sisters, Married People, Widowers, Widows, Older Boys, Older Girls, Little Boys, and Little Girls. Generally, children would live at home with their parents until they were about fourteen years old. At this time the boys would become apprenticed to any of the master workmen or Single Brothers. The girls would enter the Single Sisters House, where they would learn housekeeping, spinning, weaving, and other household duties in preparation for both married life and domestic work in private homes. Boys and girls remained in their respective choir houses until they were married.

Under the strict supervision of a *Pfleger(in)*, who served as the spiritual head of each respective house, the older boys and girls were taught restraint and control and initiative in their daily affairs. Such training, it was believed, led to the development of good moral character. Social segregation of the sexes was practiced; recreation time was often spent in reading, except on Sundays when walking was encouraged. Men and women were expected to walk in opposite directions on specifically laid-out paths, but infractions regarding this social separation were not uncommon.

Marriage proposals were made through the *Aeltesten Conferenz* (Elders Conference). Should a Single Brother desire to marry a Single Sister, he would suggest the individual's name to the members of the conference, who in turn would submit the proposal to the lot. If the answer was affirmative, a member of the conference would make the intentions known to the particular person involved. She was then free to accept or reject the proposal. If the lot were negative, nothing was said of the matter. A member was not expected to be so bound to one person that he would refuse another's hand in marriage. But, human nature being what it is, occasional secret engagements were made, despite the rigid restrictions imposed by the church. Most often these proposals were made to a person not a member of the Moravian community, in which case the church would not perform the ceremony (as was the case in any instance the lot opposed).

The Moravians of Wachovia were buried according to their choirs. *Gottes Acker*, God's Acre, an "arable field," in eighteenth-century German, where the bodies of the believers were sown awaiting resurrection, was divided into eight choirs: Little Boys, Little Girls, Older Boys, Older Girls, Single Brothers, Single Sisters, Married Men, and Married Women.

The use of the lot in Wachovia, already mentioned in connection with marriage proposals, began at Bethabara in 1757. When a situation had been approached from all possible angles and no conclusions could be reached, "in childlike faith" the conference would turn to the Lord by means of the lot. The usual procedure included slips of paper with an affirmative, a negative, and a blank. The lot was used to decide applicants for membership, the selection of sites for towns and buildings, and other important matters. The practice was not discontinued officially by the Moravian church until 1889.

On 11 November 1753 the Bethabara diarist recorded that a

neighbor had told them that the "people [of the North Carolina wilderness] lived like wild men, never hearing of God or his word." Opportunities for service to these people were numerous. Not only were regular preaching places maintained along the Yadkin River, but Moravians would and did speak wherever the settlers might request—from Haw River and Stinking Quarter Creek to as far as sixty miles away at Fox Gap. They visited Lutheran and Reformed congregations, who especially enjoyed hearing their own native tongue preached. There were also Dunkards and Baptists who requested Moravian ministers, and in most cases what they had to say was well received. The Methodists, in particular, later turned a number of the old Moravian preaching stations into regular congregations administered by their own people as more of them migrated south.

Religion and Faith in Wachovia

The religion practiced by the Moravians was "preeminently a Christ-centered faith" which called for the daily application of Christ's teaching. Instruction was by catechism, and discussions of religion and theology were common among the membership. The Brethren scrupulously avoided arguments on faith with strangers. Their religion was personal and wholly nonproselyting.

When one joined any of the Moravian communities, he had to subscribe to a set of rules and principles known as the Brotherly Agreement. Christ was accepted as the Savior, and the Bible was acknowledged as a rule of doctrine. Obedience to both temporal and spiritual rulers was required. The shifting loyalty of the Wachovia Brethren during the American Revolution was perfectly consistent with this tenet. One had to attend all services of the church, support both church and state, and avoid all political entanglements, sectarian disputes, and worldly society and amusements. Strictly prohibited were "all sorts of frolicks such as spinning and cotton picking and corn husking at night [when] intended for merryment to which numbers of people of both sexes are invited." Any offender was subject to expulsion from the congregation if the *Aeltesten Conferenz* so chose, for the elders controlled all the spiritual affairs and conditions of the congregation. It is suggested that members of the conference, however, were gentle and patient in their dealings. A deeply spiritual life was the desired result of the control maintained by the Brotherly Agreement and through acknowledgment of the elders' guidance.

The Moravians attended church frequently. Their liturgical tradition allied them closely to the established church and, even in the earliest days of settlement, services were held in English once a month for the benefit of visitors. Original sermons were delivered for the morning services on Sunday, but for evening services those of Zinzendorf and other church leaders were read. The last service was usually held at nine o'clock in the evening; this was the informal *Singstunde*, in which the members would join together and sing the familiar hymns of the church.

At home, daily texts were read. For each day there was the Scriptural Watchword from the Old Testament and the Doctrinal Text from the New Testament. Each was accompanied by an appropriate stanza of a well-known hymn. This particular practice dated from Herrnhut in 1727.

The lovefeast occurred often and was always a happy meeting for the Brethren. When Moravian visitors came to the Wachovia settlements, when new settlers joined their midst, or when any one of a number of occasions presented itself, especially church memorials, a lovefeast was held. In essence, the service signified a happy and joyous gathering and was often followed by the Cup of the Covenant, renewing the choir members' pledge. The cup might also have been used by an entire congregation as a pledge of allegiance to each other and to the Lord. Traditionally, this occasion (not considered a sacrament) consisted of sharing bread or cake and coffee, tea or wine. Much to the displeasure of some of Bethabara's earliest inhabitants, cornbread was even used out of necessity!

The sacrament of baptism was administered to infants soon after birth. Nonmembers were occasionally baptized, though this act by no means admitted them into the church. Marriages were arranged and solemnized by the church, and only communicants might attend the ceremony. Last rites were administered to dying members, and death was announced to the congregation with the playing of hymns by a brass band. To the Moravians death was not an occasion for grief or mourning, as the deceased was simply thought to be "going home." The ordination of ministers by the bishop and the reception of the lay assistants (*Akoluthie*) were both open to the attendance of the entire congregation.

The celebrations of Christmas and Easter were particularly noteworthy events in the calendar of the Moravian Church. On Christmas Eve, two lovefeasts were held, one for the children in the afternoon, when lighted candles were distributed to those present (after 1762), and another for the adults at midnight. Trumpets ushered in Christmas Day. The Easter season began with a reading of the account of Christ's entry into Jerusalem on Palm Sunday. On Maundy Thursday, a symbolic footwashing (discontinued before 1833) and communion were observed. The events of Good Friday were read at five different services during the day at approximately the times at which they originally occurred. On Saturday afternoon there was a lovefeast. Early the next morning trumpets announced Christ's resurrection and the members of the congregation gathered in the *Saal*. Together they marched to the graveyard where the Easter litany was prayed. Every Easter for more than two hundred years this ancient tradition of the Brethren, begun in Herrnhut, has been reenacted in Salem. Later in the day the story of the forty days and the resurrection were read; two sermons were preached. Occasionally, on Easter Monday, a special lovefeast was held for the musicians whose role in the Moravian services was so important.

The New Year was ushered in by three services. In one, a lovefeast was held; in a second, the congregation memorabilia was read; and in the last, a watch meeting for the new year was begun. At midnight, the sound of trumpets playing *"Nun Danket alle Gott"* ("Now Thank We All Our God") was heard throughout the community.

Other Churches and Congregations

From the earliest days of settlement, religion played a prominent role in the lives of residents of Forsyth County. The oldest Moravian congregations—Bethabara, Bethania, Salem, Friedberg, Hope, and Friedland—are discussed in Chapter 2, and the Moravian impact on the region in the years prior to the Civil War can hardly be exaggerated. Worshipers from other communions also were among the earlier settlers both within and without Wachovia and they soon began to organize churches of their own.

German Lutherans were among the first to form an organized religious group in Forsyth after the Moravians. Shiloh (formerly Muddy Creek) Lutheran Church was established in the Lewisville area in 1777. One year later, another congregation, Nazareth, was organized near what is now Rural Hall. Early in the nineteenth century Gottlieb Schober, a Moravian, became a Lutheran minister in order to serve the scattered Lutheran congregations still without pastoral service. There were so many groups who needed ministers that Schober frequently requested and received help from the ministers in Salem. One result of this cooperation was the establishment of the Hopewell Sunday School in September 1816. The Hopewell Church was formed in 1807 to serve jointly a Lutheran and a Reformed congregation. When both congregations disbanded, the church building was taken over by the Moravians. Organized Lutheran activity did not come to Winston-Salem until the late 1800s.

Methodist churches were among the earliest churches in Forsyth County and Methodists outnumbered other denominations for much of the nineteenth century. The oldest Methodist church in Forsyth County, Concord, was organized in the Lewisville community in 1781. Concord was joined by Knight's Meeting House at Clemmons in the late 1780s. A Methodist church was established in Brookstown during its early years of settlement. Love's Church, in Walkertown, traditionally recognizes 1791 as its date of organization. Its deed dates from 1797 and Bishop Francis Asbury attended a meeting at the church on 7 October 1799. In the early 1800s Old Jerusalem Church was organized on what is now the Children's Home property. These churches were among the earliest of the Methodist communions in Forsyth County.

In the Winston area the first Methodist prayer meeting of which any record has been preserved was held in the early 1840s in the old Nading home at the extreme end of what is now North

Liberty Street. As early as 1842 a Protestant Methodist congregation decided to move to the new town, purchased a lot at Liberty and Seventh streets, and constructed a frame church there in 1851.

The second Methodist church building in Winston was built by the Methodist Episcopal denomination on the corner of Liberty and Sixth streets. This congregation had begun in the 1830s as the Mulberry Tree Society, so called because of the big meetings held under a large mulberry tree on what is now the corner of Reynolda Road and Northwest Boulevard. In time the Mulberry Tree Society expanded into Old Jerusalem Church, worshiping in a stout frame building on a hill not very far from the historic tree. Shortly after the forming of Winston, the Jerusalem congregation sold its property and built a simple, unpretentious house of worship only a block away from their Protestant Methodist neighbors.

The first Baptist missionaries traveled through Forsyth County in the late 1700s and early 1800s. A number of missions were established along the Yadkin River at that time. Perhaps the first formally organized church of this denomination was New Friendship in 1827. Other early Baptist churches include Goodwill, 1846; New Bethel, 1847; Mt. Olive, 1841; and Red Bank (today, Town Fork), 1859. Not until the 1870s was there an attempt to form a Baptist church in Winston.

Throughout the early years of Forsyth's existence, until a church of their own was formed, worshipers of many denominations found a welcome at one of the nearby Moravian services. Moravian ministers held services in many of the churches when ministers of their own denomination were in short supply. Lutherans, Methodists, Baptists, Presbyterians, Episcopalians and many others found a ready welcome among fellow Christians, and joined the Moravians in the church-oriented life-style which was basic in Forsyth County.

Educational Beginnings in Forsyth

Education in colonial North Carolina is closely related to religion and must be regarded as one of the functions of the church. The

Scotch-Irish (mostly Presbyterians) and Germans (Moravian, Lutheran, and German Reformed), who came to the Piedmont in the 1740s and 1750s, gave a marked impetus to the cause of education, and without the aid of the established church. The Moravians especially fostered education among their members, and though their schools were not large, at least the rudiments of an organized instructive process were provided.

In 1761, at Bethania, a school for children was started with Ludwig Bachhoff as teacher. Throughout this early period intermittent classes in the English language had been available to those who wished to study it. Another five years saw the creation of three schools at Bethabara—one for boys, one for girls, and, in 1776, a separate one for the older boys. This last was an evening school and met from seven until nine o'clock, presumably to accommodate the apprenticeship of the older boys.

In 1770 an eleven-month school was started at Friedberg by Bethania's teacher and pastor, Ludwig Bachhoff. Except during harvest season, classes were held four days a week—two for boys and two for girls. The older children were separated from the younger children. It is known from Bachhoff's diary that there was much rote learning among the young at this school. They sang and memorized hymns and catechisms and learned Bible stories. Reading, writing, and arithmetic were studied by the older children. Schools similar to that founded at Friedberg were also started at Friedland and Hope about the same time.

Very few children lived in Salem in 1772; most of the residents were unmarried men and women. Still, the interest in education that typified the first settlements carried over into the new town. Two schools were begun that year, one for little boys which met in the home of the master carpenter, Christian Triebel, and another for little girls which met in a room of the *Gemein Haus* with Elizabeth Osterlein as their teacher.

The records suggest that the Girls School, the forerunner of Salem Academy and College, was founded by Traugott Bagge and Jacob Meyer. Its first students were ages two and one-half, four, and eight. Tuition, paid directly to the teacher, was low—one shilling per week for the two youngest girls and sixpence for the eight-year-old. So far as it is known the subjects taught during these early years were spelling, reading, writing, knitting—all of which were combined with the memorization of hymns and Bible texts.

From 1773 to 1775, seven more students entered the Girls School. One was from Salem, two were from Friedberg, two were from the farm near Salem, and one was from Friedland. Tuition for the girls, who ranged in age from four to eleven, was from fourpence to one shilling per week. The girls from outside Salem found room and board with families in the community. In return they rendered what service they could in the household.

All of the Salem girls attended this school until they were approximately twelve years old. Between 1772 and 1802 there were an estimated sixty-two students from the town and an additional thirteen who came from outside. Six teachers other than Sister Osterlein served during the school's first three decades. During this period, courses were broadened to include reading and writing (in both German and English), arithmetic, geography, biblical history, music, and probably embroidery.

The Boys School was moved to the Single Brothers House in 1774. Six years later two new teachers were hired for the older and younger boys; classes were held Monday through Friday, and tuition was one shilling per week. In 1794 the length of the boys' education was extended so that they might be "taken further in what they have been studying, that is in writing, reckoning, history, geography, geometry, Latin, and especially in English. If possible they should be taught some Greek and French. The drawing of landscapes and flowers would also be useful." The new building for the Boys School, now the Wachovia Museum, was opened for use in 1794.

Until 1792 only Moravians were educated in the Brethren's schools in Wachovia, but in that year a request for the admission of the daughter of a non-Moravian came to the elders. The general feeling was that though such a move might be good and proper, a precedent would be set and their limited facilities could not contain the probable influx of students. More and more requests came in, however, and the town's visitors continued to note with "pleasure and satisfaction" the advantages of the education being offered in Salem.

With their usual missionary zeal the Brethren did not overlook the requests of outsiders for a boarding school, particularly one for girls. The elders of the community discussed the matter with much interest and on 31 October 1802 they formally established the Girls Boarding School. Almost immediately, plans for a building that would accommodate sixty girls were made, but until the anticipated two years of construction could be completed, temporary quarters were needed. The Brethren decided to continue classes in the *Gemein Haus*, and in May 1804 the first outside boarders arrived. Four girls came from Hillsborough, two from Halifax County, one from Fayetteville, and one from Caswell County. To fill up the class two local girls were chosen by Samuel Kramsch, the school's first principal. It was hoped that these two girls would help "forge links of understanding between [the outsiders] and the unfamiliar aspects of Moravianism." Three teachers who had special training in education were hired for the girls.

Classes continued in the *Gemein Haus* until 16 July 1805, when the new building, now South Hall of the Salem College campus, was completed, at a total cost to the congregation of $6,041.50. By this time there were twenty students, and before the end of the year these were joined by twenty-one more boarders. Tuition and board per quarter was $30.00. An additional $5.00 was charged if the girl wanted to take music and drawing; most did.

Unlike the school terms of today, a girl was free to enter the Girls Boarding School at any time during the year. The course of study usually lasted from two to four years. The program of instruction included grammar and syntax, history and geography, English reading and writing, and "cyphering." Girls usually spent the afternoon hours drawing, practicing their music lessons (the school received its first pianos in 1805), embroidering, or plain sewing.

Examinations were public and served the purpose of commencement exercises. The girls would prepare by rote the answers to questions distributed at some time before the examination, and no doubt their collective show of knowledge was most impressive to those in attendance. Each girl had her own individual questions in each area of study. Handiwork was also hung or displayed at this time. Questions typical of those asked, with the prepared answers, are as follows:

Q. How was our independence established?

A. A man who was raised up by Providence to command our armies, who was able to make the best of our slender resources, & to supply their defeet [sic] by his extraordinary genius. George Washington, if any mortal man ever merited the appellation of Father of his Country, surely merits that name. He, by the united voice of his country, led its armies; trained them to the art of war; and inspired them with invincible courage.

Q. Who was appointed the [first] supreme executive officer [of the United States]?

A. The late commander in chief, George Washington, was elected the first President. . . . When Washington crossed the Delaware & landed on the Jersey shore, he was saluted with three cheers by the inhabitants of the vicinity. When he came to the brow of the hill on his way to Trenton, a triumphant arch was erected on the bridge by the direction of the ladies of the place. The crown of the arch was highly ornamented, & on its sweep beneath was this inscription: The defender of the mothers, will also protect their daughters. On the north side were arranged a number of little girls dressed in white with garlands of flowers on their heads, & baskets of flowers on their arms; in the second row stood the young ladies, & behind them the married ladies of the neighborhood. The instant he passed the arch, the young girls began to sing the following ode:

> Welcome, mighty chief once more,
> Welcome to this grateful shore.
> Now no mercenary foe
> Aims at the fatal blow.
> Virgins fair and matrons grave,
> These thy conquering arm did save,
> Build for the triumphant bowers
> Strew ye fair his way with flowers,
> Strew your Hero's way with flowers.

As they sang the last lines, they strewed the flowers on the road before their beloved deliverer.

As might be ascertained from at least the second of these questions, history was the subject most stressed at exam time. "Globes," the physiographic aspects of geography, were also studied by the girls, and questions related to the latitude and longitude were based on the location of Salisbury, North Carolina!

In 1810, at a cost of $4,850, the Inspector's House was built. This building today is the Administration Building of Salem College.

The school grew considerably and by 1814 students had to be turned away. On the other hand, teachers were becoming scarce: "All the sisters approached have refused, either for the time or absolutely. . . . Probably still more difficulty along this line will arise, and it seems that the only remaining hope is to send an urgent request [for teachers] to Pennsylvania." This crisis was in 1820 but, as the records indicate, the teacher shortage was quickly overcome. By the mid-1830s enrollment in the school had reached 137 students. Out-of-state students were coming to Salem from Virginia, South Carolina, Georgia, Alabama, Florida, Louisiana, Kentucky, and Arkansas. Some parents were actually forced to board their girls in private homes while awaiting a spot in the boarding school. Typical of literally hundreds of urgent and sincere requests for admission to the school is this excerpt from a letter dated 15 December 1835 from Edmund Ruffin of Virginia (the same Ruffin who edited the *Farmer's Register* and later distinguished himself as a leading proponent of Southern secession): "I should not hesitate to enter my daughter but for the long and uncertain delay to be encountered before she can be admitted. . . . As it is important to place my daughter in a good school, as soon as may be done, I do not like to *engage* an entrance which is so remote and so uncertain—nor have I any right to expect, & do not mean to ask any departure from your established rules as to admission."

Indeed, while many new schools were formed in the decade of the 1830s, Salem remained the choice of more parents for their daughters than there were spaces available. And despite the criticisms that at the boarding school "the discipline . . . is too *rough* for the tenderness of a female constitution," one father from Mecklenburg County, Virginia, wrote (1 December 1836): "I am a North Carolinian and am unwilling to hear our institution, one of the oldest and most respectable of the kind in the southern states thus rudely espoiled—to hear its . . . well earned and dignified character impeached by the friends of every little *mushroom* Seminary that is daily springing up and which are as *volatile* and *shortlived* as that vegetable itself."

The Girls Boarding School provided a highly substantial education for many hundreds of young ladies as they prepared for their places in homes throughout the South in the years preceding the War Between the States. This fact is attested to by numerous fathers who wrote the different inspectors of the school to say so.

A register of 329 students (called scholars) from eleven states was listed in the 1854 catalogue of the school; the faculty numbered twenty-nine. Even at this time courses of study had changed little since the boarding school was founded more than fifty years before; its goals were still the same, "to fit the scholar, by the best training, for the sober duties and the solid realities of life." A new building, Main Hall, was completed in 1856 and housed all the classrooms, dormitory rooms, the infirmary, and storage rooms. What had begun as a modest school for three little girls had grown into a formidable institution recognized throughout the South.

Newspapers in Salem

Salem's first newspaper, *The Weekly Gleaner*, appeared on 6 January 1829. John C. Blum, editor, gave assurance to the supervising board, the Collegium, that this paper "would contain nothing improper and that it would cause no offense to the congregation." The format of the paper was four pages of news, descriptions (Frederick Law Olmsted's view of Pilot Mountain, for example), and advertisements. In all probability, Blum's weekly was printed on paper made locally at the mill which Gottlieb Schober opened in 1790. According to the first issue, "Party politics, and all its train of abuses, will not occupy any portion of our columns. . . ." On 29 December 1829, the last issue of *The Weekly Gleaner* was printed. Blum explained that "to publish a larger sheet, the patronage is not sufficient; and to continue the paper in its present diminutive size, is not calculated to make it as profitable and interesting to the public as we could wish."

Brother Blum was not discouraged by the failure of his first attempt, and early in 1832 he began publishing the *Farmer's Reporter*. The following account is revealing of the paper's influence. In June of 1832 Blum's newspaper carried an advertisement for Brother Carl Eberhard for which he had not received permission from the Collegium. It seems that, according to the advertisement, Brother Eberhard intended to "carry on his shoemaking trade in his father's house and would undersell the other shoemakers in town." After much consideration the Collegium decided that Eberhard must recall his advertisement, or "it was resolved that if he would not yield to persuasion, an advertisement in the name of the Auf.[seher] Col.[legium] in 'The Reporter' would repudiate his advertisement." With the growing discontent over community control, Blum's paper could have thrived on advertisements alone, had the Collegium responded to each! Finally, after Eberhard was "lovingly admonished to desist from his intention," he "acknowledged his fault with the promise to take back the advertisement."

The name of this newspaper was changed to *Farmers' Reporter and Rural Repository*, and again, early in 1836, to the *Weekly Chronicle and Farmers' Register*. In 1827 Brother Blum also founded *Blum's Almanac*, which is still being published.

Another Salem tabloid, the *People's Press*, was published for the first time on 8 February 1851. L. V. Blum, son of Christian Blum, and E. T.'s brother, was editor. This amazing little four-page newspaper enjoyed a wide circulation and was noted for its local Salem flavor; Francis Eugene Boner received his early writing experience as an apprentice on the *People's Press*. Though it has been suggested that this Salem paper was closed down in 1866, after the war, its publication continued until December 1892.

Public Education in Forsyth County, 1840–60

Before January 1839, the state of North Carolina made no provision for the education of its youth; if one could not afford to send his children to a private academy, they did without formal training. The school law of 1839 changed this, however, by providing money from the State Literary Fund to establish free schools for all white children between the ages of five and twenty-one. There was one reservation in the law: a majority of the taxpayers of a county had to agree to pay $1.00 per year for each $2.00 provided by the state. At first this provision was not acceptable to all of Forsyth's taxpayers; many of them could not understand the value of such a school system. Ignorance quickly proved to be chief enemy of the common schools.

In 1840 the machinery for a common school system in Stokes County (of which Forsyth was then a part) was put into effect— the prescribed tax was voted in, school districts were planned, and a board of superintendents was elected with C. L. Banner as chairman. Others elected as superintendents besides Banner were John T. Blackburn, Anthony Bitting, Philip Kerner, James Davis, F. C. Meinung, and T. H. Linville. District committeemen were appointed to locate teachers for their respective districts. These men were also charged with the responsibility of periodically visiting each school to determine whether things were running smoothly.

The common schools here were greeted by mixed reactions. At Belews Creek, for example, animosity between the people living on the east and west sides of the creek prevented the early establishment of a school. The board minutes record that the "citizens on the East side are so much opposed to the school that they would not even give the names and numbers of their children." As to the location of the building, those on the west side would "not have the school on any terms on the East side of the Creek."

Forty persons from Pfafftown, Hausertown, and Old Town sent a petition to Banner in 1844 which stated that their school was too crowded. Receiving no favorable reply, they then sought to remedy the situation themselves by purchasing a piece of land and building a schoolhouse to suit their needs as they saw them. This action was clearly illegal, but there was little the school board could do to prevent it.

Besides the difficulties of poor understanding of the school law, personal animosities, and overcrowded conditions, the problem of transportation—getting to and from school—was involved. One parent whose home was just outside District 72 wrote that because the schoolhouse in his district was "three quarters of a mile the farther besides two large bottoms to cross it is impossible for children to cross in the winter season to the school house in district 72 is a good road and the nearest." Another father, Moses Smith, also wished his children to attend the school in District 72. He wrote the board that "it is two miles the farthest to go the road and to go through it is about a mile nearer but it is impossible for children to go through plantations they will have a grate many fences to clime and two bottoms to cross. I live in the very corner of my district. It is about a mile to the School House, No. 72 and it is a very good road."

Philip Kerner of District 10, on the other hand, had "good luck" in starting his school and in "getting three proper persons to act as committeemen." Moses Hasten, the teacher for District 29, conducted his school for over five months in 1843 and had an average of thirty-two students in attendance each day. In addition to the usual three Rs, Hasten taught English grammar and geography, perhaps indicative of a desire to compete with Salem's private schools that lay in his district. Districts 3 and 29 were in operation by 1843, though attendance in each was generally low.

By 1846 most of the county schools were operating on an average of sixty days per year, generally from November or December into the first two or three months of the new year. These schools benefited from increased revenue from the state, as did the students from the incorporation of an annual examining program for their teachers. When Forsyth was formally divided from Stokes three years later, the system in this county was operating quite smoothly.

The first Board of Superintendents for Forsyth County per se (1851) was made up of C. L. Banner, John Masten, William Goslin, Francis Fries, John M. Stafford, Andrew M. Gamble, Henry R. Lehman, Albert V. Sullivan, and Abraham Teague. New districts (essentially the same as the old Stokes districts) were laid off, and committeemen were appointed. The separation itself presented no problems, and of the original forty-five districts only nine were without schoolhouses in 1851. A total of 1,901 Forsyth children attended school that year.

Principally under the guidance of one man, Calvin H. Wiley,

the common schools of North Carolina were beginning to serve a valuable function to thousands of the state's youth by the early 1850s. Wiley was very popular among Forsyth's educators and his speeches and reports appeared almost in toto in the Salem *People's Press*. Despite a tacit loyalty to the Moravian academies, this paper was a staunch supporter of the common schools; according to John Yates, in "The Common School System in Forsyth County, North Carolina, from 1840 until 1884," it helped greatly to communicate Wiley's suggestions in the county. In August of 1859 Wiley was invited by J. W. Alspaugh to attend an educational meeting in Forsyth County. Those present were to be all the teachers, committeemen, and superintendents. According to Mr. Alspaugh, "We are earnestly endeavoring to raise the standards of education in our country."

The direct result of Wiley's visit and his presence at the meeting was the formation of the Forsyth County Educational Association on 27 August 1859. Resolutions passed by the new association gave teachers the right to classify their pupils "in the best manner for the convenience of the classroom" and also provided that only books recommended by Wiley would be used in Forsyth's schools. Furthermore, unless one had "good order in his school," he would not be considered a teacher by the association. School hours were standardized: classes ran from 8:00 to 11:30 A.M.; then came a break until 1:00 P.M., when classes again resumed for three more hours.

In recognition of the efforts of Forsyth's educators, Wiley wrote in the *North Carolina Journal of Education* in 1860 that "the teachers of Forsyth County deserve credit for the interest they have shown for some time past, in their own improvement as teachers and the improvements of the schools of their county. We commend their example to the teachers of other counties."

By 1860, 2,525 students were attending the common schools in Forsyth County. This was the highest number in the history of the system at that time. The school session averaged seventy-eight days, but in one district the school remained open a full 195 days. Teacher pay, still amazingly low—less than $73.00 per year, on the average—had doubled over the preceding ten-year period. An additional six districts had been added to Forsyth's system.

Yates notes that such men as John Cox, Thomas Hunter, Robert Linville, Moses H. Morris, William Swaim, and John White were at this time particularly dedicated teachers and were most influential in the maintenance of high teaching standards. And finally, without the strong interest and guidance of two men, Constantine L. Banner and J. W. Alspaugh, Forsyth's public schools would not have achieved the "stability and constant growth" with which they are credited.

Music of the Moravians in North Carolina

Their music was one of the most distinctive accomplishments of the Moravians who settled in North Carolina. Music, particularly that of a trombone choir or brass band, announced virtually every public occasion: weddings, christenings, pageants, funerals, church and community affairs, and even the special holy days of the church year. Hymns were sung by the Brothers and Sisters of Wachovia at home and on the job. Secular music likewise found its way into their lives through the *Collegium Musicum* of Salem; this "venerable old German amateur [music] society" preserved for over a century a tradition that had become extinct in Europe.

It is suggested that the corpus of the music of the Moravians in North Carolina—about 80 percent—was sacred. In contrast to the simple fugues of Billings and other New England composers, the Moravians were producing elaborate choral anthems that were frequently accompanied by strings, winds, and brass. Albeit this music was not unique in its "American-ness," it remains among the best composed in the young nation, having stemmed from the early classical tradition of Germany. The library of the Salem *Collegium Musicum* contained works—both printed and manuscript—by such composers as Abel, Haydn, Mozart, and Pleyel. Indeed, many of their copies were first editions. Later were added the compositions of Beethoven, Cherubini, Dussek, Lefevre, Méhul, Weber, Winter, and Wranitzky, among others.

The musicians themselves, all amateurs with few exceptions, were the artisans, ministers, and professional men of the community; their taste is reflected not only in the high quality of music they played but in the variety and number of instruments they owned. In 1754, when no other instrument was available, a trumpet was made from a hollow limb; three years later this single and rather makeshift instrument was replaced by two trumpets made of brass (brought from Bethlehem). In 1767 French horns and violins were added to their growing collection, and in 1768 a set of trombones was purchased. Organs found their way into their churches rather early: at Bethabara in 1762, Salem in 1772, and Bethania in 1773. Most strangely the *Zinken*, or *cornetti*, and the *viola da gamba* were added to Salem's ensemble around 1800. Both of these instruments had lost favor in Europe long before with the nominal end of the baroque period. Their use in Salem might no doubt be attributed to a general want of instruments for their larger performances, despite the already large size of the *Collegium's* collection. The *gamba*, a particularly delicate instrument, could have been used as an ersatz cello, and the *Zink* might very well have accompanied the higher of the brass or string instruments.

Conclusion

The record of the development of society in the wilderness that was Wachovia is a complex subject, taking into account the impact of that wilderness in its physical and social aspects on a group of people—essentially first-generation German colonials—as well as the impact of that group on the wilderness itself. The Brethren brought with them to Wachovia a life-style soundly based in a religion that fostered brotherhood, love of one's neighbors, and a communal selflessness. One hundred years in the North Carolina Piedmont, and exposure to its non-Moravian elements, with the unavoidable inclusion of some of those elements (both social and economic) into Moravian life, resulted in the creation of a new, amalgamated Moravian by 1860. He was a thoroughgoing Southerner who, having lost his parents' German accent, so to speak, did not forget or forsake his native traditions, heritage, or language. In religion, education, and cultural foundations the Moravians were still Moravians; and in many ways, they were still German. But in a broader sense they were irrevocably bound to their new environment and the attitudes and habits of its people.

The *Fremde*, or non-Moravian elements, likewise were influenced by the Moravians. Socially, the most notable example was in religion, as educational opportunities were largely confined to a wealthy few. The Moravians provided their neighbors with a definite religious stability that not only served to hold other non-Moravian congregations together but also witnessed the formation of new churches in the area, primarily of other denominations. The economic stability the Moravians brought to the North Carolina Piedmont would serve the *Fremde* in an infinitely greater way than the social stability, however, for the important commercial and industrial center that emerged in Forsyth County in later years had its firm base in the town of Salem before the Civil War.

CHAPTER 6

The Economic Order,
1753–1860

THE MORAVIAN SETTLEMENT IN WACHOVIA was intended by church authorities to be self-supporting and communal, and so the settlers gave immediate attention to tilling the soil as a first step towards self-sufficiency, "that as soon as possible we may be able to eat our own bread." But for the Moravians, unlike the vast majority of the inhabitants of North Carolina's Piedmont, subsistence farming was not an end in itself. Rather, within twenty years of the initial settlement at Bethabara, the Brethren had moved en masse to Salem where crafts, trade, and industry took precedence. "This town [Salem] is not designed for farmers but for those with trades," Frederic William Marshall wrote in 1765. Bethabara, or Old Town, became a small farming community, like the other outlying Moravian communities of Wachovia.

The first half of the nineteenth century witnessed definite progress towards an industrial community, especially among the Moravians, and it was through industry, not agriculture, that the Moravian and non-Moravian inhabitants of what would become Forsyth County joined together in a united effort towards prosperity.

Agricultural Beginnings

The Germans in general and the Moravians in particular produced some of the best farmers in the colony. They were thrifty, industrious, and frugal by habit and by training. In 1783 Johann Schoepf referred to the Moravians' "diligence in agriculture," a trait recognized by their neighbors but imitated by few. Another observer, Elkanah Watson, who visited Wachovia in 1786, reported that "the moment I touched the boundary of the Moravians, I noticed a marked and most favorable change in the appearance of buildings and farms; and even the cattle seemed larger, and in better condition. Here, in combined and well-directed effort, all put shoulders to the wheel which apparently moves on oily springs."

In addition to the crops, vegetables, and herbs that they planted, the first twelve Brethren to arrive in Wachovia also raised livestock, beginning a practice that continued in full force until the time of the War Between the States. The Bethabara diarist recorded on 28 December 1753, a little over one month after their arrival in North Carolina, that cattle had already been purchased. Several pigs of a "particularly good breed" were bought from a farmer on the Yadkin some four months later. In April 1754 more cattle were sought, and on 4 May "an eight acre cow pen" was completed. By the middle of September 1754 the Brethren owned 11 cows, 10 calves, 1 bull, 1 steer, and "11 old and 12 grown hogs," as well as 23 pigs. Such an interest in livestock raising is typical of the colony at large, and as Professor Cathey comments, in *Agricultural Developments in North Carolina, 1783–1860*, North Carolina's "greatest agricultural distinction in the colonial period" was as a producer of livestock, particularly cattle and swine. Both the Moravian and non-Moravian settlers in what would become Forsyth County fit into this pattern. Livestock served not only as a source of food but also provided skins which could be traded.

Equally as important as livestock to the Moravian settlers was the growing of wheat. This crop was the principal commercial product in the early days of settlement. Wheat, being the "proper grain for bread," was the first crop the Brethren planted. While "corn was . . . the grain most generally used, and the people of this country live on it," the Bethabara settlers chose to deal with corn only as a commodity. Much to their dismay, the first inhabitants of Wachovia were forced to eat bread made of corn, but within two years sufficient wheat crops allowed them to give up the former grain. Initially rye was mixed with wheat to make their bread, but in 1764, one of the Brethren cheerfully noted that "rye is used more in the distillery than for bread."

Professor H. R. Merrens states in *Colonial North Carolina in the Eighteenth Century* that it was not just this preference for wheat bread that accounted for a heavy emphasis on the crop: "In addition to satisfying their bread preferences, wheat was also an eminently salable crop." Practical economics and experience demonstrated to the Moravians that as long as their neighbors were growing corn, if they grew wheat, a higher-priced crop, it would bring them a markedly higher profit. The raw grain, as well as flour and bread, was sold to their immediate neighbors and visitors, and was also transported to outside markets. If more corn were needed than was grown, it could be purchased from their neighbors.

With the construction of the grist mill in 1765, the Moravians began a promotion of the wheat trade "within and from western North Carolina." Thus it is no wonder that in 1775 the Salem diarist recorded, "Our neighbors are steadily increasing the amount of wheat raised." Their monopoly on the wheat trade was threatened! And indeed by 1775 wheat production had become quite widespread throughout the Piedmont. It may be presumed that the Brethren grew less wheat after this time.

Slaveholding in Wachovia before the Revolution

The census returns for Rowan County in 1755 (Forsyth was then a part of Rowan, as was the western one-third of North Carolina) give a picture of the sparse settlement in the western part of the colony as well as the small number of slaves to be found: 1,116 whites and only 54 blacks. Albeit the census was far from complete, the relative guide it gives is in itself useful. Slavery was as yet confined to the eastern counties of the colony.

Because the Brethren were unaccustomed to slavery, they were definitely inclined to rely on their own labor. Both as a group and as individuals, however, the Moravians of Wachovia did own slaves. Their attitude toward the Negro from the first days of settlement was both ambivalent and paradoxical. Morally they had no objection to the institution; the use of slave labor was "a fact of life" in Wachovia as it was throughout the colonies, North and South. Therefore, as soon as construction of the tavern at Bethabara was completed, the Brethren hired several Negroes from non-Moravian slaveholders to work there. As time went on more Negroes were employed for other reasons, particularly in the performance of heavy construction, housework, and farm labor.

In 1762, one Negro by the name of Sam, who had been in Bethabara "for some time," expressed his desire "to know the Savior." With their typical missionary zeal—and the reason for their being in North Carolina was to serve as missionaries—the Moravians brought him into their community by purchase, "with the permission of the Lord." Later Sam was baptized, becoming the first Negro to enter into the Brotherhood of the Moravian church in Wachovia. Gradually several more slaves were purchased, though their number was never more than four in the early days of settlement.

When most of the inhabitants of Bethabara moved to Salem in 1772, there were only three slaves who remained behind, "one negroe who has been bought, and two maids."

The need for labor in Salem, the "commercial and manufacturing hub of the settlement," was greater than that of Bethabara. In the first year of occupation of the new town Brother Jacob Meyer brought an "old negress and her children" from Bethabara. Traugott Bagge, the store manager, purchased three slaves in his own name, though they in fact were claimed by the store. One should note at this point that slaveholding was actually prohibited by the *Aufseher Collegium* in Salem, but "necessary exceptions" were made from the beginning. Later some private individuals purchased slaves, against the express wishes of the Collegium.

As to the extent of the role played by slaves in Wachovia, an entry in the Bethabara Diary for 1773 is most enlightening. On September 20 of that year, two men from Virginia visited the settlement. The diarist noted that "they looked about with wonder and pleasure." His entry continues: "Among other questions they asked how many negroes we had? Answer, two. They were the more surprized to find that white people had done so much work."

Indeed the use of slaves seems to have merely augmented the Moravians' work force, rather than to have served in its stead. These Germans were not used to slavery and did not, from an economic standpoint, make very good masters. Quite simply the Moravians were guilty of "spoiling" their slaves by allowing them too much freedom and by spending more money on their upkeep than seemed necessary; at least it appeared so to outsiders. One observer remarked that the "Brethren cannot get as much profit out of them as other people who use them roughly and dress them poorly." No doubt his statement is true, but interestingly enough, "Moravian slaves" in Georgia sold for much higher prices than did any others.

The greatest fear that slaveholding created for the Moravians was not one of uprising or insurrection. Rather, it was fear of the possible cultural effect slave labor might create: "such workers [could] introduce into the community attitudes and habits incompatible with those of the Brethren." Nora Lee Reese's research, set forth in "The Moravian Attitude Toward the Negro and Slavery" and "Freedom and Authority in the Moravian Community of North Carolina," in fact suggests that the few slaves who did become a part of the Moravian community inspired idleness and harshness in their owners and employers, and for that reason the Collegium tended to frown upon the presence of any Negro, free or slave.

In Wachovia, as in the whole of the colony, slaves were baptized and admitted to membership in the white churches— colonial laws were such that Negroes could not form their own church organizations. Still, social intercourse was generally discouraged, and by the end of the Revolution rather strict laws limiting the privileges of Negroes had been instituted in Salem. The coming decades would see an even more open acceptance of and conformity to the Southern attitude towards its peculiar institution.

The Economic System of the Brethren and Commercial Beginnings

The Moravians wasted little time in establishing a town and a number of businesses and craft operations. While at Bethabara they lived and worked together—communally, in fact—in maintaining a very strict economic system under which everyone worked for the church. The church in turn provided for all. The land, the tools, and other means of production were all owned communally and the profits of production were shared by everyone in the settlement. This "common housekeeping" was called the *Oeconomie*.

More specifically the *Oeconomie* was such that each member of the congregation gave of his trade or labor to the general supply and requisitioned from the common store the goods he needed. Profits went into a general fund which was used to purchase livestock, building materials, and other goods and supplies which could not be produced at home. This system did not deny the individual private ownership of property or goods, but rather what he produced during the period of communal labor was added to the general fund. The business manager (*Vorsteher*) directed the efforts of the community and assigned tasks to those individuals he thought best qualified to handle them. The "common housekeeping" never existed outside Bethabara.

By the time much of the Bethabara community·had moved to Salem, all the property and debts of the *Oeconomie* were assumed by the financial administration of the entire Moravian church. Salem had its own financial organization (*Diaconie*) as did Bethabara. The supervising board (*Aufseher Collegium*) which controlled the *Diaconie* was a collecting agency of sorts and received rents and interests from individual members and in turn passed them along to the administration. The Salem *Diaconie* was self-sustaining and not dependent on any outside help.

All the expenses of the community were paid by the *Diaconie*. Also the annual quitrent was paid to Lord Granville's agents by the Salem *Diaconie*. Repairs to the *Gemein Haus* and other buildings also came from this source.

The many expenditures of the *Diaconie* were offset by rent and contributions. Brothers and Sisters alike paid a monthly fee for the upkeep of the church—the former one shilling, fourpence, and the latter, tenpence. For a house belonging to the congregation, a tenant was obliged to pay annually a rent of 6 percent of the value of the structure, or 7 percent if he were unwilling to maintain the repairs himself. Funds from profit-making businesses likewise went to the *Diaconie*.

In his book, *Myths and Realities*, Professor Carl Bridenbaugh has cited the Moravian community in Wachovia as the "best integrated and most successful . . . in the Southern colonies." This colonial success of the Brethren was due in part to their communal way of life with "common housekeeping" and in part to their natural business prowess. The Brethren, when it came to business and politics, were expedient, and in their wilderness environment they were obliged to take advantage of the opportunities afforded them. Trading with their neighbors was one of the greatest of these.

The Bethabara mill, located some nineteen miles from the next nearest mill, was of great public importance. Meal was ground for the Brethren and their neighbors here. The building also served as a sort of clearinghouse for the grain supply—when there was a good harvest the surplus was sold; when supplies were scant, it was well guarded so that distribution to members of the community and their neighbors might be controlled. This extract from the *Memorabilia* of 1766 illustrates the care with which the Moravians looked after supplies: "In the earlier months of the year we were somewhat anxious because of our small stock of grain and provision, for want and high prices increased from day to day in our neighborhood, but by the very evident blessing of God our supply lasted, not only for ourselves but for the hundreds of poor people who came here for bread, often from many miles away, and so far as we know none went away hungry." Earlier, during the French and Indian War, and later during the American Revolution, grain ground in the Bethabara mill fed refugees and soldiers of both British and American armies.

One of the craftsmen who located in Bethabara was a gunsmith, Andreas Betz. There were also Jacob Kapp, who served as a miller and turner, and Jacob Van der Merk, a turner and millwright. The organmaker, Joseph Bullitschek, came to Bethabara in

1771. The Norwegian cabinetmaker Enert Enerson established his trade in Bethabara. In 1766 he made and installed the doors for the "First House" in Salem; Enerson had an apprentice cabinetmaker, John Friedrich Beck. Coming to Bethabara in 1754 and 1755 respectively were the carpenters George Holder and Christian Triebel. Triebel aided Bullitschek in the construction of a sawmill some time later. David Rominger and his son, from Broadbay, Maine, settled in Bethania as carpenters.

Of great commercial importance to the early Moravian settlement were the potters. Gottfried Aust, a native of Silesia, came to Bethabara in 1755. In March 1756 he began to work on a "small oven" in which he "burnd some earthen-ware." The success of his small oven in testing glazes and clay encouraged him to construct a full-size pottery kiln, which he completed in July or August 1756. By the tenth day of the next month, Aust's first project was completed: "Br[other] Aust burned pottery today for the second time,—the glazing did well,—and so the great need is at last relieved. Each living room now has the ware it needs, and the kitchen is furnished. There is also a set of mugs of uniform size for Lovefeast." Continuing to fill the immediate needs of the Brethren before offering any of his ceramics for sale, Aust "burned stove tiles, and when they were ready he set up stoves in the *Gemein Haus* and in the Brothers House, probably the first in Carolina."

With the termination of Indian troubles, Gottfried Aust began to sell many of his wares to the non-Moravian neighbors or to others who came from fifty or sixty miles away, thus beginning one of the Brethren's most lucrative trades. John Bivins in *The Moravian Potters in North Carolina* suggests that the Bethabara potter filled a number of contracts with country-store owners who sold his wares. By 1770 people were coming sixty to eighty miles to buy milk crocks and pans "in our pottery." Frequently the entire stock was bought; "many could get only half they wanted, and others who came late, could find none." The profits from these sales amounted to about 50 percent. Aust had no real helpers until 1766 when Joseph Muller, Rudolf Christ, Ludwig Muller, and Henry Beroth were taken in as apprentices.

Following the construction of the first dwelling houses in

1766, a potter's shop and blacksmith's shop were built, and by the end of 1767, the town had already begun to function as a "compact, well-directed, urban center." The work of the first tradesmen who had moved to Salem was so successful that two years before the large-scale move from Bethabara, in 1770, the profits already realized had more than paid the expenses of the new town.

The first really large operation was the erection of the Single Brothers House. From the measuring of the lot on 23 July 1768 until sixteen men and four boys moved in on 27 December 1769, the Brothers House occupied the center of construction activities, and for good reason: the Single Brothers House was organized as a business establishment and each of its members paid the *Diaconie* for board and lodging. The Brothers carried on a number of trades ranging from brewing to baking; they also rented their own farm of seven hundred acres. Before 1778 journeymen were paid three shillings a day. Feeling this was too little, they went on strike as a protest to the low wages; full of shame they returned to work the next day!

The year 1772 saw much moving from Bethabara to Salem. The community store was moved into the first floor of the two-story house, and the merchant Traugott Bagge settled his family on the second floor. Gottlieb Reuter built a small house for himself and his family diagonally across from the southwest corner of the square. Matthew Miksch began to manufacture snuff and some smoking tobacco. Heinrich Herbst took charge of a tanyard just west of the village. Jacob Meyer became the tavernkeeper. Other small houses were built and by the end of the year most of the residents of Bethabara had moved to Salem. In 1775 Salem contained 125 inhabitants.

In addition to Aust, the potter, who had earlier moved to Salem, other craftsmen began to establish themselves in and around the new village. There were the gunsmiths Niels Lund, Christoph Vogler, and Andreas Betz (from Bethabara) prior to 1785. There were also sickle- and sieve-makers. Woodturners and cabinetmakers such as Kapp, Krause, Lick, Beck, Wohlfahrt, Broesing, and Stauber were all active in Salem before, during and just after the American Revolution. Bullitschek, the organmaker, had relocated in Salem by 1775.

The community store in Salem attracted a great number of trappers and hunters, who brought their hides there to sell. For many years, in fact, animal skins made up the largest export commodity of the store. Clothes and haberdashery were sold, as were pots, pans, kettles, dishes, cutlery, and various other household implements. Work tools produced by the Single Brothers were to be found at the community store, as well as products that could not be produced at home, such as glassware, rum, molasses, salt, and sugar.

C. C. Crittenden in *The Commerce of North Carolina, 1763–1789* suggests that even though Moravians of Wachovia were better supplied with cash than any other group in the backcountry, much of their trade involved barter—no one else had any money. For example on 21 February 1765 two hunters from Virginia brought 1600 pounds of skins and fur to the Bethabara store. Because Brother Gammern, the storekeeper, "could only get together £40 to pay them," the Virginians instead bought £40 worth of goods. Further the general scarcity of cash, as well as the seasonal nature of hunting, forced the Brethren to extend credit to numbers of their customers. As might be expected, this practice backfired; a few examples from the Bethabara Diary will suffice for illustration:

Sept. 23. [1766] In our store and Tavern an advertisement was posted in English and German calling on our debtors to come and pay. There are about 600 debtors, and they owe more than £1800.

Oct. 22. We hear again that certain debtors . . . have run away, and others are likely to follow them, since we have advertised that they must pay, and that we will allow no more uncertain credit.

Nov. 26. Br[other] Jacob Steiner was sent to the Yadkin etc. to see our debtors, and ascertain when and how they mean to make payment. Several that were reported to have left were still there; they have said they would pay in cattle and corn, and one man today brought two cows and two steers.

Nov. 29. A number of men came from the Town Fork with Under Sheriff Frohock and Constable Piles. Among them were a number of our debtors, as summoned. We spoke earnestly to them, and attracted the elder Pool, who is reported to have said that he would let us have corn in payment for debt at the store at 3 sh.[illings] per bushel, though the current price is 2 sh.[illings].

Despite bad credit and the barter system, the Salem store, like the Bethabara store before it, did an enviable business until the years of the American Revolution, when economic troubles resulted from high prices and fluctuating currency. The Brethren were at first understandably reluctant to accept the Continental scrip; this was not a show of unpatriotic feeling but a measure of economic necessity, as the currency was not at all stable.

A distillery, sawmill, and brewery produced additional goods which were basically intended for an export market rather than for the immediate use of the Brethren. Profits were particularly good on these items.

Transportation

Intimately related to the agriculture, commerce, and trade of the Wachovia communities and surrounding areas was transportation. Collet's map of 1770 indicates a vast network of possible routes of trade, but, as one traveler observed, "good roads are few and far between." Another visitor to this colony was less generous; he proclaimed North Carolina's roads to be the "worst in the world." The colonial assembly had passed legislation which provided for new roads and their marking and maintenance, but these laws were never enforced.

The inhabitants of the backcountry were completely isolated from ports on the coast. Moravian merchants and tradesmen found themselves about equidistant from Bolling's Point and Charleston, and almost as far from Wilmington. Roads were so bad that the trip by wagon from Wachovia to Charleston took almost one month; going to and from Cross Creek (Fayetteville) took thirteen or fourteen days. In other words, the best time a driver could make would be eighteen or nineteen miles a day. As the export trade became more and more important to the Brethren the number of side roads increased; the new roads were numerous but still poor. Brother Reuter, the court-appointed roadmaster of Dobbs Parish, took special precautions that all crossroads and distances for which he was responsible were clearly marked;

his efforts, as compared to those of overseers and roadmasters throughout the remainder of the section, were singular. Wachovia was an urban area that depended on its roads, and good maintenance was essential for ease of travel.

In the months preceding the American Revolution, it was noted by the Salem diarist that trade was largely carried on at Cross Creek rather than Charleston. A road between Salem and Cross Creek had been opened in 1770, and by 1772 a messenger was sent to Cross Creek once a month for the Wilmington newspaper. Regular trips to Cross Creek also served to keep the Brethren better abreast of prices and market conditions.

The trade carried on by the Moravians with the outside world was chiefly by wagon. Their vehicles had four wheels, sometimes were covered, and usually were drawn by two to four horses. An average load of goods would have weighed about one ton.

Tobacco Culture and Manufacturing

Tobacco was among the first crops grown in Forsyth County. It was planted before the Moravians came to the area to settle, but until the late 1850s tobacco was never widely grown in the county. The Bethabara diarist records that early in the summer of 1755 Brother Loesch acquired "a couple of hundred tobacco plants" from a Mr. Banner who lived along the Yadkin. As this was the only purchase mentioned for the year, presumably just enough tobacco was grown to fulfill the immediate needs of the Brethren, at least at this time.

In 1754 John Jacob Friis, pastor of the Bethabara Congregation, started a "Plantation for tobacco," and on 24 May he "began . . . to burn" it. The ashes of large quantities of logs and brush that were burned on the freshly cleared soil supposedly killed insects and weed seeds. Friis wrote that this planting procedure "cost me much labor & I did not understand it so well [then] as I do now." Around the first of July he cut and began to dry some of the tender young leaves from the tobacco plants. On 16 July Friis wrote in a letter, "We have smoked for a Fortnight our new Tobacco." He indicated in the same letter that it had grown "incomparably well." Throughout the 1750s and 1760s tobacco was grown in varying quantities on the Bethabara and Bethania farms.

It was not until the end of 1773 that the Brethren began to process any of their tobacco for commercial purposes. Johann Matthew Miksch, former store manager and "Shopkeeper" from Bethabara, "asked . . . if he could not have exclusive privilege in the selling of tobacco." Miksch's "poor living" had caused the Collegium much concern, but "with much pity, and with honesty," they granted him permission and wished him well in this new venture. Miksch's chief product was snuff.

By the end of the Revolution Miksch had expanded his business, and in 1782 or 1783 he constructed a manufactory behind his house on Salem's main street. Within ten years, however, he was no longer able to attend to his business, so the manufacture and sale of tobacco was passed on to other hands.

The tobacco trade of Wachovia was based largely on outside customers. During the first years of the Revolution, when the inflated Continental currency was forced upon the businessmen of Salem, the tobacco industry "felt this change most of all." The merchant simply "cannot refuse to strangers to sell them tobacco." The Brethren traded among themselves with "tickets" of their own making. Of course, it should be pointed out the actual loss suffered from the acceptance of inflated money was not limited to the tobacco merchant, but sustained by the congregation at large—the community *Diaconie* absorbed the debt.

Magnus Hulthin, like his predecessor Miksch, manufactured snuff. His recipe called for grinding both the leaves and stems into a fine powder, then adding specified amounts of salt and sugar, and finally steeping the entire mixture in tobacco juice. Later this rather liquid mixture would be strained and dried. Initially the monies realized from the sale of Hulthin's product went to the Single Brothers' *Diaconie*, but they were later used for the benefit of the congregation *Diaconie*.

When Hulthin retired in 1826, Johann Fries bought his stock and equipment. Fries was much more ambitious than his predecessor and, in an effort to expand his operation, he employed slave labor, against the wishes of the Collegium. It is suggested from contemporary sources that he did a "lively" retail business;

the quantities used in his recipe for making snuff also indicate this fact:

I take 9 lbs. tobacco and 6 lbs. stems, 15 lbs. in all, grind and mix well; take 1 gallon and 1/2 pint of water, six handfuls of salt and 1 handful of sugar; mix it well and keep it warm; in 2 to 4 weeks strain it. I take extra trouble and before straining it, put it into pots and let it sweat for a while. . . .

Johann Fries did not restrict his business interests to the manufacture and sale of tobacco. For this reason, after he had for several years maintained a corner on the Salem market, the Collegium deemed it desirable to allow Benjamin Warner to enter the trade, in 1831. Nine years later he was joined by Evan Boner, who was given permission to open a tobacco factory of his own. But by the end of the 1840s, Salem's retail-based tobacco industry was fast failing, as was the church's control of the economic life of the town.

In another part of the county, four miles north of the new town of Winston, James E. Ogburn began producing plug tobacco in 1850. Unlike the Salem manufacturers, Ogburn was buying great quantities of tobacco from his neighbors, and from 1855, some ten to twenty thousand pounds of solid plug was purchased each year until the War Between the States. Ogburn's efforts formed the real beginnings of Winston-Salem's tobacco industry.

Textile Manufacturing and Dyeing

Cotton and flax, like tobacco, were among the first crops planted by the Brethren, and were probably found in the small private gardens of most of the settlers. Cotton was never widely grown in Salem or in the Piedmont, though after the invention of the gin in 1793 experiments with the plant became more numerous. Initially the largest part of the weaving efforts of the Moravian communities were directed toward home use. Linen was most commonly used, as it was the cheapest fiber available. Wool followed linen in importance; neighboring settlers who had no accessible market for their clippings gladly sold or traded what they had for goods offered in the community stores at Bethabara and Salem. Cotton followed linen and wool in frequency of usage; it was the most expensive of the three and also the scarcest.

Gottfried Praezel initiated the first weaving efforts in Wachovia when he began experiments in processing flax in 1758. It is not known whether Praezel's cloth was dyed, but one might assume that there were some home attempts prior to 1774. In this year a dyer, Matthew Weiss of Bethlehem, came to Salem. He failed to bring his own equipment, and since none could be found in the area, it had to be sent for in Pennsylvania. By the time the materials arrived, Weiss had been found of such bad character that he was dismissed from the congregation.

No dyer could be located after Weiss's dismissal. Attempts to sell his dyeing materials were also unsuccessful. In the early summer of 1780, Johannes Schaub, then the tavernkeeper at Bethabara, was sent north to learn the trade from Weiss. He returned to Wachovia in November and "set up his kettle" in the Brothers House at Bethabara. Now the Brethren could have their spun yarn dyed at home instead of sending it to Pennsylvania, thus avoiding both the expense of travel and the loss of some of their goods.

In 1789 a fulling mill was constructed in Salem by Abraham Loesch so that the cloth could be properly shrunk and thickened. Loesch was joined by a young boy who remained at the mill only a short time, for in 1791 Loesch had to purchase a Negro boy to help him in his work. An insufficient water supply at the creek where he had located below Salem Hill forced Loesch to move his operation some two miles from the town on Brushy Creek.

The production of cloth was carried on by the Single Brothers and the Single Sisters (who also had their own *Diaconie*), particularly by the latter. The Brothers did some of their own dyeing because their wares were not being colored fast enough by Loesch. The names of C. F. Schroeter, the tailor, Jacob Vetter, a joiner, and Matthew Reuz are later associated with the Brothers' dyeing operation. Many others may have been dyers in Salem, both professional and nonprofessional, but their names are not recorded.

Van Neman (Vaniman) Zevely, "a stranger boy whose mother desired before she died that her son could find a place in Salem

Community," arrived in Salem in 1795 or 1796. After acceptance into the Salem congregation and completion of an apprenticeship in cabinetmaking with Wohlfahrt, young Zevely sought to enter a trade. By 1801 he was a journeyman joiner or cabinetmaker. Three years later Van Zevely was made a master cabinetmaker, though it was against his own wishes, for he was making more money at his old jobs as journeyman and attendant at the Salem waterworks. Zevely married Hannah Schober, the daughter of Gottlieb Schober, and moved to the paper mill of Peters Creek, giving up his position as master cabinetmaker. A large amount of land, 160 acres, was transferred from Schober's name to that of Zevely. On this land he set up and operated the first steam-powered wool-carding machine in North Carolina. This effort greatly expanded the scope of textile manufacturing in what would become Forsyth County. The land that Van Zevely received from his father-in-law was the site of his plantation, and the initial site of the oldest house in Winston (the Zevely House was moved in 1974 to the corner of Fourth and Summit streets). Built some time between 1815 and 1818, this brick structure is not unlike its two contemporaries in Salem, the Foltz and John Vogler houses.

The invention of the cotton gin had assured easier processing of the crop throughout the South and factories began to spring up in response. Some of Salem's businessmen heard of the 15 to 20 percent annual profits realized by certain North Carolina factories and decided they should build one of their own. In July 1836 the Collegium, all too aware of Salem's declining economy, determined that such a factory might "advance trade and industry anew," but care should be taken to exclude "strangers" from the profit and control of such a mill. After long and serious debate on the possible venture it was decided that a factory would be built in west Salem. Workers who could spin and weave were to be lodged in boardinghouses near the plant. A total of $50,000 was subscribed by thirty stockholders at $200 per share. Steam machinery was located and purchased in Baltimore. In the fall of 1837 the factory was completed, with operations beginning soon afterwards under the supervision of Francis Fries, the plant's first superintendent.

During the early years business at the Salem cotton factory

was satisfactory. By 1847, however, the situation had changed. Debtors were numerous and so were creditors. The panic caused by the Mexican War made it impossible to collect debts. Cotton prices were high; the costs of "domesticks" and yarn were relatively low. In November 1849 it was décided "to wind up as soon as possible." The larger stockholders protected the creditors who did not own stock, thereby taking heavy losses. In March 1854 the plant was bought by John M. Morehead of Greensboro.

Though the Salem cotton factory was less prosperous, Francis Fries, who left his position in 1840, was developing a wool mill of his own on Lot No. 103, now the northwest corner of Brookstown Avenue and South Liberty Street (then New Shallowford and Salt streets). Fries leased the lot in February 1840 and immediately began to erect a factory, placing it in the middle of the lot on the east side of the small creek which ran across the lot. A wood-burning steam engine furnished the power for the machinery. The first wool rolls were carded on 14 June and four months later spinning was commenced. Looms were added, and in May 1842 Fries could announce to the public that he expected "to keep constantly on hand a good assortment of wools, common yarn, Stocking Yarn ready twisted, and cheap Lindseys and Cloths of different colors, qualities and prices." By May of the next year "good, heavy Jeans" had been added to the line, later becoming one of Fries's most popular products.

On 5 March 1846 Francis Fries took into partnership his younger brother, Henry W. Fries, who had already been helping him in the mill; the partnership was known as F. & H. Fries. Connections were made with business firms in the North, and trade spread widely in the South. During the War Between the States the Fries mill worked largely on the cloth used for Confederate uniforms.

Wagon Manufacturing

The wagon was the most important mode of transportation before the advent of the railroad, and keeping these vehicles in good repair determined the success of Salem's businesses. Tycho Nissen worked under Brother Transou at Bethania as early as 1771 as a journeyman wagonmaker and wheelwright. Nissen sold his equipment to the Single Brothers at Salem in 1774, but in 1786, at the request of Salem's Board of Elders for him "to take up wagonmaking, in so far as to repair wagons," he reentered the trade. When Nissen died in 1789 the industry came to a temporary halt.

It was not until 1814 that another wagonmaker appeared in Salem—Johann Philip Blum. Blum had just returned from a two-year apprenticeship as a bricklayer in Bethlehem when he was approached by the board to establish himself as a wagonmaker, a trade he had also learned. It is known that Blum agreed to their request, but no reports of his work survive.

One of the Brethren at Friedberg was a wagonmaker, and in 1819 Jacob Christmann of Salem was sent to learn the trade from him. Christmann succeeded well in his apprenticeship, so that by 1824 he had established a shop in Salem. Wagons were made here, and Christmann, being something of a businessman, even proposed carriagemaking.

The real beginning of Forsyth County's wagon manufacturing, and perhaps its greatest contribution to the art, was in 1834 when John Philip Nissen established his works in a log shed on Waughtown Hill at Bagge's Town or Charlestown (some four miles southeast of Salem). Young Nissen was the grandson of Salem's pioneer wagonmaker, Tycho Nissen. Much to the amazement of his neighbors, when he was only a child he had constructed a complete wagon. Nissen's business was largely ignored by Salemites, with the exception of a warning its businessmen gave a potential apprentice, William Schulz—Waughtown was full of "many temptations," and he was advised against going there.

Another wagonworks was opened at Waughtown by William E. Spach in 1854, and both Nissen and Spach were known for wagons of superior quality and sound workmanship. Generally in the South these vehicles were called "Nissens" or "Spachs" after the builders. Elsewhere, similar wagons were known as Conestogas or Studebakers, but the most common name given was Prairie Schooner. Physically the wagons had a curved bed that was somewhat boat-shaped. Bearing distinctive colors, the Nissens and Spachs usually had shiny red running gears, green bodies, and pure black ironwork; canvas-topped curved oak bows covered the wagons.

Banking

During colonial days many of the business transactions carried on in the Wachovia communities were by barter. The financial crisis created by the American Revolution resulted in the use of scrip among the Brethren themselves, but this practice was not entirely adequate since outsiders insisted that the merchants accept the Continental currency.

The Salem store served many of the purposes of a local bank before a branch of the Bank of Cape Fear was secured for the town in July 1815. Charles F. Bagge, Christian Blum, and Emanuel Schober were named as agents. Blum promptly built himself a house, and in 1816 he became the active agent of the branch bank. For some years things went smoothly, but the income was insufficient for his needs, and early in 1827 he established a printing office. In December of that year, disaster overtook Blum. He was counting paper currency when it was time for him to go to the church and light the candles for an evening service. Leaving the bills on the table, he hastily blew out the light—or at least he thought he did. As far as could be ascertained a spark must have fallen on the paper, for he had hardly reached the church when his table at home was a mass of flames. The fire was put out before the house caught, but an estimated $10,000 in currency was burned. It looked as though Blum would be utterly ruined, for the head office in Wilmington refused at first to believe his story. A compromise was effected by Charles Bagge, and Blum was able to continue his printing business, though he lost his position as bank agent.

About the time of the fire at Blum's the banks in North Carolina were generally in financial difficulties. Men who had bought bank stock on credit lost heavily when their loans were called in, citizens of Salem among the rest. The State Bank and the Bank of New Bern liquidated. The Bank of Cape Fear also touched bottom, but held on and regained credit. In 1847 a brick building was erected in Salem for a new branch of the Bank of

Cape Fear at the southwest corner of Main Street, and the cross street thereafter was known as Bank Street. Israel G. Lash was the first banker of the new branch which served Salem and later the new town of Winston.

By 1860 there were thirty-six banks in North Carolina, half of them serving six cities. The capital stock of all the banks combined was less than $7 million and deposits amounted to $1.5 million.

Edward Belo House

In 1841 the Edward Belo home was erected. Belo was trained as a cabinetmaker, but he had ambitions to become a merchant, so he gave up his position as master cabinetmaker and opened a small store in the house on the northeast corner of Main and Bank streets, originally the "skin house," but more recently the home of his father, Frederick Belo. The small store prospered, and Edward Belo bought the home from his mother, who moved to the Widows House. He also bought the home of his brother, Lewis Belo, and in 1860 in the place of these two small houses he erected the large house which still stands. His store occupied the Main Street floor; his family lived on the second floor. The iron grillwork on the portico and in the fence and the three iron animals on the parapet beside the steps were made at his foundry north of town.

Slavery in Salem after the Revolution

The amalgamation of a unique Moravian culture with one that was American, and specifically Southern American, began to manifest itself in the years following the American Revolution. In Salem the changing position of the Negro, both free and slave, is one of the more revealing aspects of this process.

Conflicts arose between the Collegium and various members of the congregation in matters involving Negroes. In 1784 Gottlieb Krause was advised against purchasing a slave, though he did so the next year without notifying the Elders Conference. Easter Sunday 1789 found an overflow crowd that wished to attend services in Salem. Of the non-Moravian visitors, a number were blacks. The council, wary of the "customary thought of the people in this country," determined to prohibit the Negroes from sitting with the whites. Not only would such integration of the two groups be "against the way of thinking" of the visitors, but it was also felt to be "against moral principles." The black visitors were therefore held at the rear of the church until all of the white visitors had been seated, at which time they were allowed to sit on the back bench, provided there was space. By this time the Moravians were well aware of neighboring customs, habits, and ideas concerning Negroes, and a conscious effort was made to please the neighbors.

By the late 1780s Negroes in Salem were no longer allowed to carry guns, and slaves were threatened with sale if they did not obey the rules laid out for them. And though the Moravians themselves became more and more receptive to the institution of slavery, they always seemed to have treated their slaves humanely. Large numbers of blacks were baptized into the church; others who were not members of the Unity were allowed to attend lovefeasts; and some were even allowed to attend school with the white children, something quite unusual at this time in Southern history.

By the turn of the century the Collegium received an increasing number of requests for the Brethren to purchase slaves. Hiring seemed a better solution to the demands, but even this practice was discouraged by those in authority. Schemes were developed whereby slaves could be brought to Salem. For example, Brother Bagge purchased a slave but left him in another settlement until his services were needed in Salem. Finally, because the services of slaves or hired Negroes seemed to be indispensable in the tavern, the Collegium made a permanent exception to the rule banning slavery in Salem: the tavernkeeper could either own or hire slaves to work as hostlers or servants, since "it is not customary to use white persons" in these capacities.

In 1814 a rule was passed which disallowed the keeping of slaves outside the community, except by plantation owners. The Brethren recognized the necessity of slave labor "where [a planter] needs such a servant for the cultivation or for some other steady employment." No other exceptions were made at this time.

The Moravians, by 1820, wanted to purchase or hire slaves to work in the various Salem trades, and it seems that a number of the tradesmen themselves were not totally truthful as to the extent slaves were being used. As a result, on 24 February 1820 the Congregation Council actually forbade the teaching of trades to the slaves. Albeit slave labor might contribute to a "favorable growth of income" at the outset, it was thought that eventually Negroes would be the "ruin of the whole trade and community." Negro slavery led to the "sad custom of laziness," the Salem diarist wrote. Again, there appears to have been no moral compunctions as to the practice of slavery itself; the feared psychological effect and resultant indolence concerned the Brethren far more.

Opposition to Salem's slave regulations continued well into the 1820s. Francis Fries, the ringleader of the opponents, Christian Vogler, and Wilhelm Fries all bought or kept slaves without the permission of the Collegium. When the state passed laws favorable to slaveholding, it became more difficult for the church to interfere with those of the Brethren who favored the system. And as to the maintenance of the rules, when Francis Fries was asked to dismiss one of his Negro women who failed to live up to the "moral standards of the community," he refused on the basis that the rules had been broken so many times previously by other slaves they could hardly be said to be in effect. Criticism of members of the Collegium began to spread throughout the community in the late 1820s as a result of the group's continued efforts to regulate slaveholding. For all practical purposes the bonds of church control had been broken.

A sidelight to the Moravians' relationship to the Negro was the creation of the Salem Female Missionary Society on 20 January 1822. The society was organized primarily to foster religious work among the Negroes, though it was also for the support of foreign missions. As the majority of the Negroes in the Moravian community lived on the farms and not within the villages proper, the elders appointed the Reverend Abraham Steiner to take charge of the work and to begin holding meetings on the farms around Salem in particular. Three of the older Negroes were communicant members of the Salem congregation, and, with Steiner's help, a little Negro congregation was gradually assembled around them. Their first church was a small log structure, consecrated in 1823. On 4 March 1827 a Sunday school was begun for them by members of the Female Missionary Society. The new church structure that was built in 1861 and a large addition dating from 1890 were to comprise the future St. Philips Moravian Church for Negroes.

The slavery issue continued to cause agitation in Salem during the 1830s. In 1831 Francis Fries was accused of wishing "to start a kind of Negro speculation in our settlement," and the next year, another member, J. H. Schulz, was excluded from the community for his failure to sell a Negro woman when requested to do so.

By the end of the decade, however, conditions began to ease somewhat. Brother Fries was allowed to keep an unrestricted number of slaves as "ordinary casual laborers." Brother Fries, in fact, relied so much on slave labor that he established a farm for slaves who, when too old to continue working in his mill, might retire with the gift of a cow, a pig, and a place to live. Such a paternalistic gesture was to be expected of the Brethren.

Nora Lee Reese, in her "Moravian Attitude Toward the Negro and Slavery," points to the Moravians' continued concern over what their neighbors thought of them, especially in their want of slaves in the community to perform the perennial chores assigned their lot: "In a slaveholding state most of the visitors . . . expect colored people to serve them as they are generally used to them. . . ." This statement by the Collegium, though not really a total acquiescence to the institution, does at least confirm their continued cognizance of the Brethren's exclusion of black laborers in the community. The assimilation of the Moravian culture with that of their neighbors was coming in the not very distant future.

By 1842 the Collegium found it "more and more difficult" to enforce Salem's slave rules. Three years later it was suggested to the Collegium that all regulations concerning Negroes in their community be dropped; after all, the argument ran, the rules were being ignored anyway. Almost three months of debate ended in the resignation of the entire membership of the Collegium. The sides were drawn, between church control of slavery and the discretion of the individual as to the employment and treatment of slaves. A new Collegium was elected, and copies of its revised Negro Regulations distributed, but still no enforcement was practical.

After almost a century of agitation, on 14 January 1847 the Moravians unanimously abolished all restrictions on the buying, hiring, and selling of Negroes. As Nora Reese has pointed out, this decision "represented a triumph of the new leadership who believed in less community control." In fact, she continues, they had adopted "the attitudes, characteristics, and habits of their fellow Southerners, as the character of the South began to cherish the institution of slavery." Slaves were used by the Brethren in their businesses and factories and, as in the rest of North Carolina, on their farms. Reese concludes:

By the middle of the nineteenth century, the Moravians' attitude toward the Negro and slavery was much the same as that of any other true Southern farming community, whether such communities had slaves or not. The facts of slavery were not as important as the attitude toward it. In this respect, the Moravian defended his ideas, his institutions, and his home in support of the Southern cause during the Civil War. Coming from a Pennsylvania farm, the Moravian in Wachovia became a true North Carolinian.

In part this amalgamation was expedited by the Moravians' ultimate acceptance of slavery.

Agriculture in Forsyth County, 1850–60

In 1850 farmers in this portion of North Carolina's Piedmont concerned themselves more with subsistence crops than with staples such as cotton or tobacco. The 1850s in fact saw a definite trend toward the production of corn, wheat, forage, livestock, and livestock products. The per capita value of these foods for North Carolina exceeded the average for the entire country. Below is a table showing Forsyth's agricultural situation in 1850 compared to surrounding counties.

	ACRES OF LAND IN FARMS		VALUE OF FARMS AND IMPLEMENTS	
	Improved	*Unimproved*	*Cash Value of Farms*	*Value of Farming Implements & Machinery*
Forsyth	51,873	120,029	$ 593,197	$ 57,074
Stokes	33,027	132,785	451,992	24,865
Surry*	104,119	302,795	962,795	77,929
Davie	45,770	79,504	471,392	43,849
Rowan	104,157	145,157	1,071,546	84,886
Davidson	95,243	195,114	1,106,746	107,506
Randolph	96,908	262,964	1,031,503	89,066
Guilford	199,309	183,437	1,437,561	125,537
Rockingham	70,757	183,476	988,175	52,488

*Yadkin County was formed from Surry in 1850.

Some explanation is called for regarding the actual food products grown or raised. Livestock was raised with great success before 1783, but after this time, due to a general shortage of grazing lands and increasing competition with better breeds found in other states, profits decreased rapidly. By the 1850s, however, new impetus had been given livestock farmers through greater attention to selective breeding and to the general health of the animals, thus resulting in a return of high profits.

Wheat, except for the earliest days of the Wachovia settlement, was rarely a great moneymaking crop. The ease with which it could be cultivated ideally suited it to the lazier of the backcountry farmers, who received but a few bushels per acre. Whereas the average yield was usually four to ten bushels per acre in this area and westward, farmers located farther east might expect to get an average yield of fourteen or fifteen bushels per acre. Like livestock, however, by the end of the 1850s, wheat was beginning to yield greater profits; a price of as much as $2.25 per bushel might be expected.

Outside the Moravian community, corn was the most important food in the diet of antebellum North Carolinians. The forms in which this cereal might find its way to the tables of both white and black were numerous—hominy, hoecakes, grits, cornpone, cornbread, and mush, not to mention the popular potable form. Most of the corn grown was consumed at home, though in the form of whiskey, cornmeal, and corn-fed pork it frequently found its way to northern markets. At this time more than half of the farming acreage in the South was devoted to corn.

The minor cereals—oats, rye, and barley—were of slight importance as money crops. Larger amounts of rye and barley were raised and used by the Germans in the Piedmont; even they

AGRICULTURAL STOCK AND PRODUCE IN 1850

	Value of Livestock	Animals Slaughtered	Wheat (bushels)
Forsyth	$186,547	59,593	40,735
Stokes	130,697	44,213	16,004
Surry	283,275	91,668	25,412
Davie	149,212	51,977	29,076
Rowan	319,357	83,277	86,613
Davidson	319,326	89,636	82,424
Randolph	297,946	83,584	83,634
Guilford	415,155	134,851	121,379
Rockingham	227,104	64,598	44,156

	Rye (bushels)	Indian Corn (bushels)	Oats (bushels)
Forsyth	$ 4,849	349,320	97,659
Stokes	6,006	223,000	42,636
Surry	18,044	552,454	145,472
Davie	3,210	301,010	79,129
Rowan	883	540,637	141,482
Davidson	2,225	507,961	174,085
Randolph	1,559	440,086	87,247
Guilford	4,359	884,286	214,692
Rockingham	3,458	377,604	101,804

commonly fed oats to the horses. There were some two thousand horses in Forsyth in 1850.

The importance of tobacco as a cash staple decreased after the Revolution and continued to do so until around 1840. Due to trade limitations with France and England during the Napoleonic Wars—these countries stimulated tobacco cultivation in other parts of the world—and internal westward expansion after 1790, with the subsequent growing of tobacco in America's new states, the prices realized from the sale of tobacco dropped from ten to fifteen cents per pound in 1815 to an average of about four cents per pound in the years 1842–50. In North Carolina, after the invention of the cotton gin, many planters gave up the tobacco culture for cotton, though tobacco was never totally neglected, especially in the northern counties.

In 1850 Forsyth County produced 49,880 pounds of tobacco. This amount is not particularly impressive when compared to the yields of Caswell, Granville, Person, Rockingham, and Warren counties together, amounting to over ten and one-half million pounds. Of the western Piedmont counties, Forsyth ranked second after Stokes. In the state, Forsyth preceded all but nine counties in tobacco production in 1850. Perhaps most of the 1,353 slaves found in Forsyth at this time were used almost exclusively for agricultural purposes.

The discovery of the "bright" tobacco curing process by the Slade brothers in Caswell County in 1839, improved transportation, and the establishment of many small tobacco factories gave new encouragement to Forsyth's tobacco growers by the mid-1850s. Experiments with the crop in the northern part of the county proved to be highly successful, and with prices generally on the upswing, more tobacco was grown. The older tobacco-growing counties increased production two to three times; Forsyth, together with Alamance, Franklin, Guilford, and Stokes, made gigantic strides in the culture. With 551,442 pounds of tobacco produced in 1860, Forsyth ranked as the twelfth largest grower in the state.

Overall, improved farmland increased almost 50 percent in Forsyth from 1850 to 1860. During this same period the cash value of the county's farms doubled. More and more livestock was raised although a general decrease occurred in the production of other agricultural products. As Benjamin Bailey of Walnut Cove wrote to the *North Carolina Planter* in February 1858, "a disposition in many of the people to try it" [tobacco] not only resulted in greater profits to the farmers but even induced them to write and publish articles on its culture. Thus it seems that by the time of the War Between the States, Forsyth County was experiencing a heretofore unknown success in agriculture, and one that was essentially non-Moravian.

Manufacturing in Forsyth County, 1850–60

In 1850 an estimated $40,440 was invested in Forsyth County's industries, then employing sixty-two persons. The combined annual value of production was $71,838. Comparatively speaking, this manufacturing income was about average that of the other counties of the state. There were forty-four counties with less valuable production and forty-one with more valuable, ranging from a low of $2,300 for Henderson County to a high of $1,409,568 for New Hanover.

Noticeable industrial growth occurred during the 1850s in Forsyth and in the state at large. The actual number of manufacturing establishments in North Carolina increased from 2,663 in 1850 to 3,689 in 1860. Capital invested grew more than 30 percent, and the total value of the state's products rose from $9.7 million to $16.7 million. Below is a chart giving the manufactures for Forsyth County in 1860.

In terms of overall rank within the state Forsyth County fared well in those goods she manufactured. Her position among the 86 counties of North Carolina in 1860 is as follows: boots and shoes, 14; carriages, 29; cotton goods, 12; flour and meal, 38; iron castings, 6; leather, 11; linseed oil, 2; paper, printing, 4; manufactured tobacco, 11; wagons, carts, etc., 2; and woolen goods, 2. The diversity of Forsyth's industries was exceeded by only 11 counties, but in overall value, she ranked 34.

PRODUCT	NUMBER OF ESTABLISH- MENTS	CAPITAL	COST OF RAW MATERIAL	EMPLOYEES MALE	FEMALE	ANNUAL LABOR COST	ANNUAL VALUE OF PRODUCT
Boots & shoes	1	$ 2,000	$ 1,200	3	2	$ 1,020	$ 2,700
Carriages	2	7,000	1,660	11	—	3,300	7,350
Cotton goods	1	150,000	14,780	20	34	8,472	24,800
Flour & meal	1	25,000	15,000	4	—	960	16,500
Iron castings	1	1,500	120	2	—	600	1,600
Leather	4	11,600	9,080	8	—	2,100	10,800
Oil, linseed	1	1,000	200	1	—	300	2,000
Paper, printing	1	5,000	1,300	2	2	420	2,500
Tobacco, mfd.	2	17,000	5,500	10	13	3,960	11,500
Wagons, carts, etc.	4	12,700	2,430	28	—	8,460	15,100
Woolen goods	1	100,000	38,000	30	25	10,200	62,500
TOTAL	19	$332,800	$89,270	119	76	$39,792	$157,350

Forsyth County in 1860

The years immediately preceding the War Between the States represent a period of transition for Forsyth County. Successful settlement of almost one hundred thousand acres and the establishment of a civilization in the wilderness is duly credited to the Moravian founders and their "well-tried European methods." But, by the mid-nineteenth century, times and temperament had changed. Dr. John Henry Clewell, in his *History of Wachovia*, noted, "The fact that changes were necessary became apparent to many of the best minds in Wachovia, and was universally recognized by the younger people." He continued, "With the usual careful, methodical, and earnest manner in which all things were done, this matter of transition was taken up, and the decade of 1850–1860 witnessed some important modifications in the affairs of Wachovia." Of these changes or modifications, at least three are worthy of mention. First, the church's control of trades and industries was abolished in 1849. As a second important change, the old lease system under which the Brethren controlled who did or did not live in their communities was abandoned in 1856. And third, the English language officially replaced German for church services in 1855; between 1856 and 1858, all the official minutes were changed to English.

This period of transition culminated for the Brethren in the incorporation of Salem. Charles Brietz became the town's first mayor, and the Board of Commissioners included R. L. Patterson, F. Fries, A. Butner, J. R. Crist, E. Belo, T. F. Keehln, and Solomon Mickey. Again, as Clewell wrote, "the previous plans [of settlement] had been good for a certain time and for certain ends. But the time had expired, and the ends had been gained. . . . The building of the county town of Winston as a near neighbor brought with it new obligations and responsibilities. The changed conditions which followed the Civil War were approaching." Indeed, the new town of Winston was fast eclipsing the commercial importance of Salem. By 1860 the Moravians of Forsyth were thoroughly Southern and differed little in attitude and outlook from their neighbors. Salem, like Winston, was a typical North Carolina country town.

The census of 1860 reveals an aggregate population of 12,692 in Forsyth County, and, there, as in the rest of the state, the majority of the inhabitants were engaged in some form of agriculture. Experiments with the tobacco culture resulted in the first large quantity grown in 1858. The soil was found to yield rich returns of the finest "yellow-leaf" tobacco which had no superior "in texture, oil or aroma, not even in the famed leather-wood district of Henry County, Virginia." Manufacturing was on the rise in Winston and Salem, but the farmers of the county were still producing the county's most valuable commodity in 1860—tobacco.

Slavery was an accepted institution, both in and out of the Moravian communities. There were 304 slaveholders in Forsyth in 1860, each of whom owned an average of 5.8 slaves. This average, with the exception of Randolph County, was lower than any of the counties immediately surrounding Forsyth. The average number of slaves per slaveholder in North Carolina in 1860 was 9.5. No one in Forsyth owned more than one hundred slaves, but three planters did hold more than forty. Eighty-two percent of the slaveholders owned fewer than ten slaves, with 72 percent in possession of fewer than six. The peculiar institution of slavery represented an important part of Forsyth's economy in the late 1850s, with a considerable investment put forward by those persons who owned slaves.

Industrially, agriculturally, and commercially Forsyth was not the wealthiest county in the state in 1860, but even at this time it was a county on the march.

CHAPTER 7

The Formation of Forsyth County and the Founding of Winston

IMPROBABLE AS IT MAY SEEM, it is a fact that the pioneers in this immediate section of North Carolina selected their land in Anson County, settled in Rowan County, and went through the Revolutionary War in Surry County. Their descendants were in Stokes County during the War of 1812 and the Mexican War, and volunteered for Confederate service from Forsyth County, and yet the location never changed!

The explanation is that the area which is now Forsyth was always in the piece that was cut off when a large county was divided; always it saw the other part of the county keep the name and the record books; always it was in the new county, with a new county seat, and a new set of county records.

When Bishop Spangenberg surveyed the Wachovia tract, it was a part of Anson County. While he was in England reporting on his journey, Anson County was divided by an east-west line, the southern boundary of the Granville grant. The crown land to the south retained the name; the northern part became Rowan County, with Salisbury as the county seat. The Granville (or Rowan County) border remains on the map of North Carolina as the southern line of Randolph, Davidson, Rowan, and Iredell counties. The eastern boundary was made to run due north to Virginia, instead of following the watershed. The western line was still the unknown boundary of the continent.

It was into Rowan County, therefore, that the Moravian settlers came in November 1753. The Wachovia tract had been duly purchased from Lord Granville, and the original deeds were kept in England, but official copies on parchment, certified by the Lord Mayor of London, with his great seal attached, were brought to America and were recorded in Salisbury. Gradually the settlers in Rowan County increased, and those who lived in the northern part of the county found it very inconvenient to be so far from Salisbury, the county seat. They therefore petitioned the assembly to divide the county.

The Moravians by this time had founded their third village, Salem, and they asked that their convenience might be considered and that the new line should be run so as not to divide their land. Disregarding this request, the assembly ordered the new line run at a point which was supposed to cut Rowan County in half, though it also divided the Wachovia tract. The act was passed in 1771, but when the line was surveyed it appeared that it ran between Bethabara and Salem, leaving the latter in Rowan County, while only a few small villages and the scattered farms fell into the new county of Surry. Amazed consternation filled the minds of the Surry County citizens, who did not see how it would be possible to cover the expenses of the new county without the Salem taxes, and for two years there was much anxious debate.

During this period, two other Moravian centers were established, both in the Rowan section of the Wachovia tract. One group came from what was then known as the Broadbay Plantation in Massachusetts (now Waldoboro, Maine), and they settled at what is now called Friedland. The other, an English-speaking group from Maryland, settled in what is now the Hope neighborhood in the southwest part of the Wachovia tract.

In 1773 these two smaller settlements and the town of Salem became part of Surry County. The leaders of Salem agreed to join in the movement to place the county boundary six miles south of the line of 1771, on condition that the Wachovia tract as a whole should be in Surry County. This accounts for the three offsets in the present southern border of Forsyth County; a straight east-west division would have been an extension of the south line of Lewisville township.

The county seat of Rowan remained at Salisbury, but for Surry a new site was selected. It was quite near the present village of Donnaha, in the northwest corner of Forsyth County, and this was the county seat during the Revolutionary War. Court sessions were held "constantly" at the home of Colonel Gideon Wright, who was a friend of Governor Tryon and played a conspicuous role in the war of the Regulation. A few years later, during the American Revolution, Wright was considered one of the "obstinate enemies" of the cause for independence, siding with the local Tories.

It was always customary to place the courthouse as near the center of the county as possible, apparently without any regard to accessibility or the possibilities of town development. Wright, having a suitable geographic location, as well as the necessary influence with those in authority, secured the court. Soon afterwards, he built a courthouse adjacent to his own dwelling, and here the courts and musters were held until 1774. At this time, however, a rival family, the Armstrongs, who were also located near the county's center, outmaneuvered him and had the courthouse moved to nearby Richmond.

Concerning this rivalry, an interesting note appears in the Bethabara Diary for 11 March 1771: "Mr. Gideon Wright was here today, wishing to borrow £20:, in order to secure from the Governor a Charter for the new Court-House to be erected for Surry County; Mr. Martin Armstrong will also soon go thither to try to get a Charter for a Market. The diarist then somewhat humorously remarked that "it is evident that certain people are very active in looking out for their own interests in the impending County changes." Indeed the Wachovia diaries all intimate that there was great jealousy between the Armstrongs and Colonel Wright, probably because of the latter's record in the Regulator struggle. Despite this rivalry there was strong opposition to the location of the court at Wright's because it was very inconvenient. A series of rather involved arrangements for an optional site began.

Post Office, Fifth and Liberty Streets, used 1906 to 1914

*Post Office, Fifth and Liberty Streets, used from 1914
to the present*

Courthouse, Winston, used 1850 to 1897

Courthouse, Winston, used 1897 to 1926

Courthouse, Winston-Salem, used from 1926 to the present

City Hall, used from 1926 to the present

Hall of Justice, completed November 1974

Located on a hillside about two miles northeast of Colonel Wright's home was a parcel of "vacant" land that was as yet in possession of Lord Granville. Although a gentleman by the name of Snead had built a store there, John Armstrong purchased this tract, as well as a seven-hundred-acre tract, just south of Snead's store, from Major Andrew Bailie of Georgia. Bailie also owned nearly four thousand acres of additional land comprising seven tracts in Rowan and Anson counties. Power of attorney was given to Traugott Bagge to sell the Rowan lands. But, without giving notice, the Rowan County sheriff, Martin Armstrong, John's brother, offered the seven-hundred-acre tract at "publick sale." John Armstrong, being the only "publick" present at the auction, bought the land which he intended as the future site of the "County Town."

Three days after the sale, the Bethabara diarist states that the land would have to be returned to Bailie and that Brother Bagge had agreed to buy it. Brother Marshall, in a letter to the *Aeltesten Conferenz* dated August 1773, demonstrated his knowledge of the intrigue:

Br.[other] Bagge had been commissioned by a gentleman residing elsewhere to sell certain pieces of land. . ., in which Br.[other] Bagge had been partially successful. One piece remained which seemed to the Sheriff a suitable place for a town and for the Court-House, he being one of the commissioners appointed to decide on the Court-House site, so he wanted to secure possession of it, and secretly discussed it with the other Commissioners who as usual, were none too favorably inclined toward us, and some of them our bitter enemies. A small, old debt of the former owner of this land was made the pretext, suit was brought in Salisbury, and execution ordered against this tract; and without public notice given, and without notice to Br.[other] Bagge, it was put up at the auction, and as there were no other bidders it was bought in by the Sheriff's brother for a ridiculously small sum, declared the place for the Court-House, a town was laid out, and building begun. . . .

By 21 August 1772 Armstrong had proceeded with the erection of the new building, located just west of Snead's store. Richmond Courthouse was completed in 1774; Colonel Martin Armstrong had already drawn up plans for the town of Richmond, which in turn was chartered by the General Assembly in 1779. Lots were sold and buildings constructed.

The story of Richmond Town was dramatic and short, for in 1789 Surry County was divided by a north-south line, and new courthouse sites were selected—Rockford in Surry County and Germanton in Stokes County. The Surry County courthouse records were moved from old Richmond to Rockford; Stokes County set up new records on her own account. The area now called Forsyth was mostly in the new county of Stokes, but straight lines were still the custom, and the new line crossed and recrossed the Yadkin in an annoying fashion. As a result, Stokes had a long narrow strip west of the river on the Surry side; Surry had a C-shaped tract east of the river in the part of Rowan which became Davie County. In each case these detached pieces could be reached only by boat, for there were no bridges.

But what became of Richmond Courthouse? No mention of "Lots in Richmond" may be found after August 1830. Fries, in the *Moravian Records*, stated that "jealousy, rivalry, and self-seeking at the beginning, accompanied by injustice toward a neighboring land-owner" caused an "appropriate and dramatic end of Richmond Town." It had been a county seat for fifteen years, but nine years of war, combined with Tory activities along the Yadkin, took their toll. For, as Fries further stated, within a few years Richmond was a "hamlet sinking in character, and in the esteem of neighbors." Contemporary gossip asserted, "If you want to go to hell you need not go further than Old Richmond." Like a scene from the Old Testament, if tradition may be believed, the town was literally swept from the face of the earth by an intense cyclone; shingles were scattered as far as Danbury and Germanton.

An entry in the records of the Court of Pleas and Quarter Sessions of Surry County, meeting at Richmond Courthouse, 13 November 1787 reads: "Wm. Cupples and Andrew Jackson, Esqs. Each produced a License from the Hon. Sam Ashe and John Williams, Esq. two of the Judges of the Superior Court of Law and Equity, Authorizing and Empowering them to practice as Attorneys in the several County Courts, etc., with Testimonials of their having taken the necessary Oath, and admitted to practice in this Court."

In December 1796 the assembly changed the line between

Surry and Stokes, giving to Surry the long narrow strip lying on the west side of the Yadkin, the river becoming the boundary there. The Act of Assembly calls it the land "south of the Yadkin," but old deeds show that for many years everything on the right-hand bank of the Yadkin River, looking downstream, was called "south" of the Yadkin, regardless of the actual direction.

For fifty years the county of Stokes remained practically unchanged. The War of 1812 and the Mexican War made but slight demand upon the people, though the former called the attention of the nation to Colonel Benjamin Forsyth. The population increased slowly, but it did increase, and finally the General Assembly of 1848–49 was petitioned to divide it. The act dividing Stokes County bears the ratification date 16 January 1849, and is printed in full in the *Laws of the State of North Carolina passed by the General Assembly at the Session of 1848–1849*, published at Raleigh in 1849 by Thomas J. Lemay, Printer, Star Office.

The act provided for a line "beginning at the South West corner of Rockingham county, and running thence West to the Surry county line." It was further enacted "that all that part of the said county lying North of said line, shall be erected into a distinct county by the name of Stokes county; and all that part lying South of the said line shall be erected into another distinct county by the name of Forsyth county, in honor of the memory of Col. Benjamin Forsyth, a native of Stokes county, who fell on the Northern frontier, in the late war with England." A supplemental act, passed at the same session of the assembly, appointed Caleb Jones, Frederick Meinung, and John Banner to run the dividing line, named county commissioners for each county, and provided the necessary machinery for setting up the two county governments. The commissioners for Forsyth County were Zadock Stafford, John Stafford, Henry A. Lemly, Leonard Conrad, and Francis Fries, who was elected chairman.

Winston

After the formation of the new county and the naming of her commissioners, it became necessary to select and purchase a site for the county seat; a courthouse and public building had to be erected as soon as possible. Because Salem was located almost at the center of Forsyth, it seemed apparent to the commissioners that they would have to choose land in that neighborhood.

The county commissioners applied to the *Aufseher Collegium* of Salem for some thirty-one acres of land located just north of town. The Collegium refused to decide on so weighty a question and referred the matter to the Congregation Council. Two schools of thought then developed. The conservatives agreed that if the new town were located near Salem, then new settlers would come in with ideas which might possibly conflict with their own. As a result, they felt, Moravian rules and ways would be disturbed and perhaps even destroyed; therefore the courthouse should be kept as far away as possible. The progressive wing of the council thought that new settlers would rejuvenate the community; even if the new town were brought near Salem, they believed that the disturbing features would adjust themselves. The progressives won out, and on 5 February 1849 the Congregation agreed to sell conditionally thirty-one acres to the commissioners.

Before the sale was concluded the amount of land was increased to fifty-one and one-quarter acres. The price settled on was $5.00 per acre, the then-current value of unimproved land, thus amounting to a total of $256.25. The deed to this courthouse tract was dated 12 May 1849, and title was transferred from Charles F. Kluge, the proprietor (trustee) acting for the congregation, to the chairman of the Board of County Commissioners, Francis Fries.

It had been agreed between the parties that the streets of the new town should be continuations of the Salem streets and that the courthouse should be erected at the highest point on the main street. Only two conditions were written into the deed. By one, provision was made for the school committee of the district to have the lot on which a small free schoolhouse stood. By the other, Thomas J. Wilson was to have a deed for his lot as soon as he had finished paying for it. Before Winston was settled, Judge Wilson's two-story house on Second and Main streets was the only dwelling located there—Wilson wished to live in the country!

The original limits of the town were between First and Seventh streets to the south and north and between Church and Trade streets to the east and west. Seventy-two lots were drawn off, one of which was reserved for the courthouse. The remaining lots were sold at public auction. Lot 41, the first to be sold and the most expensive, was purchased by Robert Gray for $465.00 on 12 May 1849. Five weeks later, on 22 June a second sale of lots was held. The purchasers, many of whom bought more than one, were: Robert Gray, David Blum, Isaac Gibson, John S. Brown, J. Sanders, J. A. Waugh, Thomas J. Wilson, John Keller, D. Starbuck, Thomas Siddall, Thomas Ayres, A. J. Stafford, John Pepper, F. C. Meinung, John Masten, C. L. Banner, Christian Reed, David Cook, Joshua Bethel, Francis Fries, J. P. Vest, I. Golding, A. Nicholson, A. Vogler, Christian Hege, J. H. White, P. Hopkins R. Walker, D. Collins, Henry Holder, S. Mickey, Edward Reich, J. Vogler, Jacob Tise, J. Ferrabe, and Joseph Wagoner. A total of $8,833.50 was realized from the sale.

Until the new courthouse could be built, the Salem church boards allowed the courts to use the Concert Hall in Salem. The county paid a reasonable rent for it. It was expressly understood that no whippings should take place in Salem and that if any were ordered by the court, they should be administered somewhere outside the town. The sheriff "let out to the lowest bidder the furnishing of sawdust, candles, etc. for the Court at the Town Hall in Salem" at so much per court.

On 19 March 1849 sixteen "Gentlemen Justices," appointed and commissioned by the governor, met in the Concert Hall and elected for the ensuing year these officials: sheriff, William Flynt; clerk of court, Andrew J. Stafford; county attorney, Thomas J. Wilson; register of deeds, F. C. Meinung; county trustee, George Linville; coroner, John H. White; and standard keeper, Abraham Steiner. All of the justices were not entitled to sit in the Court of Pleas and Quarter Sessions, but they were permitted to elect a chairman and several members to serve for all. On 20 March, therefore, the justices elected the following as the special court: Francis Fries, chairman, Philip Barrow, Andrew M. Gamble, John Reich, and Jesse A. Waugh. The finance committee elected consisted of C. L. Banner, Israel G. Lash, and Francis Fries.

In December, F. C. Meinung, C. L. Banner, and Michael

Hauser were appointed to select a site for a "Poor House," and in May 1850 about ninety acres were bought some three and a half miles northeast of the courthouse tract on the road to Germanton.

For two years after the establishment of Forsyth County its seat of government had no name. There were some who thought it should be called Salem. But as the courthouse neared completion that idea began to cause dissatisfaction. Finally it was ordered by the court that the sheriff of Forsyth should call an election to name the new town by popular vote. This motion was somehow lost and it was not until the January 1851 meeting of the General Assembly that a name was finally decided upon for Forsyth's county seat. Colonel Marshall, who lived in the Salem Chapel section of the county, introduced a bill giving the name Winston to the town, in honor of Major Joseph Winston of Germanton, a hero of the Revolutionary War. An act was passed to this effect, and on 15 January 1851 it was ratified.

Early Days in Winston

Very little recorded evidence survives about life in early Winston. The first mention of the town is the following item from the 8 February 1851 issue of the *People's Press* of Salem:

Our young neighbor-town Winston can boast of the Hall of Justice, which stands out in bold relief—an ornament to the county and surpassed by few if any building of the kind in the State. There let justice reign supreme.

Then comes the Prison House—not yet completed, rather a gloomy looking place. May the mere sight of its grated windows prove a terror to evildoers and its cells remain tenantless!

Several dwellings, store-houses, hotels, and a Church [the Methodist on Liberty and Seventh] have been erected and in part occupied. Other buildings are in process.

Clewell states that the courthouse building mentioned in such glowing terms in the February article was so near completion by 16 December 1850 that it was formally opened with a religious service on that day. The structure was two stories tall and rectangular, forty-four by sixty feet, and faced south towards Salem.

Four thirty-foot-high pillars supported a magnificent portico. The total cost of building was $9,083.38, just $359.49 short of the amount raised from the auction of the town lots.

The first stores erected in the new town were those of Harmon Miller, Robert Gray, Sr., Sullivan & Bell, and William Barrow.

On 22 March 1851 the *People's Press* again refers to the new town across the Salem line: "A new Post Office has been established at Winston. John P. Vest, Esq. Postmaster. . . . John B. Panky, is determined to open an English and Classical School in Winston, his terms for the first five months being $15 for language, $10 for higher branches of English and $3 for lower. Outside pupils can obtain board in Salem for $5 or $6 per month." Board for Panky's outside pupils must have been in keeping with the cost of living in the community, for according to the market prices listed in the *People's Press* of the day, flour was $7.00 a barrel, lard was 8 cents a pound, butter 12 1/2 cents a pound, eggs 5 cents a dozen, and chickens were 6 to 8 cents a pound.

Slowly but steadily little Winston grew, and on 3 January 1852 editor Blum wrote in the *People's Press* that "an occasional walk to our adjoining neighbor Winston never fails to impress us with the growing importance of that place. New and tasty buildings have been erected in 1851 and others are in progress. The citizens of Winston mostly display that neatness in the erection of their dwellings which strikes the beholder."

There was little to break the monotony of everyday life in early Winston. General muster of the militia, with the marching and drilling of village and country boys and men, drew people of all classes together in friendly intercourse. A "big meeting" at the Methodist Episcopal Church with its hearty singing and shouting was also an occasion for old and young to mingle not only in spiritual fellowship but also in neighborly companionship. But the outstanding occasions in the social life of the community were the regularly recurring sessions of court, with the attendant noisy and good-natured crowds who blocked the muddy streets of the town talking politics, swapping horses, and crowding village stores.

During court week everybody came to town and everybody

in town went to courthouse square, not so much for the purpose of attending to legal affairs as to mingle with the crowds and generally have a good time. They came on horseback, on foot, and in covered wagons bearing the trademarks of the Nissen and Spach wagonworks of Waughtown; they brought fresh eggs, kegs of butter, beeswax, and dried fruit to barter at village stores for such goods as shoes, dishpans, and dress materials. If they lived at a distance, the families in wagons would come prepared to camp out at night in the vacant lot where the O'Hanlon Building now stands. Gay patchwork quilts, frying pans, huge tin coffee-pots, and lanterns hung all about the wagons.

One early case of interest that diverted the usual carefree mood of court day involved two "missionaries," or abolitionists, as they were more commonly called in the South. Adam Crooks and Jesse McBride were traveling about the "land of the bleeding slave" preaching the "strange doctrines of the abolitionists." In response to popular sentiment against their proselyting and "stirring up the slaves," the two were arrested and brought to trial at the October 1850 term of superior court in the newly formed county of Forsyth. A large crowd of anxious spectators filled the Concert Hall at Salem to witness the proceedings. McBride was accused of having given an "incendiary pamphlet" (*The Ten Commandments*) to the young daughter of a Salem resident; Crooks was charged only through his association with McBride. Crooks was acquitted by the jury and McBride was found guilty. Hanging seemed in order to the crowd, but the court ordered that McBride receive twenty lashes on his bare back, stand an hour in the pillory, and spend a year in the county jail.

The case was appealed by McBride's attorneys—a Quaker, George C. Mendenhall, and James T. Morehead, brother of the former governor. While McBride was awaiting trial, several attempts were made on his life. Finally the whole matter ended before a second trial could be held. On 25 May 1851 a mob gathered at Colfax (near Greensboro) where McBride was staying, in hopes of frightening him to leave the state. He stood his ground only until one of the mob leaders agreed to release the bondsmen from their obligation. In less than a week McBride was on his way back to Ohio. Crooks was forced to leave the state soon afterwards.

In 1854 the plank road from Fayetteville to Bethania was completed. Called the Fayetteville and Western Road, this route passed through Winston where a narrow alley from Liberty to Trade streets now separates the tall stores on either side; a spur was also run to the Fries brothers' cotton factory. This new system of land transportation, the "farmers' railroad," absorbed the attention of North Carolina legislatures from 1849 to 1856, during which time some eighty-four plank-road companies were chartered and capital stock of almost $6 million was authorized. The route from Bethania to Fayetteville (Cross Creek) was the longest and most expensive in the state, and its importance is no doubt indicated by the name it was given, the "Appian Way of North Carolina."

Throughout the 1850s party spirit ran high in the young community. Whigs of Winston and Salem formed the Chippewa Club for the purpose of boosting General Winfield Scott for the presidency of the United States and William A. Graham of North Carolina as his running mate. The club met every Monday night during the campaign. Fiery Whig speeches, interspersed with enlivening strains from the Salem Brass Band, resounded from the courthouse walls.

A typical political rally occurred on 23 October 1852, when the Chippewas had a great Scott and Graham Day. By ten in the morning the streets were thronged. Local Whigs came from all parts of Forsyth and were joined by others from Guilford, Davidson, and Randolph. Amid the firing of cannon, the procession under Chief Marshall Colonel Matthias Masten and his associate marshals—R. W. Wharton, Dr. Samuel Martin, Edwin Leight, A. Staub, and Matthew Boner—headed by the Salem Brass Band in their chariot drawn by four richly caparisoned horses, slowly moved in solid columns with banners and flags waving. Beginning at Salem Tavern, they passed up Main Street to the courthouse: "From windows and balconies, ladies waved their handkerchiefs, betokening that their cheers and smiles were for the Old Hero of Lunday's Land. The enthusiastic multitude in response burst into shout after shout for the Ladies! Scott and Graham! At the Courthouse there was great speaking; the elector for the district, Ralph Gorrell, Esq. of Guilford, enhancing the attention of the audience for two hours in a peculiarly argumentative speech." Then came the barbecue—three thousand pounds of meat, with great bowls of steaming soup and other good things in proportion spread on long tables in the square. More speech-making followed until sundown, when, after a short intermission for supper, the hearty Whigs reassembled for more speeches until far into the night.

Unfortunately, such efforts notwithstanding, the Whig party, which had been losing ground across the state since the late 1840s, suffered defeat at the polls that year. They can at least be credited with enlivening a generally quiet community's life.

On 15 April 1859 the first Board of Commissioners of Winston was elected. Members were Robert Gray, H. A. Holder, Jacob Tise, Henry Renegar, N. S. Cook, Franklin L. Gorrell, and A. J. Stafford. William Barrow, Winston's first mayor, was also elected at that time. A large portion of the business conducted by these men would be the creation of laws to govern the town.

The War, 1861–1865

IN 1860, ELECTION RESULTS INDICATED THAT North Carolina was definitely opposed to secession and dissolution of the Union. John C. Breckinridge carried the state by only 848 votes, winning all of the tobacco-planting counties along the Virginia border except Person and Granville.

By January of 1861, following the secession of South Carolina, the General Assembly began debating the possibilities of a convention of the people to consider the issue of secession. A Convention Act was passed, and the vote cast on 28 February indicated the populace was still opposed to secession, but not overwhelmingly so, the vote having been 47,323 against and 46,672 for. The events of the next two months—particularly Lincoln's decision to supply Fort Sumter, his call for seventy-five thousand volunteers, and the secession of Virginia—moved North Carolina closer to withdrawal from the Union.

At an extra session of the General Assembly, meeting on 17 April 1861, five days after the bombardment of Fort Sumter, Governor John W. Ellis responded to President Lincoln's call for volunteers "employed for the invasion of the peaceful homes of the South." He referred to the presidential action as a "high-handed act of tyrannical outrage," calling it not only unconstitutional but "in utter disregard of every sentiment of humanity and Christian civilization." This step "towards the subjugation of the whole South" caused him to request all citizens of the state "to be mindful that their first allegiance is due to the sovereignty [of North Carolina] and to the defense of Southern rights." Two days after Governor Ellis's proclamation appeared in the press, Virginia withdrew from the Union; North Carolina followed on 21 May and, with Tennessee and Arkansas, joined the Confederate States of America.

Sentiment in Forsyth County was mixed, but once secession was accomplished, the people were uniformly in favor of the new Southern Confederacy. The men of Salem, Winston, and surrounding areas prepared for military service. In the organization of the army, it was intended that the troops sent by the various states should form companies, or, if sufficiently numerous, regiments commanded by their own officers. General officers would be appointed by the government in Richmond. Clewell, in his *History of Wachovia*, notes that by early summer 1861 tents were springing up about the county, giving the countryside "a martial appearance." Companies from other sections began passing through Winston and Salem as early as the end of May. The men of Forsyth became quite restless and eager to join the troops. Virgil Wilson, writing to his "dear Aunt" in June 1861, stated that "Aby wanted to go very *badly* & if he were my *boy* I would give him a *rifle* & say 'go & die if need be in Old Dominion'. . . . He is plenty old to shoot a Yankee & protect himself."

Three companies from Forsyth—D, E, and K of the Twenty-first North Carolina Regiment—were mustered into service at Danville, Virginia, in June 1861. By this time, competitive spirit in neighboring counties was already high. One soldier wrote that "Yadkin will beat Forsyth yet." He continued that, in addition to the men already sent to Crumpler's Company in Ashe, "she will send 4 infantry Companies & one Cavalry Company." Forsyth was not to be outdone, however, and troops continued to enlist by the score.

It was a pleasant June morning in 1861 when two of Forsyth's three companies were marched to Salem Square and drawn up in a line in front of the Academy. Bishop Bahnson and the Reverend Mr. Doub, a Methodist minister, each delivered a short address from the portico of Main Hall. After Bishop Bahnson offered a "fervent prayer," those who had assembled joined together in singing the New Testament benediction, "The Grace of Our Lord Jesus Christ." Of the occasion Clewell wrote: "The entire scene was a strange one. The solemn service, with troops fully armed, drawn up in front of the ministers; the large gathering of people, some sad, some curious; the eagerness of the brave boys to go to the front, to join the gathering of the army; the songs and the hurrahs of the soldiers, as they passed down the main street, the tears and prayers of wife and mother, as with bended head they mingled their tears with their prayers in the silence of the lonely home." When the time for their departure came, many of the soldiers were accompanied by friends as far as Salem Creek.

The first year of the war found Forsyth County troops engaged at the battle of First Manassas and in subsequent skirmishes in northern and northwestern Virginia. Reports of death reached families at home and, despite the early optimism that attended Confederate victories in the field, nothing seemed to compensate for the attendant loss of life. The *Memorabilia* of 1861, "a year unexampled in the experiences of us all," expressed doubts over an early end to the conflict. And though those on the homefront were thoroughly patriotic to the Southern cause, the "mournful . . . loss" of lives seemed uppermost in their minds.

A new company of troops from Forsyth, Company I of the Thirty-third North Carolina Regiment, was mustered in at Raleigh in September 1861. In April and July 1862 they were joined in the field by Companies K and D of the Fifty-second and Fifty-seventh regiments respectively. More than one hundred Forsyth citizens enlisted in companies from other counties.

"The horrors of the battlefield," wrote Dr. J. F. Shaffner of Salem, "are bad," but, he continued, "not one particle so affecting as those of the hospital with [the] wounded." Shaffner, just twenty-two years old and one year out of Jefferson Medical College, had enlisted as a private in September 1861. He was commissioned an assistant surgeon soon afterwards. In a letter dated 27 May 1862, he wrote:

The suffering of the poor wounded soldier, his prayers, his constant calls for absent ones at home, &c., are almost heart-rending. 'Tis true we are apt to become hardened by association with these things—still humanity convinces us all that such sufferings are terrible. Surgeons are in ever-growing danger of becoming too abstract—of losing sympathy with passing emotions and sufferings, and particularly with those shared by numbers. The danger is, lest we forget that we are too mortal; subject to the same dangers, and fancy ourselves superior to our former selves, because now, at present we do not feel the pains, the agonies of the poor sufferers in our charge. But I shall never forget these scenes of anguish and pain—they make lasting impressions upon my mind.

Perhaps a somewhat happier note than Forsyth's military or medical service in the war was the contribution made by Captain Sam Mickey and the Salem Brass Band, incorporated into the Twenty-sixth North Carolina regiment. General Lee once remarked after listening to a brass serenade: "I don't believe we can have any army without music." And indeed music was one of the common soldiers' most important diversions; Julius Leinbach's written account of the Twenty-sixth Regimental Band certainly confirms this fact. Often the "boys of the band" were requested to play for the troops, particularly the wounded. The players were cheered "lustily" by all who heard them. The following excerpt from Leinbach's account begins on Christmas Eve, 1863:

We wanted something more than even what our boxes contained for our Christmas lovefeast, so we sent to town for more oysters—$20.00 per gallon, and $12.00 more for the extras. We had a jolly good time, sitting up until 1 o'clock. On Christmas morning some of the boys went to town to celebrate, but found all stores closed by order of General Lee. . . . The next night we went serenading for Major Jones, and flattered ourselves that we would get some good Christmas leavings, but came out missing.

On December 30th General Heth honôred us by stopping inside our "mansion" to see how comfortably we had fixed ourselves. On New Year's night we intended, by permission of our officers, to carry out our good Moravian custom of ushering in the New Year by playing tune 146 ["Now Thank We All Our God"] so we sat by our fires, and talked until the midnight hour when we astonished the men.

Often forgotten are the trials of those on the homefront, whose sufferings and deprivations were no less than those of the men in the field. In a poignant statement to her "dear James," E—— of Lewisville wrote in October 1864: "Well, I think the time has about come for applying the 'last man' doctrine. I have no doubt it will be one—& then comes submission, after the women & children are starved—so goes the work of desolation and ruin—I must trim my sails, put my house in order, and also prepare for marching."

Prices for once common articles were prohibitory, when they could be obtained. In Salem, salt sold for $20 per sack, corn was $10 per bushel, and bacon was $2 to $3 per pound. Clewell wrote that in estimating the cost of a lovefeast, it was figured that with the smallest size cake, and without coffee, the expense of the service would be $125. He continued:

A pleasing feature of these years of hardship appears in the earnest and self-sacrificing manner in which the church and community laboured to ameliorate the sufferings of the soldiers, especially in the latter portion of the struggle. The residents of Salem, in 1863 and 1864, will recall the long lines of cloth tacked to the fences, in the avenue, or around the private lots in the town. These long strips were being painted and made into "oilcloth," to protect the soldiers from the weather, and to serve them in other ways. The Fries mills were running day and night to weave the famous gray cloth used in the army. The clatter of the wooden shoes was heard, as the boys and girls came and went from school; and while the children rather liked them, because they did make so much noise, the real object of this use of wood instead of leather was to send so much more leather to the soldiers. Even the little folks picked quantities of lint for the wounded, while their elders wound numberless rolls of bandages for the surgeons' use.

M. Eliza Kremer, Lizetta Stewart, L. Shaub, Laura Vogler, and Margaret Clewell went to Blantyre Hospital to serve as nurses. Such service at this early date was most unusual.

Forsyth County sent its full quota of soldiers to the field, and shared in all the anxieties and privations of the times, but fortunately was spared the horror of becoming a battlefield. Parents in less-favored areas regarded Forsyth as a place of refuge and continued to send their daughters to the boarding school in Salem until it was full to overflowing and could receive no more students. Governor Zebulon B. Vance, despite some popular criticism, showed the school every courtesy in his power, supplying it with sugar and various staples from captured stores. Augustus Fogle, the steward of the boarding school, was exempted from military service in order that he might continue to serve the "daughters of the South."

According to Clewell and other writers a feeling of desperation began to fill the minds of Forsyth Countians as they began to sense the lines of opposition drawing closer and closer around them. Food was scarce, money was inflated (a silver dollar placed in the offering plate at Home Church in 1864 was estimated to be worth $40), and medicine could be secured only in very small quantities. For example, Rob Jones, who lived in Bethania, wrote his brother in the Confederate Army in Virginia of a visit he received from a cousin, Mary Ann Branson, and a friend, "Jain" Miller. They "got to talking about coffee," the shortage of which "caused more actual discomfort among the people at large" than any other commodity, and Miss Branson was suspected of being a "Union lady" because of her references to "Rio Yankee" and "Rye Rebel." But such were the times.

Directly related to the shortage of coffee, and particularly revealing of a strong tongue-in-cheek optimism concerning the end of the war is this excerpt from a letter of Edward Peterson, "one of the boys in the band." The letter is dated 18 May 1863, shortly before Lee's second invasion of the North and his high tide at Gettysburg.

We received orders last night to be ready at a moment's notice to move. I expect its to be up towards Fredsburg, at least the troops are moving that way. . . . I expect they are to invade Maryland again. If we take Wash., Baltimore, Phila., Bethlehem, and all those cities and towns, I will let you know. I could send you some coffee then. How much would you want? Perhaps Levin [a merchant in Salem] would like to engage some. New York is bound to fall, Boston, too. I will send you some soda, too, if we conquer the North, and we are bound to take mash [slang for "conquer"] with all the free states. There is no other chance for them. I am a little uneasy about Canada. We'll be in such a sweep when we take New York, that we can't stop ourselves. We'll be apt to take Canada and that will be accomplished in a short while. England will soon back up, but I think we can put her down—we'll tell her she can't get any cotton anymore and all will be right; as you know—"Cotton is King" and we'll have a powerful time from now till cool weather; you know the Northern army is almost disbanded, all gone home; so we will find no opposition and it will be quite an easy task to annihilate the vandals. I feel for them. The South is bound to have her rights. Had the North let the South alone, we would now show mercy, but that day is passed. If we shouldn't have success in annihilating the North, we'll starve them out and that we can do before fall. . . .

Exactly one year to the day later, Peterson wrote home that he and "the boys" had heard the Northern bands playing the night before. One of the tunes was "Hail, Columbia." He wrote:

I should like to hear it although it would make me sad to hear that old fashioned air as well as it [would] make me feel a quick shame as [I felt] the other day [when I saw] the Stars and Stripes that were captured in that fight. It reminded me very much of the 4th of July celebration when the Stars and Stripes used to wave over the speaker's stand in the square [in Salem].

Such nostalgia as that felt by Peterson was, of course, not so much for the former Union as it was for peace. Soldiers began to wonder exactly what it was they were fighting for. Food and clothing were scarce; battles were lost and friends dead; no intervention was forthcoming from England. To many the cause seemed already lost, although Peterson for one never wavered in his loyalty to the Southern cause. His letter is typical of thousands that were sent home during the last year of the war.

In the field one often found entire regiments without food. Dr. H. T. Bahnson, in his *Last Days of the War*, told of numerous episodes of food theft. He wrote, "I don't believe that any sane man would be fool enough to starve if he could steal anything to eat." In fact, many men—and presumably some from Bahnson's company—became quite adept at foraging. One acquaintance would crawl up to a farmhouse, make his way over to a grazing cow, and deftly "guide the milk into his canteen." Others might even kill and carry away a pig without waking the farmhouse residents. If one were particularly industrious he could catch chickens and ducks on a baited pin tied to the end of a string! But pity the poor farmers, many of whom could hardly grow enough for their own needs, when marauding soldiers came around and government agents were free to take a tithe of produce in lieu of money (which no one had anyway) for taxes. Abraham Conrad, for instance, produced a sizable harvest in September 1864. Below is a breakdown of its estimated worth as figured by Confederate officials, showing quantities, the amount of tithe, and the value of one-tenth:

PRODUCT	AMOUNT	TITHE	VALUE OF 1/10TH
Wheat	19,800 bushels	1,980 bushels	$185
Corn	195 "	19 "	152
Oats	320 "	32 "	2
Rye	1,620 "	162 "	12
Cured hay	60,000 pounds	6,000 pounds	120

Desertion from the army increased proportionately with the sufferings and privations of camp life. On 20 August 1864 the Home Guard of Salem was called out to hunt deserters. A large group of them was rounded up, and in October thirty captives passed through Salem under heavy guard as they continued their unwilling march back to the army. Dr. Shaffner recorded in his diary the pathetic letter of one enlisted man accused of desertion: "Der Sir, as i am accused of Being distant without leaf whitch is all so i now renouc the fact before the ornible Court it was on a Count of disability whitch i did not feel sofishent [for this] campaign as i hope i have as good a Suthern hart as any man ort to have i now leav it with the ornible Cort to dispenc of as tha think propper. E. Barkley—Yours Truley."

In December 1864 Forsyth Countians between the ages of forty-five and fifty were mustered into the Seventy-fifth Regiment. The "last man" doctrine was thus resorted to, and all able-bodied men from this area were marched south to protect strategic points around Salisbury. One unidentified person, writing from Salem on 6 March 1865, though "lowspirited," tried "to nerve [himself] for the day of trial." He, like many of his comrades, concluded that "to stand bravely by our Country and our principles would be safer than to creep away and try to hide."

Forsyth's military participation in the war included all of the major engagements from eastern North Carolina to Pennsylvania. The three companies of the Twenty-first, commanded by such notables as Ewell, Early, Pegram, and Ramseur, fought at First Manassas, Winchester, Harrisonburg, Cross Keys, Port Republic, Cedar Run, Second Manassas, Harpers Ferry, Chancellorsville, Gettysburg, Plymouth, New Bern, Drewry's Bluff, Cold Harbor, Monocacy, Winchester, Fisher's Hill, and Petersburg, and surrendered with Lee at Appomattox. The men of the Thirty-third added to this roster Hanover Courthouse, the Seven Days, Sharpsburg, Fredericksburg, Mine Run, and Spottsylvania. The Fifty-second saw extensive service in eastern North Carolina, Bristoe Station, the Wilderness, and Burgess Mill. The Fifty-seventh participated in the engagements at Fredericksburg, Gettysburg, Rappahannock Bridge, Winchester, and Petersburg. Dr. Bahnson concluded that most of his memories, like those of his companions, were sad, grim, and gloomy. He remembered:

The forms of my comrades and friends hurried to an untimely death by disease and wounds, left prey to the birds of the air and the beasts of the field,—at best hastily and unceremoniously shoveled into a shallow trench; if haply surviving, maimed and crippled and marred in health and usefulness;—the privations and sufferings from fatigue and hunger and heat and cold, the filth and nakedness, in comfortless camp, on toilsome march, in ruthless conflict, in loathsome hospital, in pitiless prison. . . . The abomination of desolation.

War was not without its honor, however, as an affair involving, among others, Captain A. H. Belo of Forsyth County readily demonstrates. Late in the afternoon of 1 April 1863 Federal gunboats landed a strong force of men who completely overwhelmed and captured a Confederate battery commanded by Captain Robert Stribling and two companies of Alabama troops, both of the Forty-fourth Regiment, near Suffolk, Virginia. Colonel John K. Connally's Fifty-fifth North Carolina Regiment was stationed along the Nansemond River as a part of the Confederate defense system placed there to harass Federal gunboats. Three companies of his regiment had been ordered on 16 April to protect Captain Stribling's battery. Colonel Connally stated that on 19 April "some time between four and six o'clock," General French "wished me to support the batteries," but before he could ascertain the position of the batteries and the number of men needed, "loud cheering in the direction of the river" was heard. The battery had already been captured. His intended effort to retake the fort was halted by General Law, who ordered him to rejoin his brigade.

General French blamed the Alabamians for the capture of the battery but naturally they desired to shift the blame from themselves to the North Carolinians. Resenting this malignment of their honor, the Fifty-fifth's regimental officers, all of whom were under thirty years old, demanded a retraction from the Alabamians. Major Belo delivered his colonel's challenge to Captain Cussons, an Englishman fighting with the Alabamians. Colonel Connally and Captain Terrell selected double-barreled shotguns, loaded with balls, to be fired at forty yards. Cussons, being the challenged party, selected the Mississippi rifle at the same distance against Belo. According to Captain E. Fletcher Satterfield of Person County, Colonel Connally's second, "Two spots were chosen in a large field, and forty yard markers were established to separate the two sets of officers." "I and the second of Capt. Terrell," Satterfield continued, "settled our affair without firing a shot."

Belo and Cussons had already gotten down to the business at hand. Their rifles were examined and each man assumed his station. At the appropriate signal, they fired. In the first exchange Belo's bullet pierced Cussons's coat; Belo was untouched. Another exchange—Belo this time winced from a slight wound and Cussons went unscathed. According to the narrative of another eyewitness, Colonel W. C. Oates, the captain from Alabama, with complete nonchalance, said: "Major, this is damned poor shooting we are doing today. If we don't do any better than this we will never kill any Yankees." In this second exchange Belo's neck had been grazed and he was bleeding, but he was not satisfied. Just before the third volley a messenger informed the two officers that their companions had solved the misunderstanding and there was no reason to continue. The men shook hands and each returned to his camp.

No official report of the incident was filed; such things happened in the Old South and gentlemen just did not talk about them.

On 2–3 April 1865 Forsyth County was threatened by invasion for the first time in the war. General Stoneman and a division of about six thousand Union cavalry, advancing from East Tennessee pushed across North Carolina at a rapid pace, destroying in their path much valuable property, bridges, and railroad tracks. Scouts were posted all along the road to the Shallow Ford. Preparations in anticipation of the invasion were made. The clerk of court distributed his books and papers in private homes so that if one house were burned or looted another might be spared. Cotton and cloth, according to Dr. Clewell, were stored in private houses with the same objective in view. Horses were removed to less-frequented spots and tethered until the threats had completely passed. In the vaulted cellar of the home of the principal of Salem Boarding School, a hole was dug, and money, students' jewelry, and other valuable property were buried.

The first alarms were false, but on 10 April Stoneman's entire division entered Forsyth County. About five thousand men stopped in Bethania for three hours; the general's headquarters were established in the home of Elias Schaub. The town's inhabitants were all in church, it being Monday of Easter Week, when Stoneman arrived, and by the time the Reverend Jacob Siewers dismissed the congregation, the streets were already filled with soldiers. Locked doors of private homes had been broken down, drawers and closets ransacked, but no serious damage was done. After eating everything that could be procured (somewhat reminiscent of Revolutionary days in Bethania), a portion of the party moved on to the Yadkin River and another to Salem.

Colonel Palmer was detached at Germanton to pay a visit to Salem. His orders stated that he was to "destroy the large factories engaged in making clothing for the rebel army, and send out parties to destroy the railroad south of Greensborough and Danville."

As Palmer's men approached Salem, they spotted scouts sent out from the town to warn of the expected "invasion." Following a brief race one of the men was captured. "Before we could realize it," the *Memorabilia* read, "soldiers were seen at every corner of the streets, had taken possession of the post-office, and secured our whole town." Guards were stationed at all the principal buildings in Salem. John Blackburn, clerk of court, made the following entry in the minute docket for 10 April:

Some of the most valuable papers I tumbled into a sack and left them with Mrs. Long at this time great Confusion prevailed it being certain the army was not far distant Capt. W. A. Albright Enrolling Officer had a considerable Confederate Guard in the Courthouse & they left precipitately I locked up the office and started down street to hear the news in

Salem. Met Robert DeSchweintz principal of the Female Academy in Salem Joshua Boner Mayor Salem, Thos. J. Wilson Mayor Winston and R. L. Patterson, Esq. who was on a visit to Salem, on their way up street to meet the Yankee Army. They invited me to accompany them and we went up street into Liberty in front of the house then occupied by Mr. Alexander Bevel and halted there & waited the arrival of the army which was about or near sundown. The first to come was ten or fifteen men on horse back Pistols in hand in full gallop on their arrival in forty or fifty yards we raised white handkerchiefs to let them know our mission was peace they replied all right. they was angry & inquired for Confederate or rebel soldiers said they had been fired on other parties came up soon & it was not long when one of our company introduced himself to Gen'l [C.] Palmer & then introduced the others to him & he introduced us to several of his officers &c & invited us to accompany him into town which we did the main army encamped near the Salem Bridge on the east [south] side of the Creek. Gen'l Head quarters was at the residence of Joshua Boner Esq in Salem.

In all some three thousand troops camped in and around Salem, below the creek. During the occupation one body of mounted cavalry, by some error, entered Cedar Avenue and the graveyard. Many of the men dismounted and walked through the enclosure, and in some instances, removed their caps. But, according to the *Memorabilia*, strict discipline was enforced by the officers and "very few indeed, comparatively, were the violations of proper and becoming conduct on the part of the soldiers."

News of the surrender of Lee's Army of Northern Virginia, the fall of the Richmond government, and the departure of Palmer's men left the town without organized guard, Union or Confederate. The continual stream of homewardbound soldiers, as well as the threat of marauding bands, necessitated the formation of a vigilance committee. Citizens and former soldiers patrolled the streets day and night; those persons who could not give a satisfactory account of themselves were held in custody. The committee's work was not without extreme difficulty, but order was maintained and lives were protected until the organization of a new government.

One final occupation came on 14 May 1865 when men of the Tenth Regiment of Ohio Volunteers arrived in Salem. Their commander, a Colonel Saunders, established his headquarters in the home of Edward Hege. By this time hostilities had ceased, and in general, the men behaved quite well. Most of them were awaiting orders to muster out; hence they freely fraternized with the people and were hospitably received into many of the Salem homes. The Ohioans left Forsyth County on 13 July, and "although upon the whole they had conducted themselves tolerably well as a body," reports the *Memorabilia*, "still little regret was felt at their departure, in as much as it had appeared very plainly that their presence was anything but necessary or pleasant, and their moral influence was anything but beneficial."

The South's experiment had failed and it was now time to restore the seceding states to their proper relation in the Union. On 29 April 1865 General John Schofield was placed in command of the state pending the establishment of a new civil government. Former Confederates, except the leaders, were invited to swear an oath of allegiance to the Constitution of the United States in order to receive the president's pardon. The intent of the chief executive was restoration of the Union as quickly and as easily as possible. The method was to establish a loyal government supported by at least 10 percent of the voting population of 1860, to ratify the Thirteenth Amendment abolishing slavery in the states, and to elect representatives to Congress. After these measures had been taken, peace would then be assured, the troops could be withdrawn, and the Southern states might be left to themselves, or so it was hoped.

In late May 1865 President Johnson offered a general amnesty and pardon to ex-Confederates. North Carolina simultaneously received his proclamation providing for the "reconstruction" of the state. W. W. Holden was appointed provisional governor and given the authority to call a convention which would officially restore the state to the Union. Two months passed before Governor Holden called for the election of candidates to this convention, however. Judges, magistrates, and numerous local officials had to be appointed first. Some three thousand of them, most of whom were "above criticism," received their respective appointments between June and August of 1865.

Finally on 8 August the governor called for an election on 21 September 1865 for 120 delegates who would meet in convention in Raleigh in early October to act on the president's requirements for readmission to the Union. The election "passed off quietly," as at that time there could be no question as to the extinction of slavery and the Southern Confederacy. Judge Edwin G. Reade of Person County was elected president of the body. His dramatic introductory remark bespeaks the feelings of both Presidents Lincoln and Johnson: "Fellow citizens, we are going home." This keynote established the mood and direction of the delegates who then summarily repealed North Carolina's Ordinance of Secession, declared the abolition of slavery, prepared the way for an election in November of state and national representatives, and surprised everyone by repudiating the state's war debt.

But Congress refused to seat Southern representatives in Washington, and the radical Republicans took over Reconstruction; Johnson was a "president without a party." And despite the fact that North Carolina was perhaps a bit more liberal than her sister states in granting rights to the Negro, she still refused to grant them the right to vote. Political reconstruction was to prove more difficult for North Carolinians than economic reconstruction.

CHAPTER 9

The New South, 1865–1900
The Social Order

THE WAR HAD LEFT MOST OF THE SOUTH, including Forsyth County, prostrate and broken. Many fine young men had given their lives in the four-year struggle, and now that hostilities had ceased it was time to rebuild. Those who returned home to the farm in the spring of 1865 found not only that it was too late to put in a full crop, but also that barns were in disrepair, tools had rusted, fields were overgrown, and most importantly, seed was not available. Those who returned to other pursuits, particularly business and industry, discovered that no raw materials were on hand nor could merchandise be obtained. The Union invasion and occupation of North Carolina had left in its wake destroyed and worn-out railroads, barricaded rivers, and unrepaired roads. Furthermore, the South's former farm laborers, the slaves, were now free and not especially eager to return to the plantation or the farm.

The task of rebuilding seemed gargantuan, but Forsyth County had suffered through at least two previous wars and had overcome similar hardships as those posed by the most recent conflict. Like the mythical phoenix, Forsyth was to rise from the ashes of war with youth and renewed vigor.

D. P. Robbins, in his *Descriptive Sketch of Winston-Salem* (1888), may not have typified Forsyth County sentiments, but he gave words to the principles on which leadership was acting when he stated, "Let the dead past bury its dead. Honoring it highly; cherishing it tenderly; accepting gratefully the lessons it teaches of moral and economical import—of ethics, education and business—let the record be laid aside. Let the present be grasped and so wisely wielded and worked that we may go forth to meet the shadowy future without fear and with a manly hope."

Public Education after the War

There were no common schools in Forsyth County in 1866, only private academies. Calvin Wiley's position of superintendent of North Carolina common schools had been eliminated by the Reconstruction government. And, though by the end of the war the state's literary fund was worth almost $2 million dollars, this money was soon lost when North Carolina repudiated its war debt. The literary fund had invested very heavily in banks, railroads, and navigation companies; these interests were the first to fall after the war. It was not until 1869–70 that the common schools began to reopen.

Criticism of the new government came from the Salem *People's Press* in February 1866. Unless more care in spending were taken by the legislature, said the writer, "they will fully succeed in damning themselves to everlasting fame and irrevocably ruin the people and the state." There was little money in circulation, and only a very few families—far fewer than before the war—were able to send their children to any of Forsyth's four private academies. Taking the place of the public school in Forsyth County after the war was the Sabbath or Sunday school.

Closely resembling the common schools in educational principles, Sunday schools relied on advertising and public exhibitions to provide the necessary operating funds. Most churches boasted such a school and each claimed to offer the best education. Scholastic ecumenism prevailed in Forsyth County, and by 1869 all of the county's churches had come together to form the Forsyth County Sunday School Union. A board of managers, with a member from each church represented, was presided over by E. A. Vogler, president; the Reverend W. W. Albea, vice-president; and J. T. Lineback, secretary-treasurer. Membership in the union was contingent upon a written constitution acceptable to the board's officers. Teachers generally were former common-school instructors.

Without question the most important function of the Sunday schools was in filling the educational void created by the war and the subsequent Reconstruction period for those parents who could not afford to send their children to private academies. And, even after the common schools were reinstituted, the Sunday schools continued to grow in size and strength, providing competition to the state schools. Not until the legislature passed a compulsory-education law some years later did the church schools begin to decline.

Perhaps more of a problem than education for the whites was the need for educating the thousands of freed slaves. Almost everyone feared that the carpetbag government would force racial integration on the whites, rich or poor. But the framers of the state's new constitution in 1868 managed to avoid the problem altogether. What had seemed an imminent reality was politically avoided. The next year, 1869, ex-Confederates breathed easier when S. S. Ashley, the new superintendent of public instruction, determined that "separate schools for the races are a necessity." Furthermore, "it would be folly," he said, "to attempt to establish a mixed school system." Governor W. W. Holden agreed with the superintendent, and in so many words established a "separate but equal" ideal when he said to the General Assembly in 1869, "The schools for the white and colored children should be separate, but in other respects there should be no difference in the character of the schools, or in the provision made to support them."

In Salem, before statute made education for the blacks a reality, the Friends Association for the Relief of Colored Freedmen was created to fill this need. The association established Sunday schools and a free school for the blacks in Salem in 1869. E. A. Vogler was superintendent. He conducted his classes for the black children "in the usual manner" as for whites; reading, singing hymns, and learning songs formed the basis of the curriculum.

But despite this outward appearance of good will, as early as 1866 Forsyth County whites feared outside intervention in a situation over which they felt they had complete control. The editor of the Salem *People's Press* wrote on 15 June of that year, "We are satisfied that if the Negroes were let alone, entirely free from the influences of the would-be philanthropists of the North, who know little or nothing of their habits or capacities, there would be a better feeling throughout the South." The editor got his wish as far as Forsyth County was concerned, for the important Peabody Fund which was set up to help Southern schools, both black and white, did not forward any money to this county until 1885, almost two decades after its creation.

Three years later, in 1869, when the Friends established their school in Salem, the response of the *People's Press* was more moderate in tone: "We think it of great importance that the Freedmen should be educated to the position they are expected to occupy." To the white community of Forsyth the editor spoke of "the important interest of instructing the African race. . . . In the present embarrassed condition of the South," the *Press* editor continued, "we call upon any Northern friends . . . Come over, then ye men of the North and help us."

One friend who came, a lady from Philadelphia, was given a cordial welcome by the Salem press and it was hoped that, "despite the scoffs and sneers which might, perhaps, be directed against her by the thoughtless or the shallow-brained," she might at least find the "approval of her own conscience." Books and other school needs came directly from Philadelphia.

A lack of funds and teachers, as well as inadequate facilities, greatly hindered the cause of education for the black man in North Carolina. Forsyth was more fortunate than many other counties in that as she began to prosper financially in the decade following the war, so did her citizens, black and white. In particular the school started by the Friends in Salem continued as a public common school for many years after Reconstruction ended. The Reverend Alfred Jones of Danville, Virginia, superintendent of the Colored School Association, visited this institution in March 1877 and found it to have "a more flourishing condition than any other under his control." Ten years later, in 1887, there were only two such schools left in the state; the one in Salem was counted. And, after 1873, according to Yates's graduate thesis on the common school in Forsyth County, the black schools were well attended and produced good results.

Problems of misuse of state educational funds plagued the

school system during the first half of the 1870s. Many conscientious citizens of Forsyth were extremely concerned about the future of the free schools. In 1874, amid political furor and bickering, former superintendent Calvin H. Wiley and his family returned to North Carolina from Tennessee, settling in Winston. Wasting no time in becoming active in educational matters, Wiley called a meeting of "the best citizens of the town," who in turn formed a committee of twenty to draft plans and subscribe money for a graded school in Winston. Despite the efforts and backing of such men as G. W. Hinshaw, J. W. Alspaugh, S. H. Hodges, J. A. Gray, and Martin Grogan, attempts at acquiring the necessary money came to naught.

In 1875, of 519 white children in Winston township, only 149 attended public schools, while 207 went to private schools. Of the 214 Negro children, 158 attended public schools. Conditions continued until 1877, when a new school law was passed. The county commissioners, pursuant to this law, laid off sixty-nine school districts, numbered one to fifty-five for whites and one to fourteen for blacks. Provisions for taxation were made and three committeemen were selected. Progress in public education was being made, yet this letter, dated April 1883, from a black child in Forsyth County to a Northern aid society, reveals continuing economic barriers that hindered educational advances:

I take the liberty to write you a letter, as I have been going to school nearly all term, and now as I have to leave school, I feel how much I need an education. How I am to get it I cannot tell, My father was killed two years ago last July, and there are four children of us. My mother works very hard to support us, and I try to do all I can to help her. . . . Now I am to leave school to work in the tobacco factory. I have studied arithmetic, history, grammar, and geography, besides reading and spelling. . . . I feel that what I can do will be little toward getting an education. . . . Can you tell me any way that I can do more, or any way to help myself to get what I want most in life?

This was indeed a pathetic plea, but one that delineates the educational opportunities for those who really desired to learn—black and white.

In Winston an individual effort was made in 1881 to supplement by local taxation the money provided by the state for teacher salaries as a step towards building and furnishing a graded school. An appeal "to all classes and races of our people" from the Winston *Republican* called for an affirmative vote on such a tax. When the vote was counted, however, the result was 300 against and 281 for. The *Republican*'s editor then wrote that "the Graded School project is too dead to skin."

But what element had defeated the tax? Before the vote was cast one private citizen wrote the *Union Republican* that he felt many of the town's businessmen were not concerned with education. He concluded that "Winston is already recognized as a tobacco town without schools and content therewith." Letter after letter was delivered to the local papers in reaction to the vote. Before the verbal battle became more than an exchange of words, the state passed new legislation favorable to the school system, and another vote in Winston—this time demonstrating a growing sense of responsibility—was affirmative on the graded-school issue. On 19 June 1883 five men were elected school commissioners: W. A. Whitaker, James A. Gray, Calvin H. Wiley, James Martin, and Pleasant Hanes.

Night after night during the unusually sultry summer and early fall of 1883 these five men, after long, strenuous hours in bank, factory, or office, gathered in the study of Chairman Wiley, and for hours at a time, sometimes until midnight, wrestled with figures and building plans and details which took a great deal of maneuvering to be fitted into the total educational scheme. Lots that had been suggested as suitable school sites were studied, until finally West End (for white children) was chosen. On 9 September 1884 West End School opened in regular session with 275 students. Though the total cost of lot, building, and furnishings had been $25,000, far more than was raised from the tax, private citizens borrowed and advanced the necessary funds.

Since there was little money on hand for the building of a schoolhouse for black children, the school board, by an arrangement with the trustees of First Baptist Church (black), General Barringer, Henry Pendleton, and Peter Martin converted the church into a school. Later the Depot School was erected, in part with funds personally solicited from Northern philanthropists by the chairman of the school board and superintendent Julius Tomlinson.

Winston's first public school, which was organized on a sound financial basis with an up-to-date, farsighted educational policy, attracted much attention. The editor of the widely read *New England Journal of Education*, Dr. A. D. Mayo of Boston, visited Winston four months after the opening of West End. In the *Journal* he wrote:

The new city of Winston, N.C., has done the most notable work among Southern towns of its size in the establishment of a system of graded schools. During the year it has built one of the most convenient and spacious schoolhouses in the country, and gathered the white children of the place under the superintendency of Professor Tomlinson, so well known by his excellent services at Wilson, N.C. and in the summer normal schools of the State.

Only four months from its organization, the school with all the advantages of the mixed population of a new manufacturing community is a model and is thronged with visitors from all over the Southern country. An excellent beginning has been made with the colored schools and a handsome lot awaits the next effort for a commodious school-house.

In all his labors, the indefatigable superintendent is upheld by an energetic school board, whose chairman, Dr. Wiley, was for many years State Superintendent of Education and may be called the father of the common schools in North Carolina.

Winston is a new city of remarkable growth, and in all ways a striking representation of the advancing life of the New South.

Thus another cooperative effort between business and industrial and private interests resulted in the betterment of the community. There were seventy-five schools in the county outside the Twin City by the end of the 1880s, and each had an average enrollment of forty students; Professor A. I. Butner supervised the county schools. Yet, according to Dr. Robbins in his *Descriptive Sketch*, the real educational attraction was in Winston: "If there is any one thing more than another of which Winston should feel a just pride, it is the excellency to which her graded schools have attained." "Beginning in chaos, five years since," he continued, "Superintendent Tomlinson, by the aid of well selected assistants and backed by a school board of superior intelligence, has wrought wonders and given to the Twin City a justly earned reputation of having the best graded schools in North Carolina." The T-shaped two-story brick building was as impressive as the education that went on inside it. Measuring 190 by 170 feet (including a large assembly room), West End boasted an imposing tower four stories high, that with the spire attained a height of 112 feet. Inside were nine recitation rooms, ample halls, and a "commodious library," perhaps its most valuable asset, that contained more than $4,000 worth of books. Dr. Robbins concluded: "Altogether both inside and out the building is handsomely designed and equipped and may well be termed the 'Crowning Glory of Winston.'"

Growth of the Churches

Forsyth County was well provided with churches before the Civil War, predominantly Moravian, Methodist, and Baptist. During the war years the area's first Presbyterian church was formed, largely by the efforts of Judge Thomson J. Wilson. Judge Wilson persuaded Reverend Frontis H. Johnston of Lexington to hold services in Winston, first in the Wilson home and later in the courthouse. On Sunday 6 October 1862 the small brick church on Cherry Street was dedicated on land recently purchased from the Moravians. The purchase shut off Third Street at Cherry and this was to cause much comment in later years. Over the next three decades increasing membership in Winston's First Presbyterian Church necessitated the construction of a new building in 1888–90.

In the early 1870s Negro members of First Presbyterian Church requested letters of dismissal in order to join the Negro Church of Winston, a Northern Presbyterian church. Later known as Lloyd Presbyterian Church, it was located on Chestnut Street. In 1878 the First Presbyterian Church organized a class for Negro children which was later moved to Tise Hall.

The black Methodist movement began in Waughtown when Henry Fries began holding prayer meetings in his home. In time the Methodists moved to Winston and began holding meetings under the brush arbor on North Liberty Street. Under the leadership of Reverend Isaac Wells the Methodist Episcopal Church, North, built its first building at Seventh and Chestnut streets. A year later, in 1882, the St. James Methodist Episcopal Church was built on Chestnut between First and Second streets.

Baptists, both black and white, were in Forsyth County long before the Civil War, but it was not until 1871 that Winston acquired its first organized Baptist church. Alfred Holland, the first Baptist who had located in Winston and who began the movement for a Baptist church, was one of the charter members. The First Baptist Church met at the courthouse for four years as it grew in size. It purchased a lot on Second Street in 1874 and acquired the services of its third pastor, Dr. Henry A. Brown, in December 1877.

The first Negro Baptist Church, like its white counterpart and similar to the black and white Methodist churches, came from prayer meetings in homes and in brush arbors. The Reverend George Holland, with the assistance of Reverend Henry A. Brown, pastor of the white First Baptist Church, organized the First Baptist Church for Negroes in 1879. Their first building was constructed in 1882 facing Sixth Street at Chestnut.

Both white and black First Baptist churches established missions within a short time and many of these rapidly grew into independent congregations. In the early years Salem, Southside, and North Winston churches came from the white First Baptist. First Institutional, West End, Mount Zion, and New Bethel were outgrowths of the black First Baptist.

The Episcopalians, like the Baptists, came late to Winston-Salem. In 1876 the Reverend William Shipp Bynum began to come to Winston about once a month from his parish in Greensboro. He found only one communicant in Winston and three in Salem but the congregation increased rapidly and by the next year there were thirteen communicants from three families. The small group was able to gather funds and build their first church on the corner of Fourth and Pine (Marshall) streets. St. Paul's Episcopal Church was consecrated in February 1879 and has remained an influential part of the Winston-Salem religious picture ever since.

Among the smaller denominations, the city's oldest Christian (Disciples of Christ) church was organized in 1890 by Evangelist R. W. Stancil of North Winston in the Union Grove schoolhouse. Its first building was on West Fourth Street. The earliest Roman Catholics in the area held services in the home of Francis Kesler in about 1886 with a Benedictine priest from Belmont Abbey to say Mass. Later, a priest came from Greensboro once every two months. Property was purchased for a church in 1891 at the corner of Fourth Street and Brookstown Avenue. The church, under the leadership of Bishop Leo G. Haid, O.S.B., was constructed and named St. Leo's. Shortly after the turn of the century it received its first resident priest.

Forsyth Township Lines and County Expansion

The state legislature at its special session in 1868 and at its winter session of 1868–69 provided for the regular biennial election of five men to act as a board of commissioners in each county. The legislature further defined the powers of the boards and made it "the duty of the Commissioners to exercise a general supervision and control of the penal and charitable institutions, schools, roads, bridges, levying of taxes, and finances of the county" as should be prescribed by law.

The first duty laid on the county commissioners by North Carolina's new Constitution of 1868 and the Acts of 1868 was the division of their respective counties into districts "to determine the boundaries of said districts, and to report the same to the General Assembly before the 1st day of January 1869." When the districting was done, and the reports approved by the General Assembly, the districts were "to have corporate powers for the necessary purposes of local government, and be known as Townships." The commissioners were further empowered "to erect, divide, or alter Townships," either by consent of a certain number of residents of the townships affected (after due advertisement), or by action of the legislature. Forsyth chose the latter, and on 10 April 1869, the legislature enacted "that the Districts reported by the Commissioners of the following counties of the State to the present session of the General Assembly are hereby approved, & said Districts, in obedience to Art. VII, sec. 3&4 of the Constitution, to wit . . . Forsyth . . . shall have corporate powers; shall be known as Townships, by the boundaries and by the names respectively designated in said reports."

M. H. Morris, the county surveyor, spent twenty-five days running the new township lines, for which he was paid $75.00. Morris made no map of the county, but in 1882 James T. Lineback, by independent surveys and use of the original survey notes dated 28 December 1868, constructed a large map accurately revealing the township lines for the first time.

The townships did not coincide with the earlier captain's districts, so named for purposes of militia organization and for tax assessment, but were rectangular and arranged in three tiers of four townships each. Belews Creek, Salem Chapel, Bethania, and Old Richmond were located to the north; Kernersville, Middle Fork, Old Town, and Vienna, in the center; and Abbotts Creek, Broadbay, South Fork, and Lewisville to the south. Where Middle Fork, Old Town, South Fork, and Broadbay should have cornered, Winston Township was inserted, the lines corresponding with those of the Winston and Salem corporate limits on the north and west, and extending eastward to Abbotts Creek township; the western line was identical with the original Wachovia survey.

Between Vienna and Old Town, Lewisville, and South Fork, Muddy Creek, the only natural boundary, is noted. Elsewhere naturally occurring features were not regarded. Morris's notes show that it was the original intention of the commissioners to let the Kernersville township line drop back one-third of a mile to correspond with that of Belews Creek, but Mr. Lineback found that when the line was actually run, it was carried with the Abbotts Creek line and the Wachovia survey to Belews Creek township, with the offset being made at that corner.

On 11 March 1889 Forsyth County was enlarged. Previously no attention had been paid to the inconvenient western boundary of the county. But in that year the legislature transferred from Davidson to Forsyth the land lying between Lewisville and South Fork townships and the Yadkin River. This area became Clemmonsville township. The transfer obliterated a number of angles which the Act of 1773 made in the south line of Surry County, inherited by Stokes County, and then by Forsyth County.

In 1895 another township was created in Forsyth. The name of Bethania township was changed to Rural Hall, and the new township received the old name, Bethania, and was placed at the point of meeting of Old Richmond, Vienna, Rural Hall, and Old Town. It extended two and a half miles north, south, east, and west from the town of Bethania. The east and west corners of the square fell on the line between Old Richmond and Vienna, Rural Hall and Old Town.

One more angle was wiped out by an act of the legislature of 1921 when a wedge-shaped piece of Davidson County was added to the south side of Abbotts Creek township. Also, seventy acres of "forgotten" land belonging to Forsyth County which lay south of the Yadkin River in Davie County was in 1825 transferred by the legislature from Forsyth to the county in which it belonged, geographically speaking.

This left the C-shaped segment popularly called Little Yadkin cut from Yadkin County by the river (the southern part of Surry County had by then become Yadkin County). In 1911 the legislature transferred from Yadkin to Forsyth a small triangle at the north end of the segment, in order to enable both counties to participate in the building of a bridge across the river. In 1926 the commissioners of Forsyth County agreed to buy from Yadkin County the land known as Little Yadkin. The legislature of 1927 altered the county line in accord with this agreement and authorized the Forsyth commissioners to pay the Yadkin commissioners the stipulated sum of $70,000. After 138 years the county line had ceased to run back and forth across the river, and the Yadkin became the boundary of Forsyth County on the west and southwest.

The Board of Trade and Prevailing Optimism

In his *Descriptive Sketch of Winston-Salem* (1888), Dr. Robbins wrote: "Excepting in locating a specific business or street in all our writings, when we say this city or this place, we mean both Winston and Salem, as they are practically one, and inseparable in all their movements of progression, social position, etc." Certainly the Reconstruction years had brought the two cities closer together through mutual interests and concerns, particularly those financial. When Robbins made reference to the Twin City in his *Sketch*, for all practical purposes, at least in the eyes of the members of the Board of Trade, the two cities were one.

In the development of Winston and Salem from the small country towns of the 1870s and 1880s into the one great city which exists today, the Board of Trade—now called the Chamber of Commerce—has played an important part. This organization, composed of the leading citizens of both towns, from its very beginning (circa September 1885) sought to build and improve the community, and not without Northern capital. Robbins's *Sketch*, written under the auspices of the Chamber of Commerce, pointed to "no finer chances [in the West] . . . than the 'New South' presents." Full of the optimism that prevailed in the late 1880s, he continued:

There are immediate prospects of two new railroads, the exact developments of which we shall give before closing these pages. These, with the continued progress in manufactories, etc. give to this place an exceedingly bright outlook, and in no stretch of imagination to suppose that we shall have a population of 25,000 within less than ten years from the present date. Taxes are low, real estate has not reached a speculative boom and the large amount already invested in factories and machinery will ever be a prevention from a retrograde movement. With the best graded schools in the state, and oldest and best Female Seminary in the South, together with several private schools, and excellent religious advantages, the high social and moral standing of the Twin City will always be a laurel in the crown of progress. The business men here are wide awake and pushing. While ready to welcome Northern capital and immigration, they are not Micawber-like, waiting for something to turn up, but progressive. But few cities of this size can boast of as many men who are rated in the hundreds of thousands, and the number of brick residences or costly frame mansions clearly demonstrates that we have a large per centage of well-to-do citizens in this handsome and healthful city.

Winston's *Union Republican* regularly posted the business of the Chamber of Commerce. This newspaper, in fact, contains the only record of Chamber business from its beginning to 5 February 1889 when the first minute book was destroyed in a fire. As a new organization the Chamber of Commerce was not completely embraced by the community from the beginning. The Tobacco Association, through its spokesman to the Chamber, a Mr. Morris, refused to join as a body, but urged its individual members to do so. Even the merchants were slow to recognize the new organization at first, but by the end of the first year, there were twenty firms that had signified a willingness to join (the initiation fee was

$6.00). Industrialists, particularly those in tobacco and textiles, were much quicker to see potential advantages the Chamber of Commerce had to offer. For example, among the first officers and directors were John W. Fries, W. A. Whitaker, H. E. Fries, R. J. Reynolds, P. H. Hanes, W. B. Carter, and George W. Hinshaw. After the organization was chartered, the following item appeared in the *Union Republican*: "Thirty-seven business firms were represented in the meeting and it is confidently believed and expected that others will join now that the association is permanently organized and fully officered; and upon a thorough investigation of the organization and from the character of the gentlemen enlisted, we are satisfied that it is upon a business footing, that its object is a good one and as such deserves the hearty cooperation of all."

Over the next ten years the Chamber of Commerce, with widespread support in the Twin City, was instrumental in initiating a number of improvement projects. As early as November 1885 "the matter of our public roads leading into town was discussed and the temporary president appointed a committee to raise money for the improvement of said roads and the sum of $1,600 was raised." Four years later, the Chamber was active in lobbying in Raleigh for a reduced legal rate of interest. In 1890, among other projects, the Chamber's committee on trade and transportation made a special effort to secure separate freight and passenger trains on all railroads entering Winston, as well as a more accommodating schedule. Subscriptions were raised in the amount of $6,500 to move Davis Military School from LaGrange to Winston. The possibility of free postal delivery in Winston was discussed. Nor was education ignored by the Chamber. On 30 January 1891 John Hanes, president of the Chamber of Commerce, called a meeting to consider the matter of locating an agricultural and mechanical college for blacks in Forsyth County. In June 1891 the attention of Chamber members was called to the fact that while excursion rates were given on railroads to almost all points in North Carolina, Winston was "coldly, calmly passed by." The question of a paid fire department was discussed. And twenty years before the fact, on 2 January 1893, Robert B. Glenn spoke to the Chamber of the advisability of bringing up the question of consolidation of the twin cities under the name of Winston-Salem. Thus went some of the business of a very soundly based and progressively oriented Chamber of Commerce in a growing city.

Kernersville

Kernersville, "Forsyth County's Second Town," so dubbed by Dr. Robbins in his *Sketch*, was pronounced an excellent site for those in the "northern tier of the United States" to escape the "weekly occurence of frigid waves." The salubrious climate and suitable location combined with excellent opportunities in business, industry, and agriculture were said to make the town desirable to outsiders, both for settlement and work.

The growth of Kernersville after the war very closely parallels that of the Twin City. Just a small hamlet of some one hundred inhabitants in 1870, the population had reached five hundred by 1880, and almost one thousand by 1888. Incorporation came in 1872, and as in its neighbor to the west, the arrival of the railroad in 1873 accounted for the growth mentioned above. Robbins reported that local citizens had contributed very liberally towards the acquisition of this rail connection. Kernersville in the late 1880s boasted more brick residences, stores, and factories than any town of its size in the state.

In April 1881 the *Kernersville News* was started by T. A. Lyon and H. C. Edwards. Over the next four years the paper was expanded from a five-column folio to one of seven columns. The original hand press was replaced by a Campbell Power Press, and a jobbing outfit was added. By 1888, two additional newspapers, the Thomasville *Gazette* and the Summerfield *Gleaner*, were printed in the Kernersville office. J. H. Lindsay, who bought the paper in 1883, distinguished himself as secretary-treasurer of the North Carolina Press Association.

In addition to the tobacco manufactories of Beard & Roberts, W. H. Leak & Co., Brown, Sapp & Co., J. M. Greenfield, and Lowrey & Stafford, Kernersville also boasted the carriage manufacturers Huff & Stuart and A. Lewis, as well as a variety of smaller manufacturers. As far as J. W. Beard and other town leaders were concerned, Kernersville could benefit from expansion. Beard, both a businessman and realtor, personally offered free lots adjacent to the railroad for anyone who would erect a "substantial factory." Free residence lots would be provided to those wishing to build homes in Kernersville.

Interestingly, though, Kernersville concerns in the 1880s and 1890s went beyond the usual mercantile and industrial projects of towns of comparable size. In the late 1880s there were no fewer than eight roads centering on the town, and thus easy access was afforded to surrounding farmlands. Forsyth's first inhabitants, the Indians, had exploited the abundance of wild fruits that grew there; Kernersville leaders were inclined to capitalize on the opportunity again. Dried fruit from Forsyth in particular was known for its good flavor; new farmers in the Kernersville area might couple their growing interests with a canning factory. Nutritious grasses were certainly plentiful for more stock grazing. Also, King Tobacco could be grown on what seemed to be endless acreage surrounding the town. And lastly the large outcrops of granite with opportunities for quarrying presented a fine field for development. So, asked Kernersville leaders, "Why not come while the getting's good?"

A richly prosperous "New South"—a potential recognized by Cassius M. Clay and others four decades before—seemed nowhere more likely to flourish than the Kernersville, North Carolina of 1890, according to its boosters.

"Kerner's Folly" and the Juvenile Lyceum

In January 1875, subsequent to the death of his father, Jule Kerner returned to North Carolina after a number of years of art study in Philadelphia and the Northeast and employment as an artist-designer in Cincinnati, Ohio. Establishing himself as a portrait painter and photographer in Kernersville, he quickly achieved a fine reputation. It was during his first years back home that Jule also turned his attentions to the decorative arts; a crew of workmen under his supervision completed a number of commendable jobs in the Forsyth County area. Later, as Jule's reputation spread, so did his business. With his brother Henry, he formed the Reuben Rink Decorating Company, and jobs in Durham for the Carr and Duke family residences assured his future as an interior designer.

What began in 1878 as a combination studio, office, reception hall, ballroom, carriage house and stables—all planned temporary—resulted in a spectacularly unique home in Forsyth County, "Kerner's Folly." The creative Jule could not part with his temporary quarters; more rooms were added, top and sides, until the structure was completed in the early months of 1880. Kerner immediately planned its decoration, in preparation for his marriage later that year. An Italian artist, Quintini, painted mural frescoes in the reception room, the drawing room, and the two bedrooms. The wainscoting along the stairway to the fourth-floor ballroom was frescoed by Jule himself, with designs from sketches of his travels in Florida and Louisiana. But now Jule's wife, Polly Alice Masten—the lady for whom the house was decorated—tells the story, in *I Remember*, privately printed in 1956 from her manuscript notes:

At that time [1880–81] the large room on the top floor, which is now the theatre, was unfinished except for the huge brass chandelier and chairs around the edge of the floor. It had been used for social purposes such as entertainments, parties, and dancing and the like, and was the social center of the town for the younger people, both married and single. Later, . . . Jule went to New York and brought back a German (Caesar Milch) from Berlin, who set to work to decorate all the walls and ceiling up there. He was at that job for many months and that was the beginning of a life long employment of Herr Milch, who was never out of Jule's employment as long as they both lived. . . .

Herr Milch decorated six of the high walls with allegorical paintings of cupids and flowers, while two of the walls were painted with large seascapes of Holland of which Jule had made sketches and designs. . . .

In 1896 I set up an organization which I called "The Juvenile Lyceum" composed of children of the town between the ages of 7 and 13. . . . Forty-two children were signed up and the organization was launched. [Programs were to be given fortnightly.] It was too much of a job. Then programs began to break down through failure of preparation or attendance.

So in 1897 I reorganized "The Juvenile Lyceum" and included in it only those children who had shown genuine interest, reliability, and dependability. . . .

When Jule had completed and equipped the theatre he named the fourth floor "Cupids' Park." He bought several sets of scenery from Sosman Landis of Chicago who were the famous theatrical scenery

people. Jule also painted several sets himself. He built dressing rooms.
. . . The orchestra pit was to the side of the stage and was covered with
heavy silk velour draperies. In this was the grand piano—one of the old
fashioned square type. It could not be brought up any stairs so he had to
cut trap doors through the floors beneath to get it up there. I do not
suppose it will ever come down again. Jule also bought some 75 to 100
chairs for seating the audience. . . . The curtains were silk velvet and
had lining and interlining. . . . All lighting was by kerosene lamps because there was no electricity or gas in Kernersville. . . . The footlights
were also kerosene lamps, of course, and they were guarded by metal
framework around each one.

After the reorganization of "The Juvenile Lyceum" everything went
much better. . . . Many of the plays we wrote ourselves. Some we bought
from a publishing company which made a specialty of publishing plays.

The Lyceum's programs ran the gamut of subjects, according to
Mrs. Kerner. "I tried to keep interest alive by making them topical
or current"; hence in the spring of 1898, "there was a lot to work
with" when the Spanish-American War broke out. One play was
about the Red Cross and army nurses. The assassination of Marat
by Charlotte Corday and similar historical subjects were chosen
and adapted by Mrs. Kerner. Fiction likewise found its way onto
the Kernersville stage in the form of dramatized versions of
Grimm's fairy tales and Aesop's fables adapted by Mrs. Kerner.

The orchestra, recalled Mrs. Kerner, "was a lot of fun." Since
no complete written story has survived, nor have any programs
been located for the theatre, we cannot know what was played
and with what degree of skill. But the size of the orchestra is
known, as are the names of those who played in it. Tilla Harmon
was pianist; Bessie and John Greenfield played violins; DeWitt
Harmon played the cornet; Carl Pepper and Herr Milch played
the flutes. The Kerners' dancing teacher, a Mr. Scanlon, and a
Mr. Hobbs also played violins in the orchestra. Professor Brockman, head of the Brockman School of Music in Greensboro, was
the group's leader.

The Kerner family was materially quite well off for its day,
and the age in which they lived was gilded. "My life has been
more fortunate than many others," commented Mrs. Jule Kerner.
"We had quite a gay time."

From Winston's earliest days the local newspaper played a great part in the growth of the town. F. E. Boner and James Collins began publication of the *Western Sentinel*, a weekly and Winston's first newspaper, in 1856. Before the war John W. Alspaugh acquired control of the paper, and under his leadership, the *Sentinel* became the most important tabloid in this section of North Carolina. According to W. K. Hoyt in the 1966 bicentennial edition of the *Journal and Sentinel*, the *Western Sentinel* gave "vigorous support of the Democratic-Confederate point of view" before, during, and after the Civil War. Because of other interests, however, Alspaugh was forced to seek assistance in running his paper, and in 1866 George M. Mathes, a former Confederate officer, became the *Sentinel's* editor. Mathes's "fiery" career extended over a sixteen-year period.

In 1870 another paper, the *National Advocate*, was started and financed by a small group of local Republicans. F. T. Walser was its first editor. Four years later, in 1874, Captain J. W. Goslen purchased the *Advocate*. He renamed the paper the *Union Republican* and made it the leading printed voice of the Republican party in the state.

In February 1879, Colonel James A. Robinson, popularly known as "Old Hurrygraph," began the publication of another small weekly, *The Winston Leader*. Robinson's interests were Democratic. From its first appearance until the *Leader* was taken over by the *Sentinel* in September 1885, the *Leader* was "found in the hottest of [political] fights."

An energetic young man, Edward A. Oldham, became editor and proprietor of Alspaugh's *Western Sentinel* in 1883. Oldham wanted to convert the paper to a daily but failed to get the necessary backing. He hired Zollicoffer W. Whitehead to solicit subscriptions. Whitehead was an equally ambitious young fellow, and in the early months of 1885 he joined with P. F. Doub in establishing a new paper, *The Twin-City Daily*, the city's first daily. Unfortunately the young men's enthusiasm exceeded their ability in running a paper, so they were forced to sell their modest enterprise—the paper ran only twelve inches to the page—within a few months of its appearance. Colonel H. Montague bought out Whitehead "for a very small sum." Montague then promptly sold his share to Enoch A. Griffith, who became the *Daily's* business manager. The new partnership likewise was shortlived, and in October 1885 A. M. Stack and Preston A. Snider bought the paper. Four months later operations were suspended and Stack took up the practice of law in Danbury.

Publication of the *Twin-City Daily* was resumed in March 1886 with Snider in complete control. He was joined in November by an ex-grocer, James Oliver Foy. Foy was later to become a major factor in local newspaper maneuvering.

Meanwhile, the *Western Sentinel* was taking on new life under E. A. Oldham's management. In 1883, Oldham, having acquired the interest of G. M. Mathes, placed on the dateline of his paper for the first time the hyphenated name "Winston-Salem." In 1885 Oldham merged the *Winston Leader* with his paper and introduced many new features in the staid old Democratic weekly. In 1888 Vernon W. Long, a recent graduate of the University of North Carolina, succeeded Oldham as editor. The owners of the *Twin-City Daily* acquired the *Western Sentinel* in 1890, continuing its publication as a weekly and adding the word *Sentinel* to the title of the *Daily*. In 1886 the first issues of L. L. Polk's *Progressive Farmer* were printed on the *Western Sentinel* presses.

In 1892 William F. Burbank purchased the two *Sentinels*—the weekly *Western Sentinel* and the *Twin-City Daily Sentinel*; he also purchased the venerable old *People's Press* of Salem. Then, early in 1894, after one year of consolidation, these papers were incorporated as the Sentinel Publishing Company. Burbank left for California, entrusting the care of his papers to J. B. Whitaker, Jr.

The *Winston Journal* was founded in 1897 by Charles Landon Knight. His luck was no better than some of Winston's other newspaper publishers, and he was forced to sell the operation to Wilbur C. Morrison and Silas B. Davis. The future of the afternoon daily was as yet tentative; the new owners placed the *Journal* "in the hands of our creditors" soon after they took over control. According to Mr. Hoyt, these creditors—Andrew Joyner (who became the new editor), J. O. Foy, and J. J. Darlington—used the *Journal* as a "whetstone on which to sharpen their political ax."

Joyner was chairman of the Forsyth County Democratic Executive Committee. Under new management and vigorously "waving the bloody shirt" for Furnifold M. Simmons in his white supremacy campaign in 1898, the paper found its future was assured.

After several additional changes of ownership, the *Journal* became a morning paper under the control of D. A. Fawcett and W. Lannes Foy (J. O.'s son). The *Journal*'s first Sunday morning edition appeared in December 1902. The result of such boldness, according to Mr. Foy, was immediate: "Fawcett was put out of the Presbyterian Church. . . . I was an Episcopalian [and therefore escaped church censure]."

Winston in the 1880s and 1890s

The years beginning with 1880 mark a period of expansion in the history of Winston. The mayors during this period were A. B. Gorrell, Peter A. Wilson, A. C. Buxton, Samuel H. Smith, Charles Buford, T. J. Wilson, D. P. Mast, Robah B. Kerner, Garland E. Webb, Eugene E. Gray, Paul W. Crutchfield, and John F. Griffith.

The financial center of this busy little tobacco town was the short street running from Fourth to Fifth, then called Old Town, now Trade Street. On the corner of Fifth facing west was the thriving grocery store of Vaughn and Prather; on the corner of Fourth facing west was the brick store of H. D. Poindexter, bearing on its south wall the trademark of the store, a fleet deer. Between these two stores, catering not only to the town but also to a widespread country trade, stood the mammoth brick Farmer's Warehouse of Colonel A. B. Gorrell. This building extended from Old Town Street to Liberty Street. At the time of its opening in 1881 it had the largest warehouse floor for the sale of tobacco in the world.

Across Old Town Street from the Farmer's Warehouse two more concerns carried on big business: the tobacco warehouse of Major James Scales and Captain M. W. Norfleet, called the Piedmont Warehouse and known for its reliability and popularity, and, to the north of the Piedmont, the brick tobacco factory of T. L. Vaughn. On Fourth Street facing north and causing a dead end to Old Town Street was the huge Hinshaw and Medearis store, selling everything from shoestrings to a parlor suite of furniture. It was the pioneer department store in northwestern North Carolina.

In 1893 the city occupied its new high-towered City Hall, located on the corner of Fourth and Main streets. Built at a cost of $75,000, it housed the city offices, the market, the armory, and the jail. It served the city until the 1920s when it was demolished and replaced by the Reynolds Building.

For a slant on the civic life of Winston during this period when the town was expanding in many directions, entries in the minute book of the Board of Aldermen give an interesting view. For example, in January 1882 Winston was threatened with an epidemic of smallpox. The aldermen ordered that every person in town, old and young, be vaccinated. A pesthouse was rented at $4.00 a month for those who had contracted the disease and those who had been exposed. All were to be confined in quarantine quarters under strict guard. Hence the following note from a called meeting of the Board, 14 January 1882: "Whereas it appears that the persons confined in quarantine in Winston on account of having been exposed to smallpox have become drunk and are threatening to break the grounds and spread the disease, on motion ordered that persons confined within the limits of quarantine who shall become disorderly shall be punished by having a ball and chain put on them."

In May 1882 salaries and duties were assigned to various public officials. The town constable was elected with the understanding that when he was not engaged upon the duties of constable and tax collector, he was to do full police duty; his salary was fixed at $100 per year, plus a 5 percent commission on taxes collected. The chief of police was to receive $40 per month and costs and fees not exceeding $200. The officers under him would receive $35 per month, with additional fees and costs not exceeding $200. The salary of the lamplighter, Alfred Wright, a black man, was $15 a month. A year later he was allowed $18 per month with the understanding that he devote more time to cleaning and keeping the lamps in good order. The mayor was to receive $200 per year, and the secretary-treasurer $150.

In June 1889 the aldermen received a petition reflective of the changing times in a growing town. The request, signed by "50 ladies and gentlemen asked that the old Barringer House on Liberty be removed at once as it was day by day becoming more a nuisance." The house remained for some time afterwards.

Even at that time, sewage and sanitation received a good deal of the attention of the Board of Aldermen. Meeting on 8 June 1880, at the request of Mayor A. B. Gorrell, the aldermen reported on their inspection of "privies and other foul places" in Winston. Here is part of their report:

The board found Wood's factory privies in a very foul condition, and Ham Scales factory privies in a miserable condition. Bitting and Whitaker's privy smelled very offensive, but was apparently not so foul as the others.

The next place visited was the hollow below Brown Bros. Tobacco factory over which a number of privies have been built. The board found cesspools in such a foul condition and so offensive that this secretary is not scholar enough to describe it. . . .

Three years after this report was turned in, the city began planning its first public sewage system, though it was not built until 1891.

Indeed the Winston of 1875 described in Chapter 9 in some detail had changed considerably over the following two decades. Winston was a highly prosperous, attractive city by this time.

With the increasing wealth and importance of Winston and Forsyth County, the need for bigger and better financial institutions was realized. Israel Lash died in 1879 and the First National Bank of Salem, then boasting assets of $100,000, closed its doors, thereby moving the financial center of the community into the new village of Winston. The First National Bank of Winston, with assets of $55,000, was thriving at the time of the Salem bank's move. The growing importance of Winston and the relative decline of Salem in the financial picture are highlighted by this and other changes.

The parent institution of the Wachovia Bank and Trust Company, the Wachovia National Bank, was established in June 1879. Wyatt F. Bowman was the institution's first president, Edward Belo its vice president, W. A. Lemly (formerly associated with

Israel Lash) cashier, and James A. Gray was assistant cashier. Starting business with a capital of $100,000, the bank increased capitalization to $150,000 within two months. In 1888 the bank was moved from its original building on Main Street to the corner of Main and Third, where it occupied a three-story building on the present site of the Government Center (the old Wachovia Building). Lemly was president of this flourishing institution from 1882 to 1906, and James A. Gray served from 1906 to 1911.

In 1893 the Wachovia Loan and Trust Company was organized by F. H. Fries and his nephew, H. F. Shaffner. The first Winston home of this institution was a modest one-story wooden building on the east side of Main Street between Second and Third streets. James A. Gray, J. E. Gilmer, C. H. Fogle, J. C. Buxton, J. H. Millis, T. L. Vaughn, and R. J. Reynolds were its first directors. Two of the directors, Gray and Buxton, were closely identified with Wachovia National Bank.

The movement for a public hospital was started by a group of thirty-one women who, on 27 June 1887, at the home of Dr. Henry R. Bahnson, formed themselves into the Twin-City Hospital Association. Mrs. James A. Gray was elected president of the group; Mrs. J. C. Buxton was first vice-president; Mrs. J. A. Bitting, second vice-president; Mrs. J. F. Shaffner, treasurer; and Mrs. J. M. Rogers, secretary. The old Martin Grogan home on Liberty Street was chosen by the association as their first facility. The solicitation for funds with which to furnish the beds and rooms of the house met with generous response, so that in six months' time, in December 1887, the doors of Winston's first hospital were opened. Later, when the old Grogan house was no longer adequate, the Twin-City Hospital was moved to a one-story frame building on Brookstown Avenue. It contained one ward and three private rooms, with a total accommodation of seventeen beds.

Winston's first waterworks was a private affair, with R. J. Wilson, S. E. Allen, E. A. Pfohl, W. L. Brown, G. W. Hinshaw, James A. Gray, and P. H. Hanes as directors. George Mathes of the *Western Sentinel* wrote in October 1881 that the reservoir was nearing completion and that those who saw the work through "deserve great credit." Editor Goslen of the *Union Republican*, perhaps not content with a Democrat's evaluation, decided to ride out to the waterworks and inspect the construction for himself. The result of his visit is not so much a description of the waterworks as it is a picture of the Winston of 1881.

In the heart of the town is the Farmers' Warehouse. At the corner in the rear of Mr. Sussdorff's dwelling and near the new warehouse on Old Town Street is the store house of Messrs. Vaughn and Pepper (corner of Fifth and Trade) just under cover.

On the corner of Fifth and Cherry [site of the Winston-Salem Hyatt House] we note with pride the handsome dwelling of Major T. J. Brown, built of brick and stucco-finish, with tower and porches, containing 12 rooms finished in style, with hot and cold water and gas fixtures complete.

As we drive down Presbyterian Street [now Cherry Street] we note the roomy, old-fashioned dwelling of Dr. Spencer; James A. Gray, Esq., assistant cashier of the Wachovia National Bank, we learn, has just purchased the property and will erect upon the spacious grounds a handsome, modern residence.

Further down the street, on the Winston line, is the Dr. Shelton dwelling, brick and stucco-finish, with handsome tower and porches all around, containing 15 rooms finished in the best style; the mantels are especially fine.

Going out 4th, on Shallowford Street we note the handsome residence Mr. Chamberlain is erecting. In fact, go in what direction we may, we find new building, new enterprises.

Before 1882 Winston had no fire company; the only apparatus for fighting fire were the hooks and ladders owned by the city. Early in February 1882 W. F. Keith, who represented a group of citizens interested in procuring more adequate fire protection for the town, appeared before the town commissioners with the proposal that a voluntary fire company be organized, with the town to provide the necessary equipment and station personnel. The commissioners accepted this proposition, and on 11 February 1882, Winston's first fire company—Steamer No. 1—was formally organized. In May the fire engine arrived and the young firefighters (in new uniforms furnished by the commissioners) were suitably trained. E. M. Pace was the first captain of Steamer

No. 1; he was succeeded by W. A. Bevil, and Captain Bevil was succeeded by J. H. Masten. In 1883 an Englishman, A. J. Gales, a charter member of the company, was elected to the captaincy and for twenty-one years he served most efficiently in this position.

On 2 March 1886 Winston's first fire company was incorporated by the legislature. In 1891 a second company of unsalaried firemen was organized, Steamer Company No. 2, with H. L. Foard as captain. Two years later, in 1893, a hook-and-ladder truck was added to the equipment. In this year the motorizing of the equipment was begun, though it was not until January 1913 that the first motor truck arrived.

The summer of 1887 marks the casting aside of the old gasoline and kerosene street lamps and the illuminating of Winston with electric lights. The Winston Electric Light and Motive Power Company was incorporated on 25 March 1887. The company officers were Judge D. H. Starbuck, president, and Captain D. P. Mast, treasurer; the directors were T. L. Vaughn, J. E. Gilmer, J. A. Bitting, A. Ryttenberg, and W. A. Whitaker. At eight o'clock on the evening of 26 August 1887 Colonel Bitting by a turn of the hand connected the street lines with the arch dynamo machine, and the awaiting spectators on the streets were dazzled with the first flash of Winston's electric lights.

The coming on of the lights proved a seven days' wonder to the people of Winston and the surrounding county. The battery was near the jail, and at eight o'clock each evening, when the current was on, there would be a crowd standing around to see the dazzling sight.

Some weeks after the installation of electricity, early one September during a severe thunderstorm, the people of Winston were startled by the sudden flashing on of all the thirty-seven arc street lights; for five minutes the lights burned with intense brightness, then snapped out.

Several months later Winston and Salem began the movement for an electric street railway. On 11 March 1899 the Winston-Salem Street Railway Company was incorporated. In January 1891 the Electric Company and the Street Railway Company were consolidated under the name of Winston-Salem Railway and Electric Company. The *Union Republican* of Thursday, 17 July 1890 gives the following account of the starting of the streetcars.

Monday afternoon marked another step in the ever-growing prosperity of our towns. It was the starting of the electric streetcars, an event looked for with much eagerness and expectation. President F. J. Sprague, whose system operated the plant, arrived upon the noon train. About 2 o'clock p.m. the first car made a trial trip over the line, occupied by President Sprague, Vice-President E. L. Hawkins, J. H. McClemment, Mr. Field of the Field Engineering Company, Mr. Bourn of the Sprague Company and others.

Although the machinery was all new and the track just laid, everything worked like a charm. A large company of citizens witnessed the passing of the car and the Salem Band made music as a token of appreciation for this great enterprise in our midst. It is to be regretted, however, that all the required tests were not made first and Tuesday afternoon appointed for an appropriate jollification with music, speeches, a "turnover of the line" and so forth. The citizens were eager for such a manifestation and waited for an announcement to that effect.

Tuesday, July 15, 1890, the cars began to run regularly, and the excursionists from Raleigh made free use of them as did also our visitors from Greensboro yesterday, July 16.

For the past few nights there has been a perfect jam of merry pleasure seekers spinning up and down the line, and the streets thronged with spectators.

It is certainly a great step forward, an enterprise that involved a large outlay, which signifies the confidence foreign capitalists have in our present and future welfare, and we believe that the investment will never be a cause for regret. Onward is the watchword in the Twin Cities and the entire Piedmont section has long ago caught the spirit of the times.

To the citizens in town and in country we would say that the five handsome new streetcars and two flats which will soon be operated on schedule time, the lights, the building and machinery that operates the whole, is a sight worth witnessing. It will cost nothing to look at and but a nickel to ride.

In 1902 Dr. Clewell wrote, "The march of time does not take into consideration sentiment or historical associations; hence the old court-house began to appear strange and incongruous when compared with the more modern blocks of business houses going up about it, and it fell into decided disrepute when the increased business of a growing and populous county had to be transacted in its now too small court-room and its cramped offices." Therefore plans were made for a new structure which would better

171

accommodate the affairs of local government, as well as artistically reflect the prosperity of the new town. On 9 November 1895 the county commissioners—M. D. Bailey, R. S. Linville, E. W. Hauser—commenced hearings on the subject.

Unlike the first courthouse, which was built with conveniently available funds, the proposed second building had to be paid for with the taxpayers' money, and throughout the county there was opposition to the project. It was eventually decided to issue 110 bonds in the amount of $500 each to run five, ten, and fifteen years, thereby raising a total of $55,000. In February 1896 the old courthouse was torn down, offices were moved to surrounding buildings, and work was begun on the new structure, designed by Frank P. Milburn. The contract for construction was given to L. P. Hazen & Company. Just short of one year later, on 11 January 1897 the building was declared finished and ready for use. Adelaide Fries, twenty-six years old at the time, wrote the following description: "Standing on a slight eminence in the heart of a busy little city, this handsome structure of granite, buff brick and brownstone is as great a contrast to the modest building whose place it took as is the present county seat, with its widespread suburbs, to the three streets and handful of houses of the 'county town' of 1849, and both speak eloquently of the great strides that Forsyth County has made during the fifty years of its existence." Obviously when Dr. Fries wrote these words in 1898 there was no question in her mind that Forsyth was a county on the march. Particularly interesting is the contrast that she, the young historian, poses against Dr. Clewell the older historian, and his "sentiment or historical associations."

Jones Drug Store, Fourth and Church Streets

Zinzendorf Hotel, Fourth and Grace Streets, under construction, 1890–1891

Zinzendorf Hotel fire, 24 November 1892

*Zinzendorf
Hotel saloon,
Main Street*

Hotel Zinzendorf, Winston-Salem, N.C.

Zinzendorf Hotel, Main Street

Salem Fire Company's hose and ladder wagon

Winston Fire Company Number 1

CHAPTER 10

The New South, 1865–1900:

The Economic Order

IN THE YEARS FOLLOWING THE CIVIL WAR, Forsyth County experienced great economic changes. Although the agricultural scene did not change as drastically in Forsyth as elsewhere in North Carolina and the South, still tenant farming and sharecropping came and brought their attendant problems. The available labor force increased significantly and provided a stimulus for the industrial growth which was to be the most significant development during this period.

Industry in Forsyth was already producing several items before the war began. Within a few years after the war, industrial production had increased significantly and was ready to enter a period of growth and expansion. The rate of industrial development was far higher than in surrounding areas and perhaps surpassed any part of the former Confederate states.

The role industrialization played in the rise of the New South has been debated at length by historians and others. Whether changes in society paved the way for economic development or whether industrial growth made the changes in social structure possible may be a moot point. In both areas the changes in Forsyth County were drastic and would continue into the twentieth century.

Agricultural Stagnation

In the days immediately following the Civil War Forsyth County's agricultural system went through a period which might be called the Dark Ages as far as any real achievement was concerned. Bishop Edward Rondthaler related that as he came down from Pennsylvania in 1877 to assume the pastorate of the Salem congregation he inquired about the large bundles which lay on the railway platforms in Virginia and North Carolina. He learned that these bundles were dried blackberries which had been picked by local citizens to be shipped to northern states for food and other purposes. He said that such items constituted some of the most considerable shipments going out of this section.

The inhabitants of neither Winston, Salem, nor Forsyth were large slaveholders in the period prior to the war. As a result, the freeing of the slaves was not such a severe blow to the agricultural economy of the region as it was elsewhere. The number of farms in the county in 1869 was 1,272. Almost 55 percent of these farms averaged between twenty and one hundred acres, though 30 percent contained more than one hundred but less than five hundred acres. The average size of farms in Forsyth in that year was 163 1/2 acres as compared to a statewide average of 212 acres. Actual cash value was $1,173,202, slightly less than the $1,174,800 of 1860.

Forsyth's farms grew smaller and more numerous during Reconstruction. Most of the inhabitants of the rural areas were white and most of them owned their own farms. There were few tenants or sharecroppers in the area. This should have produced an efficient agricultural operation but it did not. By the end of the century the rural population of Forsyth County was barely feeding itself and its production of foodstuffs lagged far behind the growing needs of the Twin City. The farmers of the county were well-to-do when compared to the farmers of neighboring areas, but they were losing millions of dollars a year in possible sales and were concentrating on the production of tobacco and other nonfood crops. Scientific agriculture was not being practiced and much land was not being farmed.

The Labor Market

One of the factors contributing to the slow development of agriculture in Forsyth County was the increasing opportunity for employment in the industries developing in and around Winston-Salem. The small farm was not an efficient operation, even when privately owned, and many of Forsyth's farmers looked to city and industrial employment for a way out of their poverty-level existence. As the supply of workers in the county was absorbed by the expanding industries, neighboring counties sent their young men and then their young women to fill the need for workers to operate the machines.

Forsyth's small black population was supplemented by an influx of Negro workers and their families from eastern and southern North Carolina and from South Carolina. They came in the early years on foot or riding horses or mules. Later, with the coming of the railroads, they came by train, worked for a time, and returned home to bring their families and entire households by train or by wagon to Winston-Salem.

No industrial community can survive, much less prosper, without a ready labor supply. Since Forsyth's industry did prosper, it perforce had a good labor market upon which to draw. Only the general outlines of the origins of these workers is known. More research is needed to determine the full story of both the black and white working classes in Forsyth County.

Postwar Industry

Forsyth's industries by the end of the 1860s were producing commodities the combined value of which exceeded the 1860 figure by some 33 percent. On the following page is a chart showing the county's industrial values in 1869.

Of the two central towns, Winston and Salem, little change is noted from 1865 to 1872. Small businesses eventually reopened and new stores were built, though in general no significant increase in population occurred. Some years after the war ended, however, there were two events which catalyzed a growth almost unparalleled in the Piedmont: Major T. J. Brown opened the city's first tobacco warehouse in 1872, and the Northwestern North Carolina Railroad was completed from Greensboro to Winston in 1873.

INDUSTRY	NUMBER OF ESTABLISH- MENTS	EMPLOYEES	CAPITAL	WAGES	PRODUCTS
Boots & shoes	1	17	$15,000	$7,000	$47,200
Carriages and wagons	6	29	3,400	5,330	21,000
Cotton goods	1	29	29,000	5,013	33,139
Flour mills	5	19	18,800	3,566	65,443
Woolen goods	1	50	41,000	9,310	38,129
				TOTAL	$204,911

Tobacco is King in Forsyth

The census of 1870 indicates that Forsyth's industrial evaluation was up a full one-third from 1860. Such growth without outside investment was remarkable indeed considering the financial state of North Carolina. Even more remarkable is that the $200,000 worth of manufactured goods did not include tobacco products. No available figures indicate any tobacco manufactory in operation in the five years following the war; if there was such, quantities produced were too insignificant to be recorded.

Then in 1872, using wagons of the Nissen make, Hamilton Scales hauled in equipment, machinery, and supplies to the little town of Winston and established the first tobacco manufactory there. Scales's small plant—just fifty feet square and employing twenty persons—was the beginning of an industry that within two decades would include twenty-two factories employing some four thousand laborers and producing over ten million pounds of chewing tobacco, Forsyth's chief tobacco product before the twentieth century.

Of course the growth of Winston's tobacco trade would not have been possible without large quantities of natural leaf with which to work and a means of transporting the finished products to the outside world. Major T. J. Brown, a native of Caswell County, but then residing in Davie County, saw the strong need for a tobacco warehouse in western North Carolina. After thoroughly searching this area for a suitable location he decided upon Winston in January of 1872, and by February of that year, with G. W. Hinshaw, he "extemporized" Winston's pioneer warehouse from a stable on Liberty Street. Soon thereafter these two men were joined by Colonel J. W. Alspaugh, N. S. Wilson, Colonel A. B. Gorrell, Dr. J. F. Shaffner, and several others in erecting Brown's first true warehouse on Church Street. The next twelve years of operation produced sales in excess of $2 million. By 1884, Winston also boasted the Farmer's, Piedmont, and Oronoco warehouses.

With the foundations of Forsyth's tobacco manufacturing laid by Hamilton Scales, the leaf market opened by Major Brown, and the promise of a rail connection (which was officially opened in July 1873), other energetic young men became interested in the future of tobacco manufacturing in Winston.

In 1872, when P. H. Hanes moved from Davie County to Forsyth, there were three tobacco companies in operation here. Hanes, a farmer and veteran of the recent war, had engaged in tobacco growing and peddling from 1865 to 1870. He was subsequently employed by Dulin and Booe of Mocksville to sell tobacco. But Hanes was not satisfied with the prospect of a future with his Mocksville employers, so in 1872 he moved to Winston, and with his brother, John W. Hanes, and Major T. J. Brown he formed the firm of P. H. Hanes & Company. Plug tobacco was their product. When fire destroyed the first factory—a two-story structure, forty by sixty feet—operations continued in Greensboro until a new plant could be built. Major Brown later sold his interest in the business, and the two Hanes brothers, joined for a time by another brother, B. F., continued their manufacturing until 1900, when the company was sold to the R. J. Reynolds Tobacco Company.

Three years after the Hanes brothers came to Forsyth County,

R. J. Reynolds, another Confederate veteran, erected his first Winston factory, in 1875. The son of Hardin Reynolds, one of Virginia's largest slaveholding planters, Richard Joshua began his career working at the small tobacco-manufacturing operation on his homeplace in Patrick County, Virginia. Reynolds got practical experience as a tobacco peddler traveling throughout southwest Virginia, eastern Tennessee, and Kentucky. Not content with his educational background, which included schooling at home as well as a few years of study at Emory and Henry College, and desiring to sharpen his business acumen, R. J. entered Bryant and Stratton's Business College in Baltimore in 1874. After completion of the course of study he went back to his father's farm where he took charge of the tobacco factory. The decision to establish a new factory in Winston followed much consideration as to available locations and opportunities—at that time Richmond was the leading tobacco city. So, with a capital of less than $10,000, R. J. Reynolds started a business in 1875 that was destined to become the largest manufacturer of flat-goods plug tobacco in the world. Two brothers, William N. and Walter R. Reynolds, joined Richard, and in 1888 the business was incorporated as the R. J. Reynolds Tobacco Company.

The early success of the Hanes and Reynolds family enterprises in Winston served as a catalyst to other persons wishing to manufacture tobacco. By 1878 the pioneers had been joined by nineteen other tobacco concerns. Winston, now with a population of three thousand, boasted the establishments of Sublett, Bitting, & Whitaker; Heinaman & Vickey; Hairston, Grogan, & Co.; T. L. Vaughn; Brown, & Co.; C. Hamlen; R. D. Hay; D. R. Leake; J. L. King; R. Kerner; and John King, Jr. At Walkertown there was the operation of Sullivan and Osburn dating from at least 1872. E. M. C. Doub, O. J. Lehman, and C. R. Orrender were located at Bethania. These establishments, by 1879, employed 717 adults and 354 children, and manufactured goods valued at more than $500,000 annually. Forsyth had thus plunged into the era of small-scale tobacco manufacturing.

Cigars and smoking tobacco joined the plugs and twists by the mid-1880s. A druggist, Dr. V. O. Thompson, was the pioneer cigar manufacturer in Forsyth County. His factory was first located between Fifth and Sixth streets on Main and later at 4 West Fifth, with operations covering the decade preceding 1893. His principal brands were Rough and Ready, Bethabara, Wachovia, Round Know, and Red Elephant. Another cigar manufacturer, I. Leopold, came to Winston in 1885. His factory was the old Academy building located in the block between Third and Fourth streets. Leopold imported filler from Cuba and fancy wrappers were brought in from Connecticut. Only the most skilled workers were used by the I. Leopold Company, at the sign of a large human eye with Leopold beneath it; Leopold's principal brands were Twin City, Leopold's Havana, Pine Logs, Henry Clay, John C. Calhoun, Lone Indian, and Lone Squaw. Before the turn of the century two additional cigar manufacturers entered into business: Wiggins and Jones at 414 Liberty Street in 1892, and Liipfert and Jones at 248 Liberty Street in 1895. Sy Byerly and Chesley Hamlen both were manufacturing smoking tobacco by 1885.

The close of the 1880s witnessed even greater strides in manufactured tobacco in Forsyth County than in the first years of the same decade. Of the more than thirty factories in operation two-thirds were located in newly built four- and five-story structures and were equipped with the latest machinery, steam and hydraulic attachments, elevators, and other requisites for successful manufacturing. Shipping to all parts of the South as well as to Pennsylvania, Ohio, and other Northern states, Forsyth manufacturers conducted their businesses systematically and effectively under the regulation of a Board of Trade with A. B. Gorrell as president.

Following is a descriptive listing of Forsyth tobacco manufacturers in 1888.

FORSYTH COUNTY'S TOBACCO MANUFACTURERS IN 1888

NAME	YEAR FOUNDED	APPROXIMATE NUMBER OF EMPLOYEES IN 1888	PRINCIPAL BRANDS
S. A. Ogburn (successor to his father, James E. Ogburn)	c. 1850	60	———

FORSYTH COUNTY'S TOBACCO MANUFACTURERS IN 1888 *(cont.)*

NAME	YEAR FOUNDED	APPROXIMATE NUMBER OF EMPLOYEES IN 1888	PRINCIPAL BRANDS
Sullivan Factory	c. 1860	——	Sullivan's Best, Free and Easy
Beard & Roberts (J. W. Beard and J. C. Roberts)	1866	75	Beard's Favorite, Sweet Relief, Piedmont Beauty, Old Gold, Red Devon
H. Scales & Co. (T. J. and N. S. Wilson)	1870	——	Alex Stevens, Bob Toombs, Ida Bryan, Spanker, Rabbit Gum
T. F. Leak	c. 1871	——	Southern Belle, Wide Awake
P. H. Hanes & Co. (P. H. and J. W. Hanes)	1873	300	Missing Link, Man's Pride, Greek Slave
W. H. Leak & Co.	1873	60	Leak's Best, Cock of the Walk
T. L. Vaughn	c. 1873	——	Broad Ax, Big Auger, Old Rover
C. Hamlen & Sons	1874	——	Powhatten, Volunteer, Pride of Carolina, Acme, Belle of Winston, Sunny South
R. J. Reynolds & Co.	1875	275	National, R.J.R., World's Choice
Brown & Brother (Dr. W. L. and R. D. Brown)	1876	250	Waverly, Stonewall, Cottage Home, Peace and Plenty, Slap Jacks, Little Neck, Our Q
W. W. Wood & Co. (E. A. Ebert, Dr. H. T. Bahnson, and Mr. Wood)	1878	100	Maud Miller
Ogburn, Hill & Co. (C. J. Ogburn, W. P. Hill)	1878	100	O.H. & Co.'s Choice, Dixie, Gold Leaf, Winston Leader, Eagle, Minnie Ogburn, Drummer

FORSYTH COUNTY'S TOBACCO MANUFACTURERS IN 1888 *(cont.)*

NAME	YEAR FOUNDED	APPROXIMATE NUMBER OF EMPLOYEES IN 1888	PRINCIPAL BRANDS
Red Elephant Tobacco Works (H. H. Reynolds)	c. 1878	150	Reynolds' Best, Red Elephant, Honey Dew, Peabody, City Talk, Excelsior, Reaper, Twin City, Honey Comb
S. Byerly & Son	c. 1878	10	Eagle
Bynum & Cotton (Taylor Bynum and Rod Cotton)	1879	100	Wachovia, T. Bynum's Extra Fine, Silver Wave, Mary Lee, Red Man, Nashville Chew, Smart Alex
Bailey Brothers (M. D. and P. N. Bailey)	1880	150	Nantahala, Old Bob, Ellen Fisher, Planter's Choice, O.K., Clipper, Silver Moon, May Queen, Lilac
J. M. Greenfield (with T. E. Kerner)	1881	——	Success, Reform, New Era, Free Trade
R. L. Candler	1883	100	Bonny Jean, Rebel Boy, Red Seal, Derby, Pansy Blossom, Carnival, Casino, Veto, Jubilee, Blue Stockings
Blackburn, Dalton, & Co. (Samuel Blackburn)	1883	100	Cora Moore, Come Again, Ben Hill, Bob Vance
Reynolds Brothers	1883	100	Reynolds Brothers Best, Fruit of the Farm, Minnie Reynolds, Little Pearl, Old Rattler
Lockett, Vaughn & Co. (E. L. Lockett and L. A. Vaughn)	1884	175	Limited, Red Meat, Our Peach, Brown Jug
Hodgin Brothers & Lunn (J. M. and G. D. Hodgin, L. L. Lunn)	1884	100	——

FORSYTH COUNTY'S TOBACCO MANUFACTURERS IN 1888 *(cont.)*

NAME	YEAR FOUNDED	APPROXIMATE NUMBER OF EMPLOYEES IN 1888	PRINCIPAL BRANDS
Brown, Sapp & Co. (B. A. Brown and N. W. Sapp)	1884	60	Good News, Jenny Lind, Tube Rose, Knights of Labor
S. J. Nissen	1885	——	S&W, Buncombe, Slim Jim, Old Solid Comfort
J. A. Butner	1885	——	Plug, Twist, and Smoking
Model Tobacco Works (B. F. Hanes)	1886	150	Benjamin Franklin, Carolina's Favorite, Golden Chain, Our Senator
Lowrey & Stafford (W. A. Lowrey and E. J. Stafford)	c. 1886	——	——
Bitting & Hay (J. A. Bitting and W. S. Hay)	1887	——	Zebra
W. T. Gray & Co. (Capt. Gray and Watt Martin)	——	15	Off Duty, Gray's Winston
W. A. Whitaker	——	150	White Wings, Coronet, Zip, Golden Slipper, Twin-City, Empress, Dick Graves, Peach and Honey, Olive Branch, Otter of Roses

C. Vann Woodward wrote in *Origins of the New South* that an almost phenomenal growth of tobacco manufacturing in North Carolina was due to the "aggressiveness and bold tactics of a group of young southern entrepreneurs rising with the raw towns of Durham, Winston, and Reidsville" (P. H. Hanes was twenty-seven when he came to Winston, R. J. Reynolds, twenty-five). The capital invested in tobacco manufacturing in North Carolina rose from $1.5 million in 1870 to $7 million in 1880; the value of production jumped from $2.3 million to nearly $14 million in the same period. And, while Hugh T. Lefler suggests that by 1890 most of the smaller manufacturers "had been squeezed by the competition of the larger factories," Branson's *Business Directory* for 1896 lists forty-nine manufactories for Forsyth County, double the number ten years before.

George T. Brown and R. L. Williamson started the Brown & Williamson Tobacco Company in 1894 with thirty employees and an operating capital of $10,000. They purchased the factory and machinery of H. H. Reynolds.

Before the turn of the century the standard market value of tobacco in Forsyth County was maintained largely by its leaf dealers. Their regular attendance at the market with the manufacturers created a steady and permanent demand for all grades of leaf. The leading dealers were M. N. Williamson (1881), J. B. Moseley (c. 1888), A. A. Smith with R. J. Reynolds (1876), E. C. Edmunds and Captain Gilmer (1883), and F. G. Schaum (1883).

Perhaps the greatest catalyst in Winston-Salem's multibillion dollar cigarette industry was William Cyrus Briggs's cigarette-making machine. While living in Fayetteville, North Carolina, Briggs designed the machine. Later, at the suggestion of his friend, J. R. Williams, he took the idea to Winston. Arriving there in 1892, Briggs and Williams sought and soon obtained financial backing from Colonel Francis Fries, Dr. W. T. Brown, W. F. Shaffner, and Henry F. Shaffner. The Winston-Cigarette Machine Company built its first machines in J. A. Vance's machine shop at the corner of First and Chestnut streets. The first machines produced thirty cigarettes per minute but within a short time the production rate was doubled. Recognizing the need for a machine to package the cigarettes, Briggs secured capital and the interest of W. F. Shaffner in organizing the Briggs-Shaffner Co. for developing a packer. These two improvements in the manufacturing process increased production significantly and contributed much to the growth of Winston-Salem's cigarette industry.

Railroad Mania in the 1880s

Chester Davis, writing on the early history of transportation in Forsyth County in the 1966 *Journal and Sentinel* bicentennial edition, refers to the "railroad mania" that took over Forsyth's business and industrial interests in the 1880s. The town's leading businessmen—tobacconists such as R. J. and Will Reynolds, John and Pleasant H. Hanes, the Whitakers, and the leading textile manufacturers—devoted much time, energy, and money towards the acquisition of railroad connections throughout the 1870s and 1880s. The Board of Trade (now the Chamber of Commerce) gave priority to this end, and when county and municipal taxes were not available to finance surveys, if a particular railroad were interested in a Winston connection these industrialists took on the costs themselves.

As previously mentioned, the first rail connection, that of the Northwestern North Carolina Railroad (now the Southern Railroad) reached Forsyth County in 1873. This particular route was extended westward to North Wilkesboro in the decade preceding the turn of the century. Another link, the Roanoke and Southern (now the Norfolk and Western) which, like the Northwestern, was a spur line, was completed in 1889, thus connecting Winston with the all-important markets in western Virginia. The Salem *Memorabilia* for 1888, written by Bishop Edward Rondthaler, gives a fairly sensitive view of the feeling of the times:

What has been the greatest importance to Winston and Salem from the material point of view has been the progress made toward completer railroad communication with the rest of the world. . . . Many localities have been specially favored in this respect. Railroads have come to them without their asking. With us, however, exactly the opposite has been the case. Our citizens have been obliged to work and contribute energetically for every inch of advantage to be secured. Last year we were still confronted with the prospect of being a little town at the end of a little branch road, and the whole business outlook was clouded and discouraged by this fact. The enterprise and public spirit of some of our citizens, supported by the subscription of the township, have materially changed this outlook.

Indeed, efforts to secure rail connections to this area were not without difficulty. Occasional lack of popular support, combined with the broader opening of the Danville and Henry County, Virginia, areas by new rail connections, made the task seem impossible to interested parties in Forsyth. The Winston tobacco manufacturers, against what Nannie M. Tilley in *The Bright-Tobacco Industry, 1860–1929*, called "great odds," began their campaign with renewed vigor during the 1880s. It appeared that the two important Virginia cities—Danville and Richmond— would retain control of the industry, for Winston-Salem's want of rail ties. Public pique was aroused by town leaders, and in the "remarkable fight" (again, quoting Miss Tilley) that ensued, Forsyth County citizens voted bonds freely and "tobacco manufacturers contributed without stint." Many local roads, most notably a line that connected the Cape Fear and Yadkin with Walnut Cove, sprang up during this time.

Thus in the years 1885–92, the principal cities in Forsyth, Winston and Salem, were able to achieve their end through the cooperation of citizenry and business leadership, an alliance that exists to this day. Rail connections acquired by means of this teamwork were of extreme importance to the twin cities, and in turn to the county. Miss Tilley wrote, "The history of Winston as an important manufacturing center actually dates from the completion of the Roanoke line in 1889. By securing this road Winston interests not only destroyed Danville's threat as a rival in the manufacturing of tobacco but also drew the not inconsiderable manufacturing interests of Martinsville into their orbit."

A Tour of Winston, 1875

When Henry Foltz, a slender young boy, stopped his one-horse wagon in front of the Merchants Hotel in Winston in November 1875, he seemed thoroughly impressed with what surrounded him. Winston at that time was on the verge of an expansion that is still going on. Paraphrasing Foltz's account, *Winston, Fifty Years Ago* (1925, privately printed), provides a brief tour of the town as it appeared at that time.

As one traveled from the hotel east on the north side of First Street (then the line between Winston and Salem) to a point just beyond what is now Church Street, he came first to Sylvester Miller's new brick home. Continuing along for another block he then passed the woodworking plant of the Miller brothers, who were both contractors. Next one came to the little frame station of the Richmond and Danville Railroad, which served as passenger, freight, and baggage depot, and express and telegraph office. Messrs. Polack and Brown were attendants at the station.

Back on the east side of Main Street one found the home of D. H. Starbuck, then considered the finest residence in Winston. The only other house on this block was that of Mr. Harrison Pitts; his was a frame dwelling that faced Second Street. A little futher, past Church Street, was Ed Spach's blacksmith shop. Then, on the east side of Chestnut Street was Mr. R. J. Reynolds' first tobacco plant.

Beyond Chestnut Street, on the south side of Second Street, cottages that belonged to J. W. and D. S. Reid were found. These men owned a store that was located on the corner of Second and Depot streets. Across from the Reids, on the north side of Second Street, was Mr. Dunnagan's small frame house. It was this Mr. Dunnagan who was told that Winston was *the* place to live: ". . . times were so prosperous that roast pigs were running around the streets with a knife and fork sticking in their backs, and a placard attached, inviting the hungry to come and eat." On the basis of this description Dunnagan had moved to Winston, but later bemoaned the fact that he could not find the roast pigs!

Now, proceeding westward on the north side of Second, one noted the partially constructed Baptist church that would open its doors in 1876. On the east side of Church Street, between Second and Third, was George Beck's livery stable. The rest of Winston from First to Third and east of Church was dense woods, as was the southern part of the block north of Second and between Main and Church streets. This latter section was, at that time, the town campground. It was often filled at night with covered wagons, horses, men, and dogs; wood fires burned brightly while the music of fiddles and banjos were heard late into the night.

To the north was J. E. Gilmer's store, and above it, the office and pressrooms of Winston's *Western Sentinel*. Next, and to the north was the red brick, eight-room Merchants Hotel with its four-story frame addition. The hotel had on its first floor an office, two private rooms, a kitchen, and a large dining room in which the tables extended all the way across the room. There were twenty-four small guest rooms in the frame addition: each had a wood-burning stove and kerosene lamps; water was brought in from a well in the back of the hotel.

Pfohl and Stockton's first general store was beyond the hotel and extended to Third Street. The building was wooden and rambling and very typical of the urban architecture of the day. Two years later these merchants were to erect the "first real store building in Winston," which was built under the influence of the Centennial Exposition in Philadelphia. The first telephone line in Winston was a waxed string with tomato cans at either end—one was located at Pfohl and Stockton's, and the other at J. E. Mickey's store three blocks away. In 1879 the first real telephone (of Mr. Bell's design) was installed in this store and ran to the depot.

Going on eastward down Third Street, and beyond Church Street, were several "prize houses" where Winston leaf tobacco dealers packed their hogsheads with tobacco and shipped them out. On the east side of Chestnut, near Third and below the prize house was Mr. P. H. Hanes's first factory. When this building caught fire the next year the original Salem fire engine was employed in containing the fire.

As one proceeded to the northeast corner of Church and Third he came to Winston's first tobacco sales warehouse which extended along the east side of Church Street from Third to Fourth. Major Brown was the proprietor and Mr. James A. Gray the bookkeeper.

Back at the corner of Main and Third streets was "Crosslands," a two-story frame building that contained the business of John Campbell and Nath Stockton. Next came the haberdashery of Sol and Charley Rosenthal. Beside the Rosenthals' was "Tise Hall" which housed a small furniture store on the street level and beside that the store of a Mr. Cohen. Below Cohen and to the north was the Winston post office. At the corner of Main and Fourth was the dwelling-blacksmith-wagon shop of Simeon White. Woods extended from there on.

Next across Fifth Street (on the site of the Reynolds Building) was the home of Colonel Joe Masten, and further to the north, the dwellings of O. C. Smith (then Nels Cook) and on the corner, William Beard. The only house between Sixth and Seventh at that time was that of Alex Gates, a black barber.

As one returned to First Street and began down the west side of Main Street he came to the homes of Henry Barrow and Levine Hine. Judge T. J. Wilson's two-story brick dwelling was situated beside Mr. Hine. Below Wilson was another two-story brick residence, that of James A. Gray, and beyond it, Robert Gray's paling-fence-surrounded garden.

At the corner of Main and Third was a brick store building owned by Robert Gray; this structure was rented to S. E. Allen in 1876 for Winston's first hardware store. Adjoining this building and to the west was the drugstore of Gray and Martin. In the middle of the block was the Gray family homestead. On the corner, next to Liberty Street, was a frame building soon to be occupied by Joe Jacob's clothing business.

Now to the courthouse, which was surrounded by a dilapidated paling fence whose gates were always open. Through these gates at night came numerous animals—cattle, hogs, and sheep. The sheep spent their night under the south portico of the building.

The Miller family home was located on the north side of Fourth Street, next to Main, and beside it, Chesley Hamlen, and the "old Hay building" operated by the Norwoods as a boardinghouse. Another store, that of Mr. Hall, was located next to Liberty Street.

As one proceeded north back to Main Street, and walked on the west side of the street, he came to the small frame dwelling occupied by a Mrs. Kester and her two sons. Then, between Fifth and Sixth streets there were several tenant houses. Jacob Tise's blacksmith and wagon shop was then encountered on Seventh Street; his family lived on the southeast corner of Liberty and Main.

Returning to First Street—at the corner of Salt (now Liberty) Street—and turning northward, there were no houses facing the east side of Liberty until one reached the county jail which was just north of Wall and Huske's store. The jail was two stories high, constructed of brick, and boasting a large basement. Joe Masten, the jailor, and his family lived on the first floor while the prisoners were kept on the second. On beyond the jail was the wagon and blacksmith shop of Al Bevel, and on the corner, next to Fifth Street, was a two-story frame building, the first floor of which was occupied by a tailor and a magistrate, and the upper by Walter Johnson's family.

Four private homes were seen as one passed the northeast corner of Fifth and Liberty streets. First, on the corner, was Dr. V. O. Thompson's ample brick dwelling, and beyond that, the home of Mrs. Emily Webb. Beyond Mrs. Webb was William Nelson, and beyond him, Webster Nading. Mrs. Wheeler, a widow, lived on the corner lot in a brick dwelling.

As one proceeded beyond Sixth Street he did not encounter any buildings until he came to the home of T. T. Best, a local magistrate. Next, on the corner of Liberty and Seventh, was the dwelling of J. Madison Grogan, and on the northeast corner, John H. Masten's brick residence.

Returning again to First Street, on the west side and traveling north, one came to the "free schoolhouse" which was used as a union Sunday school, with John Chitty as superintendant. Then, still going north, was J. Calvin Miller's home. On the northwest corner of Liberty and Second, one found two small houses that belonged to a Mrs. Allen. After the second of these two was passed the homes of Christian Reed and of Dietrich Tavis were seen. At the corner of Third Street was the Wilson Hotel with the little offices of a magistrate attached to the southeast corner; this hotel was a most popular resort for card players. On Liberty Street, beyond the hotel, and to the south, was the home of a contractor, another Mr. Tavis.

Next, crossing Third Street, was M. H. Langfeld's store which was the first to feature ladies' goods in the town; it was appropriately called the "Temple of Fashion." To the north as one proceeded on were the stores of S. D. Franklin (clothing) and V. O. Thompson (drugs). On the corner of Fourth Street was the two-story frame building which housed the general store of Hodgin and Sullivan. On across Fourth Street, where the O'Hanlon Building now stands, was another two-story frame store which was to be occupied by Winston's first shoe business, in 1876, that of W. S. Martin. Next was the "Holland House," a frame dwelling, and near the corner of Fifth Street, the home of Mr. Sussdorf.

Across Fifth Street, in the area now occupied by Centenary Methodist Church, was its small brick predecessor and three flanking buildings. On down, and beyond Sixth Street, was Samuel Farabee's blacksmith and wagon shop, and also his dwelling. Then came the "old Miller house" and two more dwellings. On the corner of Seventh was the Methodist Protestant church—a small frame building—and in the next block, near Eighth Street, was the Reverend John Henry White's home, store, and shoeshop. On the north side of Eighth Street were the dwellings of Melvina White, Alex Rights, and Henry Holder; on Trade Street, a short distance west, was Granville Blackburn's home.

Now from Eighth Street, east and north along Liberty (then Germanton Road) were the homes of the Reverend Howard Pegram, Dr. Bynum, a Mr. Boner, Colonel John White, Zan White, Mr. Nading and others. Farther up, in what was then called "Blumtown," between Thirteenth and Fourteenth streets, was the residence of Sanford Byerly.

Now, back to First Street again, a few houses are noted on Elm between Second and Fourth, and some on Cherry Street, but the only residents recalled were Stephen Hodgin and William Miller. Then, on the site of the Nissen [First Union] Building was a small frame Presbyterian church.

From Fourth Street along Trade, and traveling north, were the original Piedmont Warehouse, a two-story frame boardinghouse, an old barn, and a few small tenant houses on the west side of the road. Back to the block between Elm, Cherry, Third, and Fourth was the "Male Academy," the only building in the entire block. Now, on Cherry, one found the home of the Reverend W. W. Albea and several other residences north of Fourth. West of Cherry were but a few scattered homes, as no street had been opened up, except Fourth, which was then known as Shallowford Road. On the east side of Cherry Street, between Fourth and Fifth, the first tobacco factory of the Brown brothers was being built, while in the next block, to the north, was Major Ham Scales' factory, and at the corner of Sixth and Cherry the factory of Ogburn, Hill, and Company. From here we come back to the north side of First Street and the beginning point of our tour.

Wagonmaking after the War

Nannie M. Tilley suggested that Nissen wagons had been used in great numbers by the Confederate Army; more than half of Nissen's uncollected accounts at the time of his death originated during the war and were considered uncollectable. The wagon business, like all businesses in the county and state, suffered for want of raw materials and capital.

The main chance for the wagonmaker in the years following the war, however, was the undertaking chosen by many of the South's young entrepreneurs—tobacco manufacturing. Again, as Miss Tilley wrote in *The Bright-Tobacco Industry, 1860–1929*, "so essential were the Nissen wagons in marketing tobacco that they have been deemed a decisive factor in the development of the tobacco industry through the entire Piedmont area." Thus a successful relationship was established between the wagonmakers and the tobacco manufacturers and peddlers.

In 1870, five years after the end of the war, Nissen sold 250 wagons—four times more than were sold twenty years before. Twenty-four employees, twelve in the wagon shop and twelve in his blacksmith shop, accounted for almost 50 percent of the county's wagon industry operatives, producing 71 percent of the county's total annual production in that year.

Nissen's prime competitor in a field of six was the Spach

Wagon Works. Spach employed but two operatives who turned out an average of twenty wagons annually. Even this firm was dependent on Nissen's blacksmiths for its hardware. At this time the typical Spach wagon cost $100 and the Nissen $120.

By the mid-1870s the Nissen Wagon Works at Waughtown was spread over a six-hundred-acre tract of land. Business was booming and Nissen's inventory reflected this fact: on hand were "10,000 feet of lumber, 700 spokes, felloes, hubs, and wheels enough for 125 wagons." His stock in early 1874 included one four-horse wagon, seven two-horse wagons, one sulky, one ox wagon, and a two-horse carriage. But in December of that year, at the height of his career, old John Philip Nissen died of pneumonia. According to the Salem *People's Press*, his business was the "sustenance" of one hundred people. His sons, George and Will, capably assumed supervision of the wagon works and within two years they had sold 427 wagons at an average cost of $93 each. A profit of nearly $13,000 was realized. It is estimated that during the course of the first four decades of operation on Waughtown Hill the Nissens produced and sold more than five thousand wagons.

Woolens and Cottons

The F. & H. Fries cotton and wool manufactories had experienced hard times during the war, though they managed to stay open throughout the four-year struggle. Francis Fries, the company's founder, died in 1863, but his brother, Henry W. Fries, continued the operation. Francis Fries's sons joined the family business later; they were John W., Col. Francis H., and Henry E. Fries. Fortunately the textile industry had favorable publicity from both press and pulpit, and was able to continue production.

By 1870 the Fries family operation was manufacturing products valued at over $70,000 annually, just $16,000 under 1860 figures. The next ten years witnessed even greater profits, and in 1880 cotton goods realized $23,000 and woolens an all-time high of $150,000.

Arista Mills was built in 1880 for the cotton manufacturing operations of F. & H. Fries. A power plant was installed in Arista Mills, and for the first time in the history of manufacturing in the South, electric lights were used in a cotton mill.

The woolen business of F. & H. Fries operated under the name of Salem Woolen Mill for the few remaining years of its existence. In 1884 the woolen mill was running 760 spindles. A daily consumption of 700 pounds of raw material produced an average of 905 yards of cloth. One hundred operatives were earning about $16.25 each per month. At the new Arista Cotton Mills, by 1884, the steam-run 160-horsepower engine was powering 3,394 spindles and 102 looms. With a daily consumption of 2,300 pounds, Arista produced each day an average of 5,416 yards of sheeting and 300 to 500 pounds of additional yarns.

Until the turn of the century, the woolen mill held its own. Arista Mills, on the other hand, increased the number of spindles to 45,000 and its looms to 180. An increased daily consumption of 3,300 pounds of raw material was yielding 15,000 yards of sheeting in the years before the turn of the century. Remarkably, the expansion of the local textile industry was accomplished without outside financial assistance.

Forsyth County and the New South

Historians may debate over the nature and even the existence of the New South, but it is certain that Forsyth County turned increasingly to industry during the last quarter of the nineteenth century. Newcomers like Hanes and Reynolds joined Moravians Fries, Nissen, Spach, and others to produce a remarkable industrial growth. The industrialists attracted railroads, workers, and smaller competitors, and the economy flourished.

The sound economic base of the Moravian settlement, already more than one hundred years old, was probably responsible for the fact that most of Forsyth's economic development came without the importation of capital from outside the region. Most of the industries started small and grew from the reinvestment of their own resources. The emergence of several large fortunes by the turn of the century was proof not only of the favorable business atmosphere of the time and place but also of the financial acumen of many of Forsyth's early industrialists.

CHAPTER 11

The Twentieth Century, the First Fifty Years:
The Social Order

THE FOUNDING AND DEVELOPMENT OF SALEM came in the eighteenth century. The nineteenth century saw the founding and development of Winston. The first half of the twentieth century was to see the consolidation and development of Winston-Salem.

Small-Town Winston, 1900 to Consolidation

From 14 May 1900 to 12 May 1913 when by popular vote Winston ceased to be a separate municipality and through consolidation with Salem became Winston-Salem, Winston had only two mayors: O. B. Eaton and Rufus I. Dalton. In 1900 Eaton was elected for a term of two years; since, however, in 1902 Winston had no election (in compliance with state law that no municipal election could be held in the same year as the general state election), he was retained in office an additional year. Elected again in 1903, Eaton stayed in office until 1910. The 1911 municipal vote resulted in the election of Rufus I. Dalton as mayor. Serving with Mayor Dalton was the last official board of small-town Winston: Thomas Maslin, J. Walter Dalton, Garland E. Webb, J. R. Watkins, C. L. Bagby, and N. D. Dowdy.

Winston's last thirteen years witnessed the expansion of the town in many directions. Building operations were extensive and industry became more diversified. East Winston was joined to the rest of the city by streetcars; the Children's Home (at the site of the old Davis Military School) was established; the Associated Charities was organized, as was the YWCA, and the YMCA moved to new quarters. Winston's school system was expanded, especially in the erection of a separate building for the high school—the Cherry Street High School. A new city hall was erected at a cost of $75,000, and the agitation for a public library was brought to a successful conclusion in the building of the Carnegie Library on Cherry Street.

The movement for a public library began in 1903 when, through the efforts of J. C. Buxton, chairman of the City School Board, Andrew Carnegie agreed to donate to the city of Winston the sum of $25,000 for the erection of a building upon the condition that the city would furnish a lot and make an annual appropriation of not less than $2,500 for the maintenance of the institution.

Buxton acquainted the citizens with Mr. Carnegie's proposition at a mass meeting in February 1903. Time and again he appeared before the Board of Aldermen concerning the matter; he also discussed it with the commissioners of Salem. It was not until the October meeting of the Board of Aldermen, however, that official steps were taken in the matter through the appointment of a special committee to meet with a like committee from Salem. On 21 December 1903 the Winston Board of Aldermen, after an earnest appeal from Mr. Buxton, resolved "that an annual appropriation of $1,500 is hereby made for the purpose of maintaining and supporting [a] . . . library; the sum to be available when the library building is completed and turned over to the City." A reduced gift in the amount of $15,000 was forthcoming from Carnegie.

A building committee, after eliminating several suggested sites because of their distance from certain parts of the town, chose a location in the heart of Winston, at the corner of Third and Cherry. This place was accessible by foot or by streetcar to all sections of the town. In March 1904 the Board of Aldermen formally authorized the purchase of James A. Gray's lots at Third and Cherry for $2,000. Buxton's committee then appointed a group of ladies to select books for the new library and to make all preparations for the opening of the institution. Mrs. Mary Prather was asked to serve as librarian.

On 14 February 1906 the Carnegie Library was formally opened. W. A. Whitaker, who earlier had been instrumental in founding the old West End School and its fine library (which was transferred to the Carnegie Library as the nucleus of its collection) checked out the first book.

The greatest catastrophe which befell Winston in the first half of the twentieth century was the bursting of the large brick-and-cement city reservoir at the north end of Trade Street. The entire northern wall gave way unexpectedly at five o'clock on the morning of 3 November 1904. The surging torrent of 180,000 gallons of water rushed east and then north following the ravine to Belo's Pond. Eight houses were swept away; the personal effects of the families living in them were scattered everywhere. Nine persons were killed and numbers more seriously injured.

Just ten days before the bursting of the reservoir Winston's new water plant was completed and water pumped into the new standpipe. The passing of municipal bonds in January 1904 had made this construction possible.

Among the people living near the reservoir who miraculously escaped death were a black man and his wife; they were carried safely in their bed on the crest of the flood to the bottomland around Belo's Pond. A boy whose mother was crushed to death in the collapse of the wall was saved because the bed on which he was sleeping was in an upper room under the roof, where the two sides came together in a peak. When large stones hit the house, the low roof dropped over the bed, permitting the sleeping boy to continue his nap in safety.

Increasing population and growing needs brought about organized philanthropic efforts at the beginning of the twentieth century; however, philanthropy and Christian aid for victims of tragedies such as the bursting of the reservoir had always been local and disorganized. The Associated Charities of Winston, an association supported by voluntary gifts, was organized by a group of Winston women on 8 March 1905. Primarily through the untiring efforts of Mrs. R. D. Moseley and her Whatsoever Circle of King's Daughters, the new association received its momentum, and during the early years of the 1900s did a great and lasting work among the poor and underprivileged of the community. The first officers were Mrs. Henry L. Riggins, president; Mrs. D. Rich, vice-president; Mrs. James K. Norfleet, second vice-president; Mrs. J. M. Rogers, third vice-president; and Miss Annie Grogan, secretary, at a monthly salary of $20. It was thought best to have a businessman handle the financial side, so J. F. Griffith was asked to serve as treasurer.

The sum of $1,200 was set for the first year's goal. A committee headed by Mrs. James Norfleet, Mrs. R. D. Moseley, and Mrs. Henry Foltz made a house-to-house canvass with the result that by 30 May the sum of $1,080.60 had been pledged. The first annual report shows that a total of $1,170.76 was subscribed and in addition that $1,094.11 in cash had been collected, as well as $20 in wood and merchandise.

The early minutes of Associated Charities show how nobly this small group of women bearing the burden of the town's down-and-outs tried to solve the questions of segregation and care of consumptives, street begging, employment of children under the age of twelve in factories, and the perennial problem of unemployment.

The beginnings of Winston's YMCA are rooted in the late nineteenth century, though its period of greatest development came in the early 1900s.

With 129 charter members the YMCA was organized on 7 October 1888 in the annex of the old Centenary Church. Captain R. B. Crawford and W. A. Blair served respectively as acting chairman and secretary pro tem. Among the Y's first members were the Reverend E. P. Davis, Major Samuel H. Smith, Frank A. Coleman, Dr. W. J. Conrad, Rufus Spaugh, the Reverend W. E. Swaim, Eugene E. Gray, W. T. Carter, E. A. Ebert, J. C. Buxton, R. B. Glenn, and B. F. Norman.

For $25 per month (later reduced to $20) suitable quarters were obtained in the upper story of the Jacobs Building at Main and Third. E. L. Harris, a man with experience in Y work in other cities, was employed as general secretary. Within a few years a Woman's Auxiliary, consisting of representatives of different church groups, and the Boys Department were organized on a budget of $2,500.

The early membership fee was $2.00, and for an additional $2.00 the member had the use of the one small bathtub—soap and towels thrown in.

In 1897 the Association moved its quarters to Brown's Opera House, Main and Fourth. Educational classes were added to the work of the Y; and a gymnasium opened with lockers, bath, and dressing rooms. Nine years later, in 1906, under the leadership of Robert C. Norfleet, president of the Y at that time, the sum of $55,000 was subscribed in a whirlwind campaign of fifteen days for a building to be erected on the corner of Fourth and Cherry (present site of the First Union National Bank Building).

Of such public interest was this campaign for a new Y that the completion of the fund was announced in a very unusual manner. By special permission of the Board of Aldermen, at 8:15, on 7 December 1906 the fire alarm sounded fifty times, one stroke for every thousand dollars raised. In 1908 a handsome four-story stone building of colonial design was opened and occupied by members of the Winston-Salem YMCA.

On 30 January 1908 the YWCA of Winston-Salem was organized in the Presbyterian Church under the direction of Miss Anna Castle of the National YWCA Board. Mrs. E. B. Jones, who was entertaining Miss Castle in her home, and herself greatly interested in the welfare of young business girls, was elected first president of the Y.

While this was the formal organization of the local association along national lines, for two or more years a small group of young businesswomen sponsored by various groups of churchwomen had been carrying on a Business Woman's Club, an idea suggested by Miss Ada Snow. Miss Flora Leak, who knew personally almost every business girl in the small community of the early 1900s, and her mother, Mrs. Mattie Leak, became warm friends of Miss Snow. One evening around the supper table these three friends and a new one, Miss Caroline Hawkins, assistant to the pastor of the First Presbyterian Church, began to make plans for a club where working girls living in boardinghouses might spend their free hours.

With Miss Hawkins as head, the movement was soon launched. J. M. Rogers, one of the elders of First Presbyterian, donated the use of room over his hardware store and other merchants contributed heavy curtains to divide the big room into assembly, tiny restroom, and kitchenette. Interested women gave furnishings for the rooms, including a piano.

On the very evening Miss Castle was organizing a real YWCA, the Brown-Rogers store caught fire and the club rooms of the pioneer Y were completely destroyed by fire and water. New quarters were secured in a large room on the second floor of Gilmer Brothers on South Main Street. It was converted from a store room by means of beaverboard partitions into an association room (with secretary's office in one corner), a reading room, and a kitchen. Miss Anna Shaw of Pittsburgh, Pennsylvania, a trained Y official, was employed as secretary. In these rooms the association was housed until the late Mrs. R. J. Reynolds made possible a handsome and pleasant Y on First and Church Streets, which served until 1942.

A survey of Winston during the last decade of her history as a separate municipality shows the business life of the town, then with a population of some seventeen thousand persons, center-ing about the Courthouse Square, some distance down to the Union Depot, up Liberty a few blocks, and down Main to Second. Cherry Street south from Fourth, upper Liberty, Fourth and Fifth streets west from Cherry were residential sections, with tree-lined sidewalks, broad front yards, and back-yard vegetable gardens.

There were no sprawling apartment houses, no skyscrapers. The tallest, most pretentious buildings were the seven-story Wachovia Bank and Trust Company on Third and Main; the Masonic Temple, erected in 1906, on Fourth and Trade; the three-story First National Bank Building on Liberty, erected in 1890; the Masten building, Fourth and Main, erected in 1910; the Jones Building, North Liberty just north of Fifth Street, erected in 1900; and the three-story O'Hanlon Building, which was destroyed by fire after 1913 and replaced by the structure that stands there today.

The Post Office, on its Fifth Street site but then much smaller, had a working force of forty at that time. There were fourteen letter carriers and four substitute carriers; ten railway mail clerks who worked in and out of the town were paid through the local office.

The Elks Auditorium—later the State Theater at Fifth and Liberty—with a seating capacity of twenty-three hundred persons was the municipal auditorium for recreational and cultural purposes. Moving-picture theaters included the Amuzu, the Liberty, and the Rex for blacks.

Few farmers used automobiles in bringing tobacco to town. During great tobacco breaks, covered wagons crowded Trade Street, Main near Brown's Warehouse, and Fifth as far west as Spruce or even Poplar. Hundreds of farmers would sleep on the floors of the warehouses or camp out in their parked wagons, cooking their supper and breakfast by the light of the lanterns hung on at the backs of their wagons.

During the years preceding consolidation the women of Winston were, through their Women's Improvement League, waging a victorious campaign for the beautifying and upkeep of public grounds and buildings and the enforcement of sanitary measures in keeping the town clean. Not only were women aware of their responsibilities as citizens, but they realized that the town had need of more thorough official oversight of streets and public property. Among the measures urged by the Women's Improvement League were the regular flushing of the paved streets; the sweeping and sprinkling of the unpaved streets; the use of tin garbage cans in place of old barrels and boxes; the enforcement of the law against "using as enlarged cuspidors" the sidewalks and public buildings such as the Post Office and the Union Railroad Station; and the beautifying and improvement of all the city schoolgrounds, especially those of the West End School, which were about to wash away.

The minutes of the Board of Aldermen show that at the turn of the century the old question of allowing citizens to raise hogs on their town lots was still a matter of concern to the town authorities. Indeed the question of "Hogs" or "No Hogs" was made an issue in certain sections of Winston in the matter of consolidation with Salem.

The town records show that, in the months preceding the

election on consolidation, first one large group of citizens and then another group would present petitions asking to be allowed to continue raising hogs; an equally large group of property-owners would promptly petition against hog-raising. It was a delicate matter for the aldermen to decide, especially when it became evident that the vote for consolidation would be affected by the decision they made. Finally, on the evening of 7 March 1913 the aldermen cast their votes, with as many for as against. The mayor broke the tie, casting his vote for the negative. Thus from that time on it seemed the only hogs that would be found on the streets of Winston were those with knives stuck in their backs and signs reading "Eat Me" around their necks.

Legal consolidation of the Twin Cities came in 1913. Excerpts from the minutes of the Winston Board of Aldermen trace the actual course of events:

February 1, 1913. Whereas an Act of the General Assembly of North Carolina was duly passed and ratified the 27th day of January 1913 consolidating as one municipality the City of Winston and the Town of Salem in the name of the City of Winston-Salem, in accordance with the provisions contained in said Act, providing that the same should be ratified by the voters of the City of Winston in an election to be held in the City of Winston and by the voters of the Town of Salem in an election to be held in the Town of Salem.

Whereas if a majority of the votes cast in each of said elections should be in favor of the said consolidation as set forth in said Act of the General Assembly,

Be it ordained: that . . . an election shall be held in the three wards of the City of Winston on Tuesday the 18th day of March 1913 . . . that the Mayor shall give proper and legal notice of the time and place of said election by publishing in some newspaper published in the City of Winston for at least 30 days prior to the date of said election.

May 18, 1913. The returns of the election on Consolidation held March 18, 1913 having been presented, they were approved. The votes cast were: First Ward 350 For, 56 Against, total 406; Second Ward 210 For, 96 Against, total 306; Third Ward 204 For, 108 Against, total 312.

On 6 May 1913 the election of the official board for the municipality of the City of Winston-Salem was held, and the following men were elected: mayor, O. B. Eaton; aldermen, First

Ward, E. D. Vaughn, C. M. Cain; Second Ward, G. E. Webb, P. S. Bailey; Third Ward, N. D. Dowdy, G. W. Edwards; Salem Ward, H. F. Shaffner and Fred A. Fogle.

On 12 May 1913 the new board met in the council chamber of the City Hall at 8:30 P.M. and took the oath of office.

Physical Expansion of Winston-Salem

Winston-Salem's population growth from 1913 to 1920 was phenomenal. The slogan of civic leaders was "50–15," or 50,000 inhabitants by 1915. The 1920 census listed Winston-Salem's population as 48,375, representing a growth of 113 percent since 1910. Winston-Salem reigned until the 1930 census as the largest city in the state. With this population expansion the movement to the suburbs began.

Following the major trend of suburban developments in the United States, Winston-Salem built westward, and most of its suburbs were located on elevations overlooking the city. Sporadic individual home-building began early in Southside, the area south of Salem Creek and including Waughtown on the east. The Sunnyside Land Company opened up to development large areas of Southside in 1890. With paved streets, electricity, and streetcars came the people.

The eastern part of Southside was incorporated in 1891 as the town of Waughtown. Five years later, when residents refused to tax themselves enough to run the place, corporation was dissolved. The Winston-Salem Southbound Railroad was cut through Southside in 1911, dividing Waughtown from the area known as Sunnyside. Industry followed the railroad and Southside's heyday as a residential area was over. People were moving to Ardmore.

Ardmore, the namesake of a well-known Philadelphia suburb, was started in 1914 to provide for citizens overflowing the city limits. For twenty-two years, Ardmore maintained a record of one new home a week. Today the section is a large, well-developed part of the city. It has its own elementary school and its own post office, as well as its own churches. The Ardmore Methodist Church was built in 1924, followed by the Ardmore Baptist, Moravian, and Congregational Christian churches.

Originally West End was to become a resort area, or such was the intention of a number of influential Winstonians in the late 1880s. The West End Land Company was formed in 1890, with J. L. Ludlow as chief engineer. First came West End Boulevard; then came the 300-foot-long, three-story Zinzendorf Hotel (at the top of the hill west of the intersection of West Fourth Street with Glade), and along with it the inevitable streetcar line. When the Zinzendorf burned on Thanksgiving Day 1892, the builders' interests turned to residences, and for the next twenty years, West End was "the most important single residential area in North Carolina."

Other developments were also beginning west of the city. Reynolda Village began to develop around Reynolda House about 1915. The Granville section was started in 1915; a Crafton Heights section and a Melrose section were started adjoining Ardmore. In 1919 West Highlands was begun, followed by Buena Vista and later Westover, Westview, Reynolda Park, and finally the Country Club Estates in 1927. Building restrictions in these later areas confined them to larger houses, and today they contain many beautiful homes.

To the north, Montview was started in 1920 and was followed by Forest Hills and Whiteview. Bon Air, clinging to the side of a hill north of town, was begun in 1923. Anderleigh in 1928 and Konnoak Hills in 1929 were developed south of town. Alta Vista, a restricted suburb exclusively for Negroes, was begun in 1929. It was the first restricted Negro suburb in the South.

Meanwhile, the city was not unmindful of these new sections rapidly filling with potential citizens outside of the corporate limits, and Winston-Salem began gulping the new suburbs into its limits in huge bites. About 1919, the city limits were extended to include a part of Ardmore and Crafton Heights; in 1923, large sections of Ardmore and Crafton Heights, West Highlands, Waughtown, South Salem, and the Kimberly Park and Fourteenth Street School areas were annexed. In 1925 some scattered outlying sections were added, in 1926 Buena Vista and some more of Ardmore, and in 1927 another Ardmore section and Yountztown.

Following the development of the suburbs in the 1920s came

the apartment-house growth. The William and Mary Apartments, built in 1922, were the first of the modern apartment houses; the Graycourt Apartments, built in 1929, were the first of the large houses. These were followed by a number of apartment houses throughout town, including the large Twin Castles Apartments in 1938.

Major suburban development ceased after 1929 until two years or so following the Second World War. The majority of the postwar developments were in the form of huge housing projects to help correct the housing shortage that existed at that time. Among these developments were the Cloverdale Apartments, College Village, Weston Homes, Brookwood, and the Konnoak Hills expansion.

The citizens of Winston-Salem on 21 September 1948 again voted to expand their city limits, the first extension since 1927. The new extension took in, as of 1 January 1949, sections around the fairground area and sections in Konnoak Hills, Ardmore, and Buena Vista.

Winston-Salem built upward as well as outward, and by 1929 its skyline was as it would remain until the changes of the 1950s and 1960s. The Winston business district had become, before the consolidation, the commercial and financial section of the city. The Salem business section remained a quiet row of a few little businesses and shops.

In 1913 the tallest building in Winston-Salem was the seven-story Wachovia Bank Building at the corner of Third and Main streets, which had been erected in 1911. In 1915 the O'Hanlon Building was built. It became the first of Winston-Salem's skyscrapers, and remained the tallest building until 1918, when the Wachovia Bank Building added another story and caught up with it.

The next tall building was the Hotel Robert E. Lee, twelve stories and completed in 1921. In 1926 W. M. Nissen purchased the old YMCA lot at Cherry and Fourth streets and built the eighteen-story Nissen Building, completed in 1927. In 1928, the Reynolds Office Building was begun on the corner of Fourth and Main streets on the lot formerly occupied by the first City Hall of Winston. The Reynolds Building's twenty-two stories were completed in 1929, and it remained the tallest building in North Carolina until the 1950s. Also finished in 1929 was the Carolina Apartments building; later it would be called the Carolina Hotel.

Meanwhile, up and down West Fourth Street, on Fifth and on Cherry, the homes of the fathers were making way for the sons' and grandsons' businesses as the city expanded its commercial district. On the Major T. J. Brown homesite, the Hotel Robert E. Lee was built, and the Whitaker home on Fifth was replaced by a service station, as was the John W. Hanes home at Fifth and Cherry. The P. H. Hanes home on Cherry was torn down in the late 1940s and the site was made a parking lot.

The present City Hall replaced the Starbuck home on Main Street, and the lot where the R. J. Reynolds home had stood on Fifth Street became a playground beside Centenary Methodist Church, until the Forsyth County Public Library was built. The First Presbyterian Church on Cherry added to its property the site of the old Winston-Salem High School, and the Chatham Building on the northwest corner of Cherry and Fourth replaced the second St. Paul's Episcopal Church building. Walgreen's Drugstore was built on the Masonic Temple site at Fourth and Trade Street Mall.

Government buildings were keeping pace with private developments. The present City Hall was erected in 1926 on Main Street just north of the original dividing line between Winston and Salem. The second Post Office Building was built in 1914, replacing, in its site on the corner of Fifth and Liberty, the first Public Government Building, erected in 1906. The 1914 Post Office Building was enlarged and completely remodeled in 1937. The third Forsyth County Courthouse was completed in 1926 on the original Courthouse Square where the other two courthouses had stood.

Architecture and the Esthetics of Plenty

During the period 1910–31 a number of large homes were built in suburban Winston-Salem, each representative of some considerable wealth on the part of its builder. Earlier, the grand houses, according to Thomas A. Gray in his "Graylyn, A Norman Revival

Estate in North Carolina," were located in the downtown district "in close proximity to the leading tobacco companies, warehouses, and banks." With the building of "Reynolda" (1910–17), however, the suburban trend was set.

Reynolda, the spacious thousand-acre estate of Mr. and Mrs. R. J. Reynolds, was designed by Charles Barton Keen of Philadelphia. Composed of "informal" Southern bungalows, barns, stables, a church and post office, and a school, in addition to the main house itself (referred to as "the bungalow"), Reynolda marked the beginning of a successful Winston-Salem career for Mr. Keen. Many important commissions were to follow, most notably the Georgian Revival homes of Robert Hanes, P. Huber Hanes, Sr., Kenneth Mountcastle, and Robert E. Lasater. There were also the period homes of B. S. Womble (Italian Derivative) and Carl Harris (Spanish Revival). Indeed, as Gray noted, "Many of Keen's homes represented the financial and social success of both the owners and the leading industrial and banking corporations in Winston-Salem." They also rounded out the move from downtown to suburbs.

In 1925 the Bowman Grays joined the other country-home builders. A parcel of eighty-seven acres of pasture land was purchased from the Reynolda tract, and in 1927 the construction of a Norman Revival estate began. Luther Lashmit, a native of Winston-Salem, was selected as chief architect. Because of local labor problems, the chaos created by the Depression, and the ensuing temporary halts in construction, Graylyn was not completed until the end of 1932. Members of the family resided in either the main house, the gardener's cottage, or the garage-guesthouse (Bernard Cottage) for the next fourteen years. In June 1946 Graylyn was given to the Bowman Gray School of Medicine and was operated as a rehabilitation and convalescent center for a number of years.

Keen and Lashmit (Lashmit designed at least ten Georgian or Modified Georgian homes in Winston-Salem from 1927 to 1940) were joined in their work by Thomas W. Sears, a landscape designer from Philadelphia. In addition to Reynolda and Graylyn, Sears designed, between 1920 and 1950, the gardens and residential properties of twenty-four private homes; he also landscaped Reynolda Park, as well as the grounds of Forsyth County Courthouse, the Outpatient Building of North Carolina Baptist Hospital, and Wake Forest University.

From the early days of the consolidation, the need for an orderly, functional plan for the physical expansion of the city of Winston-Salem was discussed in Chamber of Commerce meetings and by civic leaders. In the 1920s, the first city plan was promoted and was instrumental in the establishment of the first through streets and in the adoption of a zoning ordinance in 1930. Although a good deal of money was spent in setting up this first plan, it was never carried through. Constant work in the 1940s resulted in the establishment in 1946 of a temporary City-County Planning Commission. The city and county governments voted to undertake a joint planning program. A city planner was employed and he, with his staff, began work on a master plan for the city and county's future growth and development. In March 1948 a permanent City-County Planning Board, made up of the mayor, the chairman of the Forsyth County Board of Commissioners, and seven citizens, was named to work with the planning staff.

City Government

Winston-Salem city government was set up at the time of the consolidation in 1913 as the mayor-alderman form of government, with a mayor and eight aldermen. The general makeup of the city government was changed little until 4 November 1947, when the citizens of the city voted to adopt the council-manager or city manager form of government. Winston-Salem's first mayor was O. B. Eaton; its first city manager was C. E. Perkins.

A comparison of the first journal entry in the books of the new city of Winston-Salem with the city's capital assets in 1948 gives a clear idea of the physical expansion since 1913. In 1913, the total capital assets were $1,314,392; in 1948, the assets were $28,527,008.

The separate water systems of the two towns remained adequate for several years after the consolidation. In 1917, however, the aldermen felt the city needed a larger water supply and purchased a 1,000-acre tract of land near the old Salem water station for an impounding reservoir. A new dam and lake were built and electric pumps and filters installed. A filter plant was built in 1925 and the pumping station enlarged then. In 1931 the dam was raised five and one-half feet and strengthened, and it was estimated that the city's water system would be adequate until about 1955. However, a greatly increased population and a greatly decreased amount of rain in the summer of 1947 nearly caused a water shortage in Winston-Salem, and the citizens in November 1947 voted a $4-million-dollar bond issue to expand and improve the water system.

A sewage disposal plant was started in 1915 and a second plant was built in 1926. Winston-Salem had 280 miles of sewage lines in 1948 covering 95 percent of the city. A city market, now gone, was built in the 600 block of North Cherry Street in 1925, an incinerator plant in 1930, and a city abattoir in 1935. The city, by midcentury, operated a large fire department with six strategically located stations.

In the fall of 1945, the Committee of 100, a body of some one hundred representative citizens, was organized at a joint meeting of the town's civic clubs. The committee was established to study problems of local municipal government and make recommendations to the public and to the Board of Aldermen. It attempted to bridge the gap between the public and City Hall.

Governor Robert Broadnax Glenn

During the years around the turn of the century, Forsyth County's most politically prominent citizen was Robert Broadnax Glenn. A native of Danbury, Glenn came to Winston in 1886. The rising young lawyer became active in church, civic, and political affairs. He took an active part in the organization of the YMCA, was an elder in the First Presbyterian Church, led the Chamber of Commerce in such actions as seeking an agricultural and mechanical school for Negroes, and was an early proponent of the consolidation of Winston and Salem. As he expanded his political activities he served as solicitor for the Ninth Judicial District; and during President Grover Cleveland's administration he was United States District Attorney.

He was elected governor of North Carolina in 1904 in a campaign in which his advocacy for temperance played a prominent role. As governor from 1905 to 1909, Glenn continued his temperance activities and led the battle which brought statewide prohibition to North Carolina on 1 January 1909. In his home community two wholesale liquor houses and twelve liquor saloons were forced to close.

Governor Glenn had been active in Winston-Salem in promoting educational excellence and had taken great pride in the new West End School just across the street from his home on Fourth Street. While continuing his interest in education Glenn worked also for better conditions in the state hospitals for the care of the insane and in the institutions for the deaf and dumb and the blind. He achieved enforcement of the laws regulating railroads and he presided over the settlement of North Carolina's long-standing debt. He remains the only governor of North Carolina from Winston-Salem.

Schools, 1913–50

At the time of the consolidation, Winston-Salem had seven schools valued with their lots and furnishings at $316,000. After the two school systems were merged, the public school system developed in a network throughout the city. In 1948 Winston-Salem operated twenty public schools valued at $5,313,640. In 1913 the annual school budget was $65,000, with 150 officers and teachers and about 5,000 pupils; in 1948 the annual school budget was $725,000 with 465 teachers and a total enrollment of 15,457 pupils.

Most of Winston-Salem's school building was done in the 1920s, when 65 percent of the school system's pre-1950 buildings were built. The oldest part of a school building in use in 1950 was built in 1910; the newest addition was built in 1939. When the Winston-Salem High School on Cherry Street (built in 1909) burned in 1923, it was replaced by the Richard J. Reynolds High School. Mrs. R. J. Reynolds, in memory of her husband, built a handsome auditorium adjoining the high school and presented it to the city as the Reynolds Memorial Auditorium. It was completed in 1924. In 1930 the North and South Junior High Schools were built. These later became the John W. Hanes High School and the James A. Gray High School when the junior high school system was dropped. Atkins High School for Negroes was built in 1931.

Since the opening of the first public school in 1884, Winston-Salem citizens have generously supported the public school system. Several bond issues were voted for public schools before 1933–34, when the state of North Carolina took over the entire support of the public schools. After two years under state support, the people of Winston-Salem saw that they could not maintain their schools at a high level on the basis of the state minimum program. Citizens again voted to tax themselves with school supplement taxes to provide for good schools.

Salem Academy, the Girls Boarding School in Salem, had been chartered for college work in 1866; in 1890 the first degrees were awarded. In 1907 the name was changed to Salem Academy and College. With the construction in 1930–31 of a new plant for the Academy, a gift of the Patterson-Bahnson-Shaffner families, the preparatory and college functions were physically separated. The Academy offered college preparatory work for girls in grades nine through twelve.

Summit School, a private institution offering two years of kindergarten and grades one through nine, was started in 1933 on Summit Street. In September 1946 it moved into a new and completely modern building and playground on Reynolda Road.

Meanwhile, higher education was keeping pace. A $640,000 endowment was completed for Salem College in 1920. The college then had twelve buildings; by 1948 it had twenty, and average enrollment was around six hundred students.

Slater State Normal School for Negroes had its name changed in 1925 to Winston-Salem Teachers College, and two more years of college work were added, thus making it a four-year accredited institution. The school had a sixty-two-acre campus, 472 students, and eleven buildings at midcentury.

In 1941 the medical school of Wake Forest College was separated from the other college departments and moved to Winston-Salem. The move was made as a result of gifts from the Bowman

Gray family and in order to coordinate the school's work more closely with the North Carolina Baptist Hospital in Winston-Salem. The hospital expanded its facilities to 300 beds and a new plant was built for the school adjoining the Baptist Hospital; the Bowman Gray School of Medicine of Wake Forest College opened in September of 1941. In 1946 an outpatient department was opened with a capacity of 50,000 patients annually.

In the spring of 1946, the trustees of the Z. Smith Reynolds Foundation offered a permanent income to Wake Forest College, a Baptist coeducational institution founded in 1834, on condition that the institution be moved within about five years from its site seventeen miles northeast of Raleigh to a new college campus in Winston-Salem. On 30 July 1946 the North Carolina Baptist State Convention met in Greensboro in special session (for the first time since its founding) and voted to accept the foundation's offer to move the college to Winston-Salem, with the provision that the college name would not be changed and that control of the college would remain with a board of trustees appointed by the Baptist State Convention.

A three-hundred acre tract of land, part of the Reynolds family estate just west of Winston-Salem, was given to the college by Charles and Mary Reynolds Babcock, and the Baptists of the state went to work to raise the money necessary to build a new college adequate for a student body of not less than two thousand. Forsyth County and Winston-Salem, in a campaign in May 1948 gave approximately $1.6 million toward the building fund goal of $6 million. The remainder of the money for building the college came from Baptist churches throughout North Carolina, from alumni and friends of the college, and from the accumulated income of the Reynolds Foundation over the stipulated five-year period.

The decision to move Wake Forest College to Winston-Salem was heralded as a great step in the city's development as well as a tremendous advancement for education in northwestern North Carolina, for the western section of the state at that time had no large college or university. Besides the commercial advantages of having a large college in the city, Wake Forest promised industrialized Forsyth County a better-rounded community life and cultural program. The large faculty and student body that Wake Forest College brought to the city also helped to round out the county's middle-income and professional groups.

Continued Growth of the Churches

As the population of Winston-Salem grew and expanded into the suburban areas, two developments occurred among the churches of the community. Downtown edifices were either newly built or enlarged to handle the increasing memberships, and mission churches were established in the suburbs.

Just before 1900, a group from the white First Baptist Church left that congregation to form Brown Memorial Baptist Church. In 1906 they built a handsome brick building on the corner of Fourth and Spring streets and worshiped there until 1935. In that year the congregation rejoined First Baptist which had constructed its present building on Fifth Street in 1925. In the years that followed both before and just after World War II, Baptist churches, black and white, were established in almost every sizable neighborhood in the city and in the county. Many flourished and in later years would construct church buildings to rival the downtown churches in size and grandeur.

The Methodists followed essentially the same pattern as their Baptist brethren. Old Centenary Church, so named because it was completed in 1884, the year of the Methodist centennial, sent out a congregation who in 1912 constructed West End Methodist Church on the corner of Fourth and Brookstown streets. In the mid-1920s West End needed additional facilities and Old Centenary was being squeezed by downtown business development. The two congregations merged and relocated at the present Fifth Street site. Methodists too, built churches in the suburbs. In 1910 the Methodist Children's Home was opened on the site of the old Davis Military School. In 1928, the Bethlehem Community Center, a kindergarten for Negro children, was established as an interracial effort. Black Methodist churches followed residential settlements in much the same way as was happening in the white communities.

Among the other denominations, Calvary Moravian was constructed in 1926; Augsburg Lutheran in 1928; and St. Paul's Episcopal in 1929. In January 1928, the cornerstone was laid for St. Leo's Roman Catholic Church at Angelo Street and Springdale Avenue. Beth Jacob, an Orthodox Jewish synagogue, was begun in 1912 and Temple Emanuel had its beginning as a Reformed congregation in the early 1920s. The Society of Friends, commonly called Quakers, was organized in 1912. The Greek Orthodox community, organized in 1926, began worshiping in the old Brown Memorial Baptist Church in 1941. As the population of Forsyth County grew, so did its diversity; and various minor religious groups began to establish places of worship. By 1950 it was easy to maintain that Winston-Salem was a city of churches.

The dominant religious orientation of the city and county was due in large part to the Moravian influence on the early settlement and the continuing impact of the Moravians on the entire region. Suburban churches served the outlying areas; but all paid homage to Home Moravian Church in Salem. The traditions and customs of the Moravians permeated the entire community. Predominant among the services which were observed by Moravians and non-Moravians alike and which quickly became a part of the lives of those newly arrived to the community were the Christmas Eve lovefeasts and candle services, as well as the famous Easter Sunrise service.

The Easter service, observed in Bethabara in 1756, traces its origin to the early Moravians in Europe and has been celebrated in Salem since 1773. The Salem service received national publicity in the 1920s and began to attract large crowds of worshipers from all over the state and the country. The Easter service was broadcast locally beginning in 1930, and in 1941 it was given national and worldwide shortwave coverage. During World War II, through the Office of War Information, the service was sent by shortwave to the United States forces overseas. Peace and the return of civilian travel increased the attendance in Salem and by 1950 many thousands of people annually visited the simple, impressive service of the Moravians in Salem.

Publishing and Broadcasting

As related earlier, Winston-Salem entered the twentieth century with a morning, an afternoon, and a semiweekly newspaper. In 1918, a newly incorporated firm, the Sentinel Printing and Publishing Company, bought the *Twin City Daily Sentinel* (an afternoon paper established in 1885) and the Sentinel Building which had been erected in 1909 at 241 North Liberty Street. The company continued operation until August 1926, when the entire property was sold to the newly organized Winston-Salem Sentinel, Inc., a corporation owned chiefly by Frank A. Gannett of Rochester, New York. The semiweekly *Western Sentinel* was merged at this time with the *Twin City Sentinel*. Gannett maintained his interest in the *Sentinel* for less than a year.

In the meantime, a morning paper, the *Daily Journal*, established in 1897, had been bought by Owen Moon, who became publisher and owner of the Winston-Salem Journal Company. In February 1927 Moon bought out the stock of the Winston-Salem Sentinel, Inc., and combined the two papers under one roof. Before the two papers were consolidated, there had been stiff competition between the *Journal* and the *Sentinel*; the *Sentinel*'s main object on Saturday night was always to get out as big a paper as possible with all the news in it because the *Journal* got out the Sunday paper. Moon in 1928 moved his two newspapers and his company into a new building built for them on Marshall Street, the Journal-Sentinel Building.

In 1937 the Piedmont Publishing Company was formed with Gordon Gray as president. The company acquired from Owen Moon the two newspapers, the building, and the equipment, and published the *Twin City Sentinel* (afternoon), the *Winston-Salem Journal* (morning), and the *Journal and Sentinel* (Sunday).

The *Southern Tobacco Journal*, founded in 1886, moved to Winston-Salem in 1932 and remained until 1963. It became a monthly magazine in 1934 and was published by the Carmichael Printing Company. *Blum's Almanac*, begun in 1828, is still a bestseller in the county.

Winston-Salem's first radio station (and North Carolina's fifth), WSJS, was formally opened on Good Friday, 17 April 1930. The radio dial was turned to 1310:

Ladies and gentlemen, good evening. This is the voice of Radio Station WSJS, Winston-Salem, North Carolina. We are operating on a frequency of 228.9 meters by authority of the Federal Radio Commission. WSJS is owned and operated by the Winston-Salem *Journal and Sentinel*. The studios and transmitter are located in the Journal Building, 416 North Marshall Street, Winston-Salem [studios were on the second floor and the transmitter on the fourth]. This is the dedicatory program of the station. Your announcer is George Cross.

A religious program was the first to be broadcast. The Right Reverend Edward Rondthaler, bishop of the Moravian church, offered the prayer of dedication and the choir of St. Paul's Episcopal Church provided appropriate music. Later in the day, in addition to local dignitaries who spoke on WSJS's first program, there were the sixteen-piece WSJS orchestra, singers Jose Bledsoe and Howard Conrad, the Piedmont Brass Quartet, the Winston-Salem Harmonica Band, the Piedmont Troubadours, the Mocksville String Band, the Radio Four Quartet, Jack Hawkins and his musical saw, and Norris O'Neil, the station's first manager.

In the early days WSJS operated seven hours per day—10 to 11 in the morning, 12 to 1 in the afternoon, and 5 until 10 in the evening. Winston-Salem's first radio station had no network affiliation until June 1933 when "Camel Caravan" (appropriate enough!) from the Columbia Broadcasting System was played for the first time.

On 24 March 1937, from the mezzanine of the Hotel Robert E. Lee, Winston-Salem's second station, WAIR, started broadcast operations. The idea for WAIR was primarily that of George Walker, who was then an engineer with WSJS. The station was daytime only at the outset, and operated on a frequency of 1250 kilocycles. Recorded dance music and thirty minutes of songs by the Lions Club Quartet (assisted by soprano Alice Blue and Charles Keaton at the organ) made up WAIR's first broadcasting schedule.

In 1937, WSJS, along with the city's newspapers, was purchased by Gordon Gray and the Piedmont Publishing Company. Five years later, FM radio came to North Carolina and the southeastern United States. The station W41MM (later WMIT) was owned by Gray and transmitted its signal from Clingman's Peak, near Mount Mitchell, though programming originated in the WSJS studio in Winston-Salem. It was not until after the war that Winston-Salem's two pioneer stations started FM broadcasting— WAIR in August 1947 and WSJS in December of that year.

James W. Coan, Robert V. Brawley, J. G. Johnson, and Archibald Craige established a new station, WTOB, in April 1947. Broadcasting from the "World's Tobacco Capital," Governor Gregg Cherry delivered the principal dedicatory address. WTOB operated as a 1,000-watt daytime station until September 1950, when its frequency was moved from 710 kilocycles to 1380, and unlimited broadcasting was made possible.

A fourth radio station, WAAA, was North Carolina's first to orient its programming towards blacks. That was in October 1950. And before the advent of the specialized programming of television, WAAA was the only Winston-Salem station to direct its broadcasts to a particular audience.

Health and Hospital Facilities

The Winston-Salem Health Department was organized in 1916 with offices in the City Hall. In December 1938 the department moved into the Health Center on North Woodlawn Avenue. In July 1945 the department was consolidated with the County Health Department, creating the City-County Health Department.

In 1914 the City Hospital was built, and in 1915 a nurses' home was built by the ladies of the Twin-City Hospital Association from proceeds of the sale of the old hospital plant on Brookstown Avenue. Later, $240,000 was bequeathed to the city by R. J. Reynolds for building two additions to the hospital. In 1922 the North Reynolds Wing for black patients was completed, and in 1924 construction on the South Reynolds Wing was finished. The Sterling Smith Annex was added later, and the name changed to City Memorial Hospital. A new home for student nurses was built in 1930. In 1941 a strip of property in front of the hospital was given to the hospital for nurses' homes and parking space.

The Baptist State Convention voted to establish a hospital in Winston-Salem, and in 1921 local citizens in a city campaign gave

$140,000 toward building the hospital. Two years later, in 1923, the North Carolina Baptist Hospital was completed on South Hawthorne Road.

A great need developed for hospital facilities for Negroes more adequate than the North Wing of the City Memorial Hospital, and in 1938 a modern hospital for the blacks, the Kate Bitting Reynolds Memorial, was built. Planning and construction was made possible by a gift of $200,000 from Mr. and Mrs. W. N. Reynolds and $125,000 from the Duke Endowment Fund.

In 1917 the first county tuberculosis sanitorium in North Carolina was opened just outside Winston-Salem. Thirteen years later, in 1930, a more modern facility, the Forsyth County Sanitorium for Tuberculosis, opened on Rural Hall Road. A building for black patients was added in 1937.

Public Health, Welfare, and Social Agencies Prior to 1950

The Associated Charities, Winston-Salem's first venture in organized, private charity, was started in 1905. Miss Annie Grogan was appointed the secretary and served until her retirement in 1936. "Miss Annie" with her horse and buggy, and later her roadster, was a familiar sight on the streets of Winston-Salem as she made her calls in the interest of charity. She became known as Winston-Salem's "mother of charity."

The Associated Charities became the pivot around which other agencies developed. The YMCA, which was formed in 1888, built its first home in 1908 on the site where the First Union National Bank Building now stands. In 1927 a new building was erected on Marshall Street at a cost of about half a million dollars. The new building was made possible through public contributions and through the sale of the old building site. A Negro branch of the YMCA had opened in 1911. The YWCA, organized in 1908, erected its first home in 1916 on the corner of First and Church streets, where the original dividing line between Winston and Salem ran. The activities of the YWCA gradually outgrew the building, and in 1942 a most attractive brick building was built on Glade Street. The Chestnut Street Branch of the YWCA was organized for Negro girls in 1918 as an outgrowth of a Negro girls' club.

The Boy Scout movement began in Winston-Salem in 1911 with the organization of the first troop. The first Girl Scout troop was organized in December 1923 at Reynolds High School.

The Winston-Salem Chapter of the American Red Cross was organized in 1917. Other organizations, such as the Forsyth County Tuberculosis and Health Association, came later.

Contemporary with the movement in the United States to consolidate fund-raising solicitations, the Community Chest of Forsyth County was organized in 1923. The Chest federated the finances of twenty local health and welfare organizations, raising the money in one campaign and distributing it according to need among its member organizations. The first Chest goal was $28,000, but $36,000 was actually subscribed. The 1948 goal was $262,000, and approximately $275,000 was subscribed.

In 1938 the Winston-Salem Council of Social Agencies was formed to coordinate the community social welfare program. This organization functioned as the Community Council and was made up of representatives from over forty public and private health, welfare, and recreation agencies and civic groups.

In 1940 the Associated Charities, which had served so well in the field of private welfare, had part of its functions absorbed by the Forsyth County Department of Public Welfare. The Family and Child Service Agency carried on the remaining work.

Winston-Salem had two institutions for the care of needy children. The Methodist Children's Home on Reynolda Road, which opened 7 September 1909, still serves western North Carolina. The Memorial Industrial School for Negroes opened in 1923 on North Main Street, then moved nine miles north of the city. It provided a home for underprivileged Negro children until 1970.

The Winston-Salem Foundation, a nonprofit organization established in 1919, manages a number of civic enterprises and works in all fields for community betterment. The foundation's funds are derived from the contributions of Winston-Salem citizens. Aiding the community in many ways, such as in providing summer camp for needy boys and girls and in helping young men and women obtain college educations, the foundation continues to make a valuable contribution to Forsyth County.

In an attempt to find some solution to the problem of the increasing number of fund-raising campaigns, the Chamber of Commerce and the Retail Merchants Association organized in the summer of 1946 the Forsyth County Committee on Public Solicitation. The committee acted as a central agency which cleared all proposals for community-wide fund-raising campaigns and made public their results. The committee was reorganized and enlarged in the fall of 1948.

Recreational Facilities

Community-wide recreation services for Winston-Salem began in 1918 when the Board of Aldermen appropriated $6,000 for park and playground services and authorized the opening and equipping of five playgrounds. In 1934 the Public Recreation Commission was organized. By 1950 the city had twenty-six parks and playgrounds, with a total of 536 acres. These parks had athletic fields, picnic areas, and special amusement features. The largest park was Reynolds, one of the South's finest municipal recreational centers. It opened in 1940. The city also provided an average of more than ten acres of playground for each public school.

Dollar train excursions, Fourth of July celebrations, summer band concerts on the Courthouse Square, and picnics in Nissen Park were Winston-Salem's idea of having fun in the early days after consolidation. Commercialized recreation began to develop with the expansion of the motion-picture theaters. In the late 1940s the city had six motion-picture theaters, two commercial and nine membership or free swimming pools, bowling alleys, and stables and riding schools. Two commercial and two membership golf courses succeeded the original Twin City Golf Club, North Carolina's first golf club, formed in Winston-Salem in 1897. Forsyth Country Club, with a clubhouse, swimming pool, and golf course, was organized in 1910. The Old Town Club, also a private country club with swimming and golf, was formed in 1938.

Bowman Gray Memorial Stadium was built as a WPA project

aided by private funds from the Bowman Gray family. The stadium, with a seating capacity of 12,000, cost almost $200,000. On 22 October 1939 the facility was dedicated with ceremonies at the annual Duke–Wake Forest football game.

Growth of Business and Service Organizations

The Chamber of Commerce of Winston and Salem, organized in 1885, became at the time of the consolidation the Winston-Salem Chamber of Commerce. Through all of the rapid development of the city it has continued its leadership in building the economic, cultural, and educational growth of the community. The Winston-Salem Junior Chamber of Commerce was formed in 1929 to organize the leadership of the young men. The Winston-Salem Retail Merchants Association, formed in 1889 as the Winston-Salem Merchants and Traders' Union, continues its services to the merchants of the city. It is the oldest organization of its kind in North Carolina.

The Winston-Salem Real Estate Exchange was organized in 1915. In 1917 the group joined the national organization and became the Winston-Salem Chapter, National Real Estate Board. The Winston-Salem Automobile Club, organized in 1911, is today the oldest in the Carolinas and one of the oldest in the South. The Winston Tobacco Board of Trade, organized in 1869, continues today its promotion and organization of the Winston-Salem market.

When Winston and Salem were young and small, businessmen could gather on the street corners and in the shops to discuss the news of the day and to exchange ideas. As the city grew, however, businessmen felt the need for a better means of getting acquainted with fellow citizens, of exchanging ideas, and perhaps of promoting community projects. So, soon after the consolidation, the civic luncheon-club movement began, following a similar pattern of development in other cities. In 1915 the Rotary Club was formed as the first, followed by Kiwanis in 1919; Business and Professional Women's Club, 1919; Civitan, 1921; Lions, 1922; Altrusa (for women), 1924; Pilot Club (for women), 1934; Exchange Club, 1935; American Business Club, 1940; Credit

Women's Breakfast Club, 1941; Cooperative Club, 1947; and the Optimist Club, 1948.

Between 1940 and 1950 there was in the city and county a movement to organize neighborhood civic clubs for the promotion of fellowship and neighborhood projects and improvements. Among these were Sun-Waugh Civic Club, North Winston Men's Community Club, North Winston Men's Brotherhood, Clemmons Civic Club, Lewisville Civic Club, Old Town Civic Club, Ardmore Civic Club, Walkertown Men's Club, Mineral Springs Civic Club, Rural Hall Civic Club, City View Men's Club, Konnoak Hills Club, South Fork Civic Club, and West Salem Civic Club.

Women's service and social organizations formed as rapidly as did the men's. A Woman's Club was organized in 1919, followed by a Junior Woman's Club. The Junior League was formed in 1923; it was the first in North Carolina. The Twin City Garden Club, organized in 1925, was the pioneer of the Winston-Salem garden clubs. It sponsored the organization of the North Carolina Federation of Garden Clubs. In 1931 the Winston-Salem Council of Garden Clubs was formed and by 1950 had nine member clubs. Book clubs led by the Sorosis Club, organized in 1895, numbered seven in 1950.

The Development of an Arts Program

Winston-Salem, since its founding by the Moravians, has always been recognized as a city sympathetic toward and active in the arts, within church, family, and school in the early days, and later with a community focus.

Several music clubs were organized in the city before 1938, but no organized arts program with a continuing pattern of development came into being until the Festival Opera Group was launched at Salem College. Two evenings of opera were brought to Winston-Salem by a Summer School of Opera, held at the Woman's College of the University of North Carolina in 1942. This opera festival program was expanded in Winston-Salem to include an evening of orchestral music and a community sing. The whole event, enlisting the support of the community's civic and art agencies, was called the Greater Winston-Salem Music Festival.

Out of this beginning was born the Piedmont Festival of Music and Arts, held for the first time in 1943. The festival was launched as a "people's art" production, designed to coordinate in a common project the various community arts groups, such as the dance studios, the Little Theater, and the various choral groups. The first festival was made up of an opera and oratorio performance, an orchestra concert, and interesting exhibits of art, photography, and handicrafts. Five hundred people took part in the first festival.

Later festivals were expanded to include a children's concert, a community sing, and a drama, and in 1948 the Piedmont Festival was successfully held for the sixth time. The "people's art" idea spread from Winston-Salem throughout North Carolina and the nation and has contributed to the development of several similar festivals and opera groups.

The Piedmont Festival stimulated the development of several arts and music groups in the community. In 1945 the Junior League sponsored the establishment of an arts and crafts center and employed a full-time director. This program led to the formation of the Arts and Crafts Association which sponsored the Winston-Salem Workshop, open to all interested in learning any art or craft.

From 1942 to 1945, several civic choral groups were organized, including the Forsyth Singers, an all-male chorus; the Maids of Melody; a boys' choir; and the Sunnyside Choral Club. In 1946 the Winston-Salem Civic Orchestra and the Winston-Salem Operetta Association were begun.

The County Centennial

On 12 May 1949 Forsyth County celebrated its first hundred years. Winston-Salem *Journal* reporter Hoke Norris wrote, "the past and the present marched one after the other down the street." And, indeed, from his description of the centennial parade, there can be no doubt as to the significance of Forsyth County's past and the impact of that past on the present:

There were top hats and bowlers, frock coats and spats, ribboned bonnets and crinoline, log cabins and at least three privies, carts, surries, fringed and unfringed, ambulances, horses, mules, goats, donkeys, hound dogs, phaetons, buggies, baby carriages, coonskin caps, wagons covered and open, fire engines, horse drawn and motorized, cows, bulls, boats, fireplaces and automatic stokers, carriages, one ricksha, cradle reaper and modern reaper, milk wagons, bicycles, jugs, tractors, trucks, tobacco hogsheads, automobiles old and new, jeeps, textile equipment primitive and modern, a horse drawn hearse, guns, beards, soldiers, sailors, marines, scouts, big and little, pretty girls, handsome men.

The past and present have traditionally walked hand in hand in Forsyth County, and the very unanimity of participation represented in the parade and subsequent centennial events pointed this up in 1949. The county was one hundred years old and halfway through a new century—and still on the march. More than a hundred thousand persons had crowded the streets of Winston-Salem. Centennial chairman James A. Gray, Jr., who with the "help of thousands" organized the event, wrote in his foreward to the 1949 edition of *Forsyth, A County on the March* (a centennial project) of the energy of the county's founders, "the surge of its new blood, and the cooperative spirit of its people."

But the centennial celebration in no way tried to cover up or gloss over any of Forsyth County's problems. In 1949 there were slum and semislum areas that needed to be cleared up; the city's municipal plant needed expanding; much could be done to improve the general appearance of the city; recreational facilities were racially segregated and inadequate. These were problems that came with Winston-Salem's rapid transition from a little town to a big city.

To offset the problems county leaders, many of whom were descendants of Forsyth's earliest settlers, encouraged growth and improvement. Forsyth County had assumed a position of leadership in the state. Winston-Salem's public school system was one of the finest in North Carolina, and the city was rapidly becoming a center for higher education. There were few counties that could boast Forsyth's economic prominence.

The second half of Forsyth's history as a county, like the first, was marked by progress and cooperation among its citizens. This tradition, which actually dates from the arrival of the Moravian Brethren two hundred years before, carried over into Forsyth's second century beginning in the 1950s.

In many ways the industrial and economic development of Winston-Salem shaped the social order of Forsyth County in the early half of the twentieth century. But it was not just the industries and the economy which extended their influence. Jonathan Daniels, writing in 1947 in *Tar Heels, a Portrait of North Carolina*, captured many of the elements:

Maybe God built Winston-Salem. It is not a blasphemous idea. In His name Moravian brothers walked down the woods from Pennsylvania to begin their skilled and God-fearing community in the wilderness. And their past is kept in Salem in the old brick and stone houses with the hooded doors and the windows made with little panes. The old trees grow green in quietness. If Winston, swollen with the wealth of cigarettes and underwear and stockings, is only across a street, sometimes it seems also across a world. It is not. There is something more than a hyphen between the two towns. There is Moravian blood in the factories and the banks. Some of the Scotch-Irish money has helped keep the old town sweet. There is a triumph in their attachment. After living together a long time the towns were formally united in 1913, the same year the first Camel cigarette was manufactured, and if it was a wedding of new-rich and old gentleness, it has been a marriage of success as well as convenience.

CHAPTER 12

The Twentieth Century, the First Fifty Years:
The Economic Order

IN THE LATTER HALF OF THE EIGHTEENTH CENTURY in England a series of inventions revolutionized industry. Most important of these inventions were the spinning jenny, the water frame, the power loom, and the steam engine. Changes were hastened by various improved processes for the production of iron and steel, and invention of the locomotive and the steamboat was equally significant. Stephenson constructed a practical locomotive in 1814; five years later the first steamboat crossed the Atlantic and ushered in fast ocean transportation.

The rest of Europe and the United States soon took note of the changes. In the early days of the American colonies manufactures were almost unknown, and such manufactured goods as were needed had to be imported, but manufacturing had begun to develop in New England before the Revolutionary War. Once the United States became independent, there was rapid expansion. Great cities, such as New York and Philadelphia, grew up along the harbors. From 1830 almost to the end of the century there was railway building and general industrial expansion, rapidly transforming the United States into a great manufacturing and commercial nation. Meanwhile, agriculture became much more productive because of improved farming methods. Thus was modern industry born in America.

The same development transformed Forsyth County from a frontier agricultural settlement to a great industrial community. The rapidity with which the development took place is even more remarkable since early settlement was 200 miles from the nearest harbor, and the roads were only trails. During the period from 1830 to 1873, when the first direct railroad connection was made, pioneers established a cotton manufacturing company, a wool mill, two wagon works, a power-driven woodworking plant, and a tobacco factory. Electricity was used to light a cotton mill by 1881. Tobacco had been rolled in hogsheads down the trail to distant markets in earlier days; in 1885 the first tobacco was shipped from Forsyth County by rail, destined for Europe.

Necessity, coupled with a progressive spirit, drove the pioneers to an early development which has continued with succeeding generations. Although the settlement was isolated 125 years ago, its inhabitants nevertheless put to good use the available products of the soil. The climate was advantageous to the cultivation of tobacco and cotton. The vast forest yielded lumber as well as food. Industry developed from within, and the community prospered.

The story of Forsyth's industry is a story of industrious men. Some of the results of their genius are the visible, tangible assets of the largest or oldest industrial establishments. Yet an appraisal of Winston-Salem and Forsyth County business development must take into account the numerous younger industries and business concerns which also play an important part in the economic life of the community. The translation of the complete story is revealed by certain facts which measure business and industrial life.

The increase in population from 1890 to 1940 is shown by the United States census figures:

YEAR	WINSTON-SALEM	FORSYTH COUNTY
1890	10,729	28,434
1900	13,650	35,261
1910	22,700	47,311
1920	48,395	77,269
1930	75,274	111,681
1940	79,815	126,475

Forsyth is one of the smallest counties in the state, with only thirty counties having less area, yet it has always been one of the most populous. In 1950 the density of population was 298.3 per square mile, nearly four times the state average. Of the county total, 63 percent resided in Winston-Salem, and of the remaining rural population 22.8 percent were classified as nonfarm dwellers. Many of the people classified as rural dwellers made their living by working in the factories. There were many factories and business concerns in Forsyth County which were not included in any incorporated town, and most of their employees were classified as rural dwellers. Also there were a great number of people living outside of incorporated areas who were employed in the towns.

The large number of Negro laborers found in Forsyth County in 1950 was due to the nature of the industries. The tobacco industry offered to the unskilled Negro the most attractive of jobs; consequently Forsyth County acquired a great many unskilled Negro laborers. It was estimated that 32.5 percent of Forsyth's population in 1949 was Negro, while in 1920 blacks accounted for 34.2 percent, and in 1930 33.3 percent. Of the total population of Winston-Salem in 1940, 36,018 were Negro.

Almost 86 percent of the population at midcentury was engaged in industry, business, and the professions. From a survey conducted by the Chamber of Commerce in 1947, it was determined that over half of this group was engaged in the manufacturing industry. The results of this survey showed the percentages according to type of work: 58 percent engaged in manufacturing, 23 percent engaged in retailing and wholesaling, 14 percent engaged in various trades and services, and 5 percent in government and the professions.

The manufactured products of ninety-seven establishments in Forsyth in 1937 had a value of $349,196,894, of which $88,-844,398 was added by the manufacturing process. Before 1950 Winston-Salem ranked first south of Richmond and east of the Mississippi in value of manufactured products, and produced seven times more goods than any other city in the Carolinas.

Winston-Salem served as the market place for eighteen tobacco-growing counties and their 98,771 acres of tobacco allotted for the 1947–48 season. Buyers came to fourteen tobacco warehouses to buy leaf for manufacture into finished products, not only in the United States but in many foreign countries. Federal legislation, first instituted in 1933, brought about government price support and also an allotment system limiting the acreage planted in tobacco. However, the local market sales for the 1947–48 season totaled 61,743,308 pounds and brought growers a return of $23,595,280, much of which was spent in the city.

In 1901 the assessed value of all taxable property in Forsyth amounted to $8,402,308. The entire state at that time had less than $300 million on the tax books. In 1949 Forsyth valuation exceeded by 20 percent the valuation for the entire state in 1901.

Because of the heavy imports incident to the tobacco industry a Port of Entry was established in Forsyth through an Act of Congress on 16 June 1916. The duty paid on goods imported into Winston-Salem for the year ending 30 June 1948 amounted to $4,988,269.34. This placed Winston-Salem in the rank of sixteenth city in the United States as a source of customs revenue.

From the foregoing description of Forsyth's economic background for the first half of the twentieth century it is evident that the foundation of the county rested on its industry. The growth was from within, with local men and local capital furnishing the leading role. It was steady, healthy, and consistent, and has been due in large measure to the type of product manufactured. Tobacco from the fields could be delivered to local factories which finished preparing it for consumer use. Cotton from the farms could be sold to a nearby mill which fabricated the garment for the consumer. Rough lumber could be delivered to the mill which made furniture for use in the home. Other local industries may have depended on supplementary processing, but the majority of Forsyth's products are definitely consumer goods. Such industry is not readily affected by economic extremes.

A Center of Industry: The First Fifty Years

At the turn of the century the Hanes brothers, Pleasant Henderson and John Wesley, who had been successful tobacconists for over twenty years, made a decision which was later to place

Forsyth County high in the textile world. The Hanes tobacco operation was sold to R. J. Reynolds, and each of the Hanes brothers went his own way—P. H. into knitting, and J. W. into hosiery.

The P. H. Hanes Knitting Company was organized in 1901 and incorporated in 1903 for the purpose of manufacturing cotton ribbed winter-weight underwear for men. Some years later boys' underwear was added to the Hanes line as were girls' and children's underclothing. About 1920, production of the now famous Hanes athletic underwear was begun.

In 1910 and 1911 the Hanes village and spinning plant were constructed. The plant produced high-grade yarn used in the Winston-Salem knitting mill. Beginning with 15,000 spindles, the Hanes spinning operation continued to grow over the next several decades into one of the nation's leading textile corporations. The village itself was a model mill town with churches, schools, and an auditorium. Near the village a twenty-acre recreation area for employees and their families was built. It included a ball park equipped with an underground sprinkler system and grandstand, bleachers, and a modern field house. Facilities for softball and employee picnics and other social events were likewise provided. By the end of the 1930s the P. H. Hanes Knitting plant was operating six factory units with some twenty-five nundred employees.

The Hanes Hosiery Mills Company had its beginning in 1900 when J. W. Hanes purchased the old Hodgin tobacco plant on Marshall Street near Second. Under the name Shamrock, this new mill was producing infants' hose and men's socks by 1902. The company was renamed Hanes Hosiery at the time it was incorporated in 1914. Within six more years, the Hanes mill, then specializing in ladies' hosiery, had outgrown its original plant. In 1926 a new plant was completed on West Fourteenth Street, and the mill was moved.

The history of the Hanes Hosiery operation is another account of rapid growth in a highly competitive market. Hanes seamless hosiery led in the transition from cotton to rayon and from silk to nylon. Emphasis was placed on quality; the product of Hanes Hosiery was undisputed. By the end of the 1940s it was the largest circular-knit hosiery mill in the world.

The Indera Mills, organized and located in Winston-Salem in 1914, manufactured as its principal products ladies' and children's knit skirts, slips, and knee warmers. From a small beginning the company had a steady demand for its product, and in 1925 the plant was enlarged by the purchase of the old Maline Mills property. Colonel Francis Fries and his nephew, W. L. Siewers, were the company's founders. Three presidents ran the company from its incorporation in 1922 to midcentury: Fries from 1922 to 1931; Mrs. R. F. Willingham from 1931 to 1954; and Frank Willingham, her son, from 1954. Production was later expanded to include nylon tricot princess slips and half slips.

The Hanes Dye and Finishing Company was organized by Ralph P. Hanes in 1924. This company, from its beginning, bleached, dyed, and finished cotton piece goods for converters located in the eastern United States.

In 1906 the Chatham Manufacturing Company of Elkin, North Carolina built a plant in Winston-Salem. The main offices were also moved to Winston-Salem in the same year. For years Chatham led the nation's production of all-wool and mixed-wool-and-cotton blankets, with the Winston-Salem factory playing a leading part in the company's output. In 1940 the company reconsolidated its manufacturing in Elkin and closed the Winston-Salem plant.

Arista Mills Co. was formed in 1903, merging Arista Cotton Mill, built in 1880, and Southside Cotton Mills. From 1915 on, its principal produce was chambray. A business descendant of Francis Fries's woolen mill of 1840, Arista was Forsyth County's oldest continuously operated manufacturing firm. Faced with increased competition from the foreign import market, Arista began to enter data processing in 1956. In early 1970 the company ended textile production and today exists in the form of Arista Information Systems, Inc.

Duplan Corp. began its Winston-Salem operations in 1942 to produce synthetic yarns, chiefly nylon, for textile manufacturers. Its general offices were moved to Winston-Salem in 1956. Its

Forsyth production facilities closed in 1974 and the general offices moved to Greensboro shortly thereafter.

The Adams-Millis Corporation located a branch in Kernersville and began manufacturing a large volume of women's and children's anklets.

The tobacco business of R. J. Reynolds and Company was chartered by the state of North Carolina in 1890 as R. J. Reynolds Tobacco Company. Reynolds was president of the company and continued in this capacity until his death in 1918. The business was operated under the North Carolina charter until 1899, when a charter was procured from the state of New Jersey.

Granulated smoking tobaccos were added to the Reynolds line in the 1890s. In 1907 the process for Prince Albert smoking tobacco was patented, and Reynolds began advertising its product on a national scale.

The first "modern-type" tobacco blend, that of Camel cigarettes, went into production on 19 October 1913. Most tobacco products before the advent of Camels depended on gimmicky advertising, but with the new blend Reynolds "warned the buyer not to expect any premium—except choice tobaccos." This straightforward pitch likewise revolutionized the sale of tobacco products. In 1930 R. J. Reynolds began packaging their Camel cigarettes in cellophane, a novel material for its day. With this additional innovation the product's position as the largest-selling cigarette in America was assured.

The Brown & Williamson Tobacco Company, which had been started in 1894, grew to such size that by 1906 it was deemed best by the directors of the company to incorporate. Capital of $400,000 was authorized, with about $70,000 paid in. Up to the time of incorporation the company manufactured only plug tobacco. But after January 1906 Brown & Williamson began manufacturing snuff. Tube Rose was B & W's brand, though Blood Hound and Sun Cured chewing tobaccos were made for some years after 1906. At one point in the company's history Old North State cigarettes were also produced with some success. In April 1927 Brown & Williamson was purchased by the British-American Tobacco Company, Ltd.

The tobacco firm of Taylor Brothers was organized in 1883 by

William B. Taylor and his brother Jacquelin P. Taylor. The business, from its beginning, manufactured plugs and twists. Conservatively managed, the company grew slowly but steadily. The original factory was enlarged more than five times by 1950. Incorporation did not come until 1921 when the business became Taylor Brothers, Inc. Its many brands include Rich & Ripe, Bull of the Woods, Taylor Made, and Ripe Peaches.

Certainly the most tenacious of the small-time tobacconists, the sons of the Taylor brothers, Harry and Arch, maintained company policy as established by the founders and refused to sell out to the larger companies until 1952, when the operation merged with the American Snuff Company. Arch Taylor, William's son, recalled the time when R. J. Reynolds was buying up all the smaller local companies. "Dick Reynolds and my father were good friends," Taylor noted. "Dad had helped Dick back in the early days and he never forgot it." While other small operations were being squeezed out of business through their inability to compete with Reynolds's low plug prices (profits were made up on smoking tobaccos and cigarettes), Taylor, through noninterference from Reynolds, stayed open.

The fine quality of leaf tobacco cultivated in this area has attracted buyers for manufacturers in other sections of the country. A considerable quantity of the tobacco sold in local warehouses is exported for use in foreign countries. In 1950 four companies led this field: The Imperial Tobacco Company of Great Britain and Ireland; The Export Leaf Tobacco Company of Richmond, Virginia; The Piedmont Leaf Tobacco Company; and The Winston Leaf Tobacco Company, both of Winston-Salem.

Cigars were made in Forsyth County after the turn of the century, though most of the operations were shortlived. In 1900 J. D. King started a small plant at 444 Liberty Street and W. J. Liipfert one at 612 Four-and-one-half Street. Two years later, in 1902, A. R. Bennett absorbed the Liipfert factory and W. A. Wiggins, formerly of Wiggins and Jones, started his own plant on West Third Street. By 1906 these manufacturers were joined by another operation, that of Terry and Leonard, located at 11 1/2 West Fourth. This business was succeeded in 1908 by J. D. Terry. And before 1930 five additional cigar manufacturers entered the

Winston-Salem market: F. S. Vernay in 1916, E. F. Spaugh in 1921, R. E. Shouse in 1922, E. J. Angelo in 1929, and G. W. Fox in 1929. Though none of these companies, or their predecessors for that matter, made any effectual impression on the international, state, or local cigar trade, William A. Blair said of their product, "Had Bulwer-Lytton sampled any cigar made by any manufacturer in Winston-Salem, he would have added something more to his well-known line, 'The man who smokes, thinks like a sage and acts like a Samaritan.'"

Of course Forsyth's industries both before and after 1950 were far more numerous and diversified than just textiles and tobacco manufacturing. The heyday of the Nissen and Spach wagons was not until the first two decades of the twentieth century. In 1919 Will Nissen was turning out more than fifteen thousand wagons a year, averaging some fifty per day, and selling them as fast as they could be made. Spach, with a smaller volume, but an equal demand, produced on the average ten wagons per day. Between the two plants there were more than 250 employees. When Will Nissen was burned out in 1919 he built a new plant that was bigger and better. He continued operations until 1925 when he sold out for close to one million dollars; the eighteen-story Nissen Building (First Union Bank Building) was constructed with this money. F. B. Reamy who bought the business produced as many as four thousand wagons annually as late as the mid-1940s.

Nissen's competitor, Spach, began to make furniture in 1925, and stopped making wagons in 1928. Furniture was produced under the trade name Unique Furniture; some of the first dinettes were made from leftover wagon parts! Taking the name Unique Furniture Makers and concentrating on bedroom and dining-room furniture the company continues to market quality products across the nation.

The B. F. Huntley Furniture Company had its origin in the Oakland Furniture Company (1898). Later the Oakland company was taken over by Huntley and renamed the B. F. Huntley Furniture Company. Manufacturing exclusively bedroom furniture in a plant with over six acres of floor space, the company advertises nationally and sells all over the United States. It has merged with

Thomasville Furniture and become a subsidiary of the Armstrong Corporation.

The Fogle Furniture Company was organized as a corporation in January 1923 with F. A. Fogle as president. It originally produced handwoven fiber furniture but began making matched living-room furniture in 1928 and abandoned the fiber line in 1936. In 1940, John D. Stockton, who had pioneered residential development on Stratford Road, bought controlling interest in the firm and was named president later that year. After Stockton's death in 1963, the company was acquired by Nicholas Martini of Meyer-Gunther-Martini of New York and continues to devote its entire production to living-room furniture.

In 1884 J. A. Vance began the manufacture of woodplaners and sawmills and added the production of metal stampings in 1936, primarily for use in the woodworking industry. Until the plant closed in the late 1960s it continued the manufacture of machine parts and the making of castings in the foundry for various industrial customers. As early as the mid-1880s, Forsyth's machinists provided a great attraction to outside industry; it was not necessary to seek repairs outside the county, thereby saving time and money. The planers and sawmills of J. A. Vance Company were well known for many years and a number of their machines were exported to South and Central America, Mexico, Africa, and the Orient.

The Bahnson Company had its beginning in 1915 under the name of the Normalair Company. A. H. Bahnson, F. F. Bahnson, and J. A. Gray founded the company to produce a centrifugal humidifier invented and patented by J. W. Fries. A few years later the name was changed to the Bahnson Humidifier Company. In 1929 the business was incorporated and became The Bahnson Company with A. H. Bahnson as president. Eleven years later F. F. Bahnson retired, and in 1946, A. H. Bahnson, Jr., became president and served until his death. The company principally manufactures and installs industrial air-conditioning equipment for the textile industry, both in this country and in several foreign countries. Currently it is a subsidiary of Envirotech Corporation.

In 1927 the Salem Steel Company was organized for the

fabrication of structural steel, and was incorporated in 1933. Rapid growth and expansion made Salem Steel one of the best equipped and most modern steel fabrication plants in the South by midcentury. The company's principal product is used in residential and industrial construction, and in the building of bridges. Salem Steel is presently a subsidiary of Carolina Steel & Iron Company of Greensboro.

In 1944 The Bassick Company, a division of Stewart-Warner Company, selected Winston-Salem as the site for their Bassick-Sack Division. The latter part of the following year, the plant, originally covering 58,000 square feet, began producing decorative metal trim used in the furniture-manufacturing industry.

Certainly the most important new industry to come to Forsyth County since World War II was Western Electric, with great social as well as economic impact. In 1956 operations started in the old Chatham Manufacturing plant, and within three years the company occupied over 800,000 square feet of manufacturing space. Land was purchased by Western Electric for the development of a new plant site with a modern building and equipment; its operations are discussed in Chapter 14.

By mid-century, Forsyth County's industries were widely diversified. Many would become leading employers over the next twenty-five years. Those manufacturing companies with a plant here before 1950 who would be among Forsyth County's one hundred largest employers in 1975 and who have not been discussed elsewhere include: L. A. Reynolds Company (1947), American Bakeries Company (1923), The Salem Company, Inc. (1946), Sealtest Foods (1918), Carolina Narrow Fabric Co. (1928), Royal Cake Co. (1925), Container Corporation of America (1913), Champion Industries, Inc. (1890), Douglas Battery Manufacturing Company (1921), and Pepsi-Cola Bottling Company of Winston-Salem, Inc. (1908).

Even the larger industries already noted included products of many types; the following list of items produced by Winston-Salem and Forsyth County industries will dispel any notion that this county has been limited in number and variety of its products. Products include awnings, tents, canvas covers and bags, automobile springs, batteries, beverages, bread and other bakery products, bricks, caskets, work clothing, fertilizer, foods, harness and saddlery, insulating yarn, lumber, machinery, mattresses and box springs, medicines, sheet metal, mirrors, books, papers, and magazines, rugs, sewer pipe, stone, tinfoil, upholstery, and veneer.

Agriculture in the First Half of the Twentieth Century

No changes in the life of rural Forsyth County people in the past two centuries, whether in politics, education, domestic facilities, communication, or transportation, have been greater than the changes in agriculture. The county advanced from the age of the bull-tongue plow through the era of the Dixie plow and the one-bottom turning plow, down to the age of heavy tractors and rotary tillers. It has exchanged the ox and skinny little mule for heavy gasoline-powered machinery. It has changed from an all-row-crop system to a day when grass farming has come into its own.

Rural Forsyth did not begin to benefit from the agricultural reawakening that started in North Carolina in the decades following the Civil War until the turn of the century. Governor Charles B. Aycock, who took office in 1900, went about the state preaching education and ultimately died on the speaker's platform with the word "education" on his lips. With education, there was a quickening of the economic pulse. Forsyth County had its share of "Farmers' Institutes." And then in the second decade of the century the Extension Service came into existence. Farm agents and home demonstration agents began to teach farmers the fundamental principles of field and animal husbandry. Throughout the early 1920s there was an industrial renaissance. Markets began to develop and with the first crude passenger automobiles and trucks pushing their way into the hinterlands, improved roads were in demand. Macadamized roads, such as the one with which C. A. Reynolds pioneered road-building in this area, began to thread their way across the country in growing numbers.

The period 1900–49 was a period of great awakening. In other words, the second half of Forsyth's first century as a county brought more development than the county ever had seen before. This was as true in Forsyth agriculture as in urban developments.

True, there were ambitious early beginnings on the part of some men and women with perspective, leaders far ahead of their day who made their mark. It was significant that as far back as 1882 and 1883, H. E. Fries and Dr. H. T. Bahnson bred registered Guernsey cattle on their farms, getting their start with Guernseys from W. P. Hazard of Chester, Pennsylvania. This was just before the beginning of the North Carolina Exposition, held in Raleigh in the fall of 1884, promoted largely by Fries, its secretary; William S. Primrose of Raleigh was president of the exposition.

Because of the close friendship between Fries and Primrose, Fries named his dairy Primrose Farm. This meant that some of the outstanding cattle from his farm carried the name "Primrose." That name continues to crop up even today among pedigreed cattle.

Pedigreed Guernsey cattle directly descended from these original brood animals on the Fries farm were being bred in 1950 on Arden Farm at Clemmons, owned by Dr. Bahnson's daughter and her husband, Mr. and Mrs. T. Holt Haywood. This pioneer work in cattle breeding, therefore, was not a wholly useless venture. It bore fruit, even though it took more than half a century to become evident.

There were pioneers also in other fields. Luther Strupe of the Tobaccoville community early in the century was producing seed corn considered the best in the South. On the basis of his seed-corn production and other farming practices, he was named a Master Farmer.

In those years between the turn of the century and the early 1930s, too, J. M. Jarvis of the Clemmons community was producing Jarvis's Golden Prolific seed corn, known throughout many of the southeastern states. He pursued the breeding of corn until the middle 1930s, when he was too old to do field work any more; when he retired, his name was synonymous with good farming practices over a wide territory.

Meanwhile, R. F. Linville, who resided a few miles east of

Winston-Salem, engaged extensively in corn breeding. He developed some of the seed strains used by Jarvis to an even greater degree than Jarvis had reached. Linville also anticipated by more than a quarter of a century the present merits of hybrid seed corn over open-pollinated corn. Before 1920 Linville was experimenting with the principle of hybrid seed production and making it work. Not until the principle was applied on a wide scale in the western states did it become nationally popular, but it should be said to the credit of the Forsyth County man that he was on the track of a great discovery. Linville appreciated its merits, although he never was able to enlist the interest of any considerable number of farmers. Thus, progress in agriculture in Forsyth County was at first sporadic, with a few individuals only here and there who were in effect lifting themselves by their bootstraps. The first farm demonstration agents in this county as well as elsewhere in the state found their work largely the work of tutor and pupil.

For approximately a quarter of a century, R. W. Pou did pioneer work as a farm agent in Forsyth County, carrying the extension service program over the period which might almost be said to bridge the space between hand tools and complete mechanization. He laid down the reins when S. R. Mitchener took over. In the women's field, the extension service program was handled largely by two home demonstration agents and their assistants. Through the 1920s and up to 1931, Miss Alice McQueen was home demonstration agent. Upon her retirement, Mrs. Elizabeth Tuttle took over. Mrs. Tuttle's leadership is attested by the fact that in December 1947 she was awarded the certificate of distinguished service by the National Association of Home Demonstration Agents at their annual convention in Chicago. The two agents were aided materially in their work by capable assistants, many of whom later served in ranking positions elsewhere in the state.

The changes in agriculture from 1930 to 1950 were extreme and the results cumulative. The system of agriculture in Forsyth County was largely a row-crop system. Small beginnings in the production of cattle and hogs were indicative of what was to come, but not of how great that progress was to be. In the space of a quarter of a century, Forsyth County became a banner county in the breeding of Guernsey and Holstein-Friesian milk cows and in the breeding of Hereford beef cattle. The expansion in the breeding of beef cattle has not been commensurate with that of the dairy breeds, but between 1940 and 1950 there was a very pronounced quickening of interest.

Meanwhile, for many years the county produced a sizable number of hogs, largely Berkshires, Poland Chinas, Duroc Jerseys, and Hampshires. In the 1940s the Tamworth hog gained wide favor in the county, with the result that from 1946 to 1948 large shipments of hogs were sent to Centerville, Indiana, to the annual National Tamworth Swine Show and Sale. In 1947 the Forsyth County consignment to the show and sale ran far ahead of any other state's consignment in the average price paid per head.

From that sale the Forsyth County delegation brought back the highest-ranking Tamworth boar in the United States, to build up the Forsyth County herds. In the 1948 show and sale, the Forsyth County consignment made an equally good showing, and again the Forsyth County breeders, this time working as an organization, brought back the top-ranking Tamworth boar. It may be said that Forsyth County was, at least in 1950, the Tamworth capital of the world.

Commensurate with the development of the cattle industry in Forsyth County was the development of the poultry industry. Forsyth County did not have any poultry-breeding establishment comparable in size to those found in Maryland and Delaware in the 1940s, but the poultry breeders who operated on a small scale made up an aggregate business that was exceedingly large. The New Hampshire breed and New Hampshire Barred Rock Crosses were favored by the Forsyth County poultrymen. At that time many breeders in the old Richmond community provided eggs for hatching.

All of these interests centralized their work in organizations. The Forsyth Guernsey Breeders Association and the Forsyth Holstein-Friesian Breeders Association are representative of the organizations through which the breeders effected group action.

The Hereford breeders set up their association in late November 1948.

An illustration of the group thinking that was going on in Forsyth County agriculture was the flourishing Forsyth Bee-keepers Association. In 1947 these beekeepers set up the Forsyth County unit and worked with such sustained interest that they were able to attract the State Beekeepers Association to Winston-Salem for its annual meeting in 1948. For two successive years, Forsyth County beekeepers swept the top prizes at the North Carolina State Fair.

There has been a general organization of the farmers and farm women of the county in the Forsyth Pomona Grange and its subordinate granges, as well as in the Forsyth County Farm Bureau, which works as a countywide unit rather than breaking its membership down into community groups.

One might think that the variety of crops produced in a county would change little through the years, since climate and rainfall are unchanging. However, crop habits have experienced extraordinary changes. The North Carolina and United States departments of agriculture have constantly sought new outlets for farmers' crops and new crops suitable for the various sections of the country. As more and more land was cleared and as stumps and rocks were removed from land already cleared, erosion became a problem. Indeed, Forsyth along with the rest of the country, lost fully one-third of its soil before the control of running water was seriously considered. One of the first crops used to aid the farmer was lespedeza. Lespedeza came to this section of the state between 1910 and 1920. The poorest farmer could grow it and it has been grown in enormous acreages ever since. Wherever lespedeza took hold, it arrested erosion immediately. Many leaders in agriculture regarded its arrival on the farm scene as the greatest single event in a hundred years. It certainly seemed so to the farmers of Forsyth County.

Other innovations came, some of them very gradually; alfalfa was one of these. While alfalfa has been widely grown throughout the United States since the 1890s, it has gained favor in Forsyth County only slowly, but consistently. In 1948 the farmers cut hay from about three thousand acres of alfalfa.

In the early 1940s a smattering of farmers obtained a small amount of Ladino clover seed; by 1948 the county had a sizable acreage in this splendid pasture crop. At first it was employed only as a grazing crop, then later as a hay crop. Around 1946 Suiter grass (fescue) began to attract attention. It gave promise of being a winter grazing crop, and many Forsyth dairymen over a period of five years or more found that grazing for most of the winter months could be assured by sowing a mixture of a variety of grasses and small grains and forcing them with heavy applications of fertilizer.

During this change in crop system, the per-acre yield of field crops continued to rise. For instance, in 1935 the average yield of corn for the state was under twenty bushels per acre. By 1950 in Forsyth County farmers averaged close to fifty bushels. Before the tobacco acreage-control program was instituted in the 1930s the average yield for tobacco was between 700 and 800 pounds per acre. In 1948 it ran close to 1,200 pounds.

Tremendous progress in agriculture was made between 1925 and 1950, not to speak of all the progress made previously. The county commissioners, James G. Hanes, chairman, Sam Craft, and Dr. D. C. Speas, in 1948 did something almost unprecedented in county government. They appealed directly to farmers to set up a board to advise the county commissioners of the needs of agriculture. As a result, the County Agricultural Board was set up. It represents every township in the county, including Winston township. Through it a great number of the pointed needs of agriculture have been brought to the attention of the county commissioners with resultant sympathetic action. In 1946 the county commissioners placed G. W. McClellan in charge of the Forsyth County Farm, a seven-hundred-acre tract. The change in the intervening period seemed almost miraculous. For example, pictures of cattle grazing on the county farm on 6 January 1948, in the dead of winter, showed the forty-cow herd of Holsteins up to their fetlocks in grass, and when the pictures were submitted to a forum of several hundred at the annual meeting of the North Carolina Dairy Council, even the experts were unable to distinguish them from pictures made in midsummer.

Meanwhile the Forsyth commissioners, on advice of the farmers, through their advisory board, started an artificial insemination program in the spring of 1946. The stud bank included some of the finest Guernsey and Holstein bulls available. It was the first such program in North Carolina and has been imitated in two-thirds of the counties of the state, with a slightly different structure in some localities.

Forsyth County's longtime interest in good roads was again reflected by farmers in the 1940s. On advice of the advisory board, the county commissioners purchased a heavy-duty motor grader to supplement and complement the heavy-duty renovations in roads and terracing on the farms of the county. Use of this machine by an expert crew met with wide approval throughout Forsyth.

Countless lesser achievements resulted from the studies of this board as it gradually got the feel of county agricultural planning. Forsyth farmers thereby overcame the financial slump of the 1920s and 1930s through cooperative efforts and strong local organization.

An Economic Overview: 1925–50

In industry, by the mid-1920s, Forsyth was the number-one county in North Carolina. In addition to primary economic standing in North Carolina, Forsyth County by 1925 had collected at least five other distinctions, as listed by Charles N. Siewers in *Forsyth County: Economic and Social* (1924): the world's largest manufacturer of tobacco products, the country's largest manufacturer of men's knit underwear, the South's largest manufacturer of knit goods, the South's largest manufacturer of woolen goods, and the South's largest manufacturer of wagons.

Forsyth County led the state throughout the 1920s in total assessed valuation of property. With almost $200 million in 1927, Forsyth was followed in this category by Guilford, Buncombe, and Mecklenburg. Forsyth and Guilford each had larger assessed value in that year than did the entire state half a century before. Even more significant, noted Professor S. H. Hobbs in *North*

Carolina: Economic and Social (1930), is the fact that these four counties in 1927 had almost as much taxable wealth as the entire state had in 1912. Indeed, recent wealth gains in North Carolina demonstrated that there were at least seven counties—again, with Forsyth in the lead—with almost as much wealth as the entire state had just eight years before.

Directly related to county wealth is county indebtedness. By the end of the 1920s the percentage range of county, district, and municipal debt, according to Hobbs's study, ranged from a low of 2.7 in Forsyth to a high of 24.8 in Carteret, with thirty-one counties in excess of 10 percent. Statewide, the average was 7 percent of the taxable wealth. And Forsyth County had the lowest tax rate in North Carolina in the late 1920s.

During the next twenty-five years, through depression and war, Forsyth was economically still on the march. In 1949 Forsyth boasted the highest assessed tangible property valuation per capita. The value of her manufactured goods was up from about $305 million in 1922 to $973,099,287 at midcentury. The median income per Forsyth County family in 1949 was $2,760, placing her seventh in North Carolina. Very much an urban community Forsyth had 96,130 city residents in the late 1940s; 36,475 nonfarm residents were found in the county, and only 13,530 farmers were noted in the county in 1949. A breakdown of employment revealed 12,122 persons engaged in the manufacture of tobacco products; 8,237 in textiles; 5,366 in machinery and electrical equipment; 1,986 in trucking; and 1,042 in furniture manufacturing.

Forsyth's heavily commercial and industrial orientation is also indicated by the fact that in 1952 there were 644 employers who hired eight or more persons, and together these firms employed 47,470 workers. At the same time the average worker earned $57.15 per week.

At least since the 1880s and 1890s agriculture has taken a back seat to industry in Forsyth County, though in Siewers's 1924 study, a renewed interest is found in farm products—"no city can grow fat in a lean countryside." In 1920 Forsyth ranked forty-first in the number of farms in the county, with a 7.6 percent increase from 1910 to 1920 as against a statewide average increase of 6.3

percent. The county's greatest problem at that time, agriculturally speaking, was that Forsyth farmers were producing only one-fourth of the food and feed supplies consumed. Siewers stated that "we have enough land to raise a large percent of our food needs if the land were properly used." Only 39 percent of Forsyth County land was under cultivation in 1920. Farming would have to be made more attractive before the county's agriculture could meet its people's needs. This was the problem facing Forsyth's agricultural leaders before and immediately after the Depression.

Also, larger farms were needed for an expanded livestock production, and more money had to be made available to farmers. "Farmers should be self-financing as well as self-feeding," wrote Siewers, and he continued, "the farmers should prepare to feed the urban population within the county."

Forsyth County's agriculture expanded. In 1920 there were 2,849 farms in the county, an increase in a decade of 7.6 percent; in 1945 there were 3,370 farm operations in the county. Farm ownership gradually increased; the number of farms operated by tenants increased only by 98, while the total number of farms increased by 521 during that twenty-five-year period. The average number of acres to the farm was 57.4 acres, with an average of 26.3 under cultivation. Of the county's 271,360 acres, 193,560 were in farms in 1945.

In 1910 Forsyth's total farm property was valued at $8,203,-133; by 1940 it had increased to $16,224,085. In 1945 farm property was valued at $21,037,418 for an average of $6,243 per farm, which placed Forsyth County second highest in the state. At that time Forsyth ranked first in the number of farms having electricity and automobiles. By the early 1950s the average value of a farm in Forsyth had again increased to $10,119, with an average size of 55.4 acres as opposed to an average state value of $6,400.

Forsyth's crop-yielding power in 1944 was as follows: value of crops harvested, $5,869,585; value of crops sold, $3,217,561; value of livestock and livestock products sold, $1,070,273.

The following comparison is based on units of comparison which do not fluctuate. No allowance need be made for the value of currency in 1860, the top prices of 1920, or parity prices of 1944.

FORSYTH COUNTY CROPS AND LIVESTOCK	1860	1920	1944
Corn, bushels	317,890	388,854	483,100
Hay, tons	5,489	19,595	20,600
Wheat, bushels	187,836	199,466	172,330
Oats, bushels	60,934	38,372	143,600
Sweet potatoes, bushels	21,001	46,531	71,400
Irish potatoes, bushels	11,869	25,143	31,960
Tobacco, pounds	551,442	4,049,428	7,151,600
Butter, pounds sold	74,681	520,242	164,378
Horses	2,275	2,533	1,878
Mules	318	2,065	2,097
Cattle	6,180	8,013	8,861
Sheep	6,386	418	89
Swine	18,942	9,127	7,648

Success in both industry and agriculture was reflected in local retail sales, which in the late 1940s and early 1950s were averaging about $138,842,000 per year. The Forsyth County trading area developed retail sales in 1947, according to Sales Managements Survey, of $264,087,000. Forsyth County alone accounted for $113,147,000, which was an increase of 246 percent over the 1940 census figure and a 44 percent increase over 1946. The same survey placed Winston-Salem as the second largest city in retail sales in North Carolina for the year (1947) with a total of $101,493,000. The wholesale sales reported by the same survey for 1947 placed Winston-Salem third in North Carolina with $125,061,000.

Financial Institutions, 1900–50

The year 1911 saw a decisive step in the financial history of Winston-Salem and Forsyth County. On 1 January the Wachovia National Bank (1897) was consolidated with the Wachovia Loan and Trust Company (1893)—then with branch offices in Asheville, High Point, and Salisbury—under the name of Wachovia Bank and Trust Company. Growth continued with the opening of a Trade Street office in 1919 and the Raleigh office in 1922. The

Forsyth Savings and Trust Company was taken over at the request of the directors of that institution in 1930 and was operated as the Third Street branch of the bank. In 1939 an office was established in Charlotte, which brought a total of eight offices in six cities before the Second World War.

Wachovia grew with the community and the state. With assets of $280 million in the late 1940s it was the largest bank between Washington and Atlanta. Also, at that time, it had the largest combined capital and surplus of all the banks in the southeastern United States.

The City National Bank was an outgrowth of the Morris Plan Bank and was established in 1917 by George W. Coan and George W. Coan, Jr. The bank enlarged the scope of its services in 1940 when it received a national charter and assumed the name City National Bank. An original capital of $40,000 in 1917 grew to total assets amounting to $8.5 million in 1948. It is today a part of the First Union National Bank.

The Hood System Industrial Bank was founded in 1925 by Gurney P. Hood and Nick Mitchell, who was elected its first president. A capital of $225,000 in the 1920s realized assets at the close of the 1940s amounting to $1.4 million. It became the Bank of Winston-Salem and then merged with the Bank of North Carolina.

The Federal Home Loan Bank of Winston-Salem was opened for business on 15 October 1932 to serve as a rediscount bank for building and loan associations and savings and loan associations. The district served by this bank included eight southeastern states. Its offices were later moved to Greensboro.

The First National Bank arose from one of the most tragic depressions in banking history. Organized on 16 May 1934, with capital, surplus, and undivided profits of $250,000, this bank grew steadily over the next fifteen years with total assets exceeding $16 million at midcentury. The original officers of First National were Charles M. Norfleet, president; Guy R. Dudley, vice-president, and Gilmer Wolfe, cashier. On 1 January 1961 it merged with the North Carolina National Bank.

In addition to commercial and industrial banks, Winston-Salem acquired two building and loan associations and two federal savings and loan associations. The oldest of these was the Winston-Salem Building and Loan Association, established in 1889, which by 1950 had total assets of over $6 million. The Piedmont Federal Savings and Loan Association was started in 1903 under a state charter. In 1935 this original charter was changed to the federal system. In 1950 Piedmont Federal was the largest of this group with assets exceeding $10 million. The Standard Building and Loan Association was organized in 1908. Assets exceeded $4 million in 1948. And finally, the First Federal Savings and Loan Association was organized originally under a federal charter in 1934, and by midcentury its total assets exceeded $5 million.

The Security Life and Trust Company (now the Integon Corporation) had its beginning in March 1920. George A. Grimsley and Collins Taylor, both of whom had many years of life-insurance experience, organized the company in Greensboro, North Carolina. Civic-minded local citizens who saw the value of such an institution to a community arranged for Security Life to move to Winston-Salem in 1923. The company had a remarkable growth over the next twenty-five years and by 1950 it had realized assets of over $20 million and insurance in force exceeding $185 million.

Transportation and Communication in the First Half of the Twentieth Century

Good transportation and communication facilities aid development and growth of cities. For example, a town may grow up where two main roads cross, a village is begun at a railroad terminal, or a city gradually comes into being around a good river harbor. But Winston-Salem had to build a dependable network of railroads, highways, and airways.

Seeing that transportation arteries could be Winston-Salem's starvation or salvation, businessmen put much stress on their development. Winston-Salem's three railroads had already been established by 1913. The Southern came into the city in 1873, the Norfolk and Western in 1889, and Winston-Salem Southbound in 1910. After 1913 the railroads began extensive expansion of their lines and stations. Southbound Railway opened an office for freight traffic; in 1916 the Norfolk and Western built a new freight station. Union Station was completed in 1926 and Southern Railroad constructed a new freight depot that same year. In 1927 and 1928 Southern and Norfolk and Western built new yards at an expense of $3 million.

Because of the vast amount of freight generated in Winston-Salem, "off-line" railways began opening offices in the city in 1929. By 1948 there were thirty-three such offices, representing 65 percent of the nation's first-class railway mileage.

The early residents of Forsyth recognized the importance of good streets and roads to economic development. The settlers in Salem had kept the paths of trade and commerce open at great expense. Cobblestone paving had been used in Salem for many years, but the first modern street-paving project began in 1890 with the laying of Belgian blocks along Main Street. Also about 1890 Charles A. Reynolds introduced macadamized roads to Forsyth County. Using convicts to crush stone and place it on the road, Mr. Reynolds made such an improvement on what is now Waughtown Street that the county constructed considerable macadamized road mileage, much of which still exists under a cover of asphalt.

One summer night in 1913 the members of the Winston-Salem Chamber of Commerce very heatedly discussed a proposed "white way" for the city. The proposition was to light and pave West Fourth Street from Liberty to and including Grace Court. The object of this proposal was to make "an evening thoroughfare for public enjoyment and an attractive advertisement to outsiders coming to the city." Among objections to the project were the expense and the thought that the "dazzling illumination" would be a discomfort to the residents of Fourth Street. After futile attempts to get the city to do so, the Retail Merchants Association installed a "white way" later that year. A permanent lighting system was later installed by the city after this first attempt met with great favor.

City streets continued to use Belgian blocks as a principal paving material as late as 1919. A short section of West First Street was laid in brick as an experiment but relatively few streets were bricked. In 1915 the city had 12.22 miles of paved streets within the city limits. In 1923 an extensive street-building program was begun and by 1948 there were 145 miles of paved streets within the city.

There was great interest in road improvement throughout North Carolina at the turn of the century. A "Good Roads Train" traveled to most parts of the state demonstrating new and improved methods of road building. The North Carolina Good Roads Association, headed by a Winston-Salem man, P. H. Hanes, likewise did much to awaken North Carolinians to the need for better roads. This group was instrumental in the establishment of the state highway commission and a state program for maintenance of highways. Wise planning of the Forsyth County commissioners brought into Winston-Salem a network of highways which often were locally subsidized, as had been the railroads. By the late 1940s Winston-Salem had more hard-surfaced roads leading into it than did any other city or center in North Carolina.

A "Romance of Transportation" pageant on 29 December 1936, sponsored by the Chamber of Commerce, marked farewell to the electric streetcar system, and the city changed to buses for its intracity transportation. Six taxicab companies also helped furnish city transportation needs.

With highway development came bus service between cities. In 1912 buses with 35-horsepower Model-T Ford engines, carrying only from seven to sixteen passengers, took travelers from Winston-Salem to High Point. About 1915 buses in the city carried around fifty passengers a day. Shortly after World War II, 240-horsepower buses carrying a maximum of thirty-seven passengers each passed through the city destined for any point or connection in the country. Some three thousand bus travelers came through Forsyth County daily.

Before 1926 a number of small bus companies operated in Winston-Salem. In that year John L. Gilmer formed the Camel City Coach Company. Gilmer had bought up a number of the smaller lines, so that by the time he formed his company he had six twenty-one-passenger buses. In 1930 the Camel City Coach Company merged with the Blue and Gray Lines of Charleston,

West Virginia, later becoming the Atlantic Greyhound Lines, with Winston-Salem as a center for its southern division.

The city's first bus station (adjoining the Zinzendorf Hotel) had an office and a waiting room to accommodate twenty people. In 1942 the Union Bus Station was built on Cherry Street between Fourth and Fifth at a cost of some $200,000. It could handle twenty-four buses and 240 persons at one time and was one of the largest and most modern stations in the nation.

Motor express transportation grew with highway development. Malcolm P. McLean started his company with a "battered old car and an equally decrepit two-wheel trailer" in 1934. Within a matter of not so many years McLean Trucking was a multimillion-dollar corporation. Pilot Freight Company, like McLean, had modest beginnings. Its founder, R. Y. Sharpe, built Pilot into a multimillion dollar line. Winston-Salem's other trucker prior to 1950, Shirley Mitchell, acquired Hennis Freight Line in 1946. At the time Mitchell purchased it the business was small but thriving, realizing gross revenues of some $282,000. By the mid-1960s Hennis revenues exceeded $51 million.

Forsyth County dedicated its first airport on 5 December 1919. The old Maynard Field, as it was called, was the first airport in the South apart from those associated with national defense needs. Some years later, in the 1920s, Winston-Salem used the Friendship Airport with Greensboro and High Point.

When it became obvious that the Friendship Airport would not serve the city's needs and that the Maynard Field was outmoded, citizens began making plans for a new field. A timely visit from Colonel Charles A. Lindbergh gave impetus to these plans, and on 14 October 1927 the Miller Airport, built on the old county farm lands just outside the city, was officially opened. That same day the field was given to the city by a public-spirited citizen, R. E. Lasater, and placed under the Winston-Salem Foundation.

In the early 1930s Miller Airport received some appropriations for grading and improvement from the Federal Work Relief Program. In 1935 the old Friendship Airport was condemned for landings by Eastern Airlines, so Miller Airport was put into shape to meet government and airline requirements. In April 1935 Eastern Airlines began Forsyth County's first commercial air service. Eight months later the service was discontinued because of inadequate facilities at the airport.

On 14 June 1941 Eastern Airlines again established regular commercial air service—direct air mail, passenger, and express service—for Forsyth. One year later, in June 1942, the new terminal, which was made possible by a gift from the Reynolds family, was finished and the new Smith Reynolds Airport officially opened. The field had Class-5 facilities (Class-6 being the highest) at that time. Capital Airlines began service through the city in June 1947, and in February of 1948, Piedmont Aviation, Inc., opened its home offices in Winston-Salem.

Piedmont Aviation was organized by Thomas H. Davis, son of Egbert L. Davis, Sr., with the help of such men as Charles Norfleet, Robert Northington, Edward Culler, and Milton Fiar. The first North Carolina-owned-and-operated airline, Piedmont broke away from the north-south transportation pattern which had handicapped the state since its earliest beginnings. Besides providing transportation across the mountains to the west, Piedmont also gave many North Carolina cities their first regular and easy contact with the outside world.

Beginning with DC-3s flying out of Smith Reynolds Airport, Piedmont flew into twenty-two cities and covered 1,686 miles. In 1948 the airline carried almost forty thousand passengers and steadily increased its passenger, air mail, air express, and air freight mileage. Its major growth was to occur in the years after 1950.

Conclusion: Economic Development, 1900–50

Forsyth County and Winston-Salem incorporated the industrial revolution into an ancient life-style. In the later half of the nineteenth century and the first half of the twentieth, industrial growth and economic development flourished in the area. Native industries expanded, some merging with outside concerns to bring in needed capital or to acquire wider markets; outside industries located within the county. The changes would intensify during the third quarter of the twentieth century. Events that once were welcomed would bring their own sets of problems. Labor difficulties, racial tensions, and economic and social changes were already visible as Forsyth County celebrated its centennial in 1949. Some of these would ease as time passed, and others would intensify. But, on the whole, Forsyth remained a county on the march.

CHAPTER 13

The Black Community

THE ASPECT OF FORSYTH COUNTY'S HISTORY which probably has been least documented is its black community. Having gained their freedom but receiving no means by which to earn a living— not even the promised "forty acres and a mule"—many Negroes migrated from rural areas to the newly industrializing cities of the New South in the late nineteenth century. Winston-Salem and Forsyth County were no exceptions to this migration and on through the first half of the twentieth century the black population was increased by Negroes coming from outlying regions. Of a total population of over 35,000 in 1900, Forsyth County had 10,543 blacks; and 1950 census figures showed a total population of 146,135 of which 41,402 were black.

The developing industrial complex of Winston-Salem provided jobs for many, both black and white. Ironically, industrialization created a need for supportive agriculture, and many blacks and whites were able to earn a living from the soil. But percentages of industrial and quasi-industrial workers remained highest among the blacks. Industry offered surer and more consistent rewards than agriculture—besides, a man could work in a factory at the same time as he and his family supported a farm or garden.

Making their way within the oppressive and discriminatory conditions typical of the post-Reconstruction South, a number of black individuals achieved some success and prominence. Receiving occasional but crucial assistance from the white community— also typical of post-Reconstruction black-white relations—blacks began to establish businesses, enter professions, provide services, and work for the improvement of their own community.

What follows is unfortunately not a comprehensive view of the black community in the first half of the twentieth century. It is instead a series of views of individuals and their work, to indicate the accomplishments made, paving the way for the rapid strides in all areas for Forsyth County's black community in the years following World War II. These are presented in hopes of encouraging the writing of a fuller history of the black community at some future time.

"Mr." George Black

George Black came to Winston-Salem in 1889 from his home in Liberty, North Carolina. His father, his brother Willie, and he traveled the fifty miles with a mule and a wagon, with the young boys walking much of the way. A few months after their arrival, their father died, and George, only ten years old, recalled his brother Willie's telling him: "We are not going to get any schooling, but we can learn a trade and people will respect us and call us 'Mr. Black.'"

Black followed his brother's advice and mastered the art and business of brickmaking so well that he lived to see his brick and his name known across the nation. He learned to make bricks by hand in the old Hedgecock Brickyard, a white-owned company where his father had worked before he died. Young George soon learned all about the craft and was frequently left in charge of the operation.

He began making brick on his own, using an old mud-mill he had been given to throw away. He fixed it up for his own use and began to make brick on his own time for his own use and for sale. Sometime in the 1920s, along with another skillful brickmaker, Alex Walker, Black established his own brickyard.

Over the years, Black's brick were used in building some fifteen banks, the Salem College Library, the Baptist Hospital, and some of Winston-Salem's finest homes. His brick—always handmade—have also been used in the restorations of Old Salem and Colonial Williamsburg. With the revival of interest in handcrafts, Black was called on by Colonial Williamsburg and others to teach his art.

In 1971, "Mr. Black" became an immediate celebrity when his work was the subject of a national television program. This led to a goodwill mission on which George Black, then in his nineties, worked to teach the people of Guyana his ancient craft of brickmaking. The trip was undertaken at the request of the United States Agency for International Development. On his return, Black was feted in Raleigh and entertained in Washington by the president of the United States. Recognized by President Nixon and other of the country's officials, his reception is typified by a letter of introduction presented by Lieutenant Governor Pat Taylor of North Carolina: "This is to introduce Mr. George Black, respected citizen and maker of bricks from Winston-Salem, N.C. Mr. Black makes bricks by hand. Through the years his bricks have been transformed into buildings that serve the uses of man. They will stand many years more in silent and useful tribute to the work of his hands. Mr. Black has worked at this handicraft all of his life. North Carolina is proud to have such a fine citizen."

Recently George Black received the Freedoms Foundation's George Washington Medal of Honor for his humanitarian mission to Guyana. Black continues to operate his brickyard.

Financial Institutions

George Black stands as an example of a successful member of Forsyth's Negro community. Another part of the business picture is illustrated by the corporate growth of Winston Mutual Life Insurance Company. As far back as 1897, young schoolteacher Robert W. Brown envisioned a plan for economic security for black people. After consulting with physician J. W. Jones, attorney J. S. Fitts, and grocer Jim Ellington, Brown brought in W. A. Jones, G. W. Hill, J. W. Lewis, John A. Blume, J. C. McKnight, L. L. Johnson, and Ed Smith to complete the organization. From these meetings, on 6 August 1906 the Winston Industrial Association came into being, based on a fraternal-order insurance plan. It grew rapidly and established an agency in Wilmington, North Carolina in 1907 and expanded by reinsuring the Piedmont Mutual Life Insurance Company of Greensboro in 1909 and the Peoples Home and Charitable Institution in 1914. In 1951, the company established an office in Asheville when it acquired Mountain City Mutual Life Insurance Company. It underwent reorganization as an assessment association and for twenty-four hours was known as the Mountain City Mutual Insurance Company. On the next day, the name was changed to Winston Mutual Life Insurance Company and so it has remained. Prior to 1915 the company had issued only health and accident policies, but in that year the first whole-life policy was written.

As the company developed it involved numerous leaders in the black communities of Winston-Salem and elsewhere. In the 1930s and 1940s, under the leadership of G. W. Hill and W. P. Hairston, the company expanded its operations to include investments in real estate and home loans. This not only gave the company a secure and profitable economic base but made it possible for thousands of black families to purchase real estate and finance their homes. G. W. Hill was elected president of the company in 1937 and served until his death when his son E. E. Hill succeeded him. He was followed as president by W. Avery Jones, and in 1971 George E. Hill, the current president, and son and grandson of earlier presidents, took office. The company occupied its new building on East Fifth Street in 1969 and continues to serve as a model of black corporate development.

The Forsyth Savings and Trust Company was organized by a group of Negro men in 1907. One of the founders and first president (1907–23) was James S. Hill. Hill was also known for his outstanding work in higher education, traveling widely to raise money for Slater Normal (now Winston-Salem State University) and Livingstone College. From 1923 until the bank closed in the early 1930s the president was W. S. Scales. The first board of directors included, along with J. S. Hill, George Reynolds, J. H. Turner, and S. G. Atkins. The Forsyth Savings and Trust Company bought out the assets of an earlier Negro bank known as the Citizens Bank. This bank was operated by Dr. J. W. Jones, a leading Winston-Salem physician in the early 1920s.

The Forsyth Savings and Trust Company served the black community well until it became one of the casualties of the Great

Depression. All of the directors of the Forsyth Bank lost much personal property and other assets when the bank was consolidated with Wachovia Bank and Trust, a move which saved the depositors' funds.

Public Transportation

Good examples of black individual and corporate progress can be found in the area of public transportation. The first cab service provided by blacks was a hack service in use at the turn of the century. Joe Martin provided a hansom carriage service. Will Davis and the Brown brothers met trains for many years with their carriages until automobiles arrived in Winston-Salem. Buster Green, Sandy Williams, Toby Lewis, and Graham Cathey operated early privately owned taxis in East Winston. In the early 1920s the Camel City Cab Company was established by the Safe Bus Company.

Public transportation in the early 1920s in the black community was a risky business, pursued mostly in dust, slush, and muck. In spite of the inconveniences private jitneys, as the early buses were called, rambled through the city picking up passengers wherever they found them. No one was ever sure when he could get a ride.

The founders of this mode of transportation were Ralph R. and Harvey F. Morgan; they provided transportation for the Columbia Heights area. Others soon followed and several jitneys served various areas of the Negro community. Arthur Hill and Eddie Richardson drove the first jitneys from downtown up Liberty Street to the corner of East Fourteenth Street where passengers waited. The Dismukes' "Blue Haven" jitney was quite a favorite in East Winston as was George Dillahunt's "Lightning Express." Fred Smith, the Morgan brothers, Charlie Peoples, and J. H. Hairston were other pioneer jitney owners.

These early jitneys could not meet the needs of a growing community, and on 14 April 1926 a group of Negro bus owners met to discuss their problems. On 26 May 1926, the state of North Carolina granted them a charter and the Safe Bus Corporation was born under the leadership of a strong business executive, C. T. Woodland. During the 1920s the company under Harvey F. Morgan made continuous progress. Under the able leadership of C. R. Peebles the company survived the Depression and World War II. For ten years John M. Adams steered the company through its most critical years until his death in 1959. Mrs. Mary M. Burns, daughter of E. H. Miller, became the first woman president in 1959. After six months she was succeeded by Mrs. Delphine Morgan as president; she served until Buster Green became president in 1961. Hampton Haith became the general manager. Haith and Green reorganized the Safe Bus Company to meet the demands of the public. The Safe Bus Company in Winston-Salem was the largest Negro transportation facility in the world. It maintained this position until it was purchased by the city of Winston-Salem during the early years of the 1970s when the company became a part of the Winston-Salem Mass Transit Authority.

Individual Business Leaders

Although the majority of the Negroes were tenant farmers, sharecroppers, or industrial workers, a few black individuals achieved much success and made a great impact on the black community, usually by providing services to the Negroes of Winston-Salem and Forsyth.

Probably the earliest funeral home operated by Negroes was owned around the turn of the century by Justus Lattie, an alderman and casketmaker. K. Howard was also among the undertakers who began operating before 1900. Grant, Smith, and Long were early casketmakers and probably did some undertaking as well. Fitch and Company were operating in 1913 as was Howard, Blackburn and Scales. The Howard-Robinson Company followed in 1917. Clark S. Brown opened Brown's Funeral Directors in 1939. Today, numerous funeral homes including Brown, Forsyth, Gilmore, Hooper, Howard-Robinson, Johnson, Russell, and Ryan serve the black community.

Rufus Foy, the owner of over forty-two acres of land in 1886 near Mickey Mill Road and Bowen Boulevard, was a successful farmer. Part of his property was Foy's Graveyard, used by Negroes until it was sold to the Smith Reynolds Airport. One of his sons, Jordon Foy, was a carpenter who built many East Winston houses between 1900 and 1920. Foytown, the section from Jackson Avenue to Woodland Avenue, was the location of many of the homes which he built and was named for him. He also made caskets in his carpenter's shop.

It was in this shop that Jordon Foy and several others in the black community laid the groundwork for Mt. Pleasant Methodist Church, which existed at Highland Avenue and East Fourteenth Street for seventy-nine years. When the church was replaced by redevelopment, most of its members went to St. Paul's United Methodist Church.

Successful contractors in the early twentieth century included Vivian C. Ramseur, John H. Smith, and John W. Hauser. Smith and Hauser were an especially competent team who served the black community for many years.

George D. Reynolds, contractor, builder, brickmaker, and banker, made bricks and built houses. He helped build the old Slater Hospital on the campus of Slater Normal and Industrial School. He gave land to the county upon which was built the Belview County School for Negroes located on Moravia Street. He was well known to both races of Forsyth County.

Morgan-Hoffman Dry Cleaners was one of the first large Negro cleaners with modern equipment and employing a large number of workers. It existed for many years on Third Street.

The Camel City Clothing Company, managed by Ernest Johnson, was established by Negroes for Negroes by 1935.

The Brown Derby Hat Works was the only Negro hat manufacturing concern in the state in 1935. It was located at 314 Patterson Avenue. Some of the managers were Tom Neely, Willie Motley, and B. C. Sanford.

Pomp Penry was reputed to be the owner of the first grocery store in East Winston. Alexander Pace, G. W. Hawkins, Joe Brim Turner, Joe Martin, Robert Warren, Thomas Hooper, Tom Toliver, Charlie Jones, Winston Rucker, and Henry Terry also operated early stores. O. A. Brown was general manager of a League Grocery Store which was a Negro community project and may be called the first supermarket for blacks in Winston-Salem during the 1920s. It was a very successful business.

Marion Dull, who operated the Little Cash Store, entered the real-estate business and was considered a progressive business-man. He owned a large amount of property during the decade of the 1920s.

Jim Ellington was manager and owner of a grocery store on Seventh at Linden Street and made successful investments in other businesses.

Negroes mastered the barber's craft before the end of slavery. Two known pioneers prior to 1900 were Alex Gates, who operated a barbershop in 1880 on the spot where the Zinzendorf Hotel was built, and the Reverend Douglas McDonald, who operated a barbershop in 1877. Some of these early barbers served whites. C. B. Cash's first barbershop was on the corner of Fourth and Liberty Streets, where the Pepper Building now stands; it was the largest shop in town. Cash and his son Artie Cash later moved the shop to Third Street, where the Wachovia Building now is located. C. B. Cash was among the first of his race to invest in the Forsyth County Fair. His wife taught music and was one of the first black teachers in the city. A. Lee Smith operated a barber-shop for whites on Main Street in Salem, near the old Post Office, before World War I. Both of these barbers were highly respected citizens of the community. By 1935 there were more than twenty-five barbershops operated by Negroes in Winston-Salem. Clients walked miles to obtain the expert services of H. A. Spencer. The Graham brothers, Will McClary, C. C. Scott, and James Wilson were all skillful barbers before World War I. Will McClary boasted of capturing the "flapper" trade. Ed Hunt was a very popular barber on Church Street, downtown. Some of these barbers worked at their trade over sixty years. The Graham Barbershop, C. E. Graham, manager, is still located downtown on East Fourth Street.

Negroes made great strides as cafe owners. Robert Shoaf, who owned the first cafe in the Downtown Garage beginning in 1928 and continuing for more than twenty years, stated that Negroes operated numerous cafes catering to the downtown fac-tory workers during the 1920s and 1930s. He recalls Will Scales's cafe on East Fourth Street as one of the largest and best, and also that Richard Moss stayed in the cafe business several years. Shoaf estimated that at least forty-five cafes were operated by Negroes.

A Negro operator of an employment office in the 1930s was rather unusual; Mollie Poag was the first such person in the city. She worked in the Bruce Building at the corner of Sixth and Patterson Avenue. From this position she became an employee of the Federal Employment Office where she continued serving the black community until her retirement.

Prior to 1910 Winston-Salem had three Negro mail carriers: John Hughes, Monroe Cuthrell, and Pete Easley. Other Negroes with the postal service worked as custodians or in the maintenance department.

The need for fire protection in the black community was met by the organization of several volunteer fire companies around the turn of the century. John Hanes organized a Hook and Ladder Company for Negroes. Its first members included Aaron Moore, Henry Neal, T. M. Hairston, and H. Seward. They were associated with the North Carolina Volunteer Fireman's Association.

Hose Reel Companies One and Two were located in Salem and Columbia Heights. John Smith was captain, Henry Elam, lieutenant, and among the first firemen were Irvin Scales, Harvey Clanton, Odell Clanton, Archie Scales, and Charles Rorie. Johnnie McKnight was reported to be the star fireman as the fastest runner and ladder climber. The volunteer companies continued until Winston-Salem could provide a full-time paid fire department authorized by the Board of Aldermen.

John Joyce was probably the first Negro policeman. The first Negro police detective in Winston-Salem was Walter Long, who served the community with pride and valor during the 1920s and 1930s until his death.

There were several short-lived newspapers published by Negroes in the early twentieth century. Perhaps the longest to survive was the *Post*, published by C. A. Ervin on Church Street. Negro columnists also began reporting news from the black community for the *Journal and Sentinel* papers in the 1920s. The first of these Negro reporters was Hoyt Wiseman, Sr., who had an office in the YMCA building. He was followed by A. A. Mayfield, a dynamic orator and community worker who covered Negro news for years. His successor was Leroy Davis, who reported local Negro news during the 1930s and 1940s.

Mildred Jacquelyn Martin, poetess and school teacher, prepared a collection of poems entitled *Wachovian Moods*. Several of her poems were published in the *Journal and Sentinel* on 11 March 1934. "At 23 her poems were unique and showed much promise," stated the newspaper reviewer.

The movement for home ownership among Negro citizens began as early as 1880. A famous two-room brick house, located on Linden and East Seventh streets, owned by Louis Heggie, was thought to be the first brick house erected by a Negro owner. John A. Blum, a pioneer citizen, said "that house was a 'sight' for pedestrians."

The old Penry House, located on East Seventh near Linden Street, was considered a palatial residence when it was built in the early 1880s by Negroes.

Dr. W. H. Goler leads the list of black realtors in Winston-Salem. Beginning about 1900, he owned a large number of rental houses on Patterson Avenue and several business buildings. Dr. Goler was also a pioneer in the establishment of Goler A.M.E. Zion Church of Winston-Salem.

Dr. H. H. Hall was the first Negro physician in the city. Dr. Hall, like most early North Carolina black doctors, was a graduate of Shaw University in Raleigh. For a while he was the only physician for the entire Negro community. After a time he secured the services of Dr. John W. Jones to assist him. Both men served Winston-Salem and surrounding community. Other early physicians included William Henry Bruce who came in 1907; John R. Henry, 1908; J. R. Hawkins, 1913; and Thomas J. Brown, 1914. Dr. Cleon O. Lee was practicing dentistry in the city by 1910 and was noted for his expert service. Mrs. Girlie Jones Strickland, Miss Daisy Teer, and Mrs. Annie K. Brown lead the list of early practicing nurses in the city.

An essential element in the Negro community was its drugstores. Dispensing medicine, sundries, and advice, the black-owned-and-operated stores served a number of community needs. In 1900 Dr. W. A. Jones became the pioneer black drugstore operator in East Winston. His store was located on Church and Third streets. In 1906 his store was joined by one operated by Drs. H. H. Hall and William Henry Bruce at the corner of Patterson Avenue and Sixth Street. Also on Church Street came the drugstore operated by Rufus Hairston and Cicero Neely. And Eureka Drugstore, owned by Dr. J. C. Williamson, another physician, was located at Eighth Street and Ridge Avenue.

Forsyth Negroes built their first hospital in 1902, adjoining Slater Normal and Industrial School. Dr. H. H. Hall and all the early doctors, both black and white, practiced at Slater Hospital. It was built with equal sums of $3,650 raised by Dr. S. G. Atkins and contributed by R. J. Reynolds. The hospital closed around 1910.

Attorney John S. Fitts was the first Negro lawyer in this city. Other early attorneys were J. S. Lanier, W. A. Jones, H. V. Price, H. O. Bright, A. R. Bridges, and F. W. Williams. Attorney J. S. Lanier was practicing law in Winston-Salem before 1900 and continued for over sixty years. The father of Mrs. J. S. Lanier operated what was perhaps East Winston's first sanitary hotel.

Many East Winston businessmen began with one trade and expanded into many others. As they prospered they usually accumulated real-estate holdings and invested in corporations which provided services for the black community. John H. Turner got his start as a schoolteacher and then began selling fish in the old City Market located in the City Hall on Church Street where the Reynolds building now stands. A popular supplier for housewives, both black and white, he also supplied fish to most cafes and big businesses. He then went into real-estate investment and banking.

Will Scales, manager of the Lafayette Theater, bondsman, cafe operator, and real-estate dealer, was especially active in the period just prior to World War I. Sam Farmer began as a Reynolds factory worker around 1900. Known for his thrift and wise investments, he purchased several low-cost homes during the Depression and became an outstanding real-estate owner before he died in the 1940s. Jeane Smith, a resourceful real-estate dealer, built a community of brick flats on Patterson and Eighth streets. C. H. Jones owned a hotel on Third and Church streets and was one of the early successful Negro hotel owners and operators. He invested in property and houses and left his widow (Savannah Jones) a large estate. She, after his death, tripled his real-estate holdings. James Madison Clanton operated a shoeshop and cafe on Main and Fourth streets, at the turn of the century, and owned the Evergreen Hotel and Sewing Shop on Fourth and Chestnut streets.

Community Service Organizations

As individuals prospered, they joined with others to provide activities for the Negro community. Around 1910 a group of black leaders formed the Piedmont Fair Association which sponsored the Forsyth County Fair. The Forsyth Fair was principally for Negroes and gave the black community an annual occasion to exhibit agricultural and home craft products and to join in the harvest merriment traditional with an agricultural community. Among the founders were R. W. Brown, general manager; J. H. Turner, president; and James Timlic, treasurer. Barber C. B. Cash was an early investor. The Forsyth County Fair continued until the late 1960s.

Another community-minded organization was the Emancipation Association, organized in the early 1900s. On 1 January of each new year the association gathered in the Forsyth County Courthouse and presented a program commemorating emancipation. Early promoters and organizers were J. S. Lanier, J. S. Hill, J. H. Turner, J. H. Alexander, and S. G. Atkins.

Many Negro women gave of their time and leadership to help the young people to read and understand the Bible. Organized prayer bands operated in almost every community. Among those dedicated souls were such women as Nora S. Bailey, who paved the way for home missionary work during the flu epidemic of the early 1920s. A devoted Christian and diligent worker, Nora Bailey began preaching in tents to those in red-light districts and in prison camps, and she traveled widely with her camp meetings. So successful was Mrs. Bailey in her ministerial endeavors that she was finally ordained to preach by the Methodist Conference.

Nora Bailey, along with the help of other dedicated women, established the Rescue Mission House on East Fourteenth Street and Claremont Avenue. So successful was her work at this mission for the poor and needy that it was renamed the Community House and subsidized by funds from the Associated Charities. The range of activities widened and the strong charitable institution survived for several years.

Another well-known community missionary was Addie C. Morris. She ran one of the first missionary houses, located at the old First Baptist Church on the corner of Sixth and Chestnut streets. She established what was probably the first kindergarten for black children in Winston-Salem. Remembered for her educational and religious contributions to the people of this area, Mrs. Morris's efforts are commemorated by the organization of Addie C. Morris Clubs which include both men and women of the community.

Mrs. Belle Campbell ran a home for the sick and aged on East Twelfth Street which was sometimes known as the Alms House.

The Phyllis Wheatley Home was established on 12 March 1918 by a group of twenty-three women who saw the need for an institution for the protection of women and girls coming to the city for employment. The idea was born with Mrs. L. B. Neal at a meeting held at the Depot Grade School, and Mrs. Neal was the first president. The institution broadened its scope to include domestic training, literary clubs, educational and business activities, with emphasis on home economics. The home housed over sixty women at a time and was located on East Fourth Street near Linden Street; it was ultimately replaced by redevelopment in East Winston.

The Colored Orphanage was established early in the twentieth century and was taken over by the civic clubs of the city in 1923. At that time the institution consisted of twenty-eight acres of land, located within the city limits. There were several buildings, including a baby cottage and girls' and boys' dormitories, farm and farm implements, livestock, and superintendent's quarters. None of the buildings was fireproof, and they had no sanitary toilets or bathrooms. The institution was badly in debt, services were poorly paid, and children were poorly clothed and fed.

In 1923 a board of directors consisting of representatives from civic clubs of the city and several white and Negro citizens incorporated the orphanage, changing the name to Memorial Industrial School. The old institution was abandoned and a new site, located nine miles north of the city in the Sauratown Mountains, was secured. The new institution covered 425 acres of land, had plenty of running water and timber, 200 acres for cultivation, boasted an administration building of brick with a slate roof, and had all other facilities for an adequate orphans' home. It included classrooms for about two hundred children, a separate dining area and kitchen, and sanitary living quarters. The Industrial School represented an investment of $175,000.

The farm was donated by W. N. Reynolds, the baby cottage by Mr. and Mrs. N. A. Gray, boys' cottage by children of the late R. J. Reynolds, and equipment for the power plant was given by W. N. Reynolds. After 1923 the orphanage was indebted to the Winston-Salem Community Chest for its yearly contributions and for contributions from the Duke Foundation. R. C. Haberkern was president of the institution and the executive board. Owen Redwine, an engineer and agricultural specialist, is credited with turning the orphanage's 200 acres into fine farmland. He employed scientific know-how to the improvement of the institution. For many years until it was discontinued in 1970 the institution served to produce useful citizens.

The city juvenile detention home for Negro boys was established on 1 January 1934. The idea originated with Chief of Police J. G. Wooten, Judge T. W. Watson, and K. W. Davis, juvenile court officials, who recognized the urgent need for a place to care for delinquent Negro boys. They worked diligently to save youthful offenders from the life of the hardened criminal.

Impetus toward the detention home grew greatly when the Forsyth County Reformatory closed its doors on 25 September 1931 and delinquent boys were rampant on the streets of Winston-Salem. Soon after the closing of the reformatory the detention of boys at the City Hall increased 250 percent in three months' time. The urgent need for an institution to care for these boys became immediately apparent. A home was established in Belview, on Moravia Street, under the direction of John C. Joyce and Mrs. Joyce, the superintendent and matron respectively.

During the first two years fifty-four inmates were sent to the home. The home had a farm and other crafts for the boys and proved to be a success immediately. It was a credit to Police Chief Wooten and all citizens interested in the lives of the delinquent boys.

On 15 February 1927, the George Moses Horton Branch Library opened its doors as a branch of the Carnegie Public Library, the branch's name being chosen in honor of the Negro slave poet who in 1829 published a book of poems, *Hope of Liberty*. Mrs. R. S. Hairston was the librarian in charge.

The Negro YWCA started in 1917, when a group of Negro girls formed a club meeting in various homes. Adventure in Christian training and other services were their goals. The group grew so large that it had to find additional space. Learning more about the ideals of the YWCA, they began calling their group YWCA. Mrs. Jane Thornton Melton headed the group for some time. Then Miss Adele Ruffin, a national traveling secretary, was called to Winston-Salem to formally organize the girls into a YWCA. On 5 January 1918, in the Pythian Hall, seventy-five women were officially enrolled in the first YWCA and Mrs. Melton became the first chairman. They met in the Little Day Nursery in the rear of the Old Depot Street School at the corner of Vine and Seventh streets. They then moved to the Old Presbyterian Church on Patterson Avenue, until it was destroyed by fire. The next move was to a garage building on Chestnut Street which cost $15,000, paid for through generous donations from white and black friends of the organizers. The Winston-Salem Branch has contributed much to the national organization since its inception. Mrs. J. H. Kyles became a national committee member. Miss Willie Mae Scales Henningburg, Miss Roberta Randolph, Mrs. Madge Neely, Mrs. Sara Hill, Mrs. Jean Pace, and Mrs. Ruby Cephas were among the tireless leaders of the beginning years.

The original committee was composed of chairman, Mrs. Jane Thornton Melton; vice-chairman, Mrs. Callie Williamson; secretary, Mrs. Lulu Sitgreaves; treasurer, Mrs. J. S. Hill Edmondson.

The YMCA for Negroes was organized in 1911 by a few outstanding citizens who realized the needs of the young adult community. These founders were J. H. Turner, J. S. Hill, J. H. Alexander, Dr. W. A. Jones, and a Mr. Edmundson. The first secretary was C. T. Woodland. The first location was on Church Street. Then it moved to the Old Depot Street School and since 1953 has been on Patterson and Sixth streets.

The Churches

Forsyth's black community has always had an active church life. St. Philip's, the Negro Moravian Church in Salem, was probably the earliest formally organized church for blacks in this region. Then in the 1870s Reverend George W. Holland pioneered the development of several black churches in Winston-Salem. In 1879 he organized the First Baptist Church at Sixth and Chestnut streets and became its first pastor. Reverend Henry A. Brown of the First Baptist Church (Fifth Street) assisted Mr. Holland in organizing the Negro church. Mr. Holland organized several Baptist churches in Winston-Salem; New Bethel Church is one of the monuments to his efforts.

Reverend J. A. Whitted succeeded Mr. Holland as pastor of First Baptist Church in 1906–7. This church at the corner of Sixth and Chestnut streets was often called the mother church of black Baptists in Forsyth County.

Bishop J. D. Diggs, religious, educational, and civic leader, was also active in the city's church life around the turn of the century. He came to St. Paul Methodist Church in February 1898. In 1904 he left the Methodist Conference and established a unit of the United Holy Church of America in this city. In 1905 he organized the Union Mission Church of God. Within this organization he became a bishop and traveled from coast to coast in the work of the church. Bishop Diggs was one of the organizers of the Ministers Union which acts as the spokesman for problems within the Negro community. He fought for better sanitation facilities and educational opportunities for the blacks.

Another prominent church leader who received national recognition for his work was Bishop Linwood W. Kyles, pastor of the Goler Memorial A.M.E. Zion Church. He was a senior bishop of the Western North Carolina Conference of the African Methodist Episcopal Zion church. He was also actively identified with interdenominational and interracial organizations throughout the country, a member of the executive committee and interracial department of the Federal Council of Churches in America, a member of the corporation of the World Christian Endeavor Society, and a member of the World Council of Churches. He addressed the World Christian Endeavor Conference in Budapest in 1936. He was the only Negro delegate from America and was officially chosen as one of the speakers for the United States delegation.

Education

The Depot Street School was one of the first city schools for Negroes and was located on Patterson Avenue and Seventh Street. Blumtown School served the children in East Winston near East Fourteenth Street and vicinity. It was located on East Thirteenth Street and Claremont Avenue. There was also a county school for Negroes located in Boston (Kimberly Park) and one on the south side of town as well.

George H. Willis established a private graded school prior to World War I in the old Citizens' Building located near Lloyd Presbyterian Church and Chestnut Street. He was the principal and his wife Hattie was a teacher. The school was destroyed by fire.

Among the early church- and day-school leaders were Israel Clemmons, the first Negro church-school teacher; Professor Martin; Sam Wall; Professor Chavis; Dr. S. G. Atkins; Professor Willis; and Professor Smith, all educators in the years before the 1920s.

The Columbia Heights graded school dates back to 1905, when the county turned over a three-room frame structure to the city. In the school year 1913–14 the school had 263 pupils. Dr. S. G. Atkins was principal and Mrs. Lillie Mebane was assistant principal. East Fourteenth Street School opened in 1924 with a large enrollment. Atkins High School opened in 1931.

Woodland Avenue School was built in 1910. This four-room frame building was erected on a site between Eleventh and Twelfth streets. The first faculty was composed of Mrs. Lillie K. Mebane, Mrs. Nora Lewis, Mrs. Zula B. Lovell, and Miss Priscilla Graham. In 1911–12 R. W. Brown became the principal.

Opportunities in higher education for Forsyth's black community were, even before the ending of educational segregation, available in the state and region. Slater Industrial Academy (now Winston-Salem State University) emerged from the work of Dr. S. G. Atkins who came to Winston-Salem in 1888 to be principal of the Colored Graded School. Educated at St. Augustine's College in Raleigh, Dr. Atkins taught at Livingstone College in Salisbury, North Carolina. While on the faculty at Livingstone and for a time after he came to Winston-Salem, Dr. Atkins assisted Dr. J. C. Price in publishing *The Southland*, a monthly magazine speaking for and to the blacks of the South.

In 1891 Dr. Atkins founded the settlement known as Columbia Heights, with himself as first settler. In this community he began Slater Industrial Academy on 28 September 1892. Throughout the 1890s Dr. Atkins was able to attract many contributions from the white and black communities and so enhanced Slater's program. Among those who contributed land and money were A. H. Eller, W. A. Blair, T. J. Brown, H. E. Fries, John W. Fries, and J. F. Shaffner.

In the first decade even the students contributed to the building of the institution. The first permanent building constructed on campus was Lamson Hall, built in 1896 of brick made by the students themselves in the Academy's brickyard. The students provided much of the labor for this and other early buildings and worked on the college farm. The farm was named the William E. Shipp Memorial Farm in honor of a young North Carolinian killed in the battle of San Juan Hill while leading Negro troops against the Spanish in Cuba. The farm was purchased in part by a special fund, more than one thousand dollars of which was collected in Winston-Salem's black community.

In the first years of development, J. S. Hill, Dr. Atkins, and others traveled widely raising funds for the school. The school was granted recognition by the state in 1895, and in 1905 it became a part of the state's system of public education under the name of Slater Industrial and State Normal School. In 1920 the institution became a standard normal school and discontinued its high-school work in 1923. This was made possible by an arrangement between Dr. Atkins and the city fathers of Winston-Salem whereby the Columbian Heights High School, the city's high school for Negroes, absorbed the high-school work of Slater. The Slater State Normal School was the first institution of higher learning for Negroes in North Carolina to restrict its work entirely to the college level. In 1925 the General Assembly of North Carolina granted the institution a new charter which changed the name to Winston-Salem Teachers College and authorized the extension of its work from two to four years above high school as well as the granting of appropriate degrees under authority from the state board of education in the field of elementary education. The Winston-Salem Teachers College was the first Negro institution in the United States to grant the bachelor's degree for teaching in the elementary grades.

The growth of Winston-Salem State throughout its history is due in large part to the support of the black and white communities of Forsyth County. But the remarkable record of the school is due in large part to the excellent guidance and formative work of Dr. S. G. Atkins. Dr. Atkins retired due to ill health in 1934. He had served as president since 1892 with the exception of the period 1904–13. His excellent leadership was followed by Dr. F. L. Atkins, his son and successor who was to lead the college until 1961. Dr. Kenneth R. Williams became president in 1961, saw the name changed to Winston-Salem State College in 1963, and since 1969, has served as chancellor of Winston-Salem State University.

Freedoms Foundation Awards

One indication of the caliber of leadership produced by the Negro community is the number of Freedoms Foundation Awards which have been bestowed on Forsyth blacks. The Freedoms Foundation at Valley Forge is an independent organization devoted to fostering an understanding of freedom and the fundamentals of a free society, and its award program seeks to identify and publicize those who have furthered this undertaking.

Dr. Kenneth R. Williams was elected to the Winston-Salem Board of Aldermen in 1947. During his four years in that office, he was active in many areas but gained nationwide recognition for his efforts to create harmony between Union Local 22 and the workers of the R. J. Reynolds Tobacco Company. The union had staged a strike at the Reynolds company but many of the striking workers, most of whom were black, wanted to return to their jobs on the basis of a company settlement offer. Williams detected Communist influences in the union and spoke out against the penetration of the union by Communists. Press and other coverage of Williams's actions brought national recognition which culminated in his being awarded the George Washington Honor Medal by the Freedoms Foundation. Dr. Williams was invited to Valley Forge, Pennsylvania, to address the foundation on his experiences and to receive his award for upholding the democratic way of life in "Main Street, U.S.A."

Columbia Heights Elementary School received the Freedoms Foundation award for promoting the ideals of democracy with a project that involved the entire school. A. B. Reynolds, school principal, Mrs. Elinor Carter Mills, project chairman, teachers Mrs. Imogene Ellis and Mrs. Flossie Pettie, and a student, F. H. Brown, Jr., went to Valley Forge to foundation headquarters to receive their award for an intensive and successful program designed to stimulate young people's belief in the American way of life, one of the primary goals of the Freedoms Foundation.

In 1958 Freedoms Foundation established the Classroom Teacher's Medal. Two teachers from Winston-Salem won the medal at Oak Grove School in Elkin, North Carolina. They were Mrs. Orressa Hauser in 1958 and Mrs. Bernice Davenport in 1959. Both teachers conducted projects featuring the importance of American ideals and the political and economic rights which protect the dignity and freedom of the individual.

In 1972 Winston-Salem State University received the George Washington Honor Medal for a classroom project, sponsored by Mrs. Louise S. Hamilton, on the theme "Democracy Confronts Communism." The project was designed for a semester in which films, debates, classroom discussions, dramas, songs, and speeches were used along with research on many constitutional concepts. A representative of the Freedoms Foundation visited the college to present the medal. He stated that Winston-Salem State University was the only college in North Carolina or South Carolina to receive the George Washington Honor Medal. Congratulated for their excellent research in American history, the class presented to the foundation a scrapbook which included all the classroom activities.

George Black received the George Washington Honor Medal in 1974, as mentioned previously, in recognition of his humanitarian mission to Guyana, South America, to teach the natives brickmaking in April 1971.

These winners of Freedoms Foundations awards typify Forsyth County's black community's involvement in public affairs and their contributions to the development of a better life for themselves and for the nation.

The first half of the twentieth century saw many changes in economic, political, and social consciousness. Much historical investigation needs to be done in these areas. When did Winston-Salem first have a chapter of the National Association for the Advancement of Colored People? Why was the city able to continue to have occasional black aldermen, black policemen, and influential black members of city boards and committees when much of the rest of the South was becoming so rigidly segregated? Just how much did the white community contribute to the development of special programs in the black community and why? The full story of the black working community in the years before and after World War II needs to be investigated while there are still those living who remember the events of those years. Some work has been done along these lines but not nearly enough. The impact of the efforts at unionization among the black tobacco workers in the 1940s needs further study. The discovery of Communist infiltration in the union hierarchy seems to have blunted the organizers' efforts, and changes on the part of management seem to have contributed also. A great many other stories of Forsyth County's black community must wait for further historical investigation before they can be fully told.

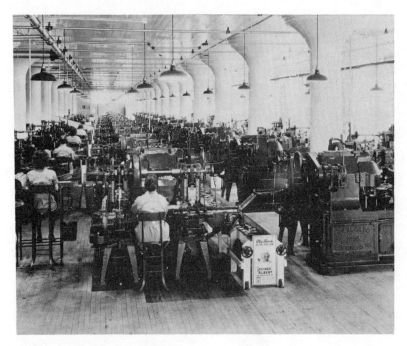

Making Prince Albert, about 1913

Old Joe, model for the Camel cigarette package, and trainer, 29 September 1913

Tobacco-selling season, Main and Fourth Streets, looking north

Nissen Wagon Works

P. H. Hanes & Co. Tobacco Works

R. J. Reynolds Factory Number 12; Reynolds Inn, for girls working in the factory, on right

First train into Winston-Salem, 11 July 1873

First depot, Chestnut Street between Third and Fourth Streets

Reynolda Road

CHAPTER 14

Forsyth County Up to Date:
The Social Order

THE HISTORY OF FORSYTH COUNTY'S growth since 1950 is the story of the expansion of principles and practices laid down by previous generations of leadership. Economically the county has continued on the march. Tremendous strides in business and industry have resulted in a more prosperous community today than ever before. City and county governments are working closely together towards a better and more effective control of their respective agencies, with complete consolidation of services a possibility. Education in Forsyth County—public and private, kindergarten through university—provides an excellent diversity of opportunities. Great improvements in the organization of the city/county school systems have been made; new and effective private schools have opened. The transplanting of Wake Forest College from Wake County to Forsyth was effected, and Salem College has successfully entered its third century. Winston-Salem State University is expanding its curriculum, and the North Carolina School of the Arts, the Governor's School, and the Advancement School have opened. The cultural advantages provided to members of this community cannot be matched—an American art museum, an excellent historic preservation, an active arts council, craft centers, and a civic symphony, to name a few. A deep-rooted religious life centered in more than 225 churches of many denominations gives a certain spiritual stability to the community. And finally, a genuine pride of long standing gives unity and direction to Forsyth.

Forsyth County Government

Although Forsyth County was created by the North Carolina General Assembly in 1849, relatively few of the services provided by the county government in the mid-1970s existed until about a century after the county's beginning.

In the historical context of the state's development, the counties were the first local governments. Communities and towns followed, some of them eventually growing into cities and major population centers. The counties are the territorial building blocks of state and nation. In North Carolina the counties grew in number from the eastern coastal area to the western mountains and today number one hundred. No two of them have exactly the same structure or the same services. Forsyth was a part of this westward movement and development.

Early public services provided by counties were rather limited, as indeed were those of other governments of the time. The principal purpose for establishing counties was defined by the Supreme Court of North Carolina in 1884: "to effectuate the political organization and civil administration of the state in respect to its general purposes and policy which require local direction of such matters as local finance, education, provision for the poor, the establishment and maintenance of highways and bridges and, in large measure, the administration of public justice. It is through them, mainly, that the powers of government reach and operate directly upon the people, and the people control and direct the government." With these rather limited beginnings, counties in North Carolina have become general-purpose local governments with most of the same powers as municipalities. Over the years the services to the public have changed. For example, counties no longer maintain highways and bridges; neither are they responsible for the administration of justice. However, counties have taken on the primary responsibility for public health, education, social services, and, in some cases, environmental protection and conservation of natural resources.

In addition to providing the countywide services listed above, counties are administrative units of the state and they usually provide law enforcement, fire protection, waste collection and disposal, recreation and parks, and zoning and building inspections.

The form of county government has undergone a number of changes. In colonial days there were justices of the peace who made up the county court, usually appointed by the governor on the recommendation of members of the General Assembly. The county courts then appointed such officers as a clerk, sheriff, and registrar. This system of county government continued until the North Carolina Constitution of 1868. The new constitution created boards of county commissioners which have continued as the governing body of the county to the present day. The most significant change in recent years has been the development of the commission-manager form of county government. North Carolina has been a leader in the movement to bring professional management to county government. It had more officially recognized professional administrators than any other state in 1975. This trend has come about because of the ever-increasing complexity of local government. Each county has intergovernmental relationships with cities, towns, the state, and the federal government. New technologies have brought new problems and those who must effectively deal with them need to be qualified through proper education and experience. The best opportunity for success comes from the proper blend of professional management and effective political leadership by the elected officeholder.

Forsyth County is governed by a Board of Commissioners, composed of five officials elected at large on a partisan basis for four-year overlapping terms by the county's voters. These individuals oversee the total operation of county government and all public funds authorized for the county government. The chairman is elected from and by the commissioners.

In 1950 the Board of Commissioners was expanded from three to five members and was composed of Dr. D. C. Speas, Roy W. Craft, William B. Simpson, Wally G. Dunham, and Carl D. Ogburn. In 1952 Craft and Ogburn were succeeded on the board by P. Huber Hanes, Jr., and Burke E. Wilson. Wilson resigned in 1953, and Howard D. Robinson was appointed to fill his unexpired term. Fred F. Bahnson, Jr., succeeded Robinson in 1954.

In 1956 Jack L. Covington joined the board to succeed Simpson; and 1958 Mrs. Bess Warren succeeded Speas on the board. In 1960, Dunham, who had served for ten years, Hanes, who had served for eight years, and Bahnson, who had served for six years, were succeeded by Fred D. Hauser, G. S. Coltrane, and E. G. Lackey.

These three new board members served with Covington and Mrs. Warren until 1964, when G. G. Reynolds succeeded Lackey. Because of a new North Carolina law that year, the five board members were required to draw lots to determine who would serve four-year terms and who two-year terms. Covington, Hauser, and Mrs. Warren drew four-year terms, requiring Coltrane and Reynolds to serve the two-year terms. In 1966 Coltrane and Reynolds were succeeded by Grover F. Shugart, Sr., and Dr. Walter L. Thompson, Jr.

Shugart and Dr. Thompson were joined by three other new commissioners in 1968, with the election of David W. Darr, Leonard E. Warner, and Grady P. Swisher. Shugart was succeeded by Henry L. Crotts in 1970. In 1972 John C. Kiger, Dr. Julian F. Keith, and John H. Tandy succeeded Darr, Swisher, and Warner. Roy G. Hall, Jr., and David L. Drummond succeeded Thompson and Crotts in 1974, to join Kiger, Dr. Keith, and Tandy on the Board of Commissioners.

The more recent chairmen of the commissioners have been Hauser, who headed the board from 1960 to 1968; Darr, from 1968 to 1972; Kiger, from 1972 to 1974; and Tandy, who assumed the chairmanship in 1974.

The actions of these different boards are perhaps most easily represented by their budgets and the county tax rates set to support them. By the late 1940s, a typical county budget was about $2 million, with the tax rate set at fifty cents per $100 assessed valuation of property. County residents outside incorporated municipalities were also charged an extra school levy of nine cents per $100 valuation.

The tax rate climbed steadily and finally jumped from eighty-five cents in 1957 to ninety-five cents in 1958 to $1.15 in 1959. The budget for the county had also climbed to $7.2 million by this time. In 1960 the tax rate dropped to $1.05 and remained at that level until 1964, when it was increased to $1.43. This increase of thirty-eight cents was approved by the voters as a special levy for the public schools and was in conjunction with the consolidation of all the schools of Forsyth County and Winston-Salem.

The tax rate was increased again in 1966, this time to $1.49, while the county budget had climbed to $25.7 million. In 1974 Forsyth County changed its percentage ratio taken of the tax rate from 58 percent to 100 percent and reduced the tax rate from $1.49 to eighty-one cents to compensate for the difference. By this time the county budget totalled $59.6 million, with much of the revenues coming from state and federal sources in addition to the property tax.

In 1961 the commissioners initiated a major change in the county government's operation by adopting the county-manager plan and appointing the first full-time professional manager, to serve on a nonpartisan basis. Previously, the county accountant or county attorney was assigned management responsibilities in addition to his other duties. Under the manager plan, the commissioners appoint the manager as the chief executive officer of the county. The board retains legislative and policy-making functions.

The Forsyth County manager is responsible for the administration of all departments over which the commissioners have authority, and the manager directs and supervises all services of the county.

Forsyth's first full-time professional county manager was G. Robert House, Jr., who served in that position from its beginning in 1961 until 1969. Roddey M. Ligon, Jr., who was county attorney, then served temporarily in the post. On 12 October 1970 Nicholas M. Meiszer was appointed county manager.

The county manager is supported by a number of administrative departments including attorney, budget and management, data processing, finance, general services, personnel, public information, and purchasing.

The physical center of county government has traditionally

been in the Forsyth County Courthouse, built in 1927–28 at a cost of $400,000, and was renovated in 1959–60 at a cost of $725,000. Even with this expansion, the demand by citizens for increased county services led to a greater demand for space. In 1966 the governments of both Forsyth County and Winston-Salem were provided office space across the street from the courthouse in the old Wachovia Bank and Trust Company Building, which became known as the Government Center.

On 13 November 1974 the Forsyth County Hall of Justice was dedicated as the center for all state courts and related offices in the county; it would house many of the administrative offices for Forsyth County government and the meeting room for the Board of County Commissioners. The area in downtown Winston-Salem bordered by Main, Second, and Liberty streets is the site of the seven-story structure, which has 162,000 square feet of floor space and was constructed at a cost of about $6.6 million. The building was first occupied in the spring of 1975.

Although the county is responsible for providing the physical facilities for the state courts in Forsyth County, the county has not actually had any courts of its own since statewide court reforms went into effect in December of 1968. A domestic relations court, previously a city function, came under county administration in 1959. It heard cases dealing with custody, delinquency, and other domestic matters. The court was housed its first year in a renovated building on Liberty Street and then moved to the third floor of the courthouse. Other courts in existence before court reform consisted of the municipal city court, which in 1963 began sitting in two divisions, one for criminal cases and one for traffic cases.

The criminal division was held in the courtroom on the second floor of City Hall (this room was later renovated into a new council chamber for the Winston-Salem Board of Aldermen). The traffic division was held in a former church building, which sat at the corner of First and Church streets before being torn down for a parking lot.

The court reform of 1968 was the result of a ten-year statewide effort by attorneys, court officials, and legislators to standardize the lower courts created over the years by special legislation.

North Carolina voters approved a constitutional amendment in 1962, and the General Assembly passed the implementing legislation in 1965.

The revision replaced justices of the peace with court-appointed magistrates. In Forsyth County, the district courts replaced municipal court, domestic relations court, and Kernersville recorder's court. The county's twenty justices of the peace were replaced by salaried magistrates. Five district court judges were authorized for Forsyth County, to be elected by all county residents for four-year terms. The first district court judges elected in 1968 were Abner A. Alexander, Buford T. Henderson, John C. Clifford, A. Lincoln Sherk, and Rhoda H. Billings. In 1972 Judge Billings was succeeded by Robert K. Leonard. The superior court judges during this time were Walter E. Johnson and Harvey A. Lupton. Upon Johnson's death, William Z. Wood was appointed to succeed him and later won election to a full term.

The clerk of superior court also was a county employee until the court reform of 1968. In 1969 William E. Church, who had served as the clerk for many years, retired. A. Eugene Blackburn was appointed to fill his unexpired term and was elected in 1970 and reelected in 1974.

Although the clerk of superior court is no longer a county employee, two other elected officials, the sheriff and the register of deeds, come under the county government system and are also considered department heads of the county.

The Forsyth County Sheriff's Department provides police protection to the unincorporated areas of the county; however, the sheriff is the chief law-enforcement officer within the county. Sheriff Ernie G. Shore headed the department for many years until his retirement in 1970. He was succeeded by Sheriff C. Manly Lancaster, who was elected in 1970, and reelected in 1974.

The sheriff's department provides a wide range of services from the serving of civil and criminal processes to the protection of citizens and their property. In recent years, the department has expanded into two new areas with a narcotic unit and a juvenile division. The sheriff's department is supplemented by reserve officers, who volunteer their time one night a week to patrol the county in a car with a regular deputy. The department also works with young people through the Sheriff's Department Explorer Post Boy Scouts of America and other programs.

The Forsyth County jail is also the responsibility of the Sheriff's Department. In 1953 Forsyth County built a new jail on Church Street behind City Hall at a cost of about $400,000, to replace a structure built in 1908. In 1967 an addition capable of housing seventy-two prisoners was added, bringing the capacity to 202 prisoners, and the county assumed custody of all prisoners including those for the city of Winston-Salem. With the county contracting to house its prisoners, the old city jail was closed.

The Forsyth County register of deeds has the responsibility for the recording and indexing of all records such as real-estate deeds, plat maps, deeds of trust, mortgages, marriages, births and deaths, and other private papers. Mrs. Eunice Ayers has served as Forsyth County register of deeds since 1949, and was reelected for a four-year term in 1972.

From the county's formation in 1849 until 1904, all recorded instruments were copied by hand. Typewritten record keeping was introduced in 1904 and continued until 1929, when photocopy equipment was first used to achieve an exact facsimile of original records. In 1954 microfilming was introduced to eliminate the large books used for recording personal property records. By 1962, marriage, birth, and death records were also integrated into this system, and in 1965 computerized indexes were installed.

The register of deeds office and Mrs. Ayers have assumed a great part in the development of a computerized land records information system to centralize records and maps formerly kept by eight different departments in three separate buildings. The new system allows both citizens and government officials to get all of the known information about any of the 118,000 parcels of property in the county by simply typing in the parcel identification number. Zoning, tax evaluation, outstanding taxes, mortgages, restrictive covenants, existing utilities and structures, and other valuable data can be displayed instantly on a video display screen, printed on a piece of paper, and given to the inquirer. An actual map of the property can also be obtained.

In addition to the Sheriff's Department and the office of the register of deeds and the county administrative departments, more than a dozen other departments or offices are connected with Forsyth County government in providing services to the residents of the county.

The Airport Commission of Forsyth County was established by the North Carolina General Assembly in 1949. The commission operates Smith Reynolds Airport and provides scheduled airline service and general aviation facilities at one of the few airports in the country operating on a self-sustaining basis. During the 1960s the commission was responsible for the construction of a new general-aviation terminal building, and the extension and strengthening of runways, taxiways, and ramps for jet aircraft. In 1974 a new waiting area and baggage-handling unit was added to the terminal.

The Agriculture and Home Extension Service was originally set up in Forsyth in 1914 to aid rural and farm areas. During the 1950s and 1960s, the service was housed in a building at the corner of Spruce and Sixth streets. In 1972 the county built a new agriculture building on Fairchild Drive next to Smith Reynolds Airport. The original programs are still provided by the Agriculture Extension Service, but there has been expansion to meet the changing needs of the community. The home economics services deal with consumer education and home management, while the youth and community development programs of the 4-H clubs are now reaching urban as well as rural areas.

The Forsyth County Animal Shelter provides countywide service twenty-four hours a day, primarily for situations where domestic animals are mistreated or where they pose a potential threat to the safety of persons or property. The shelter was built during the 1960s with county, city, and privately donated funds. It too is on Fairchild Drive and has served as a model facility in the southeastern United States. The employees of the animal shelter are responsible for enforcement of the county ordinance which requires all dogs in the county to wear a tax tag indicating payment of an annual fee and a rabies tag indicating a current vaccination against rabies. In 1975 they began enforcement of Winston-Salem's leash law which made it illegal for a dog to run loose within the city limits.

The Forsyth County Board of Elections was established in

1955 by authority of the North Carolina General Assembly. The office provides a full-time, centrally located place where qualified voters of Forsyth County may register to vote and change addresses or party affiliations. The Board of Elections is selected by the state administration, but the executive secretary and other workers in the office are county employees. The election of a Republican governor in North Carolina in 1972 led to the first Republican control of the Forsyth County Board of Elections in modern times.

The Forsyth County Emergency Medical Service was originally named the Forsyth Ambulance Service when it was established in January 1968. Until 1967 local funeral homes furnished all ambulance services within the county. However, as a result of new federal and state laws relating to minimum wages and ambulance standards, all funeral homes discontinued ambulance services. The county commissioners accepted the responsibility of providing ambulance service, and two funeral homes donated used ambulances and provided backup service until an ambulance service was operating in all areas of the county. The service began with five used ambulances and was originally based at the county fire department at Smith Reynolds Airport. In 1974 the service moved its headquarters to Reynolds Memorial Hospital, and by 1975 the fleet included four modular ambulances and five limousines. Specialized training is basic to the service, with attendants learning to administer drugs and intravenous fluids and do heart monitoring on the scene.

The Forsyth County Engineering Department is responsible for all physical structures and facilities developed or acquired by the county government, but perhaps its greatest contact with the citizens of the county is its responsibility for the county water system. By 1975 about twelve thousand five hundred residential, commercial, and industrial facilities were served by the county water system, which had been built without any tax funds. Water is purchased on a contractual basis from the city of Winston-Salem. The operating revenue of the system pays for retiring the bonds approved by the voters and issued by the county.

One of Forsyth County's major departments changed its name and expanded its functions during 1974; formerly the Air

Quality Control Department, it became the Environmental Affairs Department. The department was established by the Board of Commissioners in 1968, to prevent a serious air-pollution hazard. In addition to being responsible for countywide air-quality control, the department coordinates solid-waste management outside corporate limits in the county. The department has continued to expand its duties and responsibilities in protecting various aspects of the environment by the enforcement of federal, state, and county laws.

The Forsyth County Fire Department was established by the Board of Commissioners in 1951 and began operating with two full-time firemen. Since that time, the department has assumed the responsibility for coordinating the eighteen volunteer fire departments scattered throughout rural Forsyth County. In 1963, a new headquarters building was constructed for the county fire department at Smith Reynolds Airport. The emergency communications system housed in this building provides twenty-four-hour-a-day contact for both the county fire departments and the emergency medical service. The Board of Commissioners passed a fire prevention code in 1974 compatible with the codes of Winston-Salem and Kernersville.

The Forsyth County public library system came under the county government in 1965, after approval by the county voters, who also agreed to a five-cent special tax levy to support the countywide library system. Previously, the system was supported by the county, city, and private funds, and was operated by the city of Winston-Salem. All services and materials of the library are free to county residents, and no overdue fines are imposed. The main branch of the library on West Fifth Street was constructed in 1952; it offers reference and adult services department, children's department, and audiovisual department, in addition to its bookmobile services and outreach service to children, the homebound, and the institutionalized. Branch libraries are in Clemmons, East Winston, Kernersville, Lewisville, Reynolda Manor Shopping Center, Rural Hall, Southside, and Thruway Shopping Center. In 1974 county voters approved a $3 million bond issue for renovation and expansion of facilities for the public library system. In 1975 the main library's lower level was renovated and opened to the public, and the Bahnson House across the street was renovated to house library administrative offices, thereby freeing space in the main branch for a North Carolina room.

Recreation, while not a formally organized department of county government, has become an increasingly important demand made on the government by county residents. The county's first entry into the field of recreation came in the summer of 1974, when the county contracted with the Arts Council to provide entertainment by the Fun Center, for arts and crafts, and the Jazzmobile and Freedom Street Players, for concerts and plays. Limited recreational activities were also provided at Union Cross Radar Station, which was given to the county by the federal government in 1974 partly for recreational use. Also in 1974, county voters approved a $3 million bond issue for purchase of open-space land and the development and operation of recreational facilities by the county.

A unique recreational facility available to all the citizens of Forsyth County and surrounding areas is Tanglewood Park, the estate of the late William N. and Kate B. Reynolds. The park opened in 1954 for the use of Forsyth County's white citizens as provided in Reynolds's will. When civil-rights laws made "white only" operation impossible, the park closed briefly, but the courts set aside the restrictive clause and the park reopened and resumed the expansion of its services. Swimming, sightseeing, picnicking, camping, horseback riding, golfing, theatre, dining, and overnight lodging are available. The Barn Theatre offers live theatrical performances during the summer months. Resident and day camps for boys and girls are also offered each summer. Steeplechase and quarterhorse races attract large crowds. Golf facilities include a thirty-six-hole championship course, an eighteen-hole par-3 course and driving range, and a miniature course. The park is only minutes away from Winston-Salem and provides an excellent supplement to Forsyth County's recreation program.

Reflecting a public desire to preserve and interpret the area's historical heritage, the county began in 1970 to support the operation of Historic Bethabara Park. The park, a stabilized archaeological site with a restored eighteenth-century church and other restorable buildings, marks the site of the first Moravian settlement in Wachovia. Archaeological work and restoration has been largely supported by grants from the late Charles Babcock and the Mary Reynolds Babcock Foundation. Initial impetus came from Edwin L. Stockton, Sr., and the Bethabara Historical Society; community participation continues to play a great role in the operation of the site. The county and the city provide the funds for the interpretative and maintenance staff and the park is administered by the city recreation department.

The city and county additionally provide support for Old Salem, Inc., and the county has purchased the sites of the Wright and Richmond courthouses and is presently supporting archaeological work at these two locations.

Another joint city/county operation is the Planning Department, administered by the city and serving as the planning agency for both Forsyth County and Winston-Salem. The Planning Board was established in 1948 by the Board of Commissioners and Board of Aldermen to carry out comprehensive countywide planning. The board, as its name implies, is a full-service planning facility. It works for a comprehensive and uniform approach to zoning, provides land-use planning, gathers and evaluates census and socioeconomic data, and has provided proposals for erosion, sedimentation, and grading control. The Planning Board consists of nine members appointed by the Board of Commissioners and Board of Aldermen. The Planning Board hears requests for rezoning from county residents along with recommendations from the Planning Department. If the property is located inside the city of Winston-Salem or within one mile from the city limits, the Planning Board makes a recommendation to the Board of Aldermen. If the property lies outside the one-mile limit from the city, the Planning Board makes a recommendation to the Board of Commissioners. The Planning Department also collects, analyzes, and stores statistics needed by local, state, and federal agencies.

The Forsyth County tax offices deal primarily with the listing of property for taxes and the collection of these taxes. The office of tax supervisor was created by the North Carolina General Assembly in 1939, and is responsible for listing and assessing all real and personal property in the county and city for ad valorem taxes. The office records all real property in the county on maps with a block and lot number for each parcel. Each transfer of real property is listed on an ownership sheet showing the chain of title. In 1967 the Board of Commissioners put in a new tax listing system, permitting property owners to list by mail rather than requiring them to appear before a list taker. The office is also required under state law to conduct a revaluation of all real property in the county every eight years. The most recent revaluation was conducted in 1975. The tax collector was first appointed by the Board of Commissioners in 1929, and in 1941 the Board of Commissioners and the Winston-Salem Board of Aldermen consolidated the functions of the county and city tax offices. Each year the office averages collecting about 92 percent of the levy by the end of the calendar year.

The Forsyth County Veterans Service Office was established by the Board of Commissioners in 1951 for the purpose of assisting veterans and their dependents in obtaining benefits from the Veterans Administration and other agencies. These benefits include education, on-the-job training, compensation, pensions, hospitalization, outpatient treatment, loans, and burial expenses. The office obtains discharge, birth, death, and marriage certificates as required by the Veterans Administration in supporting claims of veterans or their dependents. By 1975 more than twenty-seven thousand veterans were living in Forsyth County, and their dependents increased the number to about seventy-five thousand residents.

The Forsyth County Youth Center was established by the Board of Commissioners in 1962. The purpose of the center is to provide temporary care for children detained for juvenile court disposition because of committing a criminal offense, running away from home, truancy, custody disputes, and maltreatment. In addition to providing and arranging counseling or psychiatric services, the center's staff provides educational and recreational programs. The center's school was brought under the Forsyth Optional School of the public school system in 1974.

Forsyth County was already responsible for providing some services in the major areas of health, education, and welfare before 1949, but each of these areas continued to be changed and improved greatly from 1950 to 1975.

Health has become a major responsibility of county government, not just in connection with the Forsyth County Department of Public Health, which was created in 1913, but also in the areas such as mental health, hospital care, and nursing-home and rest-home care.

In education, Forsyth County, like other local governments throughout North Carolina, provides a public school system. Forsyth County government has played an even more vital part in education following the consolidation of all the public schools in the county into one system in 1963.

Welfare, or the Department of Social Services, as it has come to be known today, was formally organized in 1919 to provide basic assistance to the poor, but today the department and its services have been expanded to meet the ever-growing needs of Forsyth County citizens.

Forsyth County contains three municipalities: Winston-Salem, Kernersville, and Rural Hall. In 1975 the governments of Forsyth County and Winston-Salem renewed serious discussions about the possibilities of consolidating the two governments. The governments in the past had followed a path of piecemeal consolidation of departments such as in planning, schools, libraries, and tax administration and collection. Governing officials of both governments more recently have moved in the direction of total formal consolidation of services and likewise the governments providing them.

Local government's role in society today is that of provider of public services, through any number of individual roles: social worker, public health nurse, sanitarian, inspector, farm agent, and many more. Governmental agencies in Forsyth County have tried to provide needed services, also dealing with the problems which result from continuing growth and development. Greenbelts between population centers, parks and recreation facilities, and environmental protection have become recognized goals. Imagination, innovation and experimentation mark Forsyth County's local government.

Government in the county will undoubtedly continue to

tailor its services and form to the needs of the people. Regionalism is becoming more important. Counties, cities, and towns which have already been organized into state planning regions are moving in the direction of becoming service providers. All local governments will have to cooperate in solving problems of the future. Councils of government, now only a few years old, have shown steady growth in size and influence at both state and federal levels.

There is also the question of consolidating city and county governments. Many informed citizens and students of government are asking whether both governments are really necessary in the present context. Although several attempts at consolidation in North Carolina have been unsuccessful, there is reason to believe that efforts to bring about some form of merger between the City of Winston-Salem and Forsyth County will continue in the years ahead. The record on consolidation of specific public services has been good in this community. Change is usually a slow evolutionary process building upon past successes; this is particularly true in local government and in public institutions. It will take time to convince citizens that change is a resource to be used and not something to be feared. Forsyth County is not what it was in 1849, nor what it was in 1868. The development which was slow in the beginning has become much more rapid in recent years and will accelerate as Forsyth County advances.

Winston-Salem City Government

In the twenty-five years since 1950, the city of Winston-Salem has changed from a comfortable Southern community of 87,811 persons to a front-running leader in the New South. Winston-Salem in 1975 had a population of about 138,000 and encompassed 60.66 square miles, some 41.80 square miles more than in 1950.

With the increased population, increased land to serve, and pressing complex urban needs, the city government has paced other North Carolina cities in inventiveness, responsiveness, and social awareness for its citizens. Twice it has been named an All-American city, through applications developed and presented by residents of the community. Its residents have overwhelmingly supported bond referendums to provide recreational facilities, hospital care, streets, fire, police, water, and sewer needs. Thus, Winston-Salem in 1975 is not running to catch up with its needs but rather is delivering services through well-designed systems.

The elected leaders of the community, the mayors and boards of aldermen, have provided critical farsightedness for the community. Since 1950 Winston-Salem has had four mayors: Marshall Kurfees, 1949–61; John R. Surratt, 1961–63; M. C. Benton, Jr., 1963–70; and Dr. Franklin R. Shirley, 1970–. The two-year terms of office were changed to four-year terms in December of 1966. The city is represented along ward lines, with eight wards, while the mayor is elected at large.

The Board of Aldermen has had representation from both the black and white members of the community. On 7 December 1971 the first woman, Mrs. Ernestine Wilson, was sworn in as the alderman from the South Ward. Committees of the board include: public works, finance, public safety, and a general committee. In addition to these committees, the city is persistent in its involvement of the public within governmental affairs. Winston-Salem has twenty-three various boards and commissions to provide policy guidance and to make recommendations to the Board of Aldermen for official action.

Since 1950 the city has had two city managers. John M. Gold became the city's second manager in 1951, succeeding C. E. Perkins. He provided administrative leadership for the community during the following tumultuous twenty-two years until his death in October of 1973. With vision and dedication to improvement of the community, Gold brought modernization of many city services and a tremendous increase of efficiency in the performance of these services. Orville W. Powell became the city's third city manager in 1973.

Fiscally, the city has been both responsible and liberal. It is conservative in its spending and liberal in its concepts. The city's tax rate is generally the seventh lowest of the eight major North Carolina cities; Winston-Salem survived the inflationary spiral of the late 1960s without a tax increase from 1969 to 1975. The Board of Aldermen has encouraged the development of program budgeting and has drawn the public into the budget-making process.

Each fall the finance committee holds focus hearings so the public may have an opportunity to request programs or services at the beginning of the budget preparation.

City Social Programs

While many significant changes have occurred within the services of city government, perhaps the most remarkable activity has been in the areas of social concerns. Winston-Salem, through funds from government, foundations, and private enterprise, began summer youth-employment programs in 1963 and in the following two years $162,073 was provided to furnish 608 summer jobs. Since then the federal government and the city have paid $952,639 for an additional 2,102 job opportunities.

Since 1968 the Concentrated Employment Program (CEP) has spent $7 million in federal funds to tackle headlong the unemployment programs of the hard-core unemployed. The corporate community participated fully with the program and released senior executives for six months to provide sound guidance as Mayor's Manpower Assistants. Training classes, job development, and placement of CEP graduates were the benefits of this successful program. CEP terminated in 1974 with the withdrawal of federal funds. More than two thousand past or potential public-assistance recipients were placed in permanent jobs.

The Experiment in Self Reliance (ESR) began in 1965 as a local poverty advocate agency to provide opportunities for family financing, planning, and self-sufficiency. ESR works within the community, aligning the delivery of a variety of governmental services with the needs of the city's poor.

The Urban Coalition was formed in the spring of 1968. Patterned after the National Urban Coalition, the local organization was one of forty in the nation. It was financially supported by industries, foundations, and interested citizens with gifts exceeding $1.8 million. It quickly allocated $800,000 for a housing foundation to improve housing conditions in the city; supported a privately owned bus operation until public monies became available; donated $45,000 for the development of mini-parks in low-income neighborhoods; established a youth services bureau; and contributed and catalyzed the development of day-care facilities in the community. The Urban Coalition continued its active catalytic role until 1971 when it and the Citizens Planning Council were merged to form the Citizens Coalition. Activity continued until other existing organizations had sufficiently developed their own planning and delivery systems to supersede the Citizens Coalition, and it disbanded in the early spring of 1975.

Model Cities and Revenue Sharing

In 1968 Winston-Salem was one of seventy-five cities in the country selected to receive a Model City planning grant from the federal government. The following year it received the first of five grants—ultimately totaling over $35 million—for innovative programs dealing with education, transportation, youth employment, improvements to housing and the physical environment, social problem areas, and community involvement within the Model City area. The original area, which included 1,134 acres of land just north of the central business district, was expanded to include the entire city in 1972 when Winston-Salem was one of twenty cities named nationally to serve as a laboratory for revenue sharing in a program called Model Cities Planned Variations.

Citizen participation, a crucial element in the Model Cities concept, is now designed as a structured program of Winston-Salem government. The advent of revenue sharing has not diminished the Board of Aldermen's position on citizen participation. It continues under the administrative guidance of the City-County Planning Board.

In 1975 the city completed the first application under revenue sharing, the Community Development block grants which combine the myriad applications for federal funds and programs. During 1975 Winston-Salem was one of thirteen cities to receive an additional allocation of revenue-sharing funds.

Part of the reason why Winston-Salem has received more federal funds per capita than any other city in North Carolina is its aggressiveness in seeking a return of the local dollar to its home. Another is the city's ability to complete what it sets out to do. In 1951 the city organized the first Redevelopment Commission, after waiting for the state to enact the statewide legislation. By 1975 1,960 acres of Winston-Salem were under urban-renewal planning in east and north Winston-Salem and in the central business district. All types of urban renewal are being used—rehabilitation, clearance, conservation, and code enforcement. The first three projects encompassed 440.6 acres and cost $26 million. Once the city tax yield from these areas was approximately $150,000 yearly; it is now $500,000 yearly. Such a result should probably be expected since $38 million has been spent for private, commercial, industrial, institutional, and public development occurring in these projects.

Downtown Renewal

In 1969 the Board of Aldermen approved a downtown-renewal program estimated to cost $30 million. By 1975 new development, site improvements, and rehabilitation projects have accounted for $80 million, increasing the yearly tax revenues from $120,000 to $1 million. This ninety-five-acre project has seen $40 million in private development which includes Wachovia East, NCNB Plaza and parking garage, Winston-Salem Savings & Loan Association, and the Winston-Salem Hyatt House. Another $5 million has been spent by 106 downtown businesses in rehabilitation of their facilities. The public sector has produced projects amounting to $35 million which includes the Cherry/Marshall Parking Garage, Liberty/Main Parking Garage, the new federal building, the pedestrian walkway system, and the Convention Center. Activity in the downtown area began before the official renewal program. The Wachovia Building was constructed in 1962, and in 1968 the city adopted an overhead-sign ordinance. Since that year all downtown overhanging signs have been removed, and power lines have been relocated underground.

In 1971 the city embarked on the Kimberly North Winston renewal program, which includes 646 acres at an estimated cost of $12.6 million. Finally, five sections of the city—a portion of East Winston Project 4, Northwest Boulevard, Trade Street, West 10 1/2 Street and several blocks adjoining Winston-Salem State University—have been prepared for redevelopment at an estimated cost of $3 million.

Since 1965, the city has been actively involved in a concentrated code enforcement program, the Neighborhood Improvement Program, which has seen 12,030 housing units improved at an approximate cost of $19,484,007 of private and public monies through grants or low-cost loans. Some 4,542 housing units have been demolished as unfit structures for human habitation at a cost of $1,334,913, while another 5,873 new housing units for low- and moderate-income families have been produced at a cost of $88,076,911.

Throughout this twenty-five-year period, Winston-Salem has seized the opportunity to provide a variety of public housing—apartments, townhouses, turnkey housing, leased housing, and special housing accommodations for the elderly, both in high-rise and garden apartments, for a total of 3,258 housing units (based on income).

Recreation

The city's recreation program may well be labeled the most outstanding in the nation. In 1969 the United States Chamber of Commerce, through its Urban Action Clearinghouse study, cited Winston-Salem's successful efforts of public-private action to provide sound programs and attack urban problems. It specifically commended the city for its 1964 action when a crisis developed after the state attorney general ruled that North Carolina cities could not spend their tax funds for recreation without a vote of the people. At the same time, public emotion about desegregation problems was leading many other Southern cities to abandon recreation programs in general and swimming pools in particular. The city of Winston-Salem not only approved the taxes needed but expanded the number of its public pools.

These twenty-five years of development in recreation began in 1950 with a Civitan Club donation of 23.25 acres for Civitan Park; 1974 saw the donation of 241 acres for Camp Robert Vaughan from the Winston-Salem Foundation. The first satellite park in North Carolina, Camp Vaughan is valued at $700,000. In 1975 the Board of Aldermen purchased almost 15 acres in the South Fork area for recreational development at a cost of $181,260. In between these years many private donations were made to the city for hundreds of acres of land for recreation, park development, and new programs.

Ernie Shore Field was a 50-acre gift from Charles Babcock, as was the $225,000 to develop it in 1950. In 1961 R. J. Reynolds Tobacco Company, Z. Smith Reynolds Foundation, Inc., Hanes Hosiery Mills Company, P. H. Hanes Knitting Company, Hanes Dye and Finishing, and Wachovia Bank gave $310,000 to build a swimming pool and nine additional holes to the Winston Lake Park golf course.

The next year, Hanes Hosiery Mills gave the city a lighted baseball park with grandstand and parking area amounting to 7.7 acres. Shaffner Park was a gift of 43.48 acres from the Shaffner heirs and Pilot Real Estate Company. In 1969 the Babcock Foundation provided $23,408 for the first year's operating cost of Bethabara Park and to restore the church. Under the agreement, Historic Bethabara became a park under the auspices of the recreation department and with assistance and guidance from Old Salem, Inc. Forsyth County contributes its share in the operation of the park.

With citizen support, the city has developed Winston Lake and two golf courses, built nine swimming pools and six community centers, and cosponsored swim clubs, tennis development, showmobiles, diving, special programs for the mentally and physically handicapped, senior citizens, arts, crafts, youth councils, drama, and dance. Continuous upgrading has produced new lighting at Ernie Shore Field, systematic bench replacement, the lighting of four softball fields, and an electronic spray pool at Brushy Fork, the only one of its kind in existence. Bicycling has made significant inroads in the field of recreation. Winston-Salem has provided fifty-one miles of bikeways throughout the city and enacted the first bicycle registration ordinance in the state.

Recreation in Winston-Salem in 1975 was a multimillion-dollar program encompassing 11 centers, 11 pools, 54 parks, 3,110 acres of parkland, 19 year-round and 34 summer programs, reaching 2,709,735 users yearly.

The Memorial Coliseum and the M. C. Benton, Jr., Convention Center are two operations within one department. The Coliseum was built as a war memorial with funds raised in 1946 in a campaign headed by Gordon Gray. It was given to the city by the Winston-Salem Foundation in 1969. The Benton Center was financed through public bonds at a cost of $3.5 million. These two buildings provide complete convention facilities, and the extra opportunities for various attractions including ice shows, and rodeo, as well as regional and local shows such as the Piedmont Crafts Fair. The Coliseum, the Fairgrounds, Ernie Shore Field, and Groves Stadium form a sports complex for many area activities. Groves Stadium, Wake Forest University's 30,500-seat football facility, was completed in 1968 and has hosted professional football teams, high-school playoffs, and other community activities. Winston-Salem State and Wake Forest share the Coliseum as their home basketball court. Wake Forest and the Winston-Salem Red Sox share Ernie Shore Field.

Some two thousand persons can be comfortably seated for dinner at the Convention Center, which is linked with the Hyatt House Hotel and the downtown mall system via an underground walkway beneath Fifth Street. In 1975 Beneath the Elms, a shopping and skating facility, opened adjacent to the Convention Center complex. The ice-skating rink, the same size as the one at Rockefeller Center, is in constant use and relieves the demand at the Coliseum where the local hockey club, the Polar Twins, plays.

When these facilities are combined with the Dixie Classic Fairgrounds, also donated by the Winston-Salem Foundation, eighty-seven acres are available for public/private use. The Fair itself was expanded from six days to nine days in 1975. Among North Carolina fairs, the Dixie Classic has attained a rating of 1,000 points, the highest rating any fair may receive. More than 200,000 persons attended the 1974 fair, which featured 6,139 exhibits and 25 shows and awarded over $43,189 in prize monies. The Convention Center Coliseum complex has yielded 453 bookings for 966,978 participant days in the city. The 1974 figures indicate that, based on $25 a day, these bookings have generated approximately $8.9 million in yearly revenues to the businesses and fiscal climate of the city.

Other City Services

While the foregoing discussion focuses on those programs which have captured the public headlines, many other governmental activities provide the continuing kinds of services needed in an urban society. The city's Inspection Division provides all inspection activities for the city and for the county under contractual agreement. Winston-Salem and Forsyth County were the first in North Carolina to adopt a countywide building inspection program on 1 July 1960. It was closely followed by countywide plumbing inspections in 1963, zoning in 1967, and heating in 1974. This operation, which had a budget of $73,000 in 1955–56, now has an operating budget of $614,000 and a staff of thirty-eight to enforce the various ordinances and to implement the Concentrated Code Enforcement Program.

In 1949 the city began its first computer operation for water billing. Since then the city has converted all of its record-keeping functions to computers and is developing a financial information system which not only reports on past financial activities but will indicate future allocation needs. The computer operation, under the Department of Management Services, is also developing a massive management information system, so that all departments will have the information bases needed to make accurate decisions and forecast from properly collated data.

Such management services are needed when one considers that more than three hundred miles of streets have been paved in the last twenty-five years. These streets have required the development of a computerized traffic control system supervised by the Traffic Engineering Division. The successful 1970 bond referendum made possible $2.4 million in state and federal funds for this complex operation. The division not only supervises the signal system, but also designs intersection improvements and manages the city's twelve parking facilities, which range from open-air lots to sophisticated computer-run structures.

Although the city of Winston-Salem had developed a sound system of traffic arteries throughout its limits, the public and the Board of Aldermen believed it should be engaged in other forms of public transportation—namely, the operation of a public bus system. In the bond referendum of 1972, the residents by a three-to-one vote supported the public acquisition of Safe Bus, Inc. The city had already formed a Transit Authority in 1968, and federal monies tripled funds approved by the voters. In addition, the residents approved the spending of up to five cents of property-tax funds to operate the system. Fortunately, in 1975 the federal government also authorized the expenditure of federal funds for operating costs to assist in the cost of this service.

The Utilities Division, formed in 1949, supervises the water and sewer systems for the city, and through contractual arrangements with the county provides for the water needs of all Forsyth County residents connected to the county water system. In 1950 the new raw-water supply facility on the Yadkin River was constructed. Such action provided for two sources of water, the Yadkin and Salem Lake. Fourteen years later, the Neilson Water Treatment Plant was completed and put into operation to provide for 24 million gallons of water a day. Since 1950, approximately 400 miles of water mains have been added to the system, making an approximate total of 831 miles. In 1975 the division is engaged in a program of expanded water-supply capability at the Yadkin River intake works from 26 to 95 million gallons a day, along with an expansion of the Neilson Water Plant and the Thomas Plant from 12 to 25 million gallons a day. Such action is possible because of the public's support of progressive government in various bond referendums throughout this twenty-five year period.

In 1954 the $4.5-million Archie Elledge Wastewater Treatment plant was completed and placed in operation. Twenty years later, an $8-million expansion provided for additional treatment and made possible a 95-percent contamination-free effluent from the plant. This same time period has seen 375 miles of sewer mains being constructed to provide for one of the state's most efficient operations.

An example of the city's leadership in the state was the organization of an Industrial Waste Control Section in 1955 to gather data on local industrial wastewater being discharged into the city system. In 1971 local industry contributed $150,000 to the Chamber of Commerce to provide a pretreatment aerification basin at the site of the Archie Elledge plant. That year the city

became the first in the Southeast to enclose the trickling filters—
some over 200 feet in diameter—with concrete and plastic to
increase efficiency and reduce odors. The division has also developed markets for the plant's byproduct, sludge, which it now
produces under the Organiform–SS trade name.

The City Sanitation Division continues to engage in rear-yard
collection of domestic refuse under an incentive plan frequently
studied by other municipalities. Of the city's three landfills, the
Overdale site is reserved for the Sanitation Division collections.
The other two landfills, Ebert and Hanes Mill, are open to the
general public, including the private contractors who provide
county sanitation collection.

Public Safety Program

The activities of fire and police have undergone dramatic changes.
From two separate operations, the city now has one combined
public safety operation with five departments: police, fire, communications, training, and legal. Within the public safety concept, the traditional services of fire and police remain, although a
small fire-police program had begun in 1957. The first public
safety director was James I. Waller, who served in that capacity
from 1963 until 1969. In 1973 the public safety officer program
was expanded to include all fire/police services and Justus M.
Tucker was named the second director. He served in that capacity
until his retirement in 1974. Norman E. Pomrenke was appointed
to succeed him.

A Career Development Center (CDC) was formed to train all
public safety officers in those professional techniques used by
both branches of services, and in 1975 public safety vehicles made
their appearance to replace the blue-and-white police cars and
red-and-white fire cars. The Police Academy held its first classes
in 1963. By 1974, the first class of public safety officers was
graduated from the CDC. The Harris Home Center on Cassell
Street will be renovated to replace the present police operation
center.

The public safety concept includes public safety communications, a program approved by the public and supported with

local and federal funds. The center contains sophisticated computer equipment and tracking systems to dispatch police and fire equipment, making possible an immediate response for assistance anywhere within the city, the county, and other adjoining counties in times of need. In 1974 the city formally requested Southern Bell's cooperation to implement a 911-emergency-telephone system for the city. It is anticipated that when the system becomes operational in 1978 it will be possible for anyone in the city to reach all emergency assistance by dialing 911.

Turning to the fire service, the Fire Department has undergone, since 1950, those changes which modern, well-trained departments require. Where once the work week was seventy-two hours, it has been reduced to fifty-six hours. The first black fireman was employed in 1951, and by 1967 black firemen were employed at all fire stations. Today, ten blacks are officers and two of the four assistant chiefs are black.

Winston voters have approved funds for four new fire stations and the relocation of another. Training became a consistent part of the profession in 1956 when the first organized training program for firemen recruits began. In 1964 the first snorkel company in North Carolina went into service, followed by another in 1969. Specialized needs require specialized services, and in 1975 the department accepted a truck and equipment from the Forsyth County Oil Dealers Association for use in case of oil spills. In 1966 the department developed a building and fire safety survey program. In 1971 the department abandoned the traditional red and began a transition to a lime-yellow color for its fire equipment.

The year 1975 saw implementation of the uniform fire incident reporting system—a computer program—installation of a station locator plan, plans completed for consolidation of Fire Stations Number One and Number Two and to house Engine Companies Number One and Number Two and Aerial Companies One and Two, as well as accepting the plan to solve the problems of oil spills.

All these activities are concerned with fire suppression. The department's other concern is fire prevention, an emphasis which the department began in 1950. The department adopted the national fire prevention code of 1947 and the subsequent codes of 1953, 1956, 1960, 1965, and 1970. In 1966 the department won the grand award from the National Fire Protection Association's fire safety contest for promotion and accomplishment in fire prevention. In 1970 the department organized a comprehensive inspection program for fire-company personnel, divided the city into quadrants, and assigned inspectors to each. Such action significantly reduced the number of household fires and reduced the amount of damage in commercial/industrial fires. Fire-prevention activities include the identification of the handicapped and children in homes to prevent needless loss of life and organization of an arson squad to work with counterparts from the police department's Criminal Investigation Division.

Just as the Fire Department has witnessed significant changes, so has the Police Department. It, too, has demonstrated a concern for more community involvement within its operations. The first nine school crossing guards were employed in the fall of 1950. In 1964 a youth unit was formed to handle all cases involving juveniles. This program was later enlarged and came to be known as the Community Service Division of the Police Department. This operation continues its first concern—juveniles—and also responds to family crises, boys' incentive needs, summer camp and YMCA programs for eight hundred youths, and school liaison at the city's junior- and senior-high schools. The new Office of Inspectional Services was formed in 1975. The vice, narcotics, and selective enforcement units were combined to direct all investigations of armed robbery, housebreaking, storebreaking, and auto theft. A police trailer was provided through a gift from the Exchange Club of Winston-Salem in 1967; this crime-prevention mobile exhibit is built in a burned-out sixty-foot house trailer and was initially the only such unit in the United States. Its design was copied by the Norfolk, Virginia, and Seattle, Washington police departments.

The techniques employed by the department are a string of firsts, not only in North Carolina but for most of the United States. In 1967 Police Chief Justus Tucker was called by the administrators of the Law Enforcement Assistance Act to discuss and share his law-enforcement concepts with those United States cities interested in participating in LEAA programs.

During these years, the department has also encouraged blacks and women to participate fully in departmental matters. Miss Kate Wurrescke was sworn in as a lieutenant on 1 September 1924, a position she held until 1945. The first black officer, Oscar Morris, was sworn in in 1945. The first sworn women officers, Mrs. Bobbie B. Bircham and Mrs. Lillian Bonner, were sworn in during the summer of 1966. The first woman communications officer was Mrs. Virginia Payne, who assumed her duties in 1973. By 1975, the ranks of the police department included forty-one black and thirty-five women officers.

Police activity has not been simply a matter of enforcing the law, but rather calls for a total concept of police services—enforcement, prevention, and support of its citizens. Not surprisingly, the private community has responded with support in many areas.

In 1971 the Anne C. Stouffer Foundation appropriated funds to provide a police exchange with the law officers of Great Britain. Nineteen Winston-Salem officers ultimately experienced three-week tours in four counties in England. Three British officers also visited Winston-Salem to observe American law-enforcement customs and activities.

"A City Founded upon Cooperation"

The Board of Aldermen has demonstrated it realizes that only by continuing participation in government by all people will the best ideas surface. It seeks to have each of the various boards and commissions reflect the socioeconomic mix of the community, providing a broad base for sound decisions. The city government of Winston-Salem provides opportunity for those employed in government, as well as for the public it serves. The first woman department head in City Hall, Nancy Wolfe, was employed in 1969, and the first black assistant city manager, John P. Bond, III, accepted that position in 1971.

The city has not been free of problems. It was emotionally wounded by the 1967 riots which saw 192 people arrested, $1.7 million in property damage, 47 people injured, and the National

Guard called out to restore order. Another civil disturbance occurred in 1969 but was of minimal duration and damage.

The mid-1970s pose serious challenges to Winston-Salem; difficult decisions beset its elected and administrative leaders. Policymakers are concerned about the sound delivery of basic utility services—water, sewer, sanitation. Growth, while not explosive, continues unabated, bringing with it the compounding urban problems of unemployment, urban decay, and a spiraling crime rate. As the residents increase their requests for additional services, the policymakers realize the local revenue base must be expanded or additional state and federal monies must provide relief. Rather than retreat, the many aldermen, mayors, and an involved public have laid a sound framework upon which to build into the twenty-first century.

In 1975, the business community once again joined hands with local government for an efficiency study to ensure lean and productive units of local government at the least possible cost to the public. The city continues to explore publicly its problems, reach consensus on solutions, and implement its plans. Winston-Salem prides itself in demonstrating daily its motto: *Urbs Condita Adiuvando*, "A City Founded upon Cooperation."

Health Services

Health care in Forsyth County is divided into several areas including the Health Department, Mental Health Department, Family Health Center, and Forsyth Memorial Hospital, all responsibilities of county government, and the private areas consisting primarily of Baptist Hospital, Bowman Gray School of Medicine, and Medical Park Hospital.

The Forsyth County Health Department was created in 1913 by the North Carolina General Assembly. Responsibilities of the department include communicable-disease control and promotion of improved health at the community level. In July 1964 the Health Department moved into a two-winged complex on Ridge Avenue, sharing it with the Department of Social Services. In addition to providing immunizations, venereal-disease control, and tuberculosis diagnosis and treatment, the Health Department conducts programs in diabetic screening, cervical-cancer detection, public-health nursing with home and school visits, physical-therapy services, crippled children's clinic, maternal and child health, dental health, and environmental health.

In 1974 a mobile medical unit program was set up; thus the Health Department could take clinics out to the people in the rural areas of the county rather than their having to visit the clinic on Ridge Avenue. By 1975, general health clinics were operating Monday through Friday, and glaucoma and hypertension screening clinics had been added to the previously existing ones. The environmental health bureau of the department has had the responsibility of inspecting and enforcing health regulations in such areas as restaurants, hotels, educational institutions, and septic tanks. The bureau has also had mosquito and rodent control programs.

In 1975 a proposal was advanced to consolidate all county-run health services at Reynolds Memorial Hospital including the Health Department, Family Health Center, and Mental Health Department. A citizens' study group appointed by the Forsyth Health Planning Council recommended a new board be appointed by the Board of Commissioners to govern all health matters in the county.

The Forsyth County Mental Health Department was created in 1967 by the Board of Commissioners to coordinate existing mental-health agencies. Prior to that time, mental health came under the Health Department. The creation of the Mental Health Department resulted from a recommendation in a report from the local mental health advisory committee, which had been appointed by the commissioners in 1964. Once the department was formed, a contract was made with the Child Guidance Clinic for psychiatric services for children. In 1968 the adult mental health clinic came under psychiatric direction and the adult outpatient clinic had a full-time director for the first time. The county's mental-health program has been aimed at developing and putting into operation new and improved approaches to the problems of prevention, control, treatment, care, and rehabilitation of mental patients. The department's program includes services in adult psychiatry, alcoholism, child psychiatry, mental retardation, hospitalization, education, consultation, and training.

The clinic has been located in the former nurses' quarters for the old Kate Bitting Reynolds Hospital. The department's Sheltered Workshop for the mentally retarded has been housed in the old county Agriculture Building at Spruce and Sixth streets. In November 1974, Forsyth voters authorized the issuance of up to $3 million in bonds for new mental-health facilities.

Hospitals in Forsyth County include Forsyth Memorial Hospital, North Carolina Baptist Hospital with its medical center complex, and the smallest and newest facility, Medical Park Hospital, which was constructed in the late 1960s. In 1959 the voters of Forsyth County approved a bond referendum for construction of Forsyth Memorial Hospital and authorized up to a ten-cent special tax levy to operate the hospital. The hospital began operating in 1964, and since that time has offered a wide range of medical services including cobalt therapy, radioisotopes, electroencephalography, echoencephalography, outpatient dental services, inhalation therapy, occupational and recreational therapy, inpatient psychiatric treatment, intensive care, and cardiac monitoring. The hospital provides a full-time emergency room and is supported by the John C. Whitaker Care Center adjoining the hospital and providing convalescent care. In 1975 the hospital started a $10-million expansion program for consolidating and improving health-care services.

Until 1970 the Kate Bitting Reynolds Hospital served the East Winston area. With funds from a special bond issue the city constructed Reynolds Memorial Hospital adjacent to the old structure and in January 1970 the patients were transferred to the new structure. In 1972 this new facility was closed as a general hospital and converted to the Family Health Center. In 1973 Forsyth County government assumed the responsibility for all health-care needs, and the city of Winston-Salem transferred title to the hospital to the county but continues to retire the bonds. The old City Hospital was also closed during the 1960s. Forsyth Memorial Hospital has been operated by Forsyth County Hospital Authority since the authority was created by the commissioners in 1968. With the opening of the Family Health Center at Reynolds

Memorial Hospital, the authority also took over its operation. In 1975 Forsyth County assumed control of all operations of Reynolds Memorial Hospital.

Forsyth County also provides a nursing and rest home, primarily to handle indigents who are the county's responsibility. Originally a tuberculosis sanatorium, the old Yoder home was purchased by the county government in 1958. In 1961 the county leased it to Forsyth Home, Inc., a nonprofit corporation operating the home for the county. The home, which later became Knollwood Hall, received a $3-million addition in 1975, after Forsyth voters approved a bond referendum to finance it.

Since the 1940s both the North Carolina Baptist Hospital and the Bowman Gray School of Medicine of Wake Forest University have moved together in the creation of a medical center serving its home community, its state, and a multistate region.

The hospital kept pace with the growing demand for health care by adding an additional 150 beds in 1954, by acquiring housing facilities for students in nursing and other allied health programs in 1956, and by opening its seventy-seven-bed progressive care unit in 1959. The unit, which brought national acclaim to the hospital, is designed for ambulatory patients who require less than full-time nursing and medical care.

Since opening as a four-year institution in 1941, the medical school's full-time faculty has grown from 23 to over 200 and its student body has been enlarged from 73 to 349. The M.D. degree has been awarded to more than 1,900 men and women. Over the years, the school has added new departments such as comparative medicine and community medicine, with the most recent being the department of family medicine.

Research into such problems as cancer, heart disease, kidney disease, and stroke has served to establish the medical center's reputation for contributions in both basic and applied research. In 1974 the medical center received 126 research grants totaling $3.2 million, with an additional $1.6 million received for specific training and demonstration programs, fellowships, and advanced investigator awards. The cancer research center is one of about thirty in the nation and the special center of research on arteriosclerosis is one of fifteen in the nation.

In 1948 the hospital developed the first pastoral care program for the training of ministers to work with the sick. The program has since become a model for others.

The most recent period of expansion began in 1967 with the construction program that has added a new laboratory and classroom building and an auditorium to the medical school, an allied health programs building, a fourteen-bed coronary-care unit, a power plant, and a sixteen-story hospital and clinics building (the Reynolds Tower). The new tower includes a well-equipped intensive-care nursery, considered among the best in the Southeast, and a thirty-eight bed intensive-care floor.

Construction is nearing completion on an ambulatory-care building which will house such services as a new emergency department, multidisciplinary outpatient clinics, and the cancer center. Major renovations of the hospital's older facilities are now underway.

When the hospital opened its doors over fifty years ago, it had eighty beds. Today it has 615 beds, handling over 20,000 admissions a year. The medical center has become a partner with rural communities in the development of model community-health centers. It is a major participant in a state-supported educational program for doctors already in practice, for allied health professionals, and for community hospitals which elect to take part. In Winston-Salem the medical center is involved with, among other things, programs of family planning, genetic counseling, and marital counseling.

Social Services Department

Welfare or public assistance to the needy was administered by the Department of Social Services in Forsyth County from the late 1960s. The department is responsible for providing the basic elements to sustain life and to relieve suffering. Some of the most important programs are aid to the permanently disabled, aid to the aged, aid to the blind, aid to dependent children, and hospitalization for the indigent. Other important activities include the food-stamp program, services for the elderly, day-care programs, medical screening, child welfare, and the crisis intervention unit.

The funds for these programs are provided jointly by the federal, state, and county governments. The department is housed in the south wing of the Health and Social Services Building on Ridge Avenue, where it moved in 1964.

The aid to families with dependent children is a money payment for needy dependent children who have been deprived of parental care and support because of the death, physical or mental incapacity, or continued absence from home of one or both parents, either natural or adoptive. The aid to the disabled provides a money payment to all persons under sixty-five who are physically or mentally unable to earn a living, found to be permanently and totally disabled by a medical review team, and not inmates of a public institution nor patients in an institution for tuberculosis or mental diseases.

The aid to the aged provides a money payment for any person over sixty-five years of age who is not able to provide his own necessities of life and is not an inmate in a public institution. Medical assistance is provided to anyone receiving public assistance or to others who do not meet the requirements for public assistance for living expenses but do qualify for help with medical costs only. Services covered include inpatient and outpatient hospital care, laboratory and x-ray, nursing home, physicians, dentists, optometrists, home health, drugs, eyeglasses, and services to aged patients in the state's mental hospitals. Child welfare is a major responsibility of the Social Services Department and is divided into the three programs of adoptions, foster placements, and protective services.

Education

Education, both public and private, has traditionally been of primary importance to the citizens of Forsyth County. Public education was provided separately by the governments of Forsyth County and the city of Winston-Salem with little serious thought to consolidating the systems until the late 1940s.

By 1949 many of the small schools scattered throughout rural Forsyth County were being merged into larger ones under the direction of Ralph Brimley, who took over as superintendent of the county schools in 1947. These mergers were achieved with difficulty by Brimley and his administration, who had to stand their ground when questioned by their elected board and many county residents resentful of losing their community schools.

In 1950 two reports were completed on local school problems, but neither report supported consolidation of the county and city school systems. The reports stated that consolidation of the systems would not improve the quality of education of either system.

In 1955 Brimley was unsuccessful in an attempt to bring the county school-tax rate of twenty cents up to the thirty-five-cent tax rate levied by Winston-Salem for the city school system. The first step toward consolidating the school systems was determined to be the equalization of the tax rates; only then could consolidation be considered on its own merits, disregarding the financial question.

Later the same year, the Forsyth County Board of Commissioners commissioned the Public Administration Service of Chicago, Illinois, to study the problems of the local schools and propose the methods for improving them. The report recommended the adoption of a 6–3–3 structure in the schools with six elementary, three junior high, and three senior high grades. It recommended the equalization of the county and city tax rates for schools at thirty-five cents. And, most importantly, the report recommended consolidation of the county and city school systems.

Brimley resigned in 1956, to be succeeded by T. Ray Gibbs, who had served as assistant superintendent. Gibbs continued the merging of smaller schools and soon had eight schools merged into three schools. Also, the longtime policy of eight years of elementary school and four years of high school was changed to the recommended 6–3–3 plan.

In 1957 an effort was made to have the North Carolina General Assembly enact legislation permitting consolidation of the two school systems. The city school board opposed the attempt to permit consolidation until a plan could be worked out between both boards. Work on such a plan did not begin until the summer of 1959, when both the school boards decided to get together, and it was finally announced to the public in February 1961.

A. Craig Phillips, who became superintendent of the Winston-Salem schools in 1956, was one of the strongest supporters of the plan's requirement for a countywide tax rate of fifty cents for a consolidated school system. Phillips also supported the recommendation for an appointed rather than an elected school board. The city school board was appointed, while the county school board was elected.

Residents of rural Forsyth County strongly opposed both the fifty-cent tax rate and the appointment of school board members. Winston-Salem Mayor John Surratt proposed a compromise tax rate of thirty-eight cents for a consolidated school system. The compromise on whether the board would be elected or appointed was settled by both boards agreeing to one of four plans submitted by the General Assembly in 1961. The selected plan called for the school board to be appointed for four years and then for the voters to decide if the board should continue to be appointed or be elected instead.

In 1962 Phillips was succeeded as superintendent by Marvin M. Ward, who had served as assistant superintendent under Phillips.

The question of consolidation was put before the voters on 29 January 1963 in a countywide election, which saw the consolidation of county and city schools approved by a margin of about two thousand votes. The question of setting the countywide tax rate at thirty-eight cents was also approved on the same ballot by a lesser margin.

Ward was elected in March 1963 as superintendent of the newly consolidated system by the school board. Gibbs declined the position of associate superintendent and instead became superintendent of the Iredell County schools. Raymond Sarbaugh, who had been Gibbs's assistant superintendent, shared the duties under Ward with Ned R. Smith, who had been administrative assistant under Phillips.

On 1 July 1963, the county and city school systems officially consolidated, thereby creating the second largest school system in North Carolina. Roy Ray, who had been chairman of the county board since 1960, became the chairman of the appointed board.

During the same years that consolidation of the county and city school systems was being brought about, another major change occurred in the public schools in Forsyth County. In 1954 the United States Supreme Court ordered the desegregation of all public schools, and in 1957 Winston-Salem joined Charlotte and Greensboro in admitting the first black students to previously all-white schools. Unlike the other two cities, where the change was met with resistance, the transition in Winston-Salem came about almost without incident.

When Gwendolyn Yvonne Bailey entered Reynolds High School in September of 1957 at the age of 15, she was the first black to attend any previously all-white school in the county, where blacks and whites had been previously taught separately. The event caused curious stares, and some rude signs were painted on the street near the school, but these were soon erased by the school's white students.

The pupil-assignment plan in use in the late 1950s allowed black students who lived closer to a white school than to one for black students to apply for transfer to another school within the same school district. With the consolidation of the school systems in 1963, the school board continued operating with basically the same pupil-assignment plan that had been used in the city school system. Black students from the county outside the city continued to attend Carver School, which had all twelve grades in one building.

The federal Civil Rights Act of 1964 forced the school board to change its policy, and in September 1965 the United States Office of Education approved a new pupil-assignment plan for one year based on geographic zoning with a freedom of choice for transfer. The plan came under renewed criticism, and charges of discrimination in the schools demanded more changes in the plan. From the consolidation of the school systems in 1963, much of the progress and change in the local schools was directly tied to the move toward total desegregation.

One of the first questions facing the consolidated school board was what could be done about the overcrowded conditions at Paisley Junior-Senior High School, which was predominantly black. The board first decided to build a new Paisley as a high school. The site originally selected for the school on the Methodist Children's Home property met with objections from black parents, who wanted the school located in East Winston closer to the black community. When the school board finally decided to build the new Paisley in East Winston, the decision met with protests from black leaders, who claimed that construction of the school in East Winston would perpetuate de facto segregation.

At the same time, the school board had to decide whether to close Carver School, which had served for black children living outside the city and attending grades one through twelve. The board finally decided to build Paisley and decided against closing Carver.

In the spring of 1958, a $6-million bond referendum for school construction had been approved by the voters, but the county commissioners decided to raise the county's property tax rate by twenty cents, from eighty-five cents to $1.05 per $100 valuation, and thereby decided that schools would be built on a pay-as-you-go basis. In the next five years, from 1958 to 1963, the commissioners appropriated nearly $13 million for city and county school construction when the twenty-cent increase was originally earmarked for a building program of between $6 and $7 million. With the consolidation of the school systems in 1963, the voters also approved a special thirty-eight cent tax levy for the schools, which raised the county tax rate from $1.05 to $1.43 per $100 valuation.

The early 1960s also saw the establishment of three unique state-supported schools in Forsyth County. In the summer of 1963 the first session of the Governor's School took place; it was established as a special summer program for talented junior- and senior-high school students from across North Carolina. In 1964 the Advancement School was opened in the old City Hospital building and served as a proving ground for programs dealing with underachievers in the junior-high-school level. The 1975 state legislature failed to provide funds for the Advancement School, but local support made it possible to move the school to Wake Forest University's Graylyn, continuing operations on a limited basis.

The North Carolina School of the Arts opened in the old

Gray High School in 1965, providing training in the arts for both high-school and college-level students. In order to make the school building available for the arts school, the school board approved the construction of Parkland High School in 1964. The new school, built at a cost of $1.4 million, is located in the southern part of the county at Brewer Road and N.C. 150.

The construction of Parkland followed closely the construction of three other high schools which were opened in the early 1960s. East Forsyth was built on Old Highway 421 East, North Forsyth on Shattalon Drive, and West Forsyth on the Lewisville-Clemmons Road.

Although the school system is operated by the school board, funds are appropriated to the schools by the Board of Commissioners for construction of buildings and facilities, retiring of debts, general administration, purchase of new library books and textbooks, maintenance and operation of buildings and grounds, supplementary instructional services, any increase in the number of teachers, any increase in teachers' salaries, and payment of transportation costs. The county government shares the financial responsibility for the schools with the state government.

After the closing of the old Granville School in 1963, the old building was converted to house the offices of the consolidated school system administration.

In 1965 the school board approved a plan calling for construction of five junior- or senior-high schools and six elementary schools by 1970. The plan called for spending the local system's share of $3.7 million from the statewide $100-million school-bond referendum approved by the voters in November 1964.

In 1966 school construction included the thirty-one-classroom Mount Tabor Junior-Senior High School on Petree Road, the sixteen-classroom Bolton Elementary School on Bolton Street, the twenty-four-classroom Kimberley Park Elementary School on North Cherry Street, a major renovation of Reynolds High School, and a twelve-classroom addition at Griffith Elementary School.

In April 1967 voters turned down bonds for school construction and construction at Forsyth Technical Institute and proposed increases in the tax rates to support the schools and Forsyth Tech.

By 1967 about 9 percent of the black students in the county

were enrolled in the twenty-seven previously all-white schools. Two schools, Hanes Junior High and Lowrance Elementary, were completely integrated with integrated faculties by this time.

With integration increasing in the schools, construction also continued in 1968 with the building of a twenty-four-classroom Jefferson Junior High School on Sally Kirk Road, which enabled Mount Tabor to be turned into a high school. Major classroom additions were built at North Forsyth and Reynolds, and the kitchen and cafeteria were renovated at Atkins.

In 1968 voters anticipated the need for future expansion and renovation of school facilities in Forsyth County and approved a $24.8-million general-obligation bond issue to finance new school construction and major renovation programs. These funds were tied up in the courts, however, because of the Catherine Scott desegregation suit, until 1972, when the school board and the county commissioners were once again able to develop plans for school expansions.

The late 1960s saw increased integration of the public schools, and limited trouble in the schools attributed to racial relations. North Forsyth was closed briefly because of racial unrest, but this situation and all others were settled without lasting problems.

At the time of the bond referendum in 1968, the school system had forty-two elementary, fourteen junior highs, and ten high schools for more than forty-nine thousand students. By 1969 forty-five of the sixty-six schools were integrated to some degree in the system.

A greater degree of integration in the schools was initiated on 25 June 1970, when Federal Judge Eugene A. Gordon, acting in the Catherine Scott desegregation case, approved all but two aspects of the integration plans submitted by the school board for 1970–71. He gave the board twenty days in which to file a revised plan which would not permit any child to transfer from a school where his race was in the minority to another geographic area where his race was in the majority. The order also required the reasonable integration of three all-black schools and an increase in interracial contact.

The board agreed to all requests except integration of the three schools and asked the court to reconsider the request. On

17 July Judge Gordon ordered the clustering of eight schools: Diggs, Cook, and Kimberley Park, which were black; with Latham, South Park, Speas, Sherwood Forest, and Whitaker, which were white.

In late July the board presented a revised plan to Judge Gordon, but asked that implementation of it be delayed pending an appeal to the United States Court of Appeals. On 17 August Judge Gordon ordered the implementation of a variation of the plan, which required extensive cross-busing of students across district lines. The court of appeals also denied a stay of the integration order, leaving open the way for an appeal to the United States Supreme Court.

The opening of school was delayed by the school board in 1970, while an answer was being awaited from Chief Justice Warren E. Burger on a request to delay the cluster integration plan, but the request was denied. The plan clustered five white elementary schools and three black elementary schools, and assigned all students in grades one through four to the previously all-white schools and the students in grades five and six to the black schools. The plan required busing about two thousand students.

In June 1971 the school board adopted a new desegregation plan, which was aimed at bringing the ratio of black students to white students to between 18 and 36 percent in each school. The plan, referred to as the 4–2–2–2–2 plan, placed students in five clusters of schools, all feeding into senior highs, with about seventy schools divided into five different levels.

The plan was approved on 16 July 1971 by Judge Gordon and added more than 15,000 students to the more than 23,000 already bused to school. Under the plan, the elementary school zone in which a child lived determines which schools he attends as he moves through the upper grades. The first four grades attend classes in elementary schools which were formerly white. Students in grades five and six attend classes in elementary schools which were formerly black. On 26 August 1971 the Forsyth County schools opened in a completely desegregated system for the first time.

While Forsyth County also had had many private and parochial schools in existence for some time, total integration in the public school system led to the establishment of many others. The first of the large private schools of the 1970s was Forsyth County Day School, which joined the nine-grade Summit School, four parochial elementary schools, one parochial high school, and Salem Academy. Since that time, more than a dozen private schools, many of them connected with churches, have opened in Forsyth County.

In 1972 two alternate plans were submitted to Judge Gordon, one by a majority of the school board and another one by two members of the board. Neither plan was accepted, and the school system continued to function in a similar way to the year before.

By the 1973 school year, more than twenty private schools were operating in Forsyth County with enrollment of more than 6,000 students. At the same time, public school enrollment dropped below 45,800. In November 1973 voters approved a $300-million statewide bond issue for school construction, and the local share was $12.1 million. At that same time, the county commissioners decided to issue the first $11 million of the local bonds approved in 1968 to finance four projects. The projects included a Career Center and Administrative Center complex at the south end of Miller Street near Forsyth Technical Institute, a Vocational Rehabilitation Center on South Main Street on the site of South Park School, and additions to Brown Intermediate School and Walkertown Junior High School. The commissioners later committed an additional $4 million of bond money to the school construction projects.

At the beginning of the 1974 school year, the desegregation of the school system was in its fourth year, and four of the system's sixty-two schools had a majority of black students, and five additional schools had more than 45 percent black enrollment. Public school enrollment ceased to decline. In 1975 the school board approved a $7.3-million plan to include construction of a new $2.1-million Southeast Elementary School on Nicholson Road near Parkview Shopping Center. Plans also called for a twenty-two classroom addition to replace the oldest section of Rural Hall Elementary School, and classroom additions at Bolton and Easton, libraries for Lewisville and Mineral Springs Elementary schools, a new gymnasium for Carver High School, a football field and stands for West Forsyth Senior High, and $1.5 million in equipment for the new Career Center and Administrative Center complex.

What is today known as Forsyth Technical Institute had its start in October 1960 as the Winston-Salem/Forsyth County Industrial Education Center. In 1963 the North Carolina General Assembly passed the Community College Act, and the name was officially changed to reflect its broadened goals.

Enrollment was only 150 students in 1963, but by the spring of 1975 it had climbed to 1,732 students. There are offerings for part-time and full-time students in both vocational and technical curricula. Courses range from air conditioning and auto body repair to a nursing program leading to the associate degree. The nursing degree was instituted in 1972 when the city's hospitals phased out their three-year schools, leaving Winston-Salem State's full college curriculum program as the only nurses' training program in the county. The facilities at Forsyth Technical Institute have grown steadily to meet the increasing demand, with construction of a new classroom and administration building scheduled for completion in 1977.

Higher Education

On 15 October 1952 ground-breaking ceremonies for the new campus of Wake Forest College were held on a 320-acre site provided by the late Charles H. and Mary Reynolds Babcock. More than twenty thousand persons were on hand when President Harry S. Truman began construction by shoveling the first spadeful of dirt. The next four years witnessed the erection of the fourteen original buildings designed for the campus by architect Jens F. Larsen.

Wake Forest University moved to Winston-Salem in 1956 and has made remarkable progress during the 1960s and early 1970s. Neither student unrest nor rampant inflation was a deterrent. Now, by almost any reasonable measuring stick, Wake Forest stands as one of the nation's finest small universities.

The Z. Smith Reynolds Library ranks high among the best

research libraries in the Southeast. More than 70 percent of the faculty hold earned doctorates. The student body is highly competent and diversified; 50 percent of the students come from out of state. The student-faculty ratio is fifteen to one. The cultural atmosphere is exceptionally rich; the movie series has been ranked number one in the nation and the Artists Series brings to Winston-Salem some of the world's best musicians and artists.

The University's Sesquicentennial Commission, which studied long-range goals for the institution, issued a report in 1973 which said in part: "Wake Forest University has the best of two worlds—the good qualities of both the large university and the small liberal arts college. It is the skillful blending of these qualities and a fiercely guarded spirit of proud independence that give the University its particular mystique."

In Wake Forest terms, "small" means around four thousand students, with the bulk of that group—about three thousand—in the Undergraduate College and the remainder in the School of Law, the Bowman Gray School of Medicine, the Graduate School, and the Babcock Graduate School of Management.

Wake Forest's history since the move to Winston-Salem is centered around Dr. Harold W. Tribble, who was president from 1951 to 1967, and Dr. James Ralph Scales, who became president in 1967. Dr. Tribble can best be categorized as a mover and builder. He had the unenviable task of raising the money and marshaling the human resources for building a new campus and moving books, people, and traditions from one location to another.

Under Dr. Scales, the university is acquiring national academic prominence, and there has been considerable refinement of the institution's personality. Innovations include a certain amount of cautious curriculum experimentation, a strong increase in emphasis on the fine arts, the establishment of the Babcock Graduate School of Management, and a marked increase in studies abroad, highlighted by the acquisition of the Camillo Artom House in Venice, Italy. The building is used by students for study in winter and by faculty in summer. It is named for the late world-renowned biochemist who was on the faculty of the Bowman Gray School of Medicine from 1939 to 1961.

The School of Medicine and North Carolina Baptist Hospital form one of the leading teaching and research hospitals in the Southeast. Both the School of Law and the Medical School have expanded facilities to meet an increased demand for physicians and lawyers. The Law School is known particularly for the number of graduates who are active in North Carolina politics. The new Babcock Graduate School of Management offers two-year programs for Master of Business Administration and Master of Management degrees. The Graduate School offers work leading to the master's degree in twenty-two departments and to the Ph.D. in seven.

The modern history of Salem College begins during the administration of Dr. John Henry Clewell in the late 1880s. During his term as president of the Female Academy, as it was then known, an "Industrial Department" which offered courses in sewing, home nursing, cooking, and woodcarving was established in 1889. The next year, 1890, saw the first baccalaureate degrees awarded to seven young ladies, one of whom was Adelaide Fries. Other noteworthy events during Clewell's administration included the installation of hot water and electric lights, and the removal of cattle and hogs from the campus! The school officially became Salem Academy and College in 1907, through a charter granted by the state of North Carolina.

Succeeding President Clewell in 1909 was Dr. Howard E. Rondthaler, who began a forty-year career as president of the college and academy. Throughout the Rondthaler administration one notes a definite physical expansion, beginning with the campus itself, which was enlarged from three and a half to fifty-six and a half acres. Through the magnanimity of Salem alumnae, the number of buildings increased from nine in 1909 to twenty-two in 1949. Corrin Refectory, Strong Dorm, and the Hanes Management House were all gifts.

When Rondthaler retired in 1949, he was replaced by Salem's first inaugurated president, Dale H. Gramley. Gramley, a journalist by profession, promoted the financial growth of Salem much as Rondthaler had promoted the school's physical growth. Trust funds tripled and faculty salaries quadrupled during Gramley's twenty-two-year administration. Scholarship money

327

available annually from endowments increased from $3,000 to $21,500. New buildings included two dormitories—Babcock and Gramley—the Fine Arts Center, and the Science Building. Salem College during Gramley's years also became North Carolina's first private institution to establish a nationally accredited teacher-education program. Since 1971 Salem's president, John Chandler, with the help of former vice-president James A. Gray, Jr., has led Salem into its third century, with the completion of a $3 million drive.

Originally organized as Slater Industrial Academy on 28 September 1892, Winston-Salem State University is today a leader in black education. The first one-room structure that housed twenty-five young students has been expanded to a sixty-five-acre plant including twenty-one well-equipped buildings and chancellor's home, valued at close to $15 million. Shortly after the academy was established, in 1895, the state of North Carolina recognized the educational program offered there, and two years later, in 1897, a state charter was granted under the name Slater Industrial and State Normal School. Teacher training, particularly on the elementary school level, has been the primary focus of this institution since its organization. The North Carolina General Assembly granted Slater a new charter in 1925, and until 1969 the school was known as Winston-Salem State College. Not only was it the first Negro school in the United States to grant a baccalaureate degree for teaching in the elementary grades, but today it is the only institution in Forsyth County to offer the Bachelor of Science degree in nursing. The nursing program was instituted in 1953. Today the education program at WSSU includes all levels of teacher education as well as special education and counseling. Expansion of the liberal arts program is in the offing.

In 1968, the Scholastic Achievement Program at WSSU was started with a grant of $390,000 from the R. J. Reynolds Tobacco Company, aiming for improvement of the student body, faculty, and curriculum. Three additional grants totaling over $540,000 were provided in 1970, 1971, and 1973. Under the Reynolds-instituted program, scholarships for both resident and nonresident students are provided, as well as monies for five Reynolds professors and consultants and visiting lecturers. The presidents of WSSU who have been responsible in large measure for the progress made are Dr. Simon G. Atkins (1892–1904), Cadd G. O'Kelly (1904–13), Dr. Simon G. Atkins (1913–34), Francis L. Atkins (1934–61), and Kenneth R. Williams since 1961.

According to former chancellor Robert Ward, the North Carolina School of the Arts "is dedicated to the achievement of a bold new idea in education—the idea that within the framework of public education young people with extraordinary talents in the arts can and should be given, not only the academic education, but also the artistic training which their gifts justify." This unique educational institution was established by an act of the North Carolina General Assembly in 1963 and has, since September 1965, offered a varied program of instruction in the performing arts to students both on the college level and of high-school age and younger. More than half of the student body are North Carolinians. Two academic degrees, the Bachelor of Fine Arts in drama, design, dance, and production, and the Bachelor of Music in music, are offered. The school was a project of Governor Terry Sanford's administration and was to be located in a community which would provide a site and buildings. Within forty-eight hours the citizens of Forsyth County, through a special telephone campaign, had pledged almost a million dollars and had arranged for the use of the old Gray High School on a twenty-three acre tract. A number of persons whose names are well known in the world of the performing arts have been associated with the North Carolina School of the Arts. Two distinguished American composers, Dr. Vittorio Giannini and Dr. Robert Ward, were respectively the school's first and second presidents. Ward later became chancellor when the NCSA became a part of the consolidated University of North Carolina. Dr. Robert Suderburg became chancellor upon Ward's retirement in 1974. On the advisory board are Richard Adler, Jean Dalrymple, Agnes de Mille, Paul Green, Helen Hayes, José Limón, Sidney Blackmer, Eugenie Ouroussow, James Christian Pfohl, and William Schumann. Teaching faculty includes or has included Jean Arthur, Norman Farrow, Rose Bampton, Claude Frank, Irwin Freundlich, Erick Friedman, Nicholas Harsanyi (dean of the School of Music), Louis Mennini, Norman Johnson, Pauline

Koner, Clifton Matthews, Duncan Noble, Jesus Silva, and Janos Starker.

Since the first class graduated in 1968 the number of students enrolled and graduating from the School of the Arts has increased significantly. The physical plant has been enlarged by the addition of a $1-million Commons Building, and Crawford Auditorium and the Agnes de Mille Theater have been renovated.

The Arts Council

The *Arts Council Factbook* states quite clearly the purpose and function of this organization to be in the coordination, support, and development of "a varied and comprehensive system of cultural programs" which are financed both privately and by public solicitation. Participants include professionals and amateurs. The booklet continues, "It is deemed the responsibility of The Arts Council to concern itself with the cultural interests of all segments of the community, the public at large and groups with special needs. The Council will help see that cultural traditions and cultural innovations are adequately served for all parts of the community."

The Arts Council was formally organized on 9 August 1949 and today is located in the James Gordon Hanes Community Center, a $1-million structure dedicated in 1958 (the Chamber of Commerce and United Fund offices are also located here). The wing occupied by the Arts Council is divided in such a way as to accommodate its member groups. Contained are a 420-seat theater, an art gallery, eight studio rooms for arts and crafts, a rehearsal room for the symphony and other musical groups, and a music library.

Since 1958, when the first Arts Fund Drive was conducted, the sum raised has been greater than the previous year, with the exception of only one year. Interesting too is the fact that in ten of the last seventeen drives money realized has been in excess of the set goal.

Eleven funded member groups of the Arts Council and twenty-nine associate member groups comprise the organization. The funded group includes the Winston-Salem Chapter of the

American Guild Organization; the Arts and Crafts Association, Inc. (successor to the Winston-Salem Workshop, which began in 1945); Art Gallery Originals; Associated Artists of Winston-Salem, since 1956; Children's Theater Board, Inc. (organized in 1940); Film Friends; Friends of Dance, Inc. (formerly the Winston-Salem Civic Ballet); The Little Theater; Southeastern Center for Contemporary Art (formerly the Gallery of Contemporary Art); Winston-Salem Dance Forum; and the Winston-Salem Symphony and Chorale.

In the last decade much of the work of the Arts Council has been directed towards urban arts, a concept new in arts planning. The purpose of this program is to provide cultural programs for citizens not immediately affected by existing efforts. The Urban Arts program now includes a mobile street theater, Freedom Street Players; a mobile music program, The Jazzmobile; and a mobile crafts program, Fun Center. Another current function of the Arts Council is the Northwest Arts Development, a cooperative program shared with the Northwest Economic Development Commission. Member counties (Davie, Forsyth, Stokes, Surry, and Yadkin) will be encouraged through this program "to expand the efforts of existing cultural groups and to form new ones."

Finally, the Winston-Salem/Forsyth County Bicentennial Commission, at the specific designation of the city Board of Aldermen and the Board of County Commissioners, is sponsored by the Arts Council. According to the council's *Factbook*, "The Arts Council—with its positive response from the community, in addition to being nonpartisan, including rich and poor, black and white, young and old—was the most logical and dynamic setting for Bicentennial plans and projects."

The United Way

The history of Forsyth County is filled with individuals working to serve their fellowman. Miss Annie Grogan began working with Winston-Salem's United Charities early in the twentieth century in an organized effort to care for those in need. In the 1920s came the Community Chest and its "Red Feather" drives. By 1950 there were twenty-three separate agencies conducting seventeen fund drives under the nominal umbrella of the Community Chest. In 1946 the Forsyth County Public Solicitations Committee was established to review the budgets of charitable agencies, and with its urging Mayor Marshall Kurfees appointed a committee to investigate the possibility of a consolidated fund drive.

On 25 July 1951 the United Fund was born in Forsyth County and the Community Chest with most of its member agencies was the first to join the consolidated fund. Some objections and problems with national organizations reluctant to give up separate fund drives kept many charitable agencies out of the United Fund for some years but the concept of shared responsibility and the success of the fund ultimately brought most organizations into membership.

The first United Fund Drive in 1951 had a goal of $425,376 and began with a rally at the Carolina Theater. The 15 October kickoff was spearheaded by Spike Jones, comic bandleader, who directed his barbs at Mayor Kurfees. Mrs. James DeHart headed some three thousand volunteer workers as the campaign soared some $75,000 over its goal. Throughout the 1950s and 1960s membership in the United Fund grew and membership budgets increased as the need for their services increased. Community leadership and concerned citizens joined in campaigns to meet the ever-increasing total budget, and year after year, with only one exception, the goals were surpassed as the results of the Fund Drive came in. In the mid-1950s Max Stuart became executive director of the fund. During his years with the fund, he reduced campaign expenses, continued the involvement of all levels of community leadership in United Fund campaigns, and continued the remarkable record of meeting goal after goal. The United Fund became the United Way in 1974 and John B. Goessman became executive director in 1975. The projected budget for 1976 includes funds for thirty-two agencies and a campaign goal of $1,925,000.

All-American City, 1959 and 1964

Appearing before the All-American City Awards Jury on 17 November 1959, Winston-Salem's representative Dr. Dale

Gramley—then president of Salem College—stressed Winston-Salem's interest in "restoring its past, improving its present, and blueprinting its future."

It was at the initiative of a newcomer to Winston-Salem and Forsyth County, Mrs. Peggy Bowman, that interest was aroused in the competition. R. F. Campbell, Dr. Lucia Karnes, and Mrs. Bowman (under the watchful eyes of the Chamber of Commerce and the City Planning Board) together prepared the entry application, which, after several months of consideration by the National Municipal League, was deemed one of twenty-two finalists.

Next came the trip to Springfield, Massachusetts. Dr. Gramley was accompanied by four working assistants: Fred Linton, Peggy Bowman, Ben Rouzie, and Philip Hanes. Eight accomplishments were presented by Gramley to the jury substantiating Winston-Salem's position as the "most American city." There was a keen interest in the past and tradition, as exemplified in the restoration of Old Salem. The building of the James G. Hanes Community Center demonstrated "the spirit, basic unity, and progress" of Winston-Salem in the desire of its leaders to consolidate under one roof volunteer efforts in the areas of economy, welfare, and culture. Great strides had been made in health and education: the building of a technical school, local school expansion (at a cost of $6 million), and the successful bond election for a new $10-million hospital. Also, Winston-Salem could boast the first Neighborhood Renewal Plan in the southeastern United States, a City-County Planning Board, and a general cooperation and goodwill of governmental groups in working together as a team, exemplified by the creation of an industrial park from a 600-acre county farm.

In February 1960 it was officially announced that Winston-Salem was the new All-American City. Civic pride was at an all-time high; the cooperative efforts and teamwork of what Mayor Kurfees referred to as "top industrial and business officials. . . . county commissioners, and aldermen, city and county employees and officials," and "a few just plain people" had paid off.

Again, in 1964, Winston-Salem successfully entered the All-American City competition. This time it was a Chamber of Commerce effort to help boost the forthcoming bicentennial of the city

333

in 1966. The Chamber's officials, under the leadership of William S. Yeager, chose to emphasize Winston-Salem's educational accomplishments. Dr. Gramley, again representing the city, revealed eleven accomplishments in this area, eight of which demonstrated "a united program in support of improved education opportunity," the "dollar value" of which exceeded $10,225,000.

And indeed, these accomplishments were staggering. Smith Bagley and Philip Hanes—via a two-day telephone campaign—raised $1 million in April 1964 to locate the North Carolina School of the Arts in Winston-Salem. Within ten minutes, Dale Gramley and Henry Ramm raised $225,000 at a luncheon of "the right industrial and civic leaders" to match a Carnegie Foundation Grant which would locate the North Carolina Governor's School in Winston-Salem. It was also at this time that the Winston-Salem Advancement School for underachieving students was created. A campaign to extend Baptist Hospital and Bowman Gray School of Medicine, under John Watlington, realized over $7 million. Ralph Hanes spearheaded fund raising which added $1,750,000 to the Salem College Fine Arts Center building fund. Goodwill Industries Rehabilitation Center received $250,000 for a dormitory for trainees; John W. Googe led the drive. Through the leadership of Winston-Salem's Junior League, the Nature-Science Center was established.

In addition to these educational accomplishments, Gramley had in reserve two other projects. The first was the creation of the Youth Work Corps which provided summer jobs for teenage boys. Secondly, in November 1963 the city-county school consolidation was approved as were an annexation program and a bond issue, all due to a successful voter-education campaign prior to November.

Old Salem and the Preservation of the Past

Today, twenty-five years after its beginning, it is difficult to imagine Old Salem as any thing other than what it is—the credible end result of "an adventure in historic preservation." But before the spring of 1950 there was great doubt in the minds of many local persons, Moravian and non-Moravian, that the original town of

Salem (decaying but mostly intact) could withstand the damaging effects of the machine age and commercialism.

At least eight buildings had been privately restored by individuals or institutions during the 1930s and 1940s. There was even interest in preserving the entire town along the lines of the Williamsburg restoration. As early as 1938 Charles H. Babcock, an investment broker and husband of one of R. J. Reynolds's daughters, was approached by R. Arthur Spaugh, Sr., and asked to be the "Rockefeller of Old Salem." Babcock declined, in favor of a broader-based community effort. Later Babcock was to figure prominently in the restoration, however. During World War II interest in the project was kept alive by William K. Hoyt, general manager of Piedmont Publishing Company. Then in 1948 a section was written into the Winston-Salem zoning ordinance to give some protection to "The Old and Historic Salem District."

One year later, in the fall of 1949, the planned preservation of Salem was threatened by a property owner who wanted to open an Oriental rug shop there; he was prepared to go to court to challenge the zoning ordinance. Before that time two businesses had been dissuaded from locating in the town, an automobile agency and a grocery store. In the words of James A. Gray, then with the circulation department of Piedmont Publishing and a key figure in the project, "Nothing goads people into action like a crisis." In short order money was borrowed, the proposed rug-shop property was purchased, committees were formed, and the project was well underway. Already the untiring efforts of Frank Horton and a Boston architect recommended by Colonial Williamsburg, Inc., had prepared the way for an accurate and reliable restoration of the buildings. Before her death in 1949, Dr. Adelaide Fries, archivist of the Southern Province of the Moravian Church, offered Horton her enthusiastic help in locating and translating the manuscript materials needed. On 22 May 1950, Old Salem, Inc., was formally organized with James A. Gray, Jr., as its first president. Gray was to serve and direct Old Salem in an official capacity for its formative years.

The financing of Old Salem has come largely from the Winston-Salem area, as Babcock had originally hoped. It is interesting too, as Frances Griffin pointed out in *An Adventure in Historic*

Preservation, that "no single individual, husband and wife team, corporation or foundation in the community has contributed as much as 10 percent of the total amount received." Major money-raising campaigns with the support of local foundations have figured importantly in keeping an active restoration going.

Largely under the able leadership of two men, the late Ralph P. Hanes, as chairman of the restoration committee, and Frank L. Horton, as director of restorations, forty-nine authentic restorations and reconstructions have been completed. Formal educational programs, complete with student tours and lectures and presentations, make use of these restorations as a "living museum." The authenticity of the restoration was much enhanced by the scholarship and practical ability of Dr. Frank Albright, longtime director of research, who retired in 1973. Tours of Old Salem provide an enriching experience to visitors of all ages and backgrounds.

Closely related to Old Salem physically and spiritually is the Museum of Early Southern Decorative Arts (MESDA), cited by *Antiques* magazine (1965) as "the most significant event in the field of antique collecting and scholarship in more than a decade." The idea for the museum was that of Frank Horton and his mother, the late Mrs. Theo L. Taliaferro, and MESDA is built around their own private collections of furniture, ceramics, textiles, metalwork, and art indigenous to the southern United States. Housed in a building formerly occupied by a grocery store, but tastefully renovated with funds provided by Mrs. Frank Forsyth, MESDA contains fifteen individual rooms covering the period from the 1600s to 1820. The museum is operated under the auspices of Old Salem, Inc., at the request of Horton and Mrs. Taliaferro, and Horton serves as its director.

The quality and success of the Old Salem restoration has stimulated other preservation and interpretative projects in Forsyth County. The Moravian Music Foundation was organized in 1956 to catalog, edit, arrange, and make available the thousands of manuscript copies of music brought by the Moravians to Wachovia, as well as the music composed in the eighteenth and early nineteenth centuries by Americans associated with the Moravian Church. The foundation serves as a focal point for research in early American music. Through publication, through the Early American Moravian Music Festivals, and through recordings the foundation has successfully pursued its aim.

Other preservation projects complement Old Salem's program. Historic Bethabara, discussed earlier in this chapter, has been a cooperative effort with Old Salem personnel supervising research and restoration projects. Historic Winston, a newly functioning group, has opened a Winston-Salem Museum temporarily housed in the Government Center. Dr. Frank Albright, an Old Salem staff member until his retirement and an officer of the Wachovia Historical Society, has directed the efforts of Historic Winston to begin portrayal of the early history of the town of Winston. He has supervised the acquisition and display of the Frank Jones photographic collection, which Jones left to the Wachovia Historical Society and which the society has permitted Historic Winston to use. The restoration of Kerner's Folly in Kernersville is adding yet another element to the preservation scene in Forsyth County.

Discovering Reynolda House

In June 1972 Reynolda House was evaluated for accreditation by the American Association of Museums. The visiting team reported, in part, that Reynolda House had "one of the most exciting educational experiments using original art as its basis" it had ever encountered.

Reynolda, originally built as the residence of Mr. and Mrs. R. J. Reynolds, has since 1965 served as a museum of American art and learning center. A truly remarkable collection of original paintings, noted for their quality and representing the full span of America's national artistic development, has been assembled by Mrs. Barbara Lassiter, president of Reynolda House, Inc., and granddaughter of R. J. Reynolds. American artists whose work is represented in the Reynolda House collection include Jeremiah Theus, Joseph Blackburn, John Singleton Copley, Gilbert Stuart, Thomas Cole, Frederick Church, William Harnett, Thomas Eakins, Thomas Hart Benton, Charles Burchfield, and Andrew Wyeth.

Some forty thousand visitors come to Reynolda each year. In addition to the paintings that hang throughout the house, visitors may view a complete collection of Doughty birds (donated by Mrs. Nancy Susan Reynolds, a daughter of R. J. Reynolds) and a most unusual costume museum exhibiting a changing collection of period clothes.

American Art Discovery, a "do-it-yourself" art experience, was devised six years ago by Mrs. Lassiter. It is considered the integral part of Reynolda's educational program, and executive director Nicholas Bragg states that through this discovery method one "feels comfortable in the house" and is made more receptive to the total learning experience at Reynolda.

Assisting in the educational program of Reynolda House are 125 docents who, while pursuing their own personal goals, share something of their own knowledge and experience with students of all ages who come to the house. College courses, with credit offered from each of Winston-Salem's four colleges, are held at Reynolda House throughout the year. The Reynolda Youth Committee, for teenagers, the Young Friends of Reynolda, for college students, and the Tenth Muse, for poets of all ages, function as part of the public-oriented program. Chamber-music concerts, lectures, the Festival of Spring, as well as seminars, dramas, and ballet cap off this exciting educational experience. Mrs. Lassiter spoke well when she wrote in the November 1970 issue of *Antiques* that "Reynolda House adds a new dimension to a community already well known for its interest in the arts."

Religious Life

From the earliest days of settlement religion has played a prominent role in the lives of residents of Forsyth County. Today there are more than 225 churches throughout the county, representing most of the Protestant denominations as well as the Roman Catholic, Greek Orthodox, and Jewish faiths. The period from 1950 to 1975 has seen a slight alteration of the trends of church development established between the end of World War II and 1950. The larger downtown churches, with a few exceptions, such as the First Presbyterian and the United Metropolitan Baptist churches, have not needed larger sanctuaries. They have in many cases found it desirable to expand their educational facilities to meet an expanded concept of child care, religious education, and community service.

New churches continue to follow the shift of population to the suburbs, with some of the more active new churches and some relocated downtown churches growing larger than the older downtown congregations. Smaller denominations and independents continue to make their appearance. The most identifiable concentration of the new or relocated churches is along Silas Creek Parkway, where almost twenty sanctuaries are clustered.

In addition to expanded educational programs, major shifts in the operation of many of Forsyth County's churches involve cooperative efforts on the part of many interdenominational groups to meet the social needs of the increasingly urban area. Such programs include the Downtown Church Committee, the Crisis Control Ministry, Meals on Wheels, and Contact, in addition to the individual church programs designed to meet similar needs on a specialized basis.

Interdenominational and interracial cooperation, expanded educational programs, continued growth, and a move to the suburbs seem to characterize Forsyth County's church community in the third quarter of the twentieth century. The county remains more heavily religious in orientation than similar regions elsewhere, and this produces a distinct community life-style.

The Social Order: Some Conclusions

Forsyth County has changed greatly since the days the first Moravians came to Wachovia. Planned community development and control were followed by industrial growth, bringing increased population, prosperity, diversity, and change. But many of the elements which came with the first Moravians still distinguish Forsyth County's population—religion, education, music, the arts, a reverence for the past, a cooperative attitude toward solving present problems, and looking to the future—all these remain as dominant elements in the social order.

CHAPTER 15

Forsyth County Up to Date:
The Economic Order

ECONOMIC DEVELOPMENT IN FORSYTH COUNTY from 1950 to 1975 has continued its rapid growth and change. An increasing rural nonfarm population has resulted from the shift of people to the suburbs and an increase in the number of workers employed in nonfarm jobs. Some industries which were operating within Forsyth County in 1950 no longer exist, and many have merged with larger corporations. Other Forsyth industries have expanded their operations greatly, diversifying and entering new markets. New industries have come to the region. Financial institutions have grown spectacularly. Transportation has seen remarkable changes as has the field of communications. Shopping centers have multiplied as the population has increased and moved to areas outside the central city. Downtown Winston-Salem, after a period of economic decline, has revitalized itself and is on the rise again. The face of Forsyth has changed economically as well as socially.

Population increase alone, as shown by the United States Census figures, dramatically demonstrates the rate of growth.

YEAR	WINSTON-SALEM	FORSYTH COUNTY
1950	87,811	146,135
1960	111,135	189,428
1970	133,686	215,118
1975*	140,587	229,353

*estimated

Agriculture

During the twentieth century agricultural production has increased steadily in Forsyth County. The improvement in farming methods, the use of better types of seed, and the wise use of fertilizer and weed- and pest-control chemicals brought about increased yields through the 1950s and held productions steady through the 1960s and 1970s, despite a decline in the number and size of farms in the county. Crop production per acre in Forsyth County in tobacco, corn, and wheat illustrates this increase:

CROP PRODUCTION PER ACRE

CROP	1910	1965	1974
Tobacco	517 pounds	1,740 pounds	1,528 pounds
Corn	18 bushels	100 bushels	55 bushels
Wheat	10 bushels	30 bushels	60 bushels

Because of bad weather 1965 was a poor year for wheat and 1974 saw poor tobacco and corn crops. To a considerable degree this increased production is due to the efforts of Forsyth County farm agents in urging beneficial soil and water programs. While the early agents, R. W. Pou and S. R. Mitchener, may have brought about spectacular gains through their innovative programs, it is said that farmers who introduced changes on their farms after World War II increased production by at least 35 percent by the mid-1960s.

From the early 1950s Forrest H. Harmon has been associated with the county agent's office and the Agricultural Extension Service. He became assistant to S. R. Mitchener in 1952 and was named county agent and director of the Extension Service in 1956. Harmon aided in the rapid adoption of hybrid seeds for corn growing in Forsyth County and introduced many other innovations through experimental plots and educational services. Agriculture in the county was constantly diversifying, drawing on new knowledge concerning dairy farming, turning old fields into grass pastures, and improving the culture of fruits, nuts, and vegetables as well as forestry; in recent years there has been a

341

tremendous increase in the number of home vegetable gardens.

This diversification in agriculture comes in part from the changing national agricultural picture. Mammoth farms all over the country are now producing many of the staple crops. The diversification comes also from the changing nature of farm labor in Forsyth County. As agricultural labor became scarcer, farmers turned to mechanization and diversification to meet the challenge.

Recent figures indicate a growing rural, nonfarm population, with a decrease in the number of persons engaged in agriculture statewide as well as in Forsyth County. The spread of nonfarm interests has reduced the amount of land available for agriculture in the county. Despite this reduced acreage, farm productivity in the county reached a peak in the 1960s and has remained steady ever since. Gross farm sales in 1954 totaled $5.5 million. In 1965 farm sales amounted to $17.5 million, and in 1974 total sales were $15,971,000.

A breakdown of the 1974 sales figures shows clearly the diversity and productivity of Forsyth's farms.

CROP	SALES	CROP	SALES
Field crops (including tobacco)	$7,502,000	Vegetables & berries	932,000
Poultry	2,533,000	Nursery & greenhouse	780,000
Livestock	2,223,000	Fruits and nuts	348,000
Forestry	1,589,000	Conservation programs	65,000

These figures on farm sales give a good indication of how commercial agriculture has developed in Forsyth County and what the situation is in the 1970s. They do not indicate the millions of dollars' worth of produce consumed on the farm and in the home. Farm vegetables and home gardens produce bountifully and their production has increased during the recent revival of interest in gardening. Home canning, freezing, and other means of preservation have returned as major operations in the county, a trend that is likely to continue.

It is probable that the shortage of agricultural workers will force Forsyth farmers to continue mechanization and diversification if they are to survive. Increasing population will take its toll of farmlands, and very likely the next quarter of a century will see a decline in the amount of farm production within the county. Farm productivity will, in all probability, remain high and new farm technological improvements may well increase production over present levels.

Manufacturing

Economically Forsyth's real strength still lies in its manufacturing interests. Contrary to the popular notion that the majority of the operations here have the patina of age, it is worth noting that, of Forsyth's 234 manufactories, 114—almost 50 percent—have been established since 1950. From 1950 to 1959, 45 new industries opened; from 1960 to 1969, 50 industries were established; and from 1970, 19 operations were located or started here. Maintaining her traditional lead in manufacturing activities in North Carolina, in 1967 Forsyth County asserted a dominant position. Over 12 percent of the state's entire industrial production value was amassed in this county, some $813,100,000. Forsyth's figure represents a 26 percent increase over the four-year period 1963–67. The value of products shipped from Forsyth was over $1.58 billion, representing 10.4 percent of North Carolina's total.

By the early 1970s the local labor force in Forsyth County numbered 112,200 persons. The breakdown of employment is as follows: manufacturing, 38,240; nonmanufacturing, 63,710; agriculture, 1,250; and all others (nonagriculture), 9,000. Of those persons engaged in manufacturing, over 71 percent were employed by one of three major industrial areas: tobacco, 12,510; textiles, 7,800; and electrical machinery, 6,650. Those persons engaged in nonmanufacturing pursuits are found largely in trades, with 18,140, followed by transportation, communications, and public utilities, 9,910; service (except domestic), 14,130; and government, 11,680.

Because of the large number of manufacturers in Forsyth County and because so many new industries have been established here since World War II it would be impossible to discuss each one individually. For these reasons only those industries employing 500 or more persons will be mentioned here.

By far the county's largest employer is R. J. Reynolds Industries, Inc. This diversified corporation is the parent company of R. J. Reynolds Tobacco Company; McLean Industries, Inc. (whose principal operation is Sea-Land Service, Inc., the world's largest containerized freight operation); RJR Foods, Inc.; RJR Archer, Inc.; American Independent Oil Company (Aminoil); and other new operations periodically acquired in a continuing diversification program.

R. J. Reynolds Tobacco Company, Reynolds's first and still its main operation, has changed dramatically since 1950. The company emerged at the end of World War II with its primary product the same Camel cigarette which had made the company the leading cigarette manufacturer in the United States. In 1954 the first Winston filter cigarette went on sale and by 1956 it was the top filter brand on the market. Ten years later it was the best-selling cigarette in the nation. Also in 1956 the company introduced Salem, the industry's first filter-tipped menthol cigarette. Production of the new brands increased so rapidly that expanded production capacity was essential and in April 1961 Winston cigarettes began to be produced in Whitaker Park, the world's largest and most modern cigarette plant. Since then production has continued to expand, despite the ban on radio and television advertising and the surgeon general's warning on cigarette packages. The company has acquired foreign plants and has licensed foreign companies to use its formulas and know-how and continues to expand its markets.

RJR Archer, also one of the county's major employers in its own right, produces aluminum products, flexible and firm packaging, and gift-wrap materials.

In 1950 there were two large Hanes manufacturing companies in Forsyth County, P. H. Hanes Knitting Company and Hanes Hosiery. In 1965 the Hanes Corporation was formed by the merger of these two industries. The corporation now consists of the Hanes Knitwear Division, Pinestate Knitwear, Hanes Hosiery, Inc., L'eggs Products, Inc., and the Bali Company. The hosiery company had revolutionized its industry by the introduction of seamless hosiery in 1918, and in 1970 for a second time astounded the business world with its successful L'eggs product, with hose packaged in a plastic egg and marketed through chain super-markets and drugstores.

Western Electric Radio Works came to Winston-Salem in 1946 and within a short time was manufacturing Navy and Air Force radar, vehicular radio telephones, carrier telephone sys-tems, coils, and transformers. In the late 1940s and early 1950s the company moved out of commercial radio sales, and as the Korean War began the Winston-Salem plant increased military production. In 1952 a technical publications group was formed to turn out instructional, operational, and maintenance manuals. In 1955 the Lexington Road shops were completed and occupied. In the 1950s the company devoted almost its entire operation in the county to producing advanced military electronic gear, including the Nike antiaircraft guided-missile systems. In 1960 the com-pany moved into the Reynolda Road plant, constructed by the Mary Reynolds Babcock Foundation and later given to Wake Forest University with a long-term lease to Western Electric. The early 1960s brought a reduced demand for military electronic equipment, and Western Electric's North Carolina plants began producing millions of tiny switches and circuits for the Bell Sys-tem's nationwide telephone network. Additional new products for the Bell System were added in the early 1970s and the com-pany continues to do limited work for the government in its Reynolda Road and First Union Building offices. The company employed about seven thousand workers in 1971 but has recently curtailed that work force to some degree. Western Electric con-tinues, however, as one of the county's major employers.

Of the other major industrial employers in the county, those founded prior to 1950 include the Hanes Dye and Finishing Com-pany, Thomasville Furniture Industries, Inc. (formerly B. F. Huntley Furniture Company, now a division of Armstrong Cork Corporation), and the Bahnson Corporation (now a subsidiary of Envirotech Corporation) which produces air-handling equip-ment, industrial air conditioning, textile-machine cleaners, and air-pollution control equipment. AMP, Inc., has added several manufacturing plants in the area in recent years and produces solderless connectors and other products. ITT–Grinnell Industrial Piping Company and the Fairchild-Burns Company contribute much to the county's employment picture. The Adams-Millis Corporation built a $3-million hosiery-finishing plant in Kernersville in 1965. In 1968 the Gravely Tractor Division of Studebaker Corporation constructed a $4-million world headquarters plant at Clemmons; their products include tractors, lawnmowers, and power equipment. The Joseph Schlitz Brewing Company erected a plant in Forsyth County in 1969 and is currently expanding its production facilities and constructing a plant for manufacturing cans. The Westinghouse Electric Corporation built a $47-million plant twelve miles northwest of Winston-Salem; there component parts for steam turbines are produced.

This diversification and expansion of industry in Forsyth County after 1950 continue a statewide trend towards industrialization begun in the late 1930s. North Carolina now ranks first in the nation's entire output of tobacco, textiles, and furniture; Forsyth's contribution to this accomplishment is considerable.

With the increasing prosperity of industry came larger wages to the workers; this fact is reflected in a great increase in local retail sales over the last decade. Throughout the 1960s there was a steady increase in retail sales in city and county, reflective of both the increasing importance of the urban center and the general financial stability of the county at large. From 1967 to 1974 the total amount rose from $475,877,790 to $977,980,181; the greater increase occurred outside the city.

RETAIL SALES

YEAR	INSIDE CITY	OUTSIDE CITY	TOTAL FOR FORSYTH CO.
1967	$422,009,626	$ 53,868,164	$475,877,790
1969	520,239,149	71,618,278	591,857,427
1972	689,493,035	104,419,376	793,912,411
1974	829,909,838	148,070,343	977,980,181

Financial institutions in Forsyth County have grown steadily with the city and county. By mid-1970 Wachovia Bank and Trust, with headquarters in Winston-Salem, was the largest bank in the southeastern United States, with total resources amounting to over $1.6 billion. Savings and loan associations likewise have prospered and grown with the favorable economic circumstances of the late 1960s and early 1970s. Below is a list of Forsyth's financial institutions, with total assets as of 30 June 1975.

INSTITUTION	NUMBER OF BRANCHES IN FORSYTH COUNTY	ASSETS
Bank of North Carolina	3	$ 295,291,587
Commercial and Farmers Bank	1	15,293,817
First Citizens Bank and Trust Co.	3	1,180,766,380
First Union National Bank	7	2,067,934,000
Forsyth Bank and Trust Company	3	27,603,450
North Carolina National Bank	7	3,360,663,000
Northwestern Bank	7	1,084,677,000
United Citizens Bank of Winston-Salem	2	17,320,965
Wachovia Bank and Trust Company	19	3,220,008,583
First Federal Savings & Loan Assoc.	5	123,311,108
Piedmont Federal Savings & Loan Assoc.	7	177,453,415
Standard Savings & Loan Assoc.	3	58,147,683
Winston-Salem Savings & Loan Assoc.	6	107,094,422

The county's largest insurance company, Security Life and Trust, changed its name in November 1968 to Integon Corporation. The name change reflected an expanded operation into areas other than life insurance, and today the company offers a full range of insurance services for individuals, families, and businesses, along with other insurance-related services. Insurance in force on 30 September 1975 was $5.75 billion.

Transportation and Communication

Transportation is the lifeblood of the Forsyth region and has always posed a difficult problem. The area has no rivers; it lay off the major early trading paths, missed the canals, was not located on a major railroad route, and did not easily acquire major highway thoroughfares. The plank road was an early effort to remedy this situation, but it did not survive for long. The early rail connections were obtained only by great local initiative. Rail and plane transportation finally came to the area but only by great effort on the part of those who felt the need for them.

The period following 1950 saw a continuation of this problem and the Forsyth community came up with some positive and valuable solutions. Rail transportation was already on the decline in the post–World War II period and by 1975 Forsyth County had lost all of its rail passenger facilities. Rail freight continued to be a major carrier and seems to be holding its own in recent years. But the real solution to the problem of moving goods in and out of Forsyth County has been in the use of trucks.

Along with the rest of the nation, much of Forsyth's freight was hauled by trains prior to 1950. In the years since, however, the trucking industry has grown in Forsyth at a much more rapid rate than elsewhere in the nation. The development of McLean Trucking Company has led the way in this growth. Founded in 1934, McLean established its general offices in Winston-Salem in 1943. Since 1950, mergers and acquisitions have built McLean into one of the largest trucking firms in the nation. McLean trucks and terminals serve areas from Florida to Maine, from Minnesota to Texas. The company has subsidiaries involved in refining and transporting petroleum products, in equipment repair and maintenance, and in real estate. Under the leadership of Paul P. Davis and Amory Mellen, Jr., it continues to grow.

Hennis Freight Lines, another Forsyth-based company, will shortly pass from the scene in its present corporate form, but it has become a part of another freight system almost as large as McLean. Hennis was developed by S. H. Mitchell, who sold the company to Benton-Spry Associations in 1971. M. C. Benton, Jr. has directed the company through a period of difficulty and into a merger with Spector Industries of Chicago. Hennis will become a part of the Spector Freight System, Inc. Pilot Freight Carriers, Inc., Forsyth's other major carrier, has grown materially and continues to prosper under the leadership of its founder R. Y. Sharpe.

Air transportation in Forsyth County has had a development pattern which favors local capital. In 1950 a small Smith Reynolds

Airport was served by Eastern, Capitol, and the newly formed Piedmont Airlines. Air traffic, both passenger and freight, continued to increase through the 1950s. In late 1961 Eastern and Capitol ceased serving the Forsyth airport and moved their services to the newly designated regional facility some fifteen miles away, Friendship Airport, termed the Greensboro, High Point, and Winston-Salem terminal; it continues to serve Forsyth's customers. Meanwhile, Piedmont Airlines, established primarily as a state and regional air carrier, has continued to expand and grow. After carrying fewer than 40,000 passengers in 1948, the line emplaned 1,288,825 passengers in 1965 and carried 3,821,136 passengers over almost twelve thousand route miles in 1974. Over the years it has added routes to Washington, New York, Chicago, Memphis, Atlanta, Augusta, Charleston, and many points in between. Freight and mail handling have increased at about the same pace as has passenger traffic. Piedmont still serves many communities which otherwise would have no scheduled air service and it touches the major markets of the East as well.

With a nation moving more and more of its people and freight in automobiles and trucks, Forsyth County naturally came more and more to depend on its highways. As with the railways and the airlines, Winston-Salem never seemed to be quite on the main line of highway transportation. Promise of a change came in 1957 with the opening of the first section of the East-West Expressway (Interstate 40). I-40 was completed through Winston-Salem in 1961 and now stretches westward across the state and nation with only a few uncompleted segments. The eastern portion, however, remains a dream, with a segment reaching from Raleigh toward Durham and a promise that ultimately Forsyth County will be linked by interstate highway with the eastern coast.

Plans exist to circle the city with expressways; these have encountered difficulties. Silas Creek Parkway was opened in 1961 and completed in 1969, but plans to extend the parkway through the Wake Forest campus created much opposition and were dropped. Presently on the drawing board are plans to circle the city farther to the north and to link with the North-South Expressway (Highway 52) which was completed as far south as the Schlitz plant in 1974. Plans also exist for a southern beltway, but these too have encountered opposition and show no promise of being fulfilled in the near future. Meanwhile, traffic on I-40 grows heavier, as it carries not only east-west traffic but also commuter automobiles from both directions. The city of Winston-Salem has continued its program of paving streets where needed and improving downtown traffic arteries to handle the steadily increasing flow of automobiles. Peters Creek Parkway, the Cherry-Marshall expressway, University Parkway, South Stratford Road, and the outlying reaches of Reynolda and Robinhood roads all have been widened to handle a heavier flow of traffic, only to have shopping areas develop along them, further adding to the traffic burden. In recent years such improvements have met resistance from environmental groups as well as from the residential neighborhoods involved, and frequent voices are heard demanding improved mass-transit facilities in lieu of more streets and highways.

Bus travel inside Winston-Salem has changed from two privately owned companies (one black company serving largely the Negro areas of the city, and one owned by Duke Power serving the central city and the white suburbs), to a monopoly by the Safe Bus Company (the black-owned company which took over the franchise for the entire city in 1968), to the acquisition of the entire service by the Winston-Salem Transit Authority (WSMT) in 1972. Intercity and interstate bus travel declined for a time during the 1950s and 1960s but seems to have revived in recent years. The move of the bus terminal from its downtown site to the intersection of Highway 52 and I-40 was accomplished in 1971 and the old station, long a landmark for travelers, was destroyed to make way for a parking building.

In communications as well as in other areas local ownership and control is slowly giving way to incorporation into nationwide complexes. The Gordon Gray family has sold Winston-Salem's newspapers, the *Journal*, the *Sentinel*, and the Sunday *Journal-Sentinel* to Media-General, Inc., and WSJS-TV (now WXII-TV) to Multimedia Corporation of Greenville, South Carolina. The *Suburbanite*, a weekly published for a time by Stephen Neal, was sold in 1975 to the Smiley Publishing Company, Inc. In radio all of the area's FM stations have separated from their AM affiliates. The AM stations have become oriented toward special audiences, with country and gospel broadcasting increasing notably. The county's experiment in commercial fine-music broadcasting failed in the face of economic realities, but it was replaced by increased power and new facilities for Wake Forest University's WFDD-FM. Cable television now serves most of Winston-Salem and some county areas. Summit Cable Services, along with WSJS-AM and WTQR-FM, are still owned primarily by Gordon Gray. WTOB-TV, Channel 26, broadcast from 1953 to 1957. Its channel was occupied in 1975 by WUNL-TV, a regional station of the University of North Carolina's educational television system.

The Shopping Centers

In 1950 Winston-Salem and Forsyth County had no shopping centers. The movement into suburban areas was already well under way, however, and it intensified as the years passed. In 1955 the Thruway Shopping Center opened on the site of an abandoned landfill. This was only the beginning of a great shopping-center race. Next came Northside in 1958, Parkway in 1960, Reynolda Manor in 1963, West Salem and Sherwood Plaza in 1964, College Plaza in 1965, an expansion of Thruway in 1966, and Cloverdale in 1967. Smaller centers in Winston-Salem and elsewhere in the county contributed also to the move of business and customers to the nonurban areas. Discount stores came and brought small shopping complexes to their new locations. In 1972, after a hiatus of a few years, Parkview and Pine Ridge Plaza opened on opposite ends of town. Then in 1975 came the county's shopping center to top all centers—the Hanes Mall on South Stratford Road and Silas Creek Parkway. With a potential of more than two hundred stores, the Hanes Mall has already made its impact on the shopping patterns of the county and the region.

Downtown Redevelopment

Winston-Salem is the focal point of the industry and trade of Forsyth County. With the shifting of population to the suburbs and the moving of retail stores and customers to the shopping centers, downtown Winston-Salem began to decline. This was a part of a national trend, not widely recognized even by the late 1950s, but farsighted business leaders were concerned.

In 1959 the Chamber of Commerce sponsored a Total Development Committee which visited cities where urban renewal was underway. Old Salem had already shown that an area could be profitably revitalized. By 1961 studies and plans were progressing and in 1963 plans for the Piedmont Plaza were announced. Two full blocks in the Trade Street area were to be demolished and a full-scale shopping plaza was to be constructed. It was a fascinating concept but economically unfeasible and for a time hope for the downtown area appeared to be a foolish dream.

Meanwhile the Wachovia Bank and Trust Company began constructing a modern thirty-story building on the block of Main Street between Third and Fourth. When it was completed Wachovia turned over the old bank building to the city and county government for office space. The Government Center, as it was renamed, provided much-needed room to house government offices. Behind the new Wachovia Building, one of the city's worst slums gave way to the Phillips Building, housing a computer center and offices. City planners began a beautification program which included removal of overhanging signs and placing utility wires underground.

Hope for the privately financed Piedmont Plaza gave way to plans for a downtown urban renewal program. The plan as envisioned in 1965 included such steps as wider streets, adequate parking, landscaping, and relocating industry and business which did not belong downtown. Plans were completed by 1967 but funds would be two years in coming. The Redevelopment Commission had a difficult wait.

Meanwhile, one major project was not dependent on redevelopment funds. A publicly approved bond issue made possible the construction of the M. C. Benton Convention Center across the street from the old Hotel Robert E. Lee. Complete with the most modern facilities and flexible enough to handle a large crowd or several small ones, the Convention Center was a success from the time it opened in the fall of 1969.

With the arrival of redevelopment funds, plans for the Trade Street Mall began to move. Property was acquired, Trade Street was closed between Fourth and Fifth in the summer of 1970, and the traffic congestion which it had engendered was eliminated. The Mall was landscaped and the area began to turn into an attractive gathering spot. In nearby areas mini-parks were constructed; stores on the Mall were remodeled and many of them gave their storefronts a face-lifting. Some stores closed and others opened, but on the whole retail trade in the area began to improve.

Changes in the Trade Street area were accompanied by changes in other parts of the city as well. The Nissen Building got a new owner and became the First Union Bank Building, with a new front and remodeled offices. The old First Union Building became the Bank of North Carolina's new home, after serving for a time as a meeting place for the First Presbyterian Church while their new sanctuary was under construction.

One of the most spectacular changes came across from the southwest corner of Courthouse Square. The North Carolina National Bank Company demolished its old building on Third Street and constructed a modern fourteen-story building with a large parking garage attached. The NCNB Plaza was designed as a link with the Trade Street Mall extension. Open spaces, trees, and a contemporary water sculpture all added to the beauty and made the downtown area more inviting. Across the street, Piedmont Savings and Loan constructed a building of bronze mirror glass. Further down Third Street, Winston-Salem Savings and Loan constructed a new building to blend with the NCNB Plaza concept. Governmental agencies entered the plans as well with the new Hall of Justice, discussed in Chapter 13, and the new Federal Building, to be completed in 1976.

In March 1972 the Hotel Robert E. Lee was demolished. In the place of the old ten-story hotel, magnificent in its day but defying every attempt at rehabilitation, came the new Hyatt House with indoor waterfall, hanging gardens, and glass bubble elevators—all the most modern concepts in hotel design. Behind the Hyatt House the city constructed a computerized parking deck with an ice-skating rink and spaces for retail shops. All this was connected to the Trade Street Mall and the NCNB Plaza by Freedom Walk, a new concept in downtown pedestrian systems. Nearby, the old State Theater at Liberty Street and Main was replaced by a new parking deck with hundreds of well-lighted, easily accessible spaces. One other parking area was cleared and opened, across the street from the City Hall. Only ground-level parking is provided here and it may well be the site of a new city hall sometime in the future.

The redevelopment program has been accomplished at great expense to both the public and private sectors. Money from the federal government in urban renewal funds has been supplemented greatly by private investment. Already retail trade is returning and offices are moving back to the downtown area. Within a few years it is projected that the central business district, which yielded less than one million dollars in taxes in 1969, will yield close to two and one-half million dollars. Downtown Winston-Salem is alive and well.

The Economy: Some Conclusions

Growth, diversity, and excellence: these have marked the economic community in Forsyth County since the earliest days. The blending of the careful Moravian heritage with the march of progress has proved to be a most successful combination. Industrial and economic growth, careful and planned, comes inexorably, and with it Forsyth County has retained a devotion to community which makes it a good place to live. Advances in industrial and financial wealth have brought advances in the arts, in community programs, in sports, and in preserving the region's heritage.

While it is possible to lament the growth of population and the passing of much that was pleasant in the small-town atmosphere of the pre-1950 period, it is encouraging that, as in the past, efforts are being made to retain as much of the good of those past days as is possible in Forsyth, a county on the march.

CHAPTER 16

Celebrations, Commemorations, and the Future

FORSYTH COUNTY IS CONCERNED WITH recognizing and preserving its past for future generations. This concern has taken tangible form in Old Salem and elsewhere. As a part of the hundredth anniversary of the founding of the county, *Forsyth, A County on the March* was published in 1949. The commemoration of the county centennial is recounted in Chapter 10. The city of Winston-Salem later commemorated its two-hundredth anniversary, in 1966. As a part of that celebration, formal recognition was given to the Moravians' first official celebration of the Fourth of July; and each year since, that observance has been repeated in Salem. Linked in the minds of many Forsyth citizens with the Fourth of July Service is the annual Easter Service. A quick look at these commemorations should provide a good basis for a concluding glimpse at the future of Forsyth County.

Winston-Salem's Bicentennial Celebration

The year 1966 was dedicated by the people of Winston-Salem as a "Time of Thanksgiving."

We give thanks for the courageous Moravian settlers who in 1776 carved out of the North Carolina wilderness a community known as Salem.

We give thanks for the dreams and talents of a people who gave to all generations a heritage of religion, education, music, and crafts.

We give thanks for the 1913 action that brought the communities of Salem and Winston into one great city devoted to progress in industry, education, medicine, and the arts.

For two hundred years of contributions to the history of our Nation and our State we give thanks and dedicate ourselves to a belief in mutual understanding and the desire to work together in new endeavors that will always deserve a lasting spirit of thanksgiving.

Thus read the keynote for the celebration of Winston-Salem's two-hundredth birthday.

On 6 January 1966 the celebration began with a Festival of Thanksgiving at Memorial Coliseum. Dr. Franklin Frye, president of the Lutheran Church in America, delivered the anniversary sermon. Music was provided by the combined choirs of Salem College, Wake Forest College, and Winston-Salem State College. An exhibit of historic photographs prepared by the late Frank Jones hung in the Salem College Fine Arts Center from 9 January to 9 February. Following Jones's exhibit came a folk-art collection from Colonial Williamsburg. On 13 February two hundred trees were planted and dedicated as a part of the city's continuing work in beautification and conservation. A special historical edition of the *Journal and Sentinel* was issued on 10 April. Later in the month, 22–23 April, a crafts festival was held at the Coliseum. A music and arts festival was featured at Winston-Salem State College, 28–30 April. Then, on 13 May, with tableaux and narration, massed bands and choruses involving more than three thousand public-school students performed in an original drama, *The Sound of Trumpets*, which portrayed Winston-Salem's history. May was highlighted by the Salem Flower Festival and the Metropolitan Opera's national touring company's production of *Madame Butterfly* at Reynolds Auditorium. One of the most successful events of the celebration came 12–19 June, with Dr. Thor Johnson's Early American Moravian Music Festival at Old Salem. Then on 4 July, a reenactment of the first Fourth of July celebration was given in Old Salem, and Henry H. Fowler, secretary of the treasury, unveiled a plaque commemorating the event. In July and August an outdoor drama, *Till the Day Breaks*, was staged nightly in Old

Salem. The South Hall restoration at Salem College was dedicated on 5 October. At a Festival of Thanksgiving held at Memorial Coliseum on 18 November, Dr. Billy Graham delivered a thanksgiving address. Sir Patrick Henry Dean, British ambassador to the United States, spoke to the annual luncheon of the North Carolina Literary and Historical Association, a part of the state's Culture Week (held in Winston-Salem, the first time Culture Week was ever held away from Raleigh). And finally, on 10–11 December dancers from the North Carolina School of the Arts presented with the Civic Ballet a performance of Tchaikovsky's *Nutcracker*.

Winston-Salem/Forsyth County Bicentennial Commission

As early as 1970 foresighted people in Winston-Salem/Forsyth County were contemplating plans for celebrating the nation's bicentennial in 1976. Among those actively promoting the concept of a bicentennial celebration were Dalton Ruffin, Mrs. John D. Eller, Jr., Michael Newman, and Milton Rhodes. Consequently in February 1972 the Board of Aldermen and the Forsyth County Board of Commissioners were willing to support bicentennial activities financially as well as in spirit. They designated the Arts Council as the sponsor of the Winston-Salem/Forsyth County Bicentennial Commission. Co-chairmen of the commission were M. C. Benton, Jr., and Mrs. John D. Eller, Jr., working with a steering committee and council consisting of citizens representing many interests and activities within the community.

In May 1973 seven town meetings were held to determine what citizens wanted for a bicentennial celebration. One of the first duties of the full-time coordinator, Ruth Mills Kipp, employed in June 1973, was to analyze the results of the town meetings and to conceive a workable format for the nearly one hundred ideas presented by the citizens.

At the first full commission meeting on 16 October 1973 a twelve-point master plan and a statement of goals and policies was adopted for the bicentennial of Winston-Salem/Forsyth County. On 30 January 1974, Winston-Salem/Forsyth County was officially designated a "National Bicentennial Community," the first to be so designated in North Carolina.

The Winston-Salem/Forsyth County Bicentennial was a year-long celebration from 4 July 1975 through 4 July 1976. Activities included the three thematic areas of Heritage '76, Horizons '76, and Festival USA, and participation was open to all citizens in Winston-Salem and Forsyth County.

Fourth of July at Old Salem

Attracting more and more attention since its first reenactment in 1966, the Fourth of July ceremony in Old Salem will play a major part in Forsyth County's observance of the national bicentennial.

News of the peace following the American Revolution reached North Carolina on 19 April 1783. A great wave of rejoicing and gratitude spread through the General Assembly, which was in session at that time. Before the assembly adjourned, it recommended a statewide observance of the Fourth of July as "a day of Solemn Thanksgiving," and called upon Governor Alexander Martin to issue a proclamation to that effect. This he did on 18 June 1783.

As far as is known, the Moravians of the Wachovia settlement were the only North Carolinians to respond to the governor's proclamation with a planned observance. The program in Salem on 4 July 1783, lasted all day. The people were awakened in the early morning by a trombone choir playing chorales through the streets of the town. At 10 A.M. they gathered for a worship service in the *Saal* (chapel) of the *Gemein Haus* (congregation house). In the afternoon there was a lovefeast at which the choir, soloists, orchestra, and congregation presented *Psalm of Joy*, an "ode" or cantata written especially for the occasion by John Frederik Peter, Salem minister and composer. The final event of the day was a torchlight procession through the streets of the town.

According to the Salem diaries, "hearts were filled with the peace of God, evident during the entire day and especially during the procession." Each year, before growing crowds of visitors and with the celebration's fame spreading throughout the nation, Old Salem Inc. attempts to recapture the simple, reverent spirit of the Fourth of July observed in Salem as it was in 1783.

The Easter Sunday Service

One of the most visible and meaningful remnants which the Moravians have given Forsyth County is the Easter Service at Salem. Each year thousands gather before sunrise to participate in what an April 1974 *Reader's Digest* article called "The Nation's Most Beautiful Easter Service."

Prior to Easter Day the Moravian community makes ready for the service. The Moravian graveyard, known as God's Acre, has its grass carefully trimmed, the flat stones that mark the graves are scrubbed white, and the graves are decorated with flowers. Food is prepared for the church bands which will travel through the city calling the inhabitants to the service. Each day of Passion Week is observed by church services attended by Moravians and non-Moravians.

After the bands have returned from their tours through the city, they eat a hearty breakfast and join the crowds in Salem Square waiting for the service to begin. Just as dawn's light begins to outline the buildings, the chairman of the Salem Congregation begins the ceremony by proclaiming, "The Lord is risen." Following a brief service on the square, the pastor invites the congregation to follow him to God's Acre while the bands play antiphonally. In the graveyard an Easter liturgy is conducted and it concludes, more often than not, as the sun rises on the scene. Most participants leave sensing something of the spirit of those original Moravians who emphasized the brotherhood of all Christians.

Forsyth County Today

Many of the elements that make up Forsyth County today are identified in the commemorations just discussed; many others are not. An effort has been made to pick up threads of community life in the county in these pages.

The community that began as an isolated settlement in the Piedmont wilderness has grown to include a large city and many small towns and communities in an increasingly industrial area. Forsyth County today has its problems. Rural and urban slums still exist, despite great efforts to eradicate them; there is poverty in both city and county areas; remnants of racial discrimination remain; an increasing population needs innovative solutions of transportation problems; city and county governments need to eliminate costly duplication of services and increase their efficiency. But the problems that preceded the present ones have been solved, and Forsyth's citizens are confident that the county's cooperative and progressive spirit will overcome today's problems as it did those of yesterday.

The spirit of a county is determined by the people, events, and problems which have become a part of it; so it is with Forsyth County. Salem was founded for religious purposes and religious freedom; today a deep religious atmosphere dominates community life. Winston was founded for purposes of government, as a county seat; today the county has strong city and county government and citizens show great interest in public affairs. The early Moravian settlers were firm believers in broad educational development and one of their first acts in building early Salem was the establishment of schools for boys and girls; today the Winston-Salem/Forsyth County public school system is one of the finest in the state, and the county has become a center for higher education. Salem's settlers were hard-working, industrious, farsighted men; one of Forsyth County's characteristic traits is its progressive spirit.

Forsyth County has been built by its own citizens through generations of work. The settlers of the area were family-oriented, home-loving people who believed in making their county a fit home for their children and their children's children. As a result, most of the children have stayed in the community to find opportunity and fortune. Old family names dating back for generations predominate in social and business life. The county is fortunate that the large majority of its many industries were founded and built by local citizens, and many are still home-owned. Businessmen and industrialists of the community have consistently turned their energy and their money towards building up the county. Its good roads, good government, and good schools did not come to it from outside sources or through lucky circumstances, but each had to be carefully developed by citizens willing to work and to give. If the amount of money that has been given in the county by individuals for buildings, schools, churches, and social agencies and charities could be totaled, the sum would be staggering. Forsyth County's citizens are community-minded and have been so from the time the first careful plans were laid for the settlement of Salem.

Forsyth County's future development promises to be tremendous. Its diversified industrial economy will fluctuate little with changing conditions; it will become better rounded as it develops further as an educational center. Its foundation is a rich heritage of tradition which teaches hard work, cooperation, faith in God, and faith in the ability of man. Forsyth County will stand even more firmly and grow ever stronger, for its roots are deeply embedded in the red Piedmont clay.

Selective Bibliography

IN THE PREPARATION OF THIS VOLUME, a number of sources, published and unpublished, have been consulted. Hugh Talmage Lefler's four-volume *North Carolina* (Chapel Hill: University of North Carolina Press, 1954), supplemented whenever necessary by material from the latest edition of Hugh Talmage Lefler and Albert Ray Newsome's one-volume *North Carolina* (Chapel Hill: University of North Carolina Press, 1973), served as the basic reference for background material relative to North Carolina history. Agricultural and manufacturing statistics were taken from the United States Census Bureau reports, unless otherwise stated. Recent economic and population statistics concerned with Winston-Salem were generously provided by the Greater Winston-Salem Chamber of Commerce.

Published material about the aboriginal inhabitants of this area is somewhat scant, but most helpful was Prudence Rice's master's thesis, "The Bottoms Rock Shelter: A Prehistoric Site in Forsyth County, North Carolina" (Wake Forest University, 1971). Though not specifically related to Forsyth County, Joffre Coe's book *The Formative Cultures of the Carolina Piedmont* (Philadelphia: American Philosophical Society, 1964) provides an excellent cultural study of three Indian units, one of which—the Hardaway site—is located on the Yadkin River in Stanley County. Dr. Douglas L. Rights's *The American Indian in North Carolina* (Durham, N.C.: Duke University Press, 1947) covers the folklore and mythology of North Carolina's historic Indians, as well as their customs and habits. Dr. Ned Woodall of the Anthropology Department of Wake Forest University was most helpful in answering many questions concerning the Indian inhabitants of this area and in tying together much of the material used.

Located in the Archives of the Moravian Church, South, are some two thousand volumes and ten thousand pages of manuscripts relating primarily to the Moravian settlements in Forsyth County. In this collection are church registers, account books, diaries, memoirs, letters, and manuscript music. Before 1922 the bulk of this material was inaccessible to the average researcher because it was written in German. In that year, however, the first of twelve volumes of edited translations appeared under the North Carolina Department of Archives and History imprint, as *The Records of the Moravians in North Carolina* (Raleigh: State Department of Archives and History, 1922; ed., vols. 1–7, Dr. Adelaide Fries; eds., vols. 8–12, Dr. Douglas L. Rights, Dr. Minnie Smith, and Bishop Kenneth Hamilton). These volumes constitute one of the most complete primary-source accounts of any group settling in the United States. And not only did the Moravians write about themselves, but fortunately they wrote also of the people living about them, many of whom were themselves unable to read or write. Additional sources of value in book form are Adelaide Fries's *Forsyth* (Winston, N.C.: Stewart's Printing House, 1898), Dr. John Henry Clewell's *History of Wachovia in North Carolina* (New York: Doubleday, Page & Co., 1902), and Bishop Kenneth Hamilton's *History of the Moravian Church, 1722–1957* (Bethlehem, Pennsylvania: Interprovincial Board of Christian Education, Moravian Church in America, 1965). Unpublished graduate theses containing particularly useful information related to the Moravians include: Edward Holder's "Community Life in Wachovia, 1752–1780" (Chapel Hill, 1929) and Jerry Surratt's "From Theocracy to Voluntary Church and Secular Community: A Study of the Moravians in Salem, North Carolina, 1772–1860" (Emory University, 1968). Also recommended is Adelaide Fries's little book, *Distinctive Customs and Practices of the Moravian Church* (Bethlehem, Pennsylvania, and Winston-Salem: Commenius Press, 1949). And, lastly, on file in the library of Old Salem, Inc., are a number of studies and interpretations, by John Bivins, Gene

Capps, Frank Horton, and Dr. Frank Albright of Old Salem, and others by undergraduate and graduate students, dealing with different aspects of Moravian life, particularly in Salem. Especially helpful to this work was Nora Lee Reese's "The Moravian Attitude Toward the Negro and Slavery."

Again, in the chapters on the social and economic orders in the period 1753–1860, published and unpublished materials have been used. John Yates's thesis "The Common School System of Forsyth County, North Carolina from 1840 to 1884" (Wake Forest University, 1973) provides a wealth of material and statistics gleaned from school minute and record books, listing schools, districts, teachers, and the like for the period 1840–84. On file in the Salem College Library are a number of manuscript materials (c. 1800 to date) relating to the history of that institution. Valuable books relating to artists and craftsmen (Moravian and non-Moravian) in Forsyth County are John Bivins's *The Moravian Potters in North Carolina* (Chapel Hill: University of North Carolina Press, 1972) and James H. Craig's *The Arts and Crafts in North Carolina 1699–1840* (Winston-Salem: Museum of Early Southern Decorative Arts, Old Salem, Inc., 1965). Cindy Armstrong's Wake Forest University seminar paper, "The Spach and Nissen Wagon Works," provided much interesting material on early wagon manufacturing in Forsyth County. Basic published sources include C. C. Crittenden's *The Commerce of North Carolina, 1763–1789* (New Haven: Yale University Press, 1936) and Cornelius D. Cathey's *Agricultural Developments in North Carolina, 1783–1860* (Chapel Hill: University of North Carolina Press, 1956).

The years of the war, 1861–65, found large numbers of men from Forsyth County engaged in the Confederate army. In addition to the many letters that have survived, there are several interesting and informative printed narratives: Dr. J. F. Shaffner, *Diary, Commencing September 13, 1863, Ending February 13, 1865* (Winston-Salem: Privately printed, 1936); Henry T. Bahnson, *The Last Days of the War* (Hamlet, N.C.: Capital Printing Co., 1903); and Julius Leinbach, *Regiment Band of the Twenty-Sixth North Carolina* (*Civil War History*, September 1958) reprinted as Moravian Music Foundation Publications, No. 5.

The years following the war up to the turn of the century saw the growth and expansion of industry in Winston. Slightly colored, but relatively reliable, contemporary accounts include Dr. D. P. Robbins's *Descriptive Sketch of Winston-Salem* (Winston, N.C.: Sentinel Job Print, 1888) including a good bit of county material, and Mrs. A. V. Winkler's *Souvenir of the Twin Cities of North Carolina* (Salem, N.C.: Blum's Steam Power Press, 1890). Each of these books contains industrial, business, and social material. Also there is Henry T. Foltz's *Winston, Fifty Years Ago* (Winston-Salem, 1926) which offers a very nice tour of the town in 1875, complete with names and places. For a complete listing of individual businesses and industries there is Branson's *Business Directory* (Raleigh: J. A. Jones); the years used for this volume include 1876, 1880, 1884, 1890, and 1896. Branson also lists the farmers in each township for a given county. Nannie May Tilley's thorough and unequaled *The Bright-Tobacco Industry, 1860–1929* (Chapel Hill: University of North Carolina Press, 1948) is an excellent source for information of the early tobacco-manufacturing industry. And lastly, Bishop Edward Rondthaler's charming *Memorabilia of Fifty Years, 1877–1927* (Raleigh: Edwards & Broughton Co., 1928) gives wonderful insight into the "gospel of civic pride" that was preached in the Twin Cities from the 1880s through the first decades of the twentieth century.

Worth mentioning at this point is the inestimable value of literally hundreds of historically oriented articles, some merely quaint and many hard simple fact, that have appeared in the *Journal and Sentinel* over the last thirty-odd years. Staff writers such as Chester Davis and Bill East have succeeded in doing more than just tantalizing their readers' interest in local history. Especially valuable is the bicentennial edition of the *Journal and Sentinel* which appeared in April 1966. The photographic excellence of work of the late Frank Jones enhanced in large measure the writings of these men.

In Chapter 10 two unpublished graduate theses were particularly helpful: Thomas A. Gray, "Graylyn, A Norman Revival Estate in North Carolina" (University of Delaware, 1974), and Carolyn L. Wall, "Urban Idealism: Winston-Salem's Search for the Good City" (Wake Forest University, 1974). Numerous news-paper articles were consulted as well as information generously made available by the Greater Winston-Salem Chamber of Commerce and the county manager's office. Other titles of specific interest appear throughout the text.

Photographs are from the Frank Jones Collection and are published with the permission of the Wachovia Historical Society, Winston-Salem, North Carolina.

Index

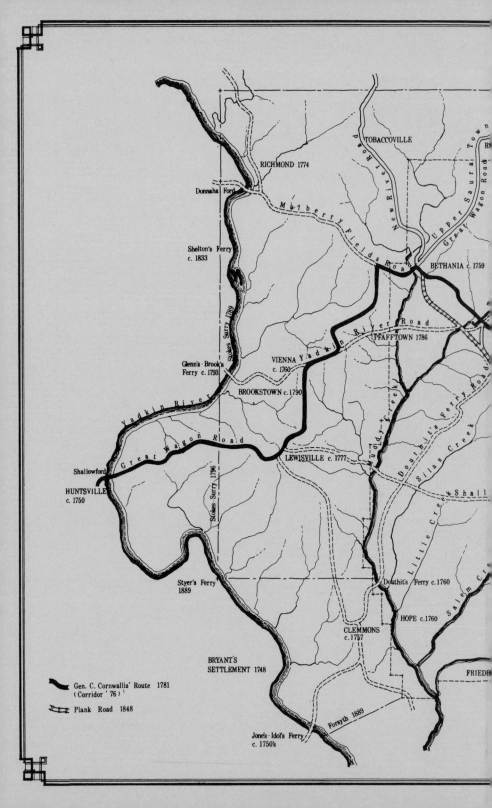